# SHIFTING
# BORDERS

# SHIFTING BORDERS

## East European Poetries
## of the Eighties

Compiled and Edited by
## Walter Cummins

Rutherford • Madison • Teaneck
Fairleigh Dickinson University Press
London and Toronto: Associated University Presses

Associated University Presses
440 Forsgate Drive
Cranbury, NJ 08512

Associated University Presses
25 Sicilian Avenue
London WC1A 2QH, England

Associated University Presses
P.O. Box 338, Port Credit
Mississauga, Ontario,
Canada L5G 4L8

The paper used in this publication meets the requirements
of the American National Standard for Permanence of Paper
for Printed Library Materials Z39.48-1984.

**Library of Congress Cataloging-in-Publication Data**

Shifting borders : East European poetries of the eighties / compiled
and edited by Walter Cummins.
    p.  cm.
    Includes bibliographical references.
    ISBN 0-8386-3497-4 : (alk. paper)
    1. East European poetry—20th century—Translations into English.
I. Cummins, Walter M.
PN849.E92S5   1993
808.81'00947—dc20                     91-58885
                                         CIP

# Contents

## Part 3: Poetry of the South Slavs

# Preface

This collection, which brings together a substantial body of east European poetry published in the eighties, began as a much less ambitious idea: to gather and expand on ten years of east European poetry translations published in *The Literary Review*. However, our compiled list made us realize how many authors and literatures we had not included in the magazine. To fill the gaps, we sought the advice of specialists for each of the languages important for east European writing. To our surprise and delight, not only were the leading poets, translators, and scholars willing to help, they were eager to participate as editors of individual sections. They chose the poets and the specific poems to be included; they arranged for translations and, in a number of cases, did all or most of the translations themselves. Even though in our initial conception of this book we had not aspired to attract the recognized experts from each literature, the result has been to bring together an ideal group of editors to make available English versions of an important body of poetry.

This collection emphasizes the decade of the eighties, the years leading up to one of the most significant turning points in the history of east Europe. For many poets, their subjects are already different because the political, social, and economic realities have changed so dramatically. Poetry is not history, and poetry, as an art, has the power to live beyond one time and one place; but, as a compilation, the poems in this book offer deep insights into a crucial period. As Burton Raffel emphasizes in his general introduction, poetry is central to the cultures of eastern Europe, and each individual poem is an event.

Because the individual editors were free to organize their sections in the manner they found most appropriate to the body of poetry they were considering, the approaches used throughout this book differ. Some sections emphasize previously published translations because those particular literatures have already received much attention in English versions, while others have had very limited exposure. Some sections devote attention to poems from decades before the eighties because their authors had such a great influence on subsequent writing. Some present groups of poems of a limited number of poets, while others present single works by a larger number. As our frequent discussions with the editors during preparations made clear, there is no one right way to compile an anthology such as this. The symmetry of uniformity would have been achieved at the expense of individual editorial visions. It seemed only fitting to encourage such personal preference for poetries that make freedom such a frequent subject.

# Acknowledgments

The following translations were first published in books and periodicals. We thanks the publishers and translators for granting permission to reprint them.

## Bulgarian Poems

Blaga Dimitrova, "Bee Lesson" and "Frost" (translated by Ludmilla Popova-Wightman) from *Poetry East*. "Amnesia in Reverse" (translated by Ludmilla Popova-Wightman) from *The Literary Review*.

## Hungarian Poems

Gyula Illyés, "One Sentence on Tyranny" (translated by Bruce Berlind with Mária Kőrösy) from *Poetry East*.
Sándor Weöres, "Seventh Symphony" (translated by Bruce Berlind with Mária Kőrösy) from *Graham House Review*.
János Pilinszky, "We and They," "December 22, 1970," "Veil," "For Life," "Here and Now" (translated by Bruce Berlind with Mária Kőrösy) from *London Magazine*.
Ágnes Nemes Nagy, "Trees," "But to Look," "Statues," "Defend It," "Crime," "Like Someone" (translated by Bruce Berlind) from *Selected Poems • Nemes Nagy*. Iowa City: Iowa Translations, 1980.
Sándor Csoóri, "Postponed Nightmare," "Questions, to Carriers of the Dead" (translated by Len Roberts and László Vertes), "A Drop of Blood on the Ground" (translated by Len Roberts) from *The Literary Review*.
László Nagy, "Cognition, Language, Poetry" (translated by Jascha Kessler), "There Is No Southern Island" (translated by Jascha Kessler with Mária Kőrösy) from *The Literary Review*.
István Vas, "October Night from the Garden," "In the Roman Forum," "I Put the Pen Down" (translated by Bruce Berlind) from *Through the Smoke: Selected Poems of István Vas*. Budapest: Corvina, 1989.
Dezső Tandori, "The Christmas of Long Walks," "Tradoni, Stress on An Abandoned Place," "What Gets Lost from the Night," "The No-Hand"

(translated by Bruce Berlind) from *Birds and Other Relations: Selected Poetry of Dezső Tandori*. Princeton: Princeton University Press, 1986.

# Lithuanian Poems

Vincas Mykolaitis-Putinas, "The Roadside Christ" (translated by R. Šilbajoris) from *International Folklore Review*.

Judita Vaičiūnmaite, "The Black Shore" (translated by R. Šilbajoris) from *Journal of Baltic Studies*.

Jonas Mekas, "Old Is the Hush of Rain" (translated by Demie Jonaitis) from *Lithuanian Writers in the West*. Chicago: Lithuanian Library Press, 1979.

Henrikas Nagys, "Laterna Obscura" "(translated by Clark Mills) from *The Green Oak*. Voyages Press, 1962, "The Sundials" (translated by R. Šilbajoris) from *Perfection of Exile: Fourteen Contemporary Lithuanian Writers*. Norman: University of Oklahoma Press, 1970.

Janina Degutyte, "My limbs are aching . . ." (translated by R. Šilbajoris) from *International Folklore Review*.

Alginantas Mackus, from "Chapel B" (translated by Mirga Girnius) from *Lithuanian Writers in the West*. Lithuanian Library Press, 1979.

Juozas Kėkštas, "Maioli Blooms with Poppies" (translated by Clark Mills) from *The Green Oak*. New York: Voyages Press, 1962.

Segitas Geda, "When Will You Take Me to Zarasai" (translated by S. Roy) from *The Amber Lyre: 18th–20th Century Lithuanian Poetry*. Moscow: Raduga Publishers, 1983.

Albinas Zukauskas, "Gifts of Autumn" (translated by Dorian Rottenberg) from *The Amber Lyre: 18th–20th Century Lithuanian Poetry*. Moscow: Raduga Publishers, 1983.

Jonas Juskaitis, "Sunday" (translated by Dorian Rottenberg) from *The Amber Lyre: 18th – 20th Century Lithuanian Poetry*. Moscow: Raduga Publishers, 1983.

Albinas Bernotas, "I Can Wait" (translated by Dorian Rottenberg) from *The Amber Lyre: 18th–20th Century Lithuanian Poetry*. Moscow: Raduga Publishers, 1983.

Kazys Boruta, "Thoughts about Eternity" (translated by Dorian Rottenberg) from *The Amber Lyre: 18th–20th Century Lithuanian Poetry*. Moscow: Raduga Publishers, 1983.

Jonas Aistis, "Saint Sebastian" (translated by Demie Jonaitis) from *The Green Oak*. New York: Voyages Press, 1962.

Bernardas Brazdžionis, "Life's Nostalgia" (translated by R. Šilbajoris) from *Perfection of Exile: Fourteen Contemporary Lithuanian Writers*. Norman: University of Oklahoma Press, 1970.

Marcelijus Martinaitis, "If I Am a Tree Someday to Be Chopped Down" (translated by Dorian Rottenberg) from *The Amber Lyre: 18th–20th Century Lithuanian Poetry.* Moscow: Raduga Publishers, 1983.

Henrikas Radauskas, "Arrow in the Sky" (translated by Theodore Melnechuk) from *The Green Oak.* New York: Voyages Press, 1962. "The Winter's Tale" (translated by Randall Jarrell) from *The Green Oak.* Voyages Press, 1962. "The Land of the Lotus Eaters," "Madonna and Fly" (translated by Jonas Zdanys) from *Selected Postwar Lithuanian Poetry.* New York: Maryland Books, 1978.

Nyka-Niliūnas, "Inferno" (translated by Clark Mills) from *The Green Oak.* New York: Voyages Press, 1962.

Tomas Venclova, "Dialogue in Winter" (translated by Jonas Zdanys) *The Green Oak.* New York: Voyages Press, 1962.

# Polish Poems

Czesław Miłosz, "They Will Place There Telescreens" (translated by the author) from *The Collected Poems 1931–1987.* New York: The Ecco Press, 1988.

Tadeusz Rózewicz, "The Tree," "The Grass" (translated by Karen Karleski) from *Poetry East.*

Miron Białoszewski, "Instinctive Self-Portrait" (translated by Peter Harris and Danuta Loposzko) from *The Literary Review.*

Ernest Bryll, "A Scene by the Fire" (translated by Daniel Bourne) from *Artful Dodge.*

Zbigniew Herbert, "A Journey," "How We Were Introduced" (translated by John and Bogdana Carpenter) from *Salmagundi.* "The Death of Lev" (translated by John and Bogdana Carpenter) from *The New Yorker.*

Stanisław Barańczak, "After Gloria Was Gone," "Setting the Hand Brake" (translated by by the author) from *Selected Poems: The Weight of the Body.* Evanston, Ill.: Triquarterly Press, 1989. Used by permission of the author.

Adam Zagajewski, "In May," "Poems on Poland" (translated by Karen Karleski) from *Poetry East.*

Ryszard Krynicki, "These Are Words" (translated by Boguslaw Rostworowski), "Tongue, This Wild Meat" (translated by Grazyna Drabik), "Much Simpler" (translated by Frank Kujawinski) from *Citizen R.K. Does Not Live.* Mr. Cogito Press.

Krzysztof Karasek, "From a Letter of Bertold Brecht to His Son," "Orpheus in the Diner," "Little Fears, Big Fears" (translated by Daniel Bourne) from *The Literary Review.*

Ryszard Holzer, "What is it like in paradise?" (translated by Daniel Bourne) from *The Literary Review.*

Marek Bienkowski, "A Pre-Christmas Toast," "The Word and the Flesh,"

"I, Peter," "Icarus Descending" (translated by Daniel Bourne) from *The Literary Review.*

Wieslaw Kazanecki, "No Smoking" (translated by Danuta Lopzyko and Peter Harris) from *The Literary Review.*

Marek Wawrzykiewicz, "The Pain" (translated by Danuta Lopzyko and Peter Harris) from *The Literary Review.*

Grzegorz Musiał, "Poem for Allen Ginsberg" (translated by Richard Chetwynd) from *Artful Dodge.*

Antoni Pawlak, "An Evening in the Veneration of the Warsaw Pact," "Visitation Rights," "In this chimney they are burning books" (translated by Daniel Bourne) from *Artful Dodge.*

Tomasz Jastrun, "Chasm" (translated by Daniel Bourne) from *Artful Dodge.* "Prose" (translated by Daniel Bourne) from *Greenfield Review.* "Prose," "Silence," "Power," "Fire," "Fatherland," "A Single Drop" (translated by Daniel Bourne) from *The Literary Review.*

Zbigniew W. Smigielski, "A Visit to the Department of Miracle-Works" (translated by Daniel Bourne) from *Artful Dodge.*

Jan Marty, "A Little Battle Hymn" (translated by Daniel Bourne) in *Artful Dodge.*

Krystyna Lars, "Seven Scenes from the Life of Men," "Those Who Come to Me in Dreams" (translated by Daniel Bourne) from *The Literary Review.*

# Romanian Poems

Cezar Baltag, "Imago ignota" (translated by Stavros Deligiorgis) from *The Altantic Review.*

Maria Banuş, "Dream with One Angel" (translated by Stavros Deligiorgis) from *Modern Poetry in Translation.*

Ana Blandiana, "In the Soul of the Land (translated by Stavros Deligiorgis) from *A Book of Women Poets from Antiquity to Now.* A. and W. Barnstone, eds. New York: Schocken Books, 1980.

Constanţa Buzea, "I'm Not Here, Never Was" and "After Snakes" (translated by Stavros Deligiorgis) from *A Book of Women Poets from Antiquity to Now.* A. and W. Barnstone, eds. New York: Schocken Books, 1980.

Ion Caraion, "Compared Treasure" and "Logos" (translated by Stavros Deligiorgis) from *100 de ani de poezie româmeasca: 100 Years of Romanian Poetry.* Jassy: Junimea Publishing House, 1982.

Nina Cassian, "Bait" and "Suave" (translated by Stavros Deligiorgis) from *100 de ani de poezie româmeasca: 100 Years of Romanian Poetry.* Jassy: Junimea Publishing House, 1982.

Leonid Dimov, "Of This World" and "Destiny on the Baobab" (translated by Stavros Deligiorgis) from *100 de ani de poezie româmeasca: 100 Years of Romanian Poetry.* Jassy: Junimea Publishing House, 1982.

Mircea Dinescu, "Metamorphosis" and "Goat of Our Times" (translated by Stavros Deligiorgis) from *100 de ani de poezie româmeasca: 100 Years of Romanian Poetry.* Jassy: Junimea Publishing House, 1982.

Stefan Augustin Doinas, "Pythia" and "Limits" (translated by Stavros Deligiorgis) from *100 de ani de poezie româmeasca: 100 Years of Romanian Poetry.* Jassy: Junimea Publishing House, 1982.

Ileana Mălăncioiu, "Bear's Blood" and "Now There Is So Much Earth" (translated by Stavros Deligiorgis) from *A Book of Women Poets from Antiquity to Now.* A. and W. Barnstone, eds. New York: Schocken Books, 1980.

Virgil Mazilescu, "Point of View nr Three" and "The Woman Always Keeps Coming" (translated by Stavros Deligiorgis) from *100 de ani de poezie româmeasca: 100 Years of Romanian Poetry.* Jassy: Junimea Publishing House, 1982.

Florin Magur, "Foot Race" and "The Clouds" (translated by Stavros Deligiorgis) from *100 de ani de poezie româmeasca: 100 Years of Romanian Poetry.* Jassy: Junimea Publishing House, 1982.

Gellu Naum, "The Eclipse" and "A Couple of Days" (translated by Stavros Deligiorgis) from *100 de ani de poezie româmeasca: 100 Years of Romanian Poetry.* Jassy: Junimea Publishing House, 1982.

Nicolae Prelipceanu, "Thrice Happy" (translated by Stavros Deligiorgis) from *100 de ani de poezie româmeasca: 100 Years of Romanian Poetry.* Jassy: Junimea Publishing House, 1982.

Nichita Stănescu, "After the Battle" and "Food Stones" (translated by Stavros Deligiorgis) in *Modern Poetry in Translation.*

Marin Sorescu, "Moveable Feasts" (translated by Stavros Deligiorgis) from *100 de ani de poezie româmeasca: 100 Years of Romanian Poetry.* Jassy: Junimea Publishing House, 1982.

Dorin Tudoran, "Poetry to Those Who Yes and Those Who No" (translated by Stavros Deligiorgis) from *100 de ani de poezie româmeasca: 100 Years of Romanian Poetry.* Jassy: Junimea Publishing House, 1982.

Daniel Turcea, "Straight Line" and "Zen" (translated by Stavros Deligiorgis) from *100 de ani de poezie româmeasca: 100 Years of Romanian Poetry.* Jassy: Junimea Publishing House, 1982.

Grigore Vieru, "Facing the Hills" and "You Bird" (translated by Stavros Deligiorgis) from *100 de ani de poezie româmeasca: 100 Years of Romanian Poetry.* Jassy: Junimea Publishing House, 1982.

# Ukrainian Poems

Lina Kostenko, "A terrifying kaleidoscope" (translated by Michael Naydan) from *Canadian Slavonic Papers.* "A shady spot" (translated by Michael Naydan) from *Nimrod.*

Natalka Bilotserkivets, "Scents, colors, lines" (translated by Vera L. Kaczmarskyj) from *Agni*.

Ihor Rymaruk, "Walk, while it's still snowing" (translated by Vera L. Kaczmarskyj) from *Soviet Ukrainian Affairs*. "Keep talking, keep talking" (translated by Larissa Onyshkevych) from *Agni*.

# Introduction

## Burton Raffel

Almost everyone who reads poetry in English knows that European poetry is different—and eastern European poetry is *very* different.

> Complacencies of the peignoir, and late
> Coffee and oranges in a sunny chair,
> And the green freedom of a cockatoo
> Upon a rug mingle to dissipate
> The holy hush of ancient sacrifice.
> > (*American:* Wallace Stevens, "Sunday Morning")[1]

> The lough will claim a victim every year.
> It has virtue that hardens wood to stone.
> There is a town sunk beneath its water.
> It is the scar left by the Isle of Man.
> > (*Irish:* Seamus Heaney, "A Lough Neagh Sequence: I")[2]

> To enter the dark
> take this mirror where
> a glacial fire
> is dying out:
>
> once you are deep
> at night's center you'll see
> reflected
> just a baptism of sheep.
> > (*French:* Philippe Jacottet, "Winter Moon,"
> > translated by Charles Tomlinson)[3]

> We must risk our lives near a downed transmission line:
> it's bad news if high voltage doesn't arc between two words . . .
> Charged myself, I too totter dizzily on the bridge between continents,
> my highest ambition to think what I think
> and not my position or, more precisely, not only that.
> > (*Hungary:* Ottó Orbán, "The Bridge,"
> > translated by Bruce Berlind and Mária Körösy)[4]

American, British, and French poetry can be singularly beautiful and wonderfully powerful, but eastern European verse has a sharp edge; it cuts and—unexpectedly—we bleed. The wounds are real and so is the blood.

Western poetry, for all its sterling qualities, does not often deal with reality in this way. Our poetry can be plain, direct, and full of right insight, but theirs has a special sad wisdom, and its echoes do not reverberate with the kind of aftershocks we expect. It is not that eastern Europe poetry is invariably grimmer—though often it is—and certainly it is not that it is sober-sided: I know of no wittier, and sometimes funnier, poetry anywhere:

> The revolution did not start this year either
> But we keep on waiting for it;
>    We are, all of us, Decembrists;
>    for this December we lacked snow
> as we lacked everything else.
> (Romania: Mariana Marin, untitled poem,<br/>translated by Stavros Deligiorgis)

> With your morning coffee bite into
> a bloody steak of fresh news
> How do you feel today my dear world?
> Are you still alive and well?
> (Czech: Jiří Žáček, "Reading the Newspaper,"<br/>translated by E. J. Czerwinski and Stana Dolezal)[5]

Perhaps the archetypical eastern European tale is Slawomir Mrozek's (Poland) "The Elephant," four taut pages in which we read of the director of a provincial zoo, anxious for status but unable to afford it. So he blows up a large elephant-shaped balloon, paints it like an elephant, and for a time is triumphantly successful—until one day, in a brisk wind, the "elephant" breaks his moorings and sails off into the sky.[6] The cut and slash of such writing is plain in almost everything Mrozek writes. His note on producing the play, *The Police*, begins: "This play does not contain anything except what it actually contains. This means that it is not an allusion to anything, it is not a metaphor, and it should not be read as such." The note ends with these ringing words:

> While I know what this little play is not, I do not know what it is, and it is not my duty to explain what it is. This must be discovered by the theatre. And if anyone imagines that these author's remarks and "nots" limit the producer or leave him without a job to do, it means that the person has no true respect for the theatre. The theatre is not so cramped and poverty-stricken as he thinks.[7]

Many of the languages of eastern Europe are spoken by relatively small numbers of people, a million or more. Many of the nationalities have no nations, but all have identities, cultures, and long-established literatures. And they have been turning out mordant, trenchant writing the whole time, much of it known and deeply influential in the West—but none more so than the work of Franza Kafka, of whom another eastern European Jew, Bruno Schulz (who wrote in Polish rather than, like Kafka, in German), has written:

Kafka sees the realistic surface of existence with unusual precision, he knows it by heart, as it were, its code of gestures, all the external mechanics of events and situations,, how they dovetail and interlace, but these to him are but a loose epidermis without roots, which he lifts off like a delicate membrane and fits onto his transcendental world, grafts onto his reality. His attitude to reality is radically ironic, treacherous, profoundly ill-intentioned—the relationship of the presdidigitator to his raw material. He only simulates the attention to detail, the seriousness, and the elaborate precision of this reality in order to compromise it all the more thoroughly.[8]

One is immediately reminded of Karel Čapek (Czech: *R. U. R.*, *War With The Newts*), Jaroslav Hašek (Czech: *The Good Soldier Schweik*), of the hard-edged music of Janáček, Bartók, and Szymanowski, and of course of the writing of Bruno Schulz himself (*The Street of Crocodiles/Cinnamon Shops*). I do not think there are many comparable figures in Western art and music: how many Western writers could cry out, resoundingly, with Bruno Schulz, that "The legend [myth] is the organ by which greatness is apprehended; it is the human spirit's reaction to greatness?"[9] Of how many poetic moments in the last century here in the West can we say, as Gertrud Graubert Champe says of Yugoslav poetry, that "during the Second World War, the ancient, vexed question of whether literature shall instruct or delight remained at rest"?[10] I suspect that any speaker at a Western literary conference who so much as raised this "ancient, vexed question" would be hooted into silence.

To bring oneself to the experience of this very different poetry is rather like coming down a perfectly ordinary road and suddenly confronting the Dead Sea in full sunlight: we could just as well be staring at the landscape of the moon or some other planet—the reflections and refractions simply do not act like those from any other earthly body of water. (I have never seen Utah's Great Salt Lake; it is possible that it produces a similar effect.)

Differentness of this kind is, of course, the farthest thing from casual; it proceeds from deep and abiding causes. The Polish poet Zbigniew Herbert, writing about the historical events underlying the scenes he sees in his travels through Western Europe, observes that "in History nothing remains closed."[11] That may weil seem an unexceptionable statement for a poet—or for Everyman—to make as he confronts the visible evidence of the past. But who in all the long roll of English and American poetry has in fact ever made it—in prose or in verse? Herbert's poetry similarly presents us with what is, to our eyes, a strange and skewed relationship between the inner man and the outer world:

> Inanimate objects are always correct and cannot, unfortunately, be
> reproached with anything. I have never observed a chair shift from
> one foot to another, or a bed rear on its hind legs. And tables,
> even when they are tired, will not dare to bend their knees. I

> suspect that objects do this from pedagogical considerations, to
> reprove us constantly for our instability.
>
> ("Objects")[12]

I do not think any poet in the English or American tradition (or for that matter in the traditions of Germany, France, Italy, or Spain) could have—or ever has—seen the relationship between outer world and inner in quite this way.

History plainly has a great deal to do with these differences. Martin Esslin nicely sums up centuries of that history, and in exactly the terms I think most relevant here:

> In their long-drawn struggles to preserve and re-assert their nationhood against the overwhelmingly powerful tides of Germans and Russians (in the case of Poland), Austrians and Turks (in the case of Hungary and the Southern Slavs) or Austrians and Germans (in the case of the Czechs) these fanatically proud nations clung to their language and literary traditions with far greater fervour and deliberate devotion than more fortunate peoples.[13]

And they *have* clung to their literatures with that sort of pride and devotion—and in particular to their poetry—for hundreds of years. Adam Mickiewicz's long narrative poem, *Pan Tadeusz* (1834), to cite only one illustration, is known as the national poem of Poland.[14] What is England's national poem? or America's? For that matter, what is France's, or Germany's? There are *needs* for literature, and for poetry especially, in eastern Europe that, for good and sufficient reason, we either do not feel or do not fulfill.

> The hour of the Word will strike
> when you don't expect it at all . . .
> And for all crimes, and for all lies,
> a retribution
> will be asked.
>
> And this retribution will not be a bloodletting,
>                         but a blood transfusion
> through the Word.
> (Bulgaria: Blaga Dimitrova, "Almost a Prophecy,"<br>translated by Ludmilla Popova-Wightman)[15]

Neither the biblical nor the poetic Word has that sort of reality, even that sort of existence, in the West. There are plainly things that eastern Europe wants and needs to have from us, but this is something that we—if we could—would do well to learn from them.

It seems to me, although I had no part in the collecting or translating of the poetry in this book, that this book itself is thus necessarily an anthology with a difference. Had I been one of its editors or translators I think

I would repeat, perhaps even as an epigraph—a kind of controlling prelimi-
nary statement—what the Hungarian scholar Linda Dégh wrote of a collection of Hungarian folk tales: "The principal goal in selecting the material
was not to assemble the most beautiful specimens from the entire body of
Hungarian folktales, but to attempt a trustworthy presentation."[16]
Whether that was or was not the editors' intention (and I do not know), it
is I think their clear achievement. It is our job, as the readers of this anthology, to try to understand what it is that this "trustworthy presentation"
offers. Some brief perspective of a general sort may be of help.

There is, in one sense, no such thing as "poetry"—some absolutely de-
finable, utterly knowable phenomenon. In this sense of the word, there are
only "poetries," phenomena that arise in particular times and places, out
of highly specific circumstances, and are expressed in words and rhythms
unique to one language and unknown to all others.

But in another, perhaps just as valid, sense, there is only one poetry—
that of the human species as a whole. The details of language, culture,
time, and even history are, in this alternative sense, inessential. It is an
incontestable, though little known or appreciated, fact that every human
culture, living or dead, of which we have knowledge—whether or not it
had writing, whether or not it had machines, whether or not it had this or
that or the other thing—has always and inevitably had poetry. The poetic
phenomenon is thus universal, endemic to the species.

Both senses of the word "poetry" are of course true, even simultaneously
true, and yet are not mutually exclusive. We can, if we choose to, talk of the
peculiar phenomenon that *is* eastern European poetry, or of the peculiar
phenomena that *are* eastern European poetry, and make sense either way.
But the choice we, in fact, make also makes a large difference in how we
approach this rich body of material. Our choice of perspective makes a
difference in how we read this poetry, what we want, and what we expect
to get from it. It also makes a difference how these poems are translated
and how we evaluate the translations after they have been made.

For most bodies of poetry, my personal inclination has always been to
stress—as English-language poetry has for two hundred years stressed—
its various esthetic dimensions. Neither I nor most others in the West are
indifferent to social and moral values in poetry. But it is not to poetry that
we primarily look for those values. Yet as Lionel Trilling wrote, in 1958,
describing an anthology of literature from modern Poland, "This book
must be thought of as an event."[17]

> . . . not even a dog can gnaw through the chain of heredity
> but it's completely different running right here in a torrent of
>     circumstances
> but it's completely different running right here in a torrent of
>     circumstances
> necessity give me your hand

> necessity here's my other hand
> I gave you the other one by being born
> necessity give me your hand
>            (*Estonia:* Paul-Eerik Rummo, "Fragments from 'Return Address',"
>                                    translated by Elmar Maripuu)[18]

This is strong poetry, strongly—and beautifully—translated. But in English, at least, its success does not depend on its beauty so much as on its substance—the *what* rather than the *how.* I suspect (heretical as it may sound) this poem would survive even a poor, distinctly unbeautiful translation. What matters most, that is, is (in Trilling's terms) the *event* of the poem, the position into which the poet has thrust the poem—a position actively pressed on by history, by nature, by mankind, and yet a position of more than mere resistance: a position of abiding, basic affirmation. Juris Silenieks, introducing this book's selections of Latvian poetry, notes that "the poet in Latvia is a much revered figure intently listened to and expected to provide comfort and guidance in times of stress and misfortune."[19] Does it matter if, in these pages and to our ears, that comfort and guidance can sometimes be heard speaking with an accent, or in a voice something less than lovely?

> If I'm a tree, some day to be chopped down,
> Don't make a stable out of me,
> Don't saw me into firewood.
>
> Make me into a bridge across a river,
> A door or doorstep
> Over which men greet each other.
>            (*Lithuania:* Marcelijus Martinaitis, "If I'm a Tree Someday To Be
>                       Chopped Down," translated by Dorian Rottenberg)[20]

There are Western poets, to be sure, who tackle themes similar to this. But their emphasis—as in Robert Frost, say, or Thomas Hardy—tends to be either the exploration of an individual existence or of a highly individualistic point of view. "If I'm a Tree . . ." is not a collectivist poem, but it clearly derives from a strong, enduring sense of communality that, I think sadly, we in the West do not often share. This book, for example, is full of many, many patriotic poems, stirringly, sometimes brilliantly evocative. How many stirring patriotic poems have been written in English in the past half-century or so? In French? In German?

Which is a good part of what I mean by appropriating Trilling's term, *event.* With even the few fragments of this book's poetic *events* that we now have had in front of us, I think it is not difficult to understand what Miklós Vajda meant when he wrote, of the role of Hungary's poets, that:

Hungarian poets in particular were subject to the relentless vicissitudes of their country's history, involving very real and immediate questions of the nation's existence. . . . Poetry had to meet the historical challenges of the political and armed conflicts of Reformation and Counter-Reformation, four hundred years of an uneasy forced marriage to the Hapsburgs, an Enlightenment carried out like a conspiracy, and two world wars in which Hungary was on the losing side, and as a consequence lost two-thirds of its territory and more than half of its population.[21]

"Relentless," "existence," "historical challenges," "conflicts," and so on: these are the intellectual terms in which Hungary's poets and critics, like all their countrymen, are forced to operate. There are no entitlements in that arena. There are choices, but they are stark and immediate, and they have equally stark and immediate consequences. The aged trainman in Jiri Menzel and Bohumil Hrabal's stunning film, *Closely Watched Trains*, dresses up in full regalia and holds a *stop* sign in front of an onrushing Nazi tank. Says Milos Hrma of his grandfather, "Grandfather wouldn't give way, but stood there, still transmitting the same message . . . [and] the tank ran him over and tore his head off."[22] "This book," declared Czeslaw Milosz (Poland), in the preface to *The Captive Mind*, "is at the same time a battlefield."[23] And there, the battles are never over—even after we may think them far behind us. Recognizing and emphasizing and struggling to understand that omnipresent fact is yet another aspect of the poet's job in eastern Europe.

> Who ever is this sweet little baby in his sleeper?
> This is tiny Adölfchen, son of the Hitlers!
> Maybe he'll grow up to be a lawyer?
> Or maybe a tenor in the Viennese opera?
> Whose little handkin is this, whose ear, whose tiny eye, tiny nose?
> Whose tummy full of milk . . .
>
> (*Poland:* Wisława Szymborska, "Hitler's First Photograph,"
> translated by Karen Kovacik)[24]

"In Central and Eastern Europe," explains Czeslaw Milosz, "the word 'poet' has a somewhat different meaning from that which it has in the West. There a poet does not merely arrange words in beautiful order. Tradition demands that he be a 'bard,' that his songs linger on many lips, that he speak in his poems of subjects of interest to all the citizens."[25] In poem after poem, repeatedly, even insistently, this book verifies Milosz's explanation:

> They are cutting down the trees
> In my town . . .
>> First they break off
>> the tongues of their leaves,
>> to silence their voices.
>> Then they cut off
>> the branches from the shoulder,
>> amputate them one by one—
>> to quell their resistance. . . .
>
> (*Bulgaria:* Blaga Dimitrova, "The Shadows of the Trees," translated
> by Ludmilla Popova-Wightman)[26]

Nor is the Eastern European formulation of poetic *events* confined to crisis situations, moments of extreme and public stress. The Hungarian poet Miklós Radnóti, murdered by the Nazis, writes in his prose memoir, *Under Gemini* (1940), of visiting Paris with his friend, Jean Citadin:

> "I can taste childhood on my tongue," Jean said one night in Paris. "I taste its flavors whenever I'm suddenly reminded of it. Often, it comes to mind from certain flavors too. And sometimes," he added shyly, "from the smells some women have."
> "With me, it's sounds," I answered, "sometimes only rustling, melodies too sometimes, then often whole dialogues will start inside me. And if I hear someone . . . has died . . . death always makes me think of it."[27]

This would be very nearly an impossible conversation for two American men—almost certainly impossible for two English men. The need to *know* is far greater, in Eastern Europe, the need to understand and to tell one's understanding, to pin the world down, to anatomize existence—for how can you take anything for granted when, suddenly, you may find yourself, as the Czech writer Jiri Mucha did, sitting quite literally at the bottom of a coal mine, unable to say when if ever you will be released? ("Where does it come from?/ The courage to be . . .," asks the Czech poet Milan Rúfus, later in this volume, in "The Snowdrop").[28] Mucha writes:

> Eighteen hundred feet below ground, in total darkness lit only by the solitary flickering light of a miner's lamp, I sit down on a log covered in coal-dust to write this diary. I carry my light around with me. I drive a nail into the mouldering wooden shuttering and hang my lamp on it. And in this uncertain glow I try to put down on paper the thoughts which, like bats roused from dark corners, flit past me, brush me with their wings and are gone.
> And in this darkness which has fallen all about me there glows like a lamp the tiny flame of faith in man—flickering, tremulous. The question is: will it survive? I shall know tomorrow.[29]

We in the West find it hard enough to contemplate being exiled to the bottom of a coal mine, let alone sitting at that blackened depth, by flickering light, writing—and asking oneself about "faith in man." The situation is very nearly unimaginable, for us; the question is, I think, inconceivable. But not in Eastern Europe. As the Czech poet Jan Skácel affirms,

> It is possible to steal the public rose in the park
> during a summer night. A rose in the vase
> is wounded and sheds the petals by morning
> like everything like human glory
> > > > (*Czech and Slovak:* Jan Skácel,
> > > > "A Sonnet Instead of a Rose,"
> > > > trans. E.J. Czerwinski and Stana Dolezal)[30]

Do we still have "public roses," here in the West? And even if we did, would we connect them to anything so grand, or so universal, as "human glory"?

The very words almost falter on our lips, and the idea has become foreign to us, even more foreign than the many languages spoken by the poets represented in this book. But Miklós Vajda (Hungary) can still declare that "Poetry, which cannot be shelled like a city, or whitewashed like murals, crushed like sculpture, closed like theaters, or even banned and censored as easily as novels and journals, can spread and be influential even without print or manuscript."[31] And we know, from the clear pages of history, that Vajda is telling the truth. When the Russian scientist Evgenia S. Ginzburg was swept senselessly but horribly into two decades of prison-camp life, she records in *Into the Whirlwind* how

> poetry united us all. In Yaroslavl I had often thought that I alone sought and found in it a way out of the closed circle of my life . . . This was a conceited illusion, I now discovered, as I listened to the floods of verse we poured out, our own and other people's, simple or sophisticated, lyrical or sardonic.[32]

Maria Kuncewicz, editor of *The Modern Polish Mind*, makes an even more resounding affirmation:

> What a contemporary Pole thinks, how he feels about life, exposed as he is to German nationalist vindications on one side and the Soviet might on the other, contributes valuable material to mankind's experience. Indeed, it might be said that after World War II, the Yalta Agreement between the Western allies and the Soviet Union had the unexpected result of transforming Poland into a laboratory retort where the most incompatible elements of human destiny are melting into new forms of coexistence. . . . Literature alone kept the dismembered nation together . . . [The] massive invasion by poetry of the field of international politics, although it did not greatly affect international politics, mobilized and electrified the originally somewhat rustic spirit of the Polish nation; it left its literature flourishing.[33]

It is to the *events* of this book that I commend you. There is beauty and to spare, in the pages which follow, but these are not "merely" poems, and their authors are not "merely" poets. In the right hands, and in the right hearts, this is a power for which men and women have died, and because of which governments and whole systems of government have been toppled. It may not happen here, nor do I think it will. But it could.

# Notes

1. Wallace Stevens, *The Collected Poems of Wallace Stevens* (New York: Knopf, 1965), pp. 66–67.

2. Seamus Heaney, *Poems, 1965–1975* (New York: Farrar, Straus and Giroux, 1980), p. 68.

3. Philippe Jaccottet, "Lune d'Hiver" ("Winter Moon"), translated by Charles Tomlinson, in *The Random House Book of Twentieth-Century French Poetry*, edited by

Paul Auster (New York: Random House, 1982; reprint, New York: Vintage, 1984), p. 469.

4. See p. 247 below.

5. See pp. 214 and 361 below.

6. Slawomir Mrozek, "The Elephant," *The Elephant,* translated by Konrad Syrop (London: Macdonald, 1962; reprint, New York: Grove, 1965), pp. 16–20.

7. Slawomir Mrozek, *Six Plays by Slawomir Mrozek,* translated by Nicholas Bethell (New York: Grove, 1967), pp. 7–8.

8. Bruno Schulz, *Letters and Drawings of Bruno Schulz,* edited by Jerzy Ficowski, translated by Walter Srndt and Victoria Nelson (New York: Harper and Row, 1988), p. 88.

9. Ibid., p. 59.

10. Gertrud Graubert Champe, "The Poetry of Postwar Yugosalavia," in *Contemporary Yugoslav Poetry,* edited by Vasa D. Mihailovich (Iowa City: University of Iowa Press, 1977), p. xviii.

11. Zbigniew Herbert, *Barbarian in the Garden,* translated by Michael March and Jaroslaw Anders (London: Carcanet, 1985; reprint New York: Harcourt Brace Jovanovich, 1986), p. 147.

12. Zbigniew Herbert, *Selected Poems,* translated by Czeslaw Milosz and Peter Dale Scott (Harmondsworth: Penguin, 1968), p. 63.

13. Martin Esslin, "Introduction," in *Three East European Plays* (Harmondsworth: Penguin, 1970), p. 7.

14. Adam Mickiewicz, *Pan Tadeusz,* translated by Kenneth Mackenzie (London: Dent, Everyman, 1966), p. xi.

15. See pp. 153–54 below.

16. *Folktales of Hungary,* edited by Linda Degh (Chicago: University of Chicago Press, 1965), p. xxi.

17. Lionel Trilling, "Introduction," in *The Broken Mirror: A Collection of Writings from Contemporary Poland,* edited by Pawel Mayewski (New York: Random House, 1958), p. 1.

18. See p. 42 below.

19. See p. 58 below.

20. See p. 136 below.

21. *Modern Hungarian Poetry,* edited by Miklós Vajda (New York: Columbia University Press, 1977), p. xx.

22. Jiri Menzel and Bohumil Hrabal, *Closely Watched Trains,* translated by Josef Holzbecher (New York: Simon and Schuster, 1972), p. 21.

23. Czeslaw Milosz, *The Captive Mind,* translated by Jane Zielonko (New York: Vintage, 1953), p. xi.

24. See p. 275 below.

25. Milosz, *The Captive Mind,* p. 168.

26. See p. 158 below.

27. Miklós Radnóti, *Under Gemini: A Prose Memoir . . . ,* translated by Kenneth and Zita McRobbie and Jascha Kessler (Athens: Ohio University Press, 1985), p. 45. I have lengthened the translation's ellipses to double ellipses, in order to keep them from being confused with deletions.

28. See p. 203 below.

29. Jiri Mucha, *Living and Partly Living,* translated by Ewald Osers (New York: McGraw-Hill, 1968), p. 7.

30. See p. 206 below.

31. *Modern Hungarian Poetry,* p. xxi.

32. Evgenia S. Ginzburg, *Into the Whirlwind,* translated by Paul Stevenson and

Manya Harari (London: Collins, 1967; reprint, Harmondsworth: Penguin, 1968), p. 224.

33. *The Modern Polish Mind,* edited by Maria Kuncewicz (Boston: Little, Brown, 1962), pp. 3–4.

# Editor's Note

All introductions for this collection were written before and during many of the changes that took place in eastern Europe at the beginning of the 1990s. Therefore, they may not reflect all the political and geographical circumstances existing at the time of publication.

# SHIFTING
# BORDERS

# Part 1
# Poetry of the Baltic Republics

# Estonia, compiled by Doris Kareva

## Estonian Poetry Today
## by Doris Kareva

To write in a language of fewer than a million speakers, and yet to write for an audience that may, at times, reach the same number of readers—that is the peculiar fate that the poets of Estonia have to face.

The urge for freedom is obviously greatest in those who have experienced liberty, but then have seen it lost. The persistence and intensity of that passion may be difficult for those who have enjoyed free existence long enough to take it for granted to imagine. Yet it is something that all small and suppressed nations share and that lies at the heart of their poetry.

Situated at the entrance to the Gulf of Finland, the maritime gateway to Russia, Estonia, throughout its known history, has had to struggle, either openly or underground, desperately for its national survival. Poetry has always been one of the few means to assure one another that we exist—that we are alive and aware of the real human values, beauty, and truth. This feeling of belonging—of inseparableness from one's country, its nature, its present and past, a deep "Estonianness"—is clearly perceptible even in the most intellectually aloof Estonian writers, no matter where or under what circumstances they live. In a way, each poem written in Estonian is a love poem, a hymn to the native language, a proclamation of resistance and remaining alive.

The brief selection presented in this anthology covers a small part of Estonian poetry, mostly from the last decade. It includes also some exile poets who escaped possible physical extermination in the forties, but had to wait for several decades before being published and openly recognized in Estonia. To render the atmosphere in which most of the poems in this selection were created, some comments will be necessary.

After the massacres and deportations, the fear and frustration of the fifties, and the short revival of hope followed by deep disappointment in the sixties, the period of stagnation seemed quite peaceful from the outside. This was the age of disillusionment: silent on the surface, but churning with inner storms, painfully awakened memories, and cunning ways to fool the censorship and to pass on a message to readers. The real meaning of censorship during those years is probably hard to grasp for those who have not experienced it. Not only was anything political prohibited, but also everything that could be even slightly associated with politics, such as certain colors or names of the months. Even the most innocent nursery rhymes were deeply distrusted and often banned for absurd reasons. Mention of an angel, for example, in one of E. T. A. Hoffmann's poems for children was found to be too dangerous, so the publisher was sent to the printing shop to tear out the blasphemous page from books ready for sale. Of course, the use of words like "God" or "Estonia" meant usually that the poem was never published and also entailed very serious problems for the author. Words like "meat" or "coffee" had to be erased from a poem if these foodstuffs were not available for sale. Emily Dickinson's verse "I taste a liquor never brewed" was banned for conflicting with Gorbachev's temperance policy. Hundreds of examples could be recounted, many of which may sound quite unbelievable. The censorship, which completely anathemized independent thought, severed people from all direct cultural contacts with the West and was especially suspicious of anything spiritually superior. Poetry had to obtain the hardness, purity, and multidimensional brilliance of a diamond in order to pass the Scylla and Charybdis of censorship without losing its significance for the reader. But, if it succeeded, there was no problem in selling forty or fifty thousand copies of a poetry book within one hour. People came to libraries to copy their favorite poets' works by hand, hour after hour, book after book. Poetry had to console and encourage those deprived of religion, politics, and national independence. The poet's role was that of a sage.

The radical changes that have recently taken place have also influenced the situation and the whole meaning of poetry. Many poets have turned into politicians. Among other problems there is a certain confusion about finding a new language. It is no longer censorship that dictates what and how to write, but rather the general material want, the desperate lack of everything from pencil to paper, as well as the commercial values that are overpowering the earlier spiritual ones. Nevertheless, the essence of poetry has not changed. New voices, forms, and aspirations continue to branch forth, gathering force from the same old roots. The new age offers new challenges to poetry—and demands as much spiritual resilience as ever. Using the most frequent metaphor for a homeland in Estonian poetry, the beehive, one could say that poetry in the present feverish and unsettled state is the healing honey, the uniting and revitalizing innermost power of the language of a small nation that still hopes to survive.

Thanks to Ivar Ivask and Mardi Valgemäe for his help in preparing this section.

# About the Poets

## BETTI ALVER

Betti Alver (1906–89), "la grande dame" of Estonian poetry, was a member of the thirties literary group, Arbujad. After publishing her first collection of poetry, *Tolm ja tuli* (*Dust and Fire*, 1936), she chose to be silent for thirty years as her way of resisting the Soviet rules. Her next book, *Tähetund* (*Starry Hour*, 1966), and the last one, *Korallid Emajôes* (*Corals in an Ancient River*, 1986), present verse that is crystal clear and intellectually flexible. She has also written novels, *Tuule armuke* (*The Wind's Lover*, 1927), poems in prose, *Viletsuse komöödia* (*The Comedy of Misery*, 1935), and several long poems, and has translated Goethe and Pushkin (*Yevgeni Onegin*).

## INDREK HIRV

Indrek Hirv (b. 1956), poet and artist, has studied ceramics and is also known as a graphic artist. He has published three books of poetry, *Uneraev* (*Dreamrage*, 1987), the bilingual *Salapainos.Pimetrykk* (*Blind-Print*, 1988 in Finland), and *Pôueoda* (*The Dagger*, 1990), and has translated French and Dutch poetry. Since 1989, he has resided in Amsterdam.

## PEEP ILMET

Peep Ilmet (b. 1948) has published four collections of verse, the titles of which all contain the word "wind"—*Tuulekanne* (1980), *Tuuletee.Ajastaja* (1982), *Tuul tuli* (1986), and a bilingual work entitled *Linnamägi tuulte vallas* (*A Drumlin in the Wind*, 1989 in Finland). He also writes children's verse. His poetry borrows images from ancient Estonian beliefs and uses an archaic vocabulary.

## IVAR IVASK

Ivar Vidrik Ivask (b. 1927 in Riga) is a poet, essayist, and scholar of literature. In 1944, he was a refugee in Germany, and he moved to the United States in 1950. He retired recently from his positions as professor of modern languages at the University of Oklahoma and editor (since 1967) of *World Literature Today*. He wrote numerous essays and reviews, encyclopedic works and symposia, and prefaces and introductory essays for a number of publications. He has also published several volumes of poetry: in Estonian, *Tähtede tähendus* (*The Meaning of the Stars*, 1964), *Elu-kogu* (*Life Collections*, 1978), *Verandaraamat ja teisi luuletusi* (*The Veranda Book and Other Poems*, 1990); in German, *Gespiegelte Erde* (1967); and in English, *Snow Lessons* (1986), and *Baltic Elegies* (1987). In 1985, he published a bilingual collection in Estonian and Italian, *Il libro della veranda*. He has illustrated his own and his wife's books of poetry, and his art has been exhibited in Oklahoma, Wisconsin, Helsinki, Stockholm, and Tallinn.

## MERLE JÄÄGER (MERCA)

Merle Jääger (b. 1965), a poet and actress, uses "Merca" as her pseudonym. She has published two slim volumes of poetry, *Merca by Air Mail* and

*Mercamerka* in Canada in 1989. She is the central figure of a "punk" movement in Estonia, "the bard of protest."

## JAAN KAPLINSKI

Jaan Kaplinski (b. 1941) is probably the most widely known Estonian poet and essayist. *Tolmust ja värvidest* (*Of Dust and Colors,* 1967), *Valge joon Võrumaa kohal* (*White Line over Võrumaa,* 1972), *Ma vaatasin päikese aknasse* (*I Looked into Sun's Window,* 1976), *Uute kivide kasvamine* (*The Growing New Stones,* 1977), *Tule tagasi helmemänd* (*Come Back Ancient Pine,* 1984), and a collection of poems, *Käoraamat* (*Fragrant Orchid,* 1986), as well as the autobiographical *Kust tuli öö* (*From Where the Night Came*) are among his books. He has also written plays, children's verse, and several essays about language, literature, ecology, nature, and philosophy. He has translated works from French, Spanish, English, Polish, and other languages, including Li Bo and Du Fu from Chinese. Many of his own books have been translated into Swedish, Finnish, Polish, and other languages. *The Same Sea in Us All* (Portland, Oregon, 1985) and *The Wandering Border* (Port Townsend, Washington, 1987) are available in English.

## DORIS KAREVA

Doris Kareva (b. 1958) has published six books of poetry; *Puudutus* (*Touch,* 1981), *Salateadvus* (*The Secret Consciousness,* 1983), *Vari ja viiv* (*Shadow and While,* 1986), and *Armuaeg* (*Days of Grace,* 1991) are among them. She has also translated works by Emily Dickinson, Anna Ahmatova, and others.

## HASSO KRULL (MAX HARNOON)

Hasso Krull (b. 1964), one of the modernists among the younger Estonian poets, used "Max Harnoon" as a pseudonym for his first collection of poetry, *Must-valge* (*Black-and-White,* 1986). His next book of poems was *Pihlakate meri* (*The Sea of Rowans,* 1988). He has also written several critical essays on art and literature and has translated French poetry.

## ILMAR LAABAN

Ilmar Laaban (b. 1921), poet and essayist, is the most outstanding surrealist of Estonian poetry. A refugee in Sweden since 1944, he works as a freelance writer and art critic. His first book of poems, *Ankruketi lõpp on laulu algus* (*The End of the Anchor Chain Is the Beginning of the Song,* 1946), was followed by a slim volume of witty linguistic experimentation, *Rroose Selaviste,* in 1957. His last book, *Oma ja võõrast luulet* (*Own and Others' Poetry,* 1990) contains his own poems in Estonian and Swedish and also his translations of others' poems. In Sweden, a three-volume set of his works is being published, the first volume containing his poetry and translations, the second collected articles on literature, and the third articles on art. Laaban has written several essays, among them works on Baudelaire and Sartre, has translated French poetry into Swedish, and has created a new form of auditive poetry, "häälutused," which he performs in person.

## KALJU LEPIK

Kalju Lepik (b. 1921), a refugee since 1944, lives in Sweden. Since 1987, he has been president of the Exile Writers' Union—the central figure in Estonian poetry-in-exile. Among his books are *Nägu koduaknas* (*Face in the Home Window, 1946*), *Mängumees* (*The Fiddler,* 1948), *Kerjused treppidel* (*The Beggars on the Stairs,* 1949), *Merepõhi* (*Sea Bottom,* 1951), *Muinasjutt Tügrimaast* (*A Tale of Tigerland,* 1955), *Kivimurd* (*Stone Quarry,* 1958), *Ronk on laululind* (*The Raven Is a Singing Bird,* 1961), *Kollased nõmmed* (*Yellow Heaths,* 1965), *Marmorpagulane* (*A Marble Refugee,* 1968), *Verepõld* (*Blood Field,* 1973), *Klaasist mehed* (*Glass Men,* 1978), *Collected Poems* (1980), *Kadunud külad* (*Lost Villages,* 1985), *Rukkilille murdmise laul* (*Song of Breaking a Cornflower,* 1990), and several deluxe editions.

## VIIVI LUIK

Viivi Luik (b. 1946) has won much attention and interest not only for her poems, but also for her novels, *Seitsmes rahukevad* (*The Seventh Spring of Peace,* 1975) and *Ajaloo ilu* (*The Beauty of History,* 1991), which were published first in Finnish. Her books of poems include *Pilvede pyha* (*The Feast Day of Clouds,* 1965), *Taevaste tuul* (*The Wind of Heavens,* 1966), *Lauludemüüja* (*The Songseller,* 1968), *Hääl* (*Voice,* 1968), *Ole kus oled* (*Be Where You Are,* 1971), *Pildi sisse minek* (*Entering the Picture,* 1973), *Põliskevad* (*Ancient Spring,* 1975), *Maapäälsed asjad* (*Terrestrial Things,* 1978), and *Rängast rõõmust* (*From Grave Joy,* 1982). She has also written books for children.

## ENE MIHKELSON

Ene Mihkelson (b. 1944) has written poetry, prose, and essays on literature. She has published many books of poetry: *Sele talve laused* (*The Sentences of that Winter,* 1978), *Ring ja nelinurk* (*Circle and Quadrangle,* 1979), *Algolekud* (*Primary Beings,* 1980), *Tuhased tiivad* (*Ashy Wings,* 1982), *Igiliikuja* (*Perpetuum mobile,* 1985), *Tulek on su saatus* (*Coming Is Your Fate,* 1987), and *Võimalus õunast loobuda* (*Chance to Discard the Apple,* 1990). Her novels include *Matsi pôhi* (*Ground of Bumpkin*, 1983), *Kuju keset väljakut* (*Monument in the Square*, 1983), and *Korter* (*The Flat*, 1985).

## PAUL-EERIK RUMMO

Paul-Eerik Rummo (b. 1942) is the central figure of the wave of the sixties. He has written numerous books of poetry: *Ankruhiivaja* (*Heaver of Anchor*, 1962), *Tule ikka mu rôômude juurde* (*Keep Coming to My Joys*, 1964), *Lumevalgus . . . . Lumepimedus* (*Snow Light . . . . Snow Blindness*, 1966), *Saatja aadress* (*Return Address*, 1972 and published partly in the collection *Ajapinde ajab* [*Splinters of Time*, 1985]), and *Oh et sädemeid kiljuks mu hing* (collected poems, 1985). He has also written several plays—among which is *Tuhkatrii-numäng* (*Cinderellagame*, 1969), which has been staged in New York City, at La Mama in 1971, and elsewhere—filmscripts, essays, and other works. He has produced recordings of poetry and has translated Dylan Thomas, R. D. Laing, Tuomas Anhava, and others. At present, he works at the cultural council in the Estonian government.

## HANDO RUNNEL

Hando Runnel (b. 1938) is a very popular Estonian poet and essayist. Most of his poems have been set to music. He has published several books of poetry for adults and children: *Avalikud laulud* (*Public Songs*, 1970), *Laul-uraamat ehk Môôganeelaja ehk Kurbade kaitseks* (*Songbook, or Sword Swallower, or In Defence of the Sad*, 1972), *Môru ja mööduja* (*Bitter and Passer*, 1976), *Kodu-käija* (*Home-Ghost*, 1978), *Punaste ôhtute purpur* (*The Purple of the Red Evenings*, 1982), and *Laulud eestiaegsetele meestele* (*Songs for Men of Good Old Times*, 1968). He has also published two collections of essays, *Ei hôebdat, kulda* (*No Silver, No Gold*, 1984) and *Môôk ja peegel* (*Sword and Mirror*, 1988), a recording of his poetry, and several articles on literature, ethics, and other topics.

## MARI VALLISOO

Mari Vallisoo (b. 1959) has published three collections of poems: *Kallid koerad* (*Dear Dogs*, 1979), *Kônelen sinuga kevadekuul* (*Speaking to You in Spring*, 1980), and *Rändlinnud kôrvaltoas* (*Migratory Birds in the Next Room*, 1983). The original force of her balladlike verse springs from the very soul of the northern spirit.

## JUHAN VIIDING (JÜRI ÜDI)

Juhan Viiding (b. 1948) works as an actor and producer in the Tallinn Drama Theater. His poetry became the leading voice of the seventies. He has published several collections of verse poems, *Detsember* (*December,* 1971), *Käekäik* (*Course of Life,* 1973), *Selges eesti keeles* (*In Clear Words,* 1974), *Armastuskirjad* (*Love Letters,* 1975), *Ma olin Jüri Üdi* (*I Was Jüri Üdi,* 1978), *Elulootus* (*Hope for Life,* 1980), *Tänan ja palun* (*Thanks and Pleads,* 1983), and *Osa* (*Part,* 1991) among them. He has also performed his poetry and songs with Tônis Rätsep in the form of a literary cabaret; they have been recorded. Together, they also have written a play, *Olevused (Beings),* which was staged in 1980. A collection of Viiding's poetry has been translated into Finnish.

# Estonian Poems

### FROM "BALTIC ELEGIES"
Ivar Ivask

Strange to hail from almost anonymous shores
in overexplored Europe where the Baltic
still hides a lunar side, unilluminated
except for subjugations, annexations
which continue unabated for centuries.
No problem for anyone to name the Nordic countries
from Iceland to Finland,
but how about the Baltic ones?
Surely one and the same language
is spoken there? If not Russian,
at least something akin to German?
You will never guess unless we unravel
the skein of Indo-European and Finno-Ugric
language families, ponder Babel
to clear up the Baltic,
and who has time for such marginal myths?
We persist with the subsoil. Grass is another
favored metaphor (trampled upon, it springs back),
or limestone cliffs filed away by gales
yet undefiled, withstanding millennia.
It is strange to hail from the dark side of the moon
while supposedly we inhabit the same planet.
There are Third World pockets inside Europe
one tends to overlook, anonymous shores
marked with an x or a mental question mark.

If only you incline in the Baltic direction,
you begin to hear the dirge of a beehive
and perceive in underwater outline
an amber chamber built with pollen of grief.

(Written in English)

## THE STELLAR HOUR
### Betti Alver

The wind won't ask: to what did life amount?
To your own self you'll render your account.

However long, however dark the night—
your forehead bears your name in plain, clear sight.

Each leaf that sees the sunlight falls unknown
with all the rest. Yet each one falls alone.

No shining goal, no star to travel toward?
Consumerism brings its own reward.

Do you know how kindness grows, unseen and gentle?
Why cruel deeds are never accidental?
Why helmets rust unless they bloom and flower?
Why life can never repeat its star-bright hour?
Why tiny flames withstood the snow-storm's test
and flickered on within the human breast?

Go ask your betters, do their bidding.
Go ask the dead. And then go ask the living.

But never ask a long-lost yesterday
for those who took the circumstantial way
across the sandy marsh to pitch black night.

It's all the same to them—was it spite
that made the boatman take his chance
without a light, or was it happenstance?

Translated by Elmar Maripuu

# THE DEBT
Betti Alver

My soul owes a debt, a constant reproach.
First to be taken
were my shawl
and my brooch,
my magic mirror, my mandrake root,
my silver-voiced
enchanted flute.
Then the claimant took my festive hours,
took away my joy and my vital powers,
took away my home,
all shelter and shade—
> but my debt,
> o my debt
> can never be paid.

Whatever I hoped for, today it's quite plain
that the claimant can claim my most harrowing pain.
My bitterest tears
must all be conveyed—
> but my debt,
> o my debt
> can never be paid.

In my dreams I still dream
the impossible,
eternity's made
comprehensible,
blossoms and blooms
of exuberance,
ducats, doubloons, endless opulence,
singing and soaring, with stars arrayed—
> but my debt,
> o my debt
> can never be paid.

Translated by Elmar Maripuu

## CORALS IN AN ANCIENT RIVER
### Betti Alver

A shimmering rainbow's high ridge
arched over the river that day.
We stood on the cast-iron bridge;
ahead lay your iron-paved way.

Time's treasures were spilled at my feet;
ahead lay your iron-paved way.
I turned and, with no need to speak,
threw my red coral necklace away.

Time's treasures have lost all their lustre,
God's truth has a dull, lifeless glimmer;
but the river flows stronger and faster
where beads of red coral still shimmer.

Translated by Elmar Maripuu


## BY THE WATERS OF TOONELA
### Kalju Lepik

Faint distant stars are shining,
And the night wind blows rank.
Here I am stalking the death-bird
On this dead bank.

Tipped in a Karjala smithy,
This is the shaft I have chosen,
Knowing the bird of death
Waits for death from my bowstring.

Now in their final flight,
See how the great wings quiver.
God! I am borne into night,
Borne down the darkened river.

Translated by W. K. Matthews

---

(NOTE: The translator has slightly changed the original title "Corals in Emajôgi." The Emajôgi is the major river of Estonia.)
(NOTE: Toonela: The Estonian Hades, or abode of death, known also as Manala. Karjala: Carelia.)

## WOODEN CROSSES
Kalju Lepik

At thickets of wooden crosses
The moon's bloodless snout
Barks out its aching lustre.

Helmets with noiseless mouths
Open in frozen laughter.

Tempests of February
Strive with the brass of words
Over heroic blood fallen.

Snowdrifts smother each laugh
In thickets of wooden crosses,
Meaningless wooden crosses.

Translated by W. K. Matthews

## TO LIVE FREE OR DIE
Ilmar Laaban

To weigh the sun on scales of leaves
To shout the truth to every wind
To mirror fountains on one's brow
To live free or die . . .

To see tall Dawn's coruscant tree
Rise on the mountain range of hate
Find man in hail in mothlike wings
To live free or die . . .

To sprout and deck a murderer's tomb
To balance blocks of rock with joy
To seek the waves deep undulant heart
To live free or die.

Translated by Ivar Ivask

## FRAGMENTS FROM "RETURN ADDRESS"
### Paul-Eerik Rummo

+

I don't suppose the world understands me much
I'm talking about Estonia

I don't suppose Estonia understands me much
I'm talking about myself

I don't suppose I understand myself much
I'm talking about the world

+

on at least two sides of good and evil
always within the reach or the grasp
      of my inner universe's firm handshake
in the thickets of my private life, in Estonia

+

now god grant me strength to run in a torrent of circumstances
and to recognize necessity among the multitude
who assume her appearance by force

suffering nest in the memory
not even a dog can gnaw through the chain of heredity
but it's completely different running right here in a torrent of
circumstances
but it's completely different running right here in a torrent of
circumstances
necessity give me your hand

necessity here's my other hand
I gave you the other one by being born
necessity give me your hand

Translated by Elmar Maripuu

## WE'RE HERE TO HOLD FAST TO EACH OTHER
Paul-Eerik Rummo

We're here to hold fast to each other
a clan of wild bees swarming free
we're here to hold fast to each other
and pass through the turbulent sea
and pass through the turbulent sea
that rises in anger to thwart us
and pass through the turbulent sea
with no other strength to support us
with no other strength to support us
but shoulders as one to the load
with no other strength to support us
but mutual debts gladly owed
but mutual debts gladly owed
that bind to their own joyful ends
those mutual debts gladly owed
that the sea has no power to cleanse

Let me feel the wind on your breast
understanding what you understand
let me feel the land your heels press
and stand on the soil where you stand
and stand on the soil where you stand
and think of all lands the sky covers
the land on whose soil we both stand
is given forever to lovers

Then love me if through all reverses
you see the bright sky in my eyes
then love me and sing these my verses
entangled in heartache and sighs
entangled in heartache and sighs
sensing dangers unseen, undiscovered
my verse tells of heartache and sighs
can we learn to hold fast to each other
can we learn to hold fast to each other
a clan of wild bees swarming free
can we learn to hold fast to each other
and pass unafraid through the sea

Translated by Elmar Maripuu

## OUTLINE
Hando Runnel

Father drank; mama
was good as good can be,
the kids grew up to join
the petty bourgeoisie.

The daughter's nouveau riche,
the son's idealistic views
have made him anchorman
for prime-time TV news.

Pa deceived the people,
Ma deceived papa,
the children, worldly-wise,
trust no one very far.

Translated by Elmar Maripuu

## I FINISHED LUNCH
Hando Runnel

I finished lunch, put down my spoon
and took the prompt my heartstrings gave.
I went to . . . where? . . . the cemetry,
to sit beside my father's grave.

I went to air my troubled thoughts,
unburden every hope and care;
my father always hears me out,
he's got the time, and more, to spare.

But now the graveyard's leafy maples,
lofty ashes, linden trees
seemed strange and unfamiliar,
peculiar currents stirred the breeze.

Yes, there it was: my father's grave,
the vase of water overturned,
the flowers broken, trampled, stolen,
shame unleashed and honour spurned.

Translated by Elmar Maripuu


## SONS AND DAUGHTERS: CON AMORE
Hando Runnel

Honored and loved,
invited and seated,
salved and anointed,
blessed and cherished,
selected and tested,
trusted and committed,
commanded and controlled,
rejected and forgotten,
cheated and swindled,
toppled and punished,
degraded and insulted,
disgraced and hated,
tortured and terrified,
exterminated, compensated,
demoted, promoted,
amnestied, rehabilitated.

Translated by George Kurman


## THE EAST-WEST BORDER
Jaan Kaplinski

The east-west border is always wandering,
sometimes eastward, sometimes west,
and we do not know exactly where it is just now:
in Gaugamela, in the Urals, or maybe in ourselves,
so that one ear, one eye, one nostril, one hand, one foot,
one lung and one testicle or one ovary
is on the one, another on the other side. Only the heart,
only the heart is always on one side:

if we are looking northward, in the West;
if we are looking southward, in the East;
and the mouth doesn't know on behalf of which or both
it has to speak.

Translated by the author with Sam Hamill and Riina Tamm

## EVERYTHING IS INSIDE OUT
### Jaan Kaplinski

Everything is inside out, everything is different—
colorless, nameless, voiceless—
the sky overhead is an axe-blade. No one knows
that what mirrors the stars and the Milky Way is an axe.
Only those who love see, and remain silent
while in the sky the mirror-blade gets loose and falls
through us, a black starry dark
falling through a blacker dark, and nothing can stop it.
It falls no matter how we turn, always,
it hits us and divides head from body.
The sound of the abyss rises like clouds through us.
Twin stars are overhead: one light, one dark.
Everything else is illimitable void and distant,
dust motes whirling through a dark cathedral, everything else
is a black shawl where the fine old fire has written our names too.

Translated by the author with Sam Hamill and Riina Tamm

## NEW BUTTERFLIES ARE MADE
### Jaan Kaplinski

New butterflies are made of dust and color, but we
are planted in the ground like broken bones to replace ourselves.
Somewhere in storm and darkness, waves lap newborn islands
    like the lioness licks her cubs.
Words take their first steps on the darkness of white pages
    where there are no shadows, no depths, no distances
until something utterly new is born co-ordinate with Aurora Borealis
    and silver-starred hammer-blows fall through deep sleep,
walls touch fingers and syrup hums in the maple's virgin heart.
Once we were to meet our children's, our parent's blood.

Red strawberries stretch out their hands and geraniums are
strangely silent.
Dunes grow here as if white sand remembered the murmur
    of the rivers of paradise. Lone ants lose themselves in the wind,
    carnations
blaze up on beaches, something burns unavoidably, and night sleeps
    in the moor's warm lap while nearby star clusters break in its hair.
Fleet memory filled with ancient waterfall roars, seashells,
    and bees asleep behind dark walls—
will anything be reborn? Everything burns deep, deep,
    coals blanch and arteries harden,
and when the time comes to rise, ashes won't let go' our hands,
    wing-feathered spring fog freezes.
How does a child's smile lose itself in the king's chamber,
    where does clover, that four-leafed fortune, find courage to grow
    beneath these forbidding pillars
when even the black inscriptions on the birches fade and the leaves'
    green flight
    wearies before clay becomes clay and the bloody mud sinks back into
    the soil?
No, no one anywhere needs your history, your ends and beginnings.
Peace. Simple peace to the jellyfish, and to grouse eggs; peace,
    to the ant's rushing pathways; peace, to birds of paradise and to the
    ginko
peace, to apples, pears, plums, apricots, oranges,
    wild roses growing in the railroad guardshack:
Requiem, Requiem aeternum.

                                   Translated by the author and Sam Hamill


### [UNTITLED]
### Viivi Luik

Across the empty page moves a human hand,
skin, flesh, fingernails and bones.
But held by three fingers, slanted toward the good
and evil of the world, is the pencil, firm and true.

Outside howls the wind or the city or history.
The gazing eyes have become inscrutable.
The heart beats against the chest ceaselessly,
but the mouth is mute and cannot explain

why every moment contains a special misery
felt by everything that breathes. The hand writes.
And the time will come when this dark pain
will rise from the page and bring us back to life.

Translated by Billy Collins and Mardi Valgemäe


## [UNTITLED]
### Viivi Luik

The century of darkness snaps the spine's puppet wires straight,
its paws manipulate dances of discord, enmity and hate.

It spills its shadow into souls. What secrets does it bury there?
What things does it make unlike themselves? Whom does it choose to
    spare?

High above a skittish glittering in ancient starry skies.
One acquainted with its signs would raise his hands to hide his eyes.

Local bars and stores as always help the idle hours pass,
picking at another's faults distracts you from your own distress.

Nothing's changed to look at it, the snow still falls, the rain still pours.
people come and people go, attending to their daily chores.

But in the night someone tosses, turns, his body drenched in sweat,
raves of a great judgment day and asks if it's approaching yet.

Into the winds of time a window crashes, bursts open wide.
With parted lips, you gasp for breath to scream. Lightning strikes
    inside.

Translated by Gabriella Mirollo and Talvi Laev


## WING SHADOW
### Viivi Luik

Say it: "Verdant fir, you dark celestial angel."
Say it poignantly. Unmockingly. With grace.
Words infuse the air with white enchanted circles.
Don't observe the manner of your voice or face.

Stars that never tarnish, pious Christmas light
lay their curses on a land already damned.
All too clear the end, the start not yet in sight.
Nations scattered at the slightest gust of wind.

'Til death's magic mountain rises and explodes,
wear the century like a dark engagement ring.
All is possible. This too, that heaven's host
may rally from its ashes without warning.

> Translated by Gabriella Mirollo and Talvi Laev

## [UNTITLED]
### Juhan Viiding

Tall grass, vast calm, a tiny man
listens to time passing, his eyes on the clouds.
Summer swelters, the air shimmers, all is in its place,
but already the calm has changed. . . .

Completely changed. And he sees lying in the grass
a man like a dark speck or comma on time's page.

> Translated by Gabriella Mirollo and Talvi Laev

## PHARMACY
### Juhan Viiding

The night bell—what magic words.
Black letters on a white enamel sign.
Dusk. A closed door. A glow coming
from the back room. Night light.
Perhaps a desk lamp,
with a hanging brass chain . . .
an arm holding a torch?
A marble counter.

If the night could only ring the bell,
I wondered, but I knew that night
does not have hands. Night has wings,
a bosom, a shadow.

Black letters on a white sign;
four screws, their slotted heads
pointed upward, parallel.

The night bell—I didn't touch it.
There were many who rang.
Unto them it was opened.

Translated by Billy Collins and Mardi Valgemäe

## REGIONAL STUDIES
### Juhan Viiding

One midwinter evening two men met on a downtown street.
A lamp on a corner house provided them with light.
They had not been face to face for quite some time.

They stood opposite each other—not too close—
with hands deep in their pockets. It was extremely cold.
One of the coldest winters on record. Perhaps the coldest
night of that winter.

The bigger of the two had just returned from a trip,
having spent some time in a complicated city.
And he talked about how to tie a knot—
how a necktie was worn in a faraway land.
It was a complicated, special cravat.

The bigger man talked, the smaller (bespectacled) listened.
Neither used hands during all the talking.
But the talk was, as before, of how to tie this knot.
The bigger explained. Repeated a few things
when the smaller had asked questions.
The extreme cold became even colder.
The men parted. The street remained empty.

The smaller man—the listener—walked home.
Warmed up his nearly frozen body.
Took a necktie
and, remembering the description,
with a single try,
tied the knot.

Translated by Billy Collins and Mardi Valgemäe

[UNTITLED]
Ene Mihkelson

Tell me frankly don't evade do we still have hope
When bright happiness blinded our eyes
soul knew soul When over more than half the edge
eternity's inviting radiance slipped yet
we believed the feast cannot last long at our place
and sticking to the facts we once shall speak the truth
But now our bread is bitter words cut
to the bone even when remembered The newspaper
glows with pain Isn't perhaps our endurance
nothing but illusion since it's so hard
to bear this knowledge across time
Time is open   Flowers sprout from black earth
Begin with the beginning   Don't trample them

Translated by Ivar Ivask

A DRUMLIN IN THE WIND
Peep Ilmet

*

The present is like   sailcloth
                Fluttering in the winds of past
All of life is woven in this cloth
No thread of this cloth can come loose
And live.

*

We have aged prematurely
Though you might not notice it
Maybe it isn't old age at all
Maybe it is a certain set of truths

Which change you in the course of recognition
And in some it can be seen from their bearing
And in some from hair turned grey too soon
And in some from their features
And in some from the eyes
But surely in all of us
From our silence.

*

In a bright clear autumn day
Two men made a halt on a drumlin
One of them young, lithe and laughing
One old, hunched and sad
Catching their breath they looked across
At the land sloping down to lake Peipsi.
This land is beautiful, murmured the young one,
It is worth dying for.
This is a beautiful land, sighed the old one,
It is worth living for.

Translated by Krista Kaer

## THREESOME
### Mari Vallisoo

One has wings of air.
One has a light laugh and
from them winds begin.

Early in the morning
three women come downtown
from the Angel Bridge
white dresses flowing

Doors are still locked
on the town's oblivion.

(NOTE: Lake Peipsi is the largest lake of Estonia.)

Bird heart and bone
hide in the three.
Of this
nails, fingers, face
and hair want to speak.
But the mouth won't tell.

Translated by Gabriella Mirollo and Talvi Laev

## [UNTITLED]
### Indrek Hirv

All of your frightening frigidity
will one day be gathered
on the moon-landscapes of your light-hued retinae
to be set ablaze

Sparks flying like red corpuscles
will beat against the lenses of your eyes
until huge bell jars fracture
and a gust of the odor of love
wafts in through your splintered irises

Hundreds of mouths will open
in the soft fogs of the clouds
their breath will mingle
with your odorless coolness
in the bonfire's glow
and the incandescent starry sky
will whisper to you the first word
of the Unabridged Book of Self Deceit

Translated by George Kurman

## THE SILENT ONE
### Doris Kareva

Viewing the rainbowing world, I chose black
for my badge; the throbbing truth at the bottom
of false worlds—mother-blind, prior
to love and knowledge—right
behind the eyes.

Everything comes to an end, decays, recurs,
presents a different face—but I know that;
even with my eyes closed, I know the stony hand,
the fathomless womb.

Amid the thrashing abundance of colors,
of exuberant radiance, a figure stands,
straight and black, enroute to nothingness.

The bundle at its feet suddenly becomes
the point of an exclamation mark.

Translated by Billy Collins and Mardi Valgemäe

## [UNTITLED]
### Hasso Krull

I don't ask anybody why I waver
on the brinks of warfare and of extinction. The green telephone
warbles—proclaimer of the spring. "Hello!" Snow,
the sun, lemons. I did what I did for
our relationship.

Long ago, I abandoned hope
but not hopelessness.

Glorious patterns coruscate. Very quietly.
The floor glimmers through the carpets—transparent,
cold, and cosmic. It's there where I'll
finally fall. Through the carpets, free from disease
and from self-awareness.

Free from nature.

(Nature is free from naturalness:
artificial, salon-like.)

Snow. You. My mighty fortress.
I rest beneath you. In the spring
I'll rot (and the ravens
are sure to harvest me, the tiny birds
to devour me); in the summer I'll reek,

I'll smell, I'll blossom. Come on,
touch me. How soft and
rotted I am. How
young.

Snow:
don't leave me alone
in the sunlight.

Translated by George Kurman


## HERMAN'S THIRD DREAM
### Hasso Krull

I love you, floor. I want you, floor. I
press myself against your meek sleek body but
you're cold and hard to me. I can only imagine
your breasts' gentle contours. I can't cover
you with my hands, I can't cover you with my
body.
Ah, I suffer for you, floor. Ah, I die
for you, floor.

Translated by Gabriella Mirollo and Talvi Laev


## BIRCH-TREES
### Merle Jääger

Across the meadow, treading through
the pure wetland, drenched with dew,
each foot-print plants an empty space,
wild raspberry bushes—in this place
a house once stood—overgrown.
Birch trees, birch trees, oh my home.

Among the roots the weeds grow higher,
round the treetrunk—coiled barbed wire—
a chastity-belt's protective mesh—
pointed barbs stab pale, white flesh.

Tender craving virgins groan:
birch trees, birch trees, oh my home.

A gun is pressed against my spine.
Hell, I'm not afraid to die.
Can you see those birth trees too,
see, like me, the sky's bright blue
and shoot me in the back, unknown?
Birch trees, birch trees, oh my home.

Blood on grass, on growing green,
blood on birthbark, white and clean,
bullet-notches on the tree,
old harrows where the house should be. . . .
The dawn pours down its copper glow.
Birch trees, birch trees, oh my. . .

Translated by Elmar Maripuu

# Latvia, compiled by Aina Kraujiete

## Introduction
## by Juris Silenieks

Any introduction to Latvian poetry is likely to start with the statement that the roots of Latvian poetry are to be found in the Latvian folk songs, *dainas*, an immense corpus of some 2 million songs, whose origins, in many cases, date back to the darkest periods of the feudal period when the Latvian serf was subjected to untold physical brutalization and spiritual dehumanization. But somewhat paradoxically, the suffering of the people is very much muted in the *dainas*. Contemporary Latvian poetry so often harks back to *dainas* in its mood and form. We find much stoic forebearance as well as direct quotes from *dainas*, well-known lines paraphrased, or motifs interwoven into a contemporary setting. Andrejs Upits, the ersthwile most prominent arbiter of social realism and a writer of some merit himself under the Soviet regime, once said, in one of his more morose moods, that by his very nature every Latvian poet is condemned to love his people. And indeed, nationalism was the initial impetus that gave rise to Latvian literature and has been, by and large, its essence, for better or for worse.

The history of Latvia offers a clear refutation of historical determinism. Chance and accident have woven the fabric of the past in the Baltic region, a much-coveted piece of real estate at the crossroads between the West and the East. The Russians, the Germans, the Swedes, and the Poles have intermittently invaded, conquered, colonized, and dismembered the region since the beginning of the thirteenth century when the Teutonic Order and German bishops arrived to christianize, "with fire and sword," the heathens of the Baltic region. Though the region was under the Russian domination for the last three centuries, culturally it was not *ex oriente lux*, for light came from the West. The Enlightenment and the French Revolution spawned currents that eventually reached the Baltic region and shaped the cultural contours there.

The first impulse to authentic Latvian writing came with the wave of nationalism that swept over Europe and arrived in Latvia, which was treated not unlike a colony of the tsarist Russia, in the middle of the nineteenth century. It precipitated what is now considered to be the first national awakening. Its main goal was to create an authentic Latvian literature expressed in the Latvian language, which was yet to be developed into a subtle and forceful means of artistic communication. For its subject matter, Latvian literature was expected to mine the rich lodes of folklore and history. Following the vicissitudes of World War I, Latvia achieved independence, which the successive governments aspired to extend to cultural matters. Therewith came the second renaissance period—abruptly terminated with the occupation of the country by the Soviet Union on the eve of World War II. The Soviet rule was interrupted for almost four years by the German conquest and occupation of the land. The return of the Red Armies precipitated an exodus of some two hundred thousand Latvians, particularly professionals, writers, and artists, toward the West.

For this moment until the third renaissance, occasioned by the advent of *glasnost*, Latvian literature found itself between a rock and a hard place, or, as the late Latvian playwright, Martins Ziverts put it, "at home with no air to breathe, in exile with no soil to grow roots in." Fueled by exile or occupation, the patriotic afflatus is almost invariably present, but its intensity may vary from loud lamentations to much-muted feelings of bondage with the land and its people. In exile, particularly, the paths diverged. While all bemoaned the loss of the native land and the suffering of the people, some poets of the younger generation also celebrated the freedom from tradition—from the tribe's convention—and rejoiced in the nomad's life that brought them spiritual enrichment by coming in contact with other cultures.

In Latvia, although poetry may not be subject to as much censorship as prose, the poet was well aware of the ideological requirements and had to invent ways of obviating the strictures imposed by the demands of socialist realism. Hence, pre-*glasnost* poetry may exude the strain that comes from toeing the line. Currently there is little overt effort on the part of the central Soviet authorities to stop free expression. Among other *glasnost* effects, there was an explosion of pent-up nationalist sentiments and, with it, the return to the pre-Soviet cultural orientation of Latvia. "Latvians of all lands must be reunited again and develop our European consciousness, Latvia must again and finally return to Europe," as the editor of a recent anthology put it. The poet in Latvia is a much revered figure, intently listened to and expected to provide comfort and guidance in times of stress and misfortune. The poet is also the curator of the language, which, as in all colonized lands, is constantly threatened with assimilation. Today, a number of poets, such as Peters, Ziedonis, Čaklais *et al*, occupy important political and cultural posts. New poetry volumes are eagerly awaited and so often become best-sellers.

The situation in exile is quite different; for one thing, after some forty-five years of residence outside Latvia, the term "exile" now may appear somewhat inappropriate. One description of exile, which takes into account the inner life of the exile, not his or her political stance, may be quite convenient here. An exile writer never leaves his homeland in his memories or imagination since everything he writes harks back to the lost place. This dictum was quite true during the first decades of residence outside Latvia. In most instances, the inner landscape was distinctly Latvian. Now "the siren call of the Elsewhere" has precipitated other sensibilities. Unlike the poet in Latvia, his or her counterpart in the outside world is, for the most part, marginalized. The exile poet, by and large, has disdained commitment. Poetry does not sell well, being in competition with pot boilers and television. There are, nonetheless, poetry prizes, well-recognized and annointing the laureate with a special distinction. The present selection includes exile poets who have received the coveted Zinaida Lazda poetry prize. But these days the principal editors and publishers outside Latvia prefer to leave poetry to samizdat efforts.

The chronological arrangement of the selections according to the birth dates of the poets coincides with other diachronies. Andrejs Eglitis, the elder dean of Latvian poetry, was already a well-known figure in Latvia prior to his exile. His thunderous "God, Thy land is aflame," is likely to remain one of the most famous lines in Latvian poetry. By and large, he is followed by the next generation whose poetic fortunes came to the fore in exile in the fifties and sixties. Some of them belonged to a coterie called "Hell's Kitchen," named after the Manhattan neighborhood where these poets would gather. They were viewed as an iconoclastic group that shied away from traditional forms and the self-righteous proclamations of patriotism of their elders. Their verse is shaded with subtleties and ironies. They are the first—and most likely the last—generation in exile. During his first years of banishment, Josif Brodsky insisted that the exile poet must hear his people speak the language in taverns, buses, and grocery stores to replenish his linguistic resources, to attune his poetic ear to the linguistic genius of his people. Now Brodsky writes in English. The next generation, if there is one, educated in the often improvised Latvian schools, is not likely to engender a poet.

The poets from Latvia, aligning in a neat chronological sequence after the exile group, were, for the most part raised and educated in the midst of the stagnation period. Brezhnev had announced that, once and for all, the nationality question was finally settled and the arrival of the new *homo sovieticus* would be imminent. *Homo sovieticus* was, of course, stillborn. This group of poets represents so well the resilience and vitality of poetic creativity. Before the advent of *glasnost,* they managed to be published without writing odes to the Red Flag or "praising the bosses in a manner comprehensible to the bosses," as some have defined socialist realism. In their midst is the late Klavs Elsbergs, whose untimely death—officially labeled as suicide, but suspected as being the result of defenestration—reminds us of the precariousness of life in this century of ours (quite likely to be recorded as the bloodiest in the history of mankind). Yet as in the *dainas,* these poets express themselves in a manner much restrained and laconic. Apart from the differences of their geopolitical situations, Latvian poets, both at home and elsewhere, share the trauma and nostalgia of the past, but their poetry is more than preoccupation with what is Latvian. It speaks to the world, to people everywhere. Pasternak is reported to have said that Latvian poets have remained where poetry itself still lives: close to the grass.

# About the Poets

## VIZMA BELŠEVICA

Vizma Belševica (b. 1931) is one of the most popular poets in Latvia. She studied at the Latvian State University in Riga and the Gorki Institute of Literature in Moscow. Belševica's writing spans forty years. For periods of time, however, she was forced, by an official reprobation that was followed by a heart ailment, to suspend her creative work. She has published several volumes of poetry and a book of short stories; she has also written film-scripts and translated works by Russian, British, and American authors into Latvian. Belševica's own work has been translated into more than a dozen languages.

## BAIBA BIČOLE

Baiba Bičole (b. 1931 in Riga, Latvia), residing in the United States since 1950, has published five books of poetry. The last one, *Atgriežos (I Return)* was published in Latvia in 1991. Bičole is the fourth recipient of the Zinaida Lazda Biennial Poetry Prize. Since 1985, she has been writing in English. She is now a teacher of Latvian literature to young Latvians in exile and the associate editor of the Latvian newspaper *Laiks (Time)* in New York.

## MĀRIA ČAKLAIS

Māria Čaklais (b. 1940) lives in Riga and has published more than ten volumes of poetry. He has been active as an essayist, novelist, and translator. Recently he was honored with an Armenian prize for his translations of P. Sevak's poetry. He has made recordings of his own works and has traveled abroad, including several appearances in the United States. Čaklais is the editor-in-chief of *Literātūra un Māksla (Literature and Arts)*.

## ANDREJS EGLĪTIS

Andrejs Eglītis (b. 1912), the son of a musician killed in World War I, often sings his poems as his way of creating them. In 1943, Eglītis wrote the libretto to the powerful cantata *God, Thy Earth Is Aflame;* set to music by Lucija Garuta, it was performed in a church in Riga in 1944 and has resounded again in churches there in 1990. This work is an example of how a poem can document the events of an epoch without losing any of its absolute artistic merit. Eglītis is one of Latvia's great poets. To continue the fight for Latvia's freedom, Eglītis has lived in Sweden since 1945. There he established the Latvian National Foundation. He is the author of thirty books, some in English, German, or Swedish. His book of poems, *Svešais Cirvis Cērt un Cērt,* was issued in Riga in 1990.

## KLĀVS ELSBERGS

Klāvs Elsbergs (1959–87) died mysteriously in a fall out of what was then the Soviet writers' residence hotel near Riga. Few in Latvia believe that he died accidentally or of his own free will. Despite appeals, however, an investigation never took place. During his brief life, Elsbergs published two collections. The selections here are from his posthumous collection *Velci, tēti (Pull, Dad,* 1989). Elsbergs represents an uncompromising "I say 'No!'" position among the pre-*glasnost* generation of Latvian poets in Latvia.

## ASTRĪDE IVASKA

Astrīde Ivaska (b. 1926) has published five collections of poetry in Latvian. A bilingual chapbook, with English translations by Inara Cedrins, was a Small Press Book Club selection. *Oklahoma Poems* was written in English. She has received the Zinaida Lazda Biennial Poetry Prize and the Latvian Cultural Foundation Prize, as well as the Janis Jaunsudrabins Prose Prize for poetic travel sketches. She has been active as translator, critic, and author of children's literature. Her own work has appeared in a dozen languages.

## AINA KRAUJIETE

Aina Kraujiete (b. 1923), after studies in medicine at the W. von Goethe University in Frankfurt, Germany, worked at the Sloan-Kettering Institute for Cancer Research and other similar institutions. She is the author of five collections of poetry. Her poems have been translated into several languages, and she has translated works by E. Pound, M. Moore, C. Sandburg, R. Frost, O. Paz, C. Milosz, and A. Vosnesensky. Kraujiete is the editor of poetry for the Latvian literary journal *Jaunā Gaita (New Way)* and was the recipient of major Latvian literary awards, including the Zinaida Lazda

Biennial Poetry Prize. She resides in New York and writes critical essays and scripts for Radio Free Europe.

## ROBERTS MŪKS

Roberts Mūks (née Avens, b. 1923 in Latvia) studied philosophy and the humanities at universities in Germany and Belgium. He received additional degrees from the University of Michigan and Fordham University (Ph.D. in history and phenomenology of religion). Mūks has published four volumes of verse and is the recipient of the Zinaida Lazda Biennial Poetry Prize. His scholarly work in English consists of three books: *Imagination Is Reality* (also translated into Italian and Japanese), *The New Gnosis*, and *Imaginal Body*.

## ANNA RANCĀNE

Anna Rancāne (b. 1959 in Latvia) graduated in economics from the University of Latvia and, with distinction, from the Faculty of Literature at the University of Moscow. Rancāne has published two collections of poetry, *Lūgšanas mājai (Prayers to a House*, 1982) and *Piektdiena (Friday*, 1986). Her third book is being prepared for publication.

## GUNARS SALIŅŠ

Gunars Saliņš (b. 1924 in Latvia) is one of the founders of the so-called "New York Hell's Kitchen" school of Latvian poetry. Author of three volumes of verse, he is the recipient of major Latvian literary poetry awards. Translations of his poems have appeared in English, German, French, Spanish, Norwegian, Swedish, Estonian, Lithuanian, and Hungarian. He has translated R. M. Rilke, T. S. Eliot, Robert Frost, and Dylan Thomas, compiled and edited several books, and published essays and literary criticism in both Latvian and English-language periodicals. He is professor of psychology at Union County College in New Jersey.

## VELTA SNIĶERE

Velta Sniķere (b. 1920) studied philosophy at Riga University, worked as an interpreter for the British Army in Austria, is a member of the Chartered Society of Physiotherapy, and was a founding member and tutor for the British Wheel of Yoga. Sniķere studied Indian dancing with Ram Gopal and was a member of his troupe. She has evolved an original form of reciting poetry, illustrating it with mudras, or gestures. Apart from some poems in French and German, Sniķere writes in Latvian and English and has translated other poets into one or the other language. She is president of the PEN Centre for Writers in Exile, London. Her book of poems, *Lietu mutes,* was published in 1991 in Riga, where she gave her poetry readings after fifty years of exile.

## AINA ZEMDEGA

Aina Zemdega (b. 1924 in Talsi, Latvia) went to school and studied music in Jelgava. She fled Latvia in the fall of 1944 and went to Sweden. In 1950, she arrived in Toronto, Canada, where she studied literature, fine arts, and music. She presently lives in Ontario and teaches music. She has four collections of poetry and three volumes of prose. She is the recipient of the Zinaida Lazda Biennial Poetry Prize.

## IMANTS ZIEDONIS

Imants Ziedonis (b. 1933) is a prolific writer and immensely popular, both in Latvia and among exiles, as poet, essayist, and translator. He earned a degree in philology at the Latvian State University. After his first volume of verse in 1956, more than a dozen have followed. The poetry of Ziedonis has been translated into many languages and has been adapted for stage presentation. He is also known for his children's poetry and has written philosophical meditations, critical essays, and film scenarios. Ziedonis travels abroad frequently and has visited the United States, presenting recitals in Latvian communities.

# Latvian Poems: Poets-in-Exile

### NOON ON THE LAKE
Andrejs Eglītis

Winds subside into sleep.
Fierce resplendence descends from the sky.
I shield my eyes, shield them in vain.

Winds stir and awaken the deep.
Steep brilliance outdazzles the sky.
To love you means to court pain.

Translated by Velta Sniķere and Robert Fearnley

## PERISHABILITY
Andrejs Eglītis

The dust of dissolution blows off me
like smoke from yellow catkins,
And the clouds burn with sombre purple.

I am in love; the willow of the dead rustles,
Springs murmur midst the graveyard sedges:
Everything changes to dust with time.

You smile at me in the harshness of mortality
With an avid craving for life.—
My love for you is heartache.

Around me blows the dust of dissolution,
The clouds burn in a sombre purple.—
Like golden smoke we evaporate.

Translated by Velta Sniķere and Robert Fearnley

## THE WIND OF BLOOD
Andrejs Eglītis

In remembrence of the battle of Kurzeme

I again sense that rustling sound of yours
with breathing oppressive and fierce, when
the dead regiment looked towards me
with eyes all filled with sand, yet alive, when
you tidy for some the singed hair, for some
the tattered coats. And it seems to me that
once more I see countless coffins being carried
which are unburied year after year.
The wind of blood goes again to hunt for itself
fresh battlefields and to quench its thirst for new
wounds in terrible laughter and moans.
Those that have died meet those that have died
in their smiles.

Translated by Velta Sniķere and Robert Fearnley

## THE NINETEENTH BATTALION
### Andrejs Eglītis

The nineteenth. Where does the battalion of God's country
              rest its head today
When in soft birch woods birds flutter and with suspended breath
              warble in song?
Is it by the earth of our fathers' graves, or are their breasts
              weighed down by mouldering alien feet,
Does the green garland of grass of forgetfulness meander
              through death's deep winters?
What an honour it was to die together on battle's stretchers, and
              in dark tongues of fire,
Time, fleeting from the past, impassively fences in the wounds
              of death.
All the more splendid will be the white expanse of flowers, where
              in murderous battle blood has flowed.
The great nineteenth. It seems to me—from atop a golden
              catafalque
And in proud silence you are teaching us: Desiring freedom,
              embrace death.

              Translated by Velta Sniķere and Robert Fearnley

## RED-WHITE-RED
### Andrejs Eglītis

Weave me into red-white-red,
Weave me into our flag.
Then, as heaven weaves white morning flax
And the evening plaits its blood red tresses,
let us gather flags, more flags, more flags than we are.
To be carried in the hands of all our dead,
Flags to flutter in the smiles of our unborn.
Weave me into our flag.
Our red-white-red,
Our sacred home.
It is there we dream.
In thinking of that, we wake.

              Translated by Velta Sniķere and Robert Fearnley

## [UNTITLED]
### Andrejs Eglītis

While ever the earth will revolve round the sun,
we turn ourselves in imperceptible movement
towards the shore of our ancestral home—
bones eternally sleeping in a mouldering foreignness,
a child's cheek, receiving a mother's breast—
Do you feel it?
Unperceived, both in birth and in death,
all turns towards our beginning and our ending,
like a child's cheek taking its mother's breast—
towards the shore of our ancestral home.

Translated by Velta Sniķere and Robert Fearnley


## KALI
### Velta Sniķere

Snake fire eyes,
Truth's tongue.

Blaze with my eyes,
Freedom,
A trail to truth,
Laugh with my mouth,
Freedom,
Shatter untruth;
Laugh with my eyes,
Freedom,
Set life alight,
Speak with my tongue,
Speak,
Freedom.

Translated by the author

## THINGS
Velta Sniķere

What are the things
That are things
As they are?

If one were to see them
As they were
Or will be?

Things opened like clams
Disclosing tenderness,
But my sympathy,
My approaching caress
As if by spells
Distilled them:

As if poured out of glass,
Without shells,
Through each other
Transparent, outlines.

Translated by the author

## THE DANCER
Velta Sniķere

Upon an evening, upon dusk descending,
You rose and turned, and turned and leapt
And we new moment upon glorious moment
Join glittering infinity.

First you were like a mirror,
Reflecting a glint,
Then a shaft,
Then a flood of light.

You blazed.
But now,
The light that you were
Turns to darkness,

As through you,
Who have become transparence,
There steps into the night
Of our consciousness
Pure lustre.

And we too
Have become windows
For the whirling presence
As it sweeps
Round and round
As it sweeps
With tongues of fire
Round your ecstasy.

Translated by the author

## LIGHT
### Velta Sniķere

Glittering sandals upon water,
Over water
Light wades into me;
Nothing protects my heart.

Depth protects the deep,
Lids protect the eye;
Nothing protects my heart.

Translated by the author

## LAPIS
### Velta Sniķere

Light poured out, to be attained within,
Innermost juice of pulsating;
Deeply silent
Until solidified:
Amber.

Translated by the author

[UNTITLED]
Velta Sniķere

Vanquish in love.
Let your turtle doves land on my shoulders and arms—
I will not startle them by turning sharply.
Let your flowers arise from my open palms—
Your butterflies will not alarm me,
Nor your nightingales . . .

Translated by the author

SYMBOLS AND POLITICS
Velta Sniķere

Hammer of Thor, hammer of Mars;
Sickle of death, sickle of Saturn:
Mars and Saturn conjoint in a red field—
Death and destruction.

Hammer and sickle conjoint
in a red flag:
mass graves and heaps of rubble.

Translated by the author

COMMON CURRENCY
Velta Sniķere

Molotov Ribbentrop
Stalin Roosevelt
Gorbachov Bush
Pacts:

Buying and selling Balts.
Blood ECU.

Translated by the author

## HAIKU ON THE THOUGHTS OF CHAIRMAN MAO
### Velta Sniķere

In China
The bandages taken from women's feet
Now bind
Men's minds.

Translated by the author

## GAIA
### Velta Sniķere

A horse and a cow
Wrinkle their skin
To shake off insects.

Let us pray
Earth continues
Tolerating humanity.

Translated by the author

## FROM ANCIENT TIMES
### Roberts Mūks

From ancient times, moldering times
Old Prussians speak to me—
Brother tribe, shadow tribe.

These shadows are strong—
These shadows are fruitful—

They grow within me, outgrow me
As if to show me how to grow

How should I grow?
With frequent drinks
From Death's vessels.

Translated by Guna K. Chaberek

## PEACE
### Roberts Mūks

May my soul yield to the barren hills,
May it flow away with the steely waters,
May it merge at night with the dark and the wind
With the bark of the dog and the jackal
With the mute wilderness and
The echoless scream—

May my soul be whole, a hill without valleys,
A mask on a face that doesn't exist,
A mask to remind of itself alone,
And other masks, other hills—
May my soul know peace.

Translated by Guna K. Chaberek

## REFLECTING
### Roberts Mūks

I'm translucent. Sometimes heavy, thick like a coal tar
Vat—still, translucent. I shine my insides with coal
Tar. The sun, terrible, irresistible,
Springs up inside me, I melt, and flow
Out in the four directions of heaven, searching for
Salvation, I stick to the wind.

I can only shine through—
Through wind, a casual song, a hint from the future.
Yoked to my nightmare, two eyes in my head,
Unseeing, I teleologically, apocalyptically
Move on all sides.

Perhaps I am already dead or simply undone,
Until death puts its period (which would be one and the same).
But, perhaps, another way out—no way out:
Not to count on the sun, the wind, or that hint from the future,

To stick to absolutely nothing,
To be absolutely nothing.
Not to shine through, but reflect—
An empty mirror, never stained by
Something strange.

Translated by Guna K. Chaberek

### NARCISSISM
### Roberts Mūks

Safety lies in
Loving what you do not have:
Women, birds of paradise,
Flying fish, saucers,
And so on, and so on.
While Love
Itself is safest.
Then, I'd be Narcissus.

But
Looking into water
I'd see only you
Your face traced
In the clouds
Your name inscribed
In empty sky

I would carry you up to
Heaven, never let your
Eyes give way, no matter
What Jerusalem or Rome
May say

Because of eyes
Only because of eyes
Does the idea of
Heaven
Abide

Translated by Guna K. Chaberek

## TO MY TRANSLATOR
### Roberts Mūks

Oh, if only you could
translate my words into some unheard-of tongue, some
sounds or images only you
can understand. Then I could talk as one
who isn't there, until there could be only you,
until you were my final myth. Then

I would burn gladly at the stake, a happier
Heretic than
our tortured God.

Translated by Guna K. Chaberek

## A DIFFERENT VISION
## (TO LATVIAN POETS)
### Roberts Mūks

From afar I see you all as
One tree stretching to the heavens.
But your own heaven is far different—
No angels, and, oh lord,
Not even God.
        Then, whatever are you doing there?
        In such a heaven forever desolate?
                        —forever tiresome?
                        —forever divine?

I know:
You do not need a visa
        For Paradise
Or an opiate called
        Utopia.

You are beset by a strange vision—
    To sing of the earth so
    It would be our first
    And last
    love
    To sing of the heavens so
    They also would be
    Full of
    Blunders.

Translated by Guna K. Chaberek

## AMRITA; OR, HOW TO DIE
### Roberts Mūks

Birds and other flying things
    die quietly
making no noise about life
and death, no "last words"
leaving no trace
    this, then, is the mystery—
    to die, leaving no trace
as the wind, rushing over the plain
as the arrow, piercing yet not harming the sky
    the person vanishes
    selflessly having loved
    the earth
only thus can we die undying—
life's elixir, begrudged by the gods,
nectar, inspiring the intoxication
of the wind, of the loosed arrow
of the bird's last song

Translated by Guna K. Chaberek

---

(NOTE: "AMRITA" is the Sanskrit word for "immortality"; or "the drink of immortality")

## MIRROR, MIRROR, REVEAL YOURSELF
Aina Kraujiete

1

into the brightness slides
a shadow
                —my own?
And the splendid time-walked
mirror, set toward a window,
with a reflected ray tethers
a falling star, stirs up
                            the clouds—
but beneath the dull silver coat,
in the center,
aren't clotted centuries
darkening?
        I call:
                mirror, reveal yourself,
                reveal what you've seen
                in other eras,
                in other lifetimes.

2

And  yes—
            faces   faces   faces
        return in the mirror as in a silver canvass
        and paint themselves over mine.

        Bodies, regaining contour
from times past, straighten.

        Candles in fanciful chandeliers
        begin to flame, to reveal
        unfamiliar  smiles
                        and tears.

        Eyes spilled out long ago watch me,
and throats once choked by fire want to speak.

I brush the antique glass with my arm,
to ward off the   dead scenes—

oh!

a moan,
and the ancient-day curtain bursts.

In the apocalypse of the past, haphazard
flags
        diadems
                spears
                    goose quills.

Piecemeal faces zigzag like lightning,
on   slivers
            an eye
        an ear
                half a nose
        half a cheek

while distant mouths cry without sound,

wait!
give us a moment
more, a moment of life
through you!

But the wars
and revolutions
sweep themselves back into the mirror.
Nothing is in shards. Having met me,
the ancient glass is generous:
I see myself whole and alone,

and weary clouds

and stars in a hurry

Translated by Bitīte Vinklers Bluķis

[UNTITLED]
Aina Kraujiete

with a bright silk scarf Aphrodite
dries her tears in the mirror
over the loss of her divine beauty

look—the delicate skin,
like a Pompeiian fresco,
has begun to crack

or does the mirror lie,
blackening
from the scratches of time,
and the image of the goddess is
every woman
in love
but no longer young?

Translated by Bitīte Vinklers Bluķis


A WOMAN MADE OF GLASS (selections)
Aina Kraujiete


1


Neither of clay nor porcelain, a woman
made of glass:
                someone shaped her
                with his breath, this sparkling
                woman of glass,
                releasing her
                graceful and fragile
                to uncertain
                eternity.
                        Like dreams, everything—
doors walls slivers of light through
Venetian blinds
birds at the window
passersby
time—
slides through her.

4

She is too fragile
to be of this century—her delicate form
is the sure work of a master,
a Venetian glassblower masterful
in his art
and in love

her pose, with arms upraised
in yielding invitation,
is the creation only of one
who still loves
and whom his beloved awaits with passion.

7

at night when darkness spreads like Medusa
unwinding her snake hair, and the sound of
slapping oars in canals reaches far
while the gondoliers' voices linger

the woman made of glass darkens—

a dream lowers her from her pedestal
and lays her down for her first sleepless night

        the darkness doesn't hasten away,
        it fastens itself on her upraised arms,
        presses against her breasts, and slides
        down over her body
                wrapping her
           in cool
      snake spirals

8

She is not his only
beloved, not the only one
he's loved or might love (bride?
wife? no!)
       He is in love
with figurines, small and expensive,
he is aged but his eyes will always stay
young. In his gallery of art
the woman made of glass
belongs—

      a light touch of his fingers
      leaves a pleasant warmth of life
      on the cool glass body

        at that moment
        even a woman made of glass
        might feel as Eve once did.

Translated by Bitīte Vinklers Bluķis

## MIRRORS
### Aina Kraujiete

I

I stand between two mirrors,
repeating myself endlessly,
as if turning back,
as if in a hurry—
not to arrive
but to stay close behind myself

walking farther and farther
from one mirror into the other,
in their infinity
I meet myself

II

        The mirrors
reflect each other over and over, they toss me
back and forth
        I study
my multiplied look
of surprise:
from the mirror corridors
the eyes of my father
look back at me. Around the mouth,
on the forehead
weave the lines on the faces
of my ancestors

III

        But even the mirrors can't reveal
how I'll join my forebears: with the features
of ancestral faces or
with features I have formed myself.
        I do not know
how much I'm theirs,
how much my own.

Translated by Bitīte Vinklers Bluķis

## REPORT OF AN ARREST
### Gunars Saliņš

When arrested he was wearing—
no, not the uniform of the home guard or of the Boy Scouts, or the
  4-H Club—
he wore an off-white summer suit.
Sprawled in the rye, he was reading
a book of poems. Under his lapel they found
not a concealed pin with Latvia's coat of arms,
no, just a dried-up daisy stalk.
The cartridge-shaped objects inside the lining
proved to be pebbles,
while from the left pocket of his trousers
—an adult's pocket, mind you—

they took a slingshot in good working order.
There wasn't one political pamphlet,
not one subversive document
—just some tobacco crumbs, and, covered in the crumbs,
a piece of black bread for fish bait
and a cork still smelling of red currant wine,
In his breast pockets, programs
from song fests, dances, and Memorial Days.
The guardians of security
rummaged in this material evidence and said,
"Public enemy number 1!"

And as the prisoner was led away along a river bank profuse with
    flowers,
one of the guards nervous and boyish-faced,
shuddered, "This air,
even this air smells of subversion. It's
like religion. Like the opium of the people. And then all these
haze-filled horizons. And the brightness. . . ."

He squinted at the river surface—
then jerked the barrel of his submachine gun upward
and let off seven bursts of bullets
into the white summer clouds shimmering in the water

Translated by Ilze Mueller Kļaviņa

## A CHRISTMAS LETTER
### Gunars Saliņš

Yes—we'll celebrate Christmas Right in the stable. We'll wait
for the Virgin who has conceived
the Son of God from the Holy Spirit.
    Here I stopped writing and looked at the old family Bible in its
        wooden
    covers: what times we live in! any newborn child
    is such a wonder now it seems from the Holy Spirit. And isn't it so?
    Blasphemous talk, and yet

_____

(NOTE: Italicized lines are from a Latvian folk song)

*What will you do, dear God,*
*After all of us die?*

You speak of Epiphany. The Three Wise Men. Whence would they
   come?
From the lands of the East? From the West? From the
Arctic Circle? No, not those, they won't make it back any more
As for ourselves, where would we find three? We have
just two,
the third is a simpleton. Or is that from another tale?
   But welcome, holy night!
And the stable too, with every smell!
                         The lantern is throwing shadows
before us. Barefoot we feel our way
through the hay, the straw—among the muzzles, the flanks of the cattle.
   We listen
to their breathing,
              mooing,
                   bleeting—
                        where,
where in this stable will the star shine forth? where
will arise the cry of the
CHILD?

Translated by Bitīte Vinklers Blukis

## THE ARCHITECTURE OF RIGA
### Gunars Saliņš

I

One Riga—a city of friendly cobblestoned streets from days gone by, of
   stone
         walls, of crumbling stone steps, of towers and steeples,—
the other—a city of fear,
fear in the steeples, in walls, in crumbling stone steps, in cobblestone
   streets,—
coursing in eyes and fingertips
fear

II
We're walking—
coming towards us, the Laima clock and the lindens, swans on the
   canal and
the Opera, the Statue of Freedom—as though on a postcard. But then
we cross Lenin Boulevard—and the asphalt crackles, caves in, we drop
down into an underground world.
                            Those are shafts,
those are coal mines—and, in the center of Riga, we're suddenly
at a vast distance from Riga. We're walking
through mines, in the Arctic—stooping, signalling to each other,
   whispering.
        The lindens,
the Statue of Freedom are a vast distance away—as though on an old
postcard.
        As though on an old
postcard that faded ages ago, somewhere at a distance,
at a vast distance somewhere above our heads—
Riga?

Translated by Ilze Mueller Kļaviņa

BALLET
(a half-crumbled mural)
Gunars Saliņš

A heavenbound
Christ with eyelids closed as if still in a dream.
with nail-perforated feet—
                   a dancer
springing away from the world.
But the midriff is gone—in its place,
already invisible to me,
dances
the flesh of God

Translated by Bitīte Vinklers Blukis

## A VISION
### Gunars Saliņš

My mother carries me in my cradle on her head.
She walks like an Indian woman, without holding her load.
I trust this balance.
This balance between her and me.
Balance between her and the earth.
Balance between us and the earth and the stars.

My mother carries me in my cradle on her head

My mother carries me in my coffin on her head

Translated by Bitīte Vinklers Bluķis

## [UNTITLED]
### Gunars Saliņš

Unmade beds
and a broken door swung out across the waters—

where,

where have you gone?

And these abandoned clothes,
these lips thrown across them—what else?

And then I hear
singing over my head, as if in the clouds.

As if in the clouds
your voice

Translated by Bitīte Vinklers Bluķis

## MYSTIFICATIONS
### Gunars Saliņš

She lives on sixteen.
Each morning a yellow tomcat sits in the window
and licks the rising sun—
and then, with radiant whiskers and tongue, he jumps into her bed
  and licks

her cheeks
and shoulders
and breasts
and hips—
that is her morning
toilette


    +

The building has thirty floors,
and when her suitor, with Dantesque profile and carnation in hand,
    calls from
            the street below,
she leans out of all the windows
on all the floors.
Giddy, he heads inside—but every door
is opened in wonder
by someone else


    +

The street darkens.
A beat of distant drums.
Has she flown
to Africa?
            No, her face appears
in the dark-blue sky as in an outdoor movie:
"Don't dream—move lightly,
as if from a dream yourself."

Translated by Bitīte Vinklers Bluķis


## SING
### Gunars Saliņš

Sing—sing so that stars
press against the windowpanes
and the sun and the moon
and from the stars our grandmothers
our grandfathers

Sing—sing so that bird's milk
begins to flow
from women's breasts
and from men's
also from men's

As we drive across the bridge you sing
and the river sits up and looks at us in wonder
as we speed away faster than sound
your voice streaming like red roses behind us
like red wind

You sing and our flesh turns transparent
until it vanishes and we see
in your voice as in a flowing mirror
our souls so long unseen
and dazed we rub our eyes that are no more

Sing—sing for those
who cannot, who are dead—their non-singing
is more like our singing than we realize
if our singing is true—as true
as their silence

Then sing—sing so that children are born—
and children to those children—and grandchildren. Sing,
sing so that we see ourselves—
see ourselves
through death

Translated by Bitīte Vinklers Bluķis


IN HER GARDEN
Aina Zemdega

She walked under the fern trees
and trees with leaves like the wings of butterflies
with a garment of rainbow-mist over her shoulders
and called:
          "Come with me!"
My friend, my guide,
she who walks on water,

having left the earth to those who guard it
and the keys to the keepers of keys,
led the way
     and taking
     all the directions of the sky and earth
     in her hand
     divided them
     between us.
"Be not afraid," she said,
"I shall not divine your fate,
but remember—
     you must not touch the walls!
     The walls should open by themselves
     as medieval paintings open
     and parachute silk."

Translated by M. Zariņa

## DEATH AT YOUR FEET
### Aina Zemdega

1.

As yet you do not know,
as yet I may not tell
the hidden reality—
     life will not take roots
     in this place.
In the shadows of the fir trees,
in the sun on the threshold,
in the melancholy of the jamsnins
     your summer weaves
     her last loom.

2.

Give me the craft of a sorcerer
that will melt all the crossing shadows of death
into only one and put it under a stone
till the remembrance day;
the words that can summon
and place into one accord
all the stray voices
making them sing in unison

from beginning to end.
Give me the gentle strength of the wise
to unravel all the tangled dead-end streets
and leave only one.

Translated by M. Zariņa


## SUMMER IN THE CITY
### Aina Zemdega

We do not speak of it.
It is something each one of us knows:
the city is torn from its foundations
and hopelessly nearing the sun.

Our hair and the streets are full of ashes,
the walls of the buildings melt,
shoulders burn
and the wind does not reach us anymore,
neither the sprays from the sea-thrown waves.
With growing impatience,
with greater and greater force,
its desire aflame with abandon,
the sun draws us closer and closer,
and people leave their homes and flee—
to return—
or so they say.
But we—the forever homeless wanderers—
we know better.
Those of us, who live with love,
remain.

Translated by J. Kļaviņš


## BY THE WATERFRONT
### Aina Zemdega

What fantastic fungus, quaint mushrooms and lichens
grow by the waterfront
where the streetcar tracks loop
and make their journey back!

There the sweating, sinking shacks
have thrown wide open their doors and windows,
shirts, blouses and mouths
of caged birds and children.

I stop on the well-worn threshold
where oriental grandfathers sit and smoke
and trace my name in the soot with a finger
as if I were a part of this place
or signing up for a journey.
I touch the notches on the door-posts
that chronicle the years and growing-heights,
I feel the spots where the foreheads pressed—
some smooth and warm, some dark and grooved
as tree fungus illuminated by white lichen,
and touching I read from a book for the blind:
no noisy Noah's ark will save us
but these broken down porchless ferries
with sides full of holes.

Translated by J. Kļaviņš

## MOON POEM
### Astrīde Ivaska

Sometimes you gaze at me like that,
when it is Fall, and the nights are long.
Huge and inquisitive you hang
in the peartree's branches,
and your gaze holds out to me
the polished silver disk
that a Roman woman put
to her dying lover's lips,
till his breath
could cloud it no more.

You gaze and ask, you await
my breath against yours,
my outstretched hand groping for you,
and my tears clouding your face:

look, I am living.

Now and then
through the autumn night
a pear falls. Slowly
you turn toward morning,
and I—
    look, I am still living.

Translated by the author

## LADY IN THE MIRROR
### Astrīde Ivaska

1.

When I was small,
I was often told—
Be patient, it is not yet time.
    A little while I'll be patient
    between two darknesses,
    but not much longer.
    What will remain
    between two darknesses
    to be told?
Don't ask now, be patient,
    it is not yet time.

2.

Time to go,
only allow me to thank
the lady who always
looked at me from the mirror.

For weeks sometimes there was no one,
only she did not disappoint me.
Always close, that friendly lady,
who knows who'll greet her now?

3.

The meadows—

beginning with cowslips
and anemones,
they adorn   themselves
with one summer shawl
after another,
until that very last one,
edged in madder and covered
all over
with little white daisy stars—

in that one, you will wrap me.

4.

But it's nothing, if I don't manage
to await it. Much remains
not understood, like the blunt
cold pain in one's chest in leaving,
                that jerks
like a dog run over at the roadside,
looking out with broken eyes,
unable to die.

5.

Come along, little one—
and then they put
a leash around its neck.
They pulled, but it resisted,
dug nails into the slippery floor.
I saw only something greyish
moving in the mist.
I stood with hanging head:
it will be best that way for us all,
we had often said it.

6.

It will be better that way sooner or later,
don't worry. But into this hollow
> between three pine forests
> and two darknesses,
> into this hollow
> all flows
> that could have been—
> but was not,
> yet can not be denied,
> can not be expressed,
> can not be laid aside.
Flows together and reflects darkly
the rainy horizon.

7.

Once more, with feeling,
let's act our parts
without mistakes to the end.
Again let's look
past one another,
reluctant to touch
and afraid to remember
it is possible
to wake, hearing cranes
in the middle of an autumn night

8.

On the lady in the mirror
let's put a summer hat,
so we don't have to fear any longer
the cavities of her eyes.
> Surely that way
> it will be best for us all
> and no more questions have to be asked.

Translated by Inara Cedriņš

## WALK/HEAT/DEATH
### Baiba Bičole


—a day in the month
      of March:
thermometer's tiny red tongue
                  quivers
         at the 80° mark
—fever runs through
   every tree—every branch
   and every twig
            feels
   a feverish coursing
               of sap
   towards the buds
      : hard-swollen nipples
      of a child-girl
—too early—too early—
—death still hovers
               around—
      —a fever of eighty degrees—
—the wisps of grass still
   as fine as embryo's hair
               in the womb—
—too soon—it's still too soon
            to be born—
   —death still hovers
               around—
      —fever of eighty degrees—
—clouds bulging
      like glands
      the white blood-cells
               multiplying
            at an alarming rate—
—a house stands still
               in fright
   pale sweat drips
               down
   its windowpanes
      —a shaking hand
      locks the door
      rocks the crying
                  child—

—death still hovers
              around—
—and then : silence
        —silence
        —silence—
     : anticipation stretched taut
       : a peel—a skin—membrane
       stretched taut
     over
    something
   something
  expanding
growing
EXPLODING
    : a sudden boom
     a thunderclap
       —a red-hot lightning-bolt
        —a red-hot erect penis
         pierces the earth
          (the virgin earth
             of March)
   —fever of fire—
    —fever of death—
    —fever of life—
      of life—
 : crocus bleeding purple and yellow
  tree bleeding—coagulating—green
  rain cloud's blood runs
  through the throbbing vein
       of a street—
—blood—life—life-blood—
  —death still hovers
       around—
—and I remember
  I remember :
   the newly dug grave
   the freshly laid flowers
   glittering in sun through
        the snow:
       the splendid jewels
       of death—
 —and I remember
  I remember
    the casket:

and now:
how does the rain
            sound
                down
                    there?—
—like whispers? like tiptoes?
like faraway laughter? or cries?
timid knocking on door? or
a feverish dance of despair?
        —how does it sound
                down
                    there?
—death still lingers
                nearby—

Translated by the author

## AN AMERICAN, A NEW YORKER, AN INMATE IN A SOVIET LABOR CAMP; A NOTEBOOK
### Baiba Bičole

### I

—this distance
        of thousands of miles
                between:
    : thousand tomahawks
                dancing
                    on my skull—
    : a shot in the dark
        & the last bullet
                    spent—
    : an amber-colored Vermont maple-syrup
                                stream
                        over
                    pancake-mountains
        suddenly rearing up suddenly
                    turning into
                        charging
                        anger-steaming
                                buffaloes—
    : a flock of birds
            gliding over

New Jersey's Meadowlands
            disappearing
                    towards
                        the west
                    a trace-less track-less
                                        trail—
—and *I* dream—
            *I* dream
                about
                    New York—
                        —a jagged abrasive
                                        dream:
                    : the skyline-slash
                    the color-smash
                    sunset crashing
                        into millions of windows
                    the mad dash
                        of the broken glass
                    subway's brash song—
—longing's black rain—
            —black soot-covered
                            beads
                                rolling
                                    down
                                        my face—


                            II
—a liquid morning slowly sloshing against
    the barbed-wire fence
                    —puddles—
                        grey-white-film-covered tongues
                        lazily touching—tasting—licking
                        the torn slivers of leather
                        around the shivering toes
                        bluish-red skin black crumbling toenails
                        (a sudden flashback:
                        Robert Rauschenberg's, Jasper John's
                        paintings—Pop-art—ha! art-Pop-
                        art-pop!—ha!)
                        —saliva floods the hungry mouth
                            —each movement each footstep
                                    opens the pores
                        as the weakened bodies shower
                                            themselves

                        in their own sweat—
—a liquid morning—
            —I swim on my swollen belly
                            —slowly—
            I'm a puffed-up toad
            too heavy too exhausted
                        to leap—
            —I'm creeping I'm trickling
                                along—
—breakfast: the cup in my hand
                    turns into liquid
                    & floats
                            away—
            my lips keep dripping
                        down
                            my chest—
            my tongue falls out &
                        floats away
                        on the murky
                                    liquid
                                    floor—


                                Translated by the author




                        [UNTITLED]
                        Baiba Bičole


                            I


—bird-beak-scissors shredding the silence into
    rainbow-colored-confetti streams : the singing tree—


                            II


—wind-wave flowing through the shrubs—the submerged
    buds suddenly revealed : flying-fish suspended in leap—


                            III


—the heartbeat that whispers like a drum and
    screams like a dandelion seed—

IV

—the pale cheeks—closed eyelids' snow-clad fields—
white lips trembling in submission—in fright—the
sudden burst of a burning-red well : mouth open in kiss—

V

—a kneeling tree : the tusk-less elephant in pain—
the darting monkey wind and : a black bird—a black
flower—its darkly glistening petals opening like an
upward-shooting parachute—

Translated by the author

## Latvian Poetry: Poets in Latvia

### I CARRY MY LOVE
### Vizma Belševica

I carry my love
As a child—a one year old—
Carries a chestnut leaf:
So seriously holds the outstretched hand—
It is so difficult to balance the tiny step
With giant autumn all around.—
From the trees
Fall and fall
Rustling golden secrets
And confuse his steps.
But the little one does not slip.
He holds on to his leaf
And elegantly walks into the blizzard of leaves.

Translated by Astrida Stahnke

## SILENCE
### Vizma Belševica

I am a woman.
                    I am silence.
And silence must not say, "I love you."
Silence is the first to know
That when the acorns falling on the streets drum in
        the autumn
The oak tree is already on his way to winter's white aloness;
Likewise he knows that silence will bear another spring
And labor hard in the floods' desolate contractions
Until with one long moan the ice will break.
A woman is the first to understand that.
                    And silence also.

★ ★ ★

I put upon your palm the heart of the woods
And the tiny loganberry told you what depth
Lies in the intricate entanglement of its roots.
You did not understand.

I reached to you the silent longing of the heather
And for loyalty—a green pine branch
That would endure the most outrageous frost.
You did not understand.

I sought out an empty bird's nest;
The down was full with love's warm simplicity
and the gentle presence of each daily care.
You did not understand.

★ ★ ★

Have you ever seen how the coke swamp burns?
Neither flames moan nor sparks fly spitefully—
There is only bitter silence,
            so bitter that it takes one's breath away.
Without a sound inside the querulous marsh inebriation
Sink down the white burned-up stars of moss.

Without a sound the fir tree folds her needle hands
Over the sinking earth and with the earth dies silently.

But when at last you will hear, will understand
Why silence choked the throat so bitterly
It will be too late.

Translated by Astrida Stahnke


## BLESSED ARE THE POOR IN SPIRIT
### Vizma Belševica

Blessed are the poor in spirit
Their minds like a meadow in evening fog—
For theirs is the kingdom of heaven
Since they do not recognize their weakness.

You say you are strong. Then be to the end,
And there is no need to lie that God drives you:
Since you began to separate good from evil
There is no paradise. You simply—know.

Hence, in the mind's stony desert
You now have to struggle by the sweat of your brow
To cultivate a small illusion,
Some transparent, fragile blossom of faith.

So you cup your palm and blow your breath around
     the bud
To protect it against the draft's icy laughter
In order to be happy for that short moment
When you will succeed in deceiving yourself.

Translated by Astrida Stahnke

## RELATIVES IN SAMARKANDA
Vizma Belševica

Brother jackass, if in the gall of your stagnant cry,
Out of your deeply bitter chest
you would permit it, let's cry together, brother,

Hard.

I see that slanting load
Insensibly high over your ears,
But, brother, you're not the only one
Who is fed stingily and whipped lavishly.
Generally speaking, it won't help.
How did you put it?

*Ars longa vita brevis?*

Cry or don't—it's all the same.
There won't be another to pull your load,
But, instead and for sure, someone will add to it
Even while I cry and wallow in my bitterness.

Better let's take up the yoke together
And then plod on
Straight into the traffic's deluge of sin,
And, whether or not we'll get through
Is besides the point.
In this world everyone has his load
And his place, brother jackass.

Translated by Astrida Stahnke


## AN ARGUMENT BETWEEN A BLOSSOM AND AN AX
Vizma Belševica

Don't scream at the linden.
She will bloom in her time.
If you like it—look at her blossoms;
If you don't—don't look.
That is all you can do.

And, of course,
At any moment you can cut the tree down:
In an argument between a blossom and an ax
The winner will always be the ax.

But after that, don't forget
To wipe your boots in the blossoms.
No silk in the whole world
Is gentler than linden blossoms.

And do not be afraid of those bees
That your boots crush into the ground.
For her stinging your boot
The bee pays with her life.

Translated by Astrida Stahnke

## PROMETHEUS SPEAKS TO THE EAGLE
### Vizma Belševica

Eagle,
    You have never belonged to them.
Every day you drink my blood.
Every day you tear my flesh.
You sharpen your claws on my heart.
Eagle, you are mine—
        from your eyes glaring in hatred
to your soft dawn under your wings.

Eagle,
    They think
That your hard copper beak can pluck out
        the conscience like liver.
But you know, as I do,
        that it will never happen.
In my torture-dialated eyes
        flash like lightning
            the world's pain, despair,
                bitterness, injustice.

You never let me shut my eyes in peace and happiness.
Eagle, thank you for letting me see everything,
    that my suffering lets me listen to lovers' whispers,
    to infants' whimpering at their mothers' breasts flooded
    with milk, to the firm hand gripping the handle of a hoe
    that turns the earth.

Eagle, as long as you will torture me,
    they will not break us.—

Never.

Translated by Astrida Stahnke

## THROUGH EVENING TWILIGHT
Imants Ziedonis

Through evening twilight,
through cool evening mists
we pass
and gradually become shadow.

We pass.
And no one any longer sees our profile.
There remains only a sense
that someone has gone by somewhere.

As though a door has creaked.
As though a rustling leaf has flown up.
As though a sorcerer
wanted to patch your heart.

As though from the summits had flown
the last flocks of leaves.
Someone wanted to caress you,
but passes . . .
and did not touch.

Translated by Inara Cedriņš

## I LOVE AN APPLE
### Imants Ziedonis

I love an apple in the night, that floats
without any branch and without any tree.
I love an apple tree in night, that floats,
bending its branches in the dark, without roots.

And the whole earth that floats in night
is not erected nor propped by anything.
I love darkness that will not disappear
when I rise again tomorrow morning.

But will stand away, unseen,
and near when the sun sets.
I see a person, approaching now,
come from darkness, to go again into the dark.

Translated by Inara Cedriņš

## FIRST
### Imants Ziedonis

First, when I switch on the light
I see my pencil's end.
In what strength does it live?
How does it see the hurdles while leaping?

White page like a bog—
tundra, in which one vanishes.
How does it find a place to hold on—
those tiny words?

A dog skims over the bog,
over the white page.
When I went there alone
I met nothing.

Translated by Inara Cedriņš

## SMALL WINDOW
### Imants Ziedonis

small window of the sauna
and wormhole in mushroom
and the tunnel into which the mountain train vanishes
                how I long for home!
                to go still deeper
                and find the old beer drinkers
                who I've not been with so long, long
small window of the sauna
and the hole made by mice in the chaff
and the tunnel into which the mountain train vanishes

                                    Translated by Inara Cedriņš

## TRY TO FIND
### Imants Ziedonis

    try to find
    a neutral apple

    they've all struggled heavily
    against the heavy earth
    and have fallen heavily

    those green grafted branches
    are witness
    that a neutral apple
    isn't possible.

                                    Translated by Inara Cedriņš

## MEANWHILE
### Māris Čaklais

While lead purposefully flows
all together toward mankind
drive the slave out from our minds
hearts and livers, Blow Wind Blow!

Over Kurland, our Kurland—
Star of Morning—dear Kurzeme.
Frightened or not scared at all—
still just fall in one direction.

Still just rise in one direction—
Once arisen, already phantom.

That's OK—but while lead flows
all together toward mankind
drive the slave out from our minds
hearts and livers, Blow Wind Blow!

Translated by Guna K. Chaberek


## CAMEO. FINAL LONGING
### Māris Čaklais

Traces of beauty in marble.
Traces of mildness in gypsum.
They're all together in the Great Score,
in the impossible-to-adore Styx.

Do not fear carrying on.
Repetition overcomes in waves.
Do not fear waves—
a wave heals a bruise.

How easily the boat sails,
shines like muscles of bronze! . . .

But, to see one spring butterfly
at my oar-tip! . . .

Translated by Guna K. Chaberek

---

(NOTE: "Blow Wind Blow" refers to an old Latvian folk song that has surged in popularity during the renascence of nationalism in Latvia.)

## LUSH ARE A YOUNG GIRL'S EYELIDS
### Māris Čaklais

Lush are a young girl's eyelids
markings on the skin of a serpent

A guitarist loves his guitar
water is adored by a duck

A lot must be witnessed
before the world becomes a friend

When all is seen, then
you and she must part

Translated by Guna K. Chaberek


## OBSERVATIONS
### Māris Čaklais

I. Distances—like flutterings—wear down.
Wake up—happy there's water in the bowl.

In the window, sun, not bars.
Uncertain, who do you embrace?

Nothing added. Nothing taken away.
Gone too the player opposite—

Yesterday's cheat, and the day's before—
did he suspect what this smithy would forge?

In the frigid room, anxieties
cover us—a worn fur coat.

II. Not one poor soul
not one little babe
unstuffed to the marrow
with foul, sour rain.

We felt, we felt—God will protect—
the nightmare would pass.
Black Angel (how long?)
do not fly down.

III.  Liberty, liberty—dynamic dactyls
rock us like swings throughout the night.

Liberty—to shake hands or not . . .
to lift a lid or lift a hat . . .

Tin head, club in hand.
A woodpecker pecks in radiowaves.

Dancers drag on toward morning,
like bulky bags, like lame legs.

IV.  Look—after broken bones and smashed fates—
embracing waves rush in.

Sun-singed pines stand as if nothin's happened.
Lower limbs fill with groans, fringe roots embrace death.

Alone, Latvian rocks sit on their sorrows, while
bureaucrat-Wind sews a record-book of sand.

Behind dunes, too late, a seagull shrieks,
is one unseen being strangled?

Unexpected Baltic snow rasps on abraded souls.
Disinfection? eagerness for vengeance? ever-enduring joy of being?

V.  Again, by the shattered trough
Rodin's Thinker sits . . .
Delighting ducks, the wind
flaps flimsy facades.

Tattered scourge, wearied by lies
shakes in offended rage.
Cardboard arch raised in honor
of the long-forgotten, still invites.

A dung-heap is still a dung-heap,
let it explain why it crawls.

Black clouds with polished snouts
speed over sudden awakenings.

Translated by Guna K. Chaberek


## DARKNESS THICKENS BLACK-GREEN
Māris Čaklais

Darkness thickens black-green
pines melt in

a wall of darkness
with a pine relief

but there are
there really are pines

the sea sighs three times
together with me
the mournful tune it plays
is already something else

the sea cannot be discerned
but I know it
is there

jerked up out of the ground
my beloved shoulders can
be seen only
on a map

but I shut my eyes and
they are there

shoulders are there
ground is there

Darkness thickens black-green
pines melt in

perhaps it is the new-year
of the pines, of the sea, of the ground
perhaps they pour luck out
of darkness
as we do from lead*

Surely it is also my new-year
for
hear
my heart
tolls—
a bell.

Translated by Guna K. Chaberek

[UNTITLED]
Anna Rancāne

To see oneself more clearly. To draw one's features
in the dark of night that smarts salty in the eyes.
To bite into the bread of darkness without hesitation,
to swallow it, even if it sticks in the throat.

To look at one's reflection without turning away
for a long time, as into a bottomless, borderless well.
Until tears sprout like flowers behind lashes,
until you see in your own eyes clearly those of others.

To listen to oneself, as if standing on the threshold
of an abandoned house. Without screaming for fear.
To squeeze the scream tightly in one's palm,
hide a sharp thorn deep in one's breast.
To listen to oneself, until in solitude
one hears other voices.

---

(*NOTE: On New Year's Eve, Latvians traditionally pour lead to divine their luck
in the coming year.)

To pronounce the word Death with calm lips,
to smile quietly and put out the reflection in the dark.
To smile quietly and say the words: I am.
To look at passers-by in the morning as if looking into a mirror.

Translated by Astrīde Ivaska

## NOVEMBER
### Anna Rancāne

Nobody will come any more. Mittens have a pattern of crosses
and the road has set under my feet.
Treetops in the woods hurt. Blood in the temples
rustles with the linden boughs. It is fall.

Jagged, thorny treetops in the woods
surround me, do not let anybody near.
Only death by my left hand, solitary and close,
meant for me. Only the earth. Nothing else.

Only the earth, hiding precious souls in its lap,
its features mark my numb face with pain and light
awaiting frost and snowstorms. Lighting a fire,
calmly celebrating within myself the only feast that will come.

Ice flowers slowly cover the feast to which no one will come.
Logs form a cross in the stove. A thread runs black and red.

Translated by Astrīde Ivaska

## IN THE ABSENCE OF PERIODS
### Klāvs Elsbergs

I will express you in the absence of periods
yes before they—and commas—
            have crawled into the lines
like an ugly *nota bene*

we all will kick off
only you I will express
only you I will surround with greenish flower garlands
only for you I will wait with love's hatchet
hiding cozily around the corner of dispassion

you will be expressed
hush
the periods are coming already—
the small stupid grave mounds . . .

Translated by Valters Nollendorfs

## [UNTITLED]
### Klāvs Elsbergs

\* \* \*

it seems there is the smell of garbage somewhere
it seems there is the sound of poems in the air

how unhappy are those who are indentured
to this here subservient literature
\* \* \*

Translated by Valters Nollendorfs

## WOLF!
### Klāvs Elsbergs

\*

*the Romans*

if in the world a single
wolf will remain and
if in crossbreeding
this wolf with various
bitches

anything but a wolf
will come about

      the Romans will never forgive us

I would not recommend
annoying the Romans

*

*the wolf's present*

it suffers
from a total
lack of
      weapons and ammunition

*

*the future*

under normal circumstances
man
      will live longer than wolf

but it can happen
that the wolf
      will not yet have succeeded
      in extinction

      Translated by Valters Nollendorfs

## MADDY
### Klāvs Elsbergs

the parquet gives off a faint reflection
the moonlight falls upon it silently
girlie *geh zum Teufel geh zum Teufel*
*geh zum Teufel.* Maddy walks out the
gate of the estate her
heart collapses the end is near
on the lakeshore there's no soul

to talk to her. The lord has done
what every lord has
title to do. Maddy
too Maddy too Maddy too
Maddy too

Translated by Valters Nollendorfs

## "BACK IN THE USSR"
### Klāvs Elsbergs

this land is as strong as death
as the cloud of a slowly gathering
storm

and every cloud
has a silver lining

and we live
in that lining

but let's better remember Dante:
hell too has a lining around it
there howling circle around
those who in life
those who in their
those who in their only life
have been such:
neither fish nor fowl

to be sure
to be sure
I do not think about
those touched by eternity
and those touched by cult

but I think about me
and about you
and about many bosses
I think indeed too

Translated by Valters Nollendorfs

# Lithuania, compiled by Rimvydas Šilbajoris

## Lithuanian Poetry
## by Rimvydas Šilbajoris

Much of the contemporary Lithuanian poetry sounds an echo of native woodnotes, even if they are no longer wild. The instinctive turns of poetic idiom, the roots of imagery, the worldview, do not automaticly go back to the centuries of written tradition—the anchorbed of the old literatures of the West—but rather to an unconsciously shared self-perception and font of poetic language stemming from an oral, folkloric heritage. Thus Vincas Mykolaitis-Putinas (1893–1967), poet and playwright, whose creative imagination passed over time through the mesh of French and Russian Symbolism, has retained in his poem "The Wayside Christ" the intonations and references of country folk whose faith has dotted the Lithuanian land-scape with wayside crosses of Catholic devotion.

A much younger poet, Judita Vaičiūnaitė (b. 1937), known for her spell-binding reveries of love in sunlit urban settings, has nevertheless reached down to the depths of Lithuanian mythological beginnings and observed how the roots of primeval awe before the world from time out of mind have branched out in the contemporary self-awareness of her nation. Across the waters, the New Yorker Jonas Mekas (b. 1922) still feels in every capillary of his soul that ancient country life of his native Lithuanian home coursing through the blood. His years as a filmmaker and underground-cinema critic have only enriched his inborn village-lad integrity. The hush of rain in his poem whispers the same things we might hear from Vaičiūnaitė's ancient amber god.

Small nations placed at the crossroads of history tend to have old and bitter memories of their encounters with the large forces that, in their mutual conflicts, have shaped today's world. Foreign occupation, enslave-ment, exile, and death have all cast their long shadows over Lithuanian poetry. Every century has had its victims, and every successive generation has stood in silence in their dark remembrance; there were always poets who articulated the measure of this pain. Henrikas Nagys (b. 1920) is a poet who remained steeped in the past of his nation and in its proud, unbroken spirit, even while he developed his Romanticism in the West

115

European mode. Here he recalls the Tsarist Russian empire and its cossacks who crisscrossed their own Mother Russia and all the subject lands with bloody punitive expeditions.

In Stalin's reign of terror, the massive brutalities were aggravated by the fierce and prolonged guerilla resistance against the regime; often there was no one left in the family to weep for the victims, or no one dared to approach bodies dumped without burial in the market place for all to see. Janina Degutytė (1928–90), a gentle poet deeply in love with her land, was a witness to it all. Like Antigone of old, she performed the poetic ritual of love for all those who perished, without counting friends or enemies. Her poem speaks in a folkloric mode, referring to the tulip designs in national dress, to an ancient myth of a lover killed, and to a maiden, wronged by the gods, who could only get her consolation in the nonexistent land of nine rivers and nine dawns.

Algimantas Mackus (1932–64) was the darkest witness of exile, of the Lithuanian diaspora under the hollow eyes of death. With bitter nobility, he challenged the exiles to strive toward a tragic dimension of their experience. The excerpt here is from a narrative poem dedicated to his friend, the writer Antanas Škėma, who, like Mackus himself, died arbitrarily, in a traffic accident. Mackus gives a meaningful context to this event by relating it to the deathly landscape of Lithuania in the aftermath of Stalin's terror.

This aspect of Lithuanian poetry—its confrontation with history—may well be best represented in the poet Juozas Kėkštas (1915–81) who took part in the allied campaign in Italy. The poem is in its way a liberation from Lithuania's exclusive concern with its own wounds, an opening toward the universal tragic story of all humanity.

Life resembles a cliché in that it does "go on." In the shadow of history, Lithuanian poets have tended to their own landscape as if it were an ancient pagan garden full of trees, fruit, sun, and shade, dotted with mushrooms, trolls, flowers, and fairies, heavy with harvests, and light on the wing. Sigitas Geda (b. 1943) is an old magician of myth and nature—a mystic and a humorist in one—whose subtly refined, complex verse often comes from his ability to think simply—like a child. He sings of nice and silly things, like an impish folk bard, and yet, history is there, brooding darkly behind. Henrikas Nagys takes a deep, sweet breath of a summer day from long-gone childhood. Albinas Žukauskas (1912–90), a crusty old farmer of a poet, known especially for his rich country-bred poetic language—and the headstrong proletarian convictions to go with it—offers a goodly wallop of his magic brew. Jonas Juškaitis (b. 1933), like many other Lithuanian poets, moves in a dreamy, limpid aura of nature, but, unlike some, he is a master of the delicate nuance, of an almost oriental calligraphy of feeling for just the right touch to make a fairy tale out of mere remembrance. Albinas Bernotas (b. 1934) may be said to continue this delicate calligraphy unto the cobwebs of time. His poetry in general is distinguished by great concern for the survival of green things—birds, water, air—because he feels that there is a holiness in earth that our harsh world no longer knows.

Time is both the main enemy and the theme in the works here cited by the next group of poets: Kazys Boruta (1905–65), Jonas Aistis (1904–73) and Bernardas Brazdžionis (b. 1907). All three are venerated pillars in the edifice of Lithuanian poetry, very different in their talents and inclinations but equal in achievement. Boruta acquired much of his iron will, sardonic humor, and uncompromising rebellious urge from German Expressionists and Russian Futurists like Mayakovsky, but, instead of both proclaiming and damning the City, he chose to worship the monumental, completely invented, figure of the "Village Lad," a giant of honesty and strength and a martyr carrying the flag of future revolutions. Aistis made his tortured emotions matter to more readers than any other Lithuanian poet between the wars and afterwards (from exile). We learned from him that (his!) disappointment in love was tragically important, no less than the lyrical pain of loving a spare, long-suffering place—his native country—or the vague, exciting reveries of beauty, life, and death, evoked in Aistis' Lithuanian soul by his encounters with beautiful and decadent things in the Western, particularly French civilization. Bernardas Brazdžionis (b. 1907), the most rhetorical of Lithuanian poets, always replete with yearning for a beautiful death in God, became the flag-bearer—indeed, the banner itself—of the protesting Lithuanian spirit clamoring in the voice of martyrs and prophets for freedom from the Soviet grip of tyranny. We should add that on his recent trip to the still-Soviet Lithuania, he was mobbed by adoring crowds. By an ironic contrast, the radical modesty of Marcelijus Martinaitis' poem embodies the very essence of Brazdžionis' striving to be a bridge for his people across the sea. Martinaitis (b. 1936) is a fascinating poet, as much in love with nature as with Man and a spinner of fantastic, amusing, and biting peasant yarns of the time and tide of all things human that are like a beam, well, splinter in the eye of God.

The last group of authors presented here are most of all engaged in playing the poet's games of the mind. Henrikas Radauskas (1910–70) is, possibly, the best player of them all. For him art is of itself a value and stands in the relationship of master over ideas and feelings outside its proper sphere, as in the poem "Arrow in the Sky" in which an aesthetic gesture leads to a confrontation with the horror of eternity. In his other moments, Radauskas is playful, sometimes cheerfully cruel in his images, sardonic about society and erudite about art, and always supremely skillful with words. Alfonsas Nyka-Niliūnas (b. 1919) is not always as darkly brooding as presented here, but he does transform the artistic experience into one of profound, complex existential thought about the human condition—and the condition and meaning of all other things—in what he calls the "theology of the poetic word." Tomas Venclova (b. 1937) is also, even predominantly, an intellectual poet, approaching the complex issues of existence in the mode of intense analytical inquiry, in the course of which the mysteries of all being become transformed into one poet's art; we cannot ask for more.

The choice of the poets represented here depended to a large extent upon the realities of available translated material and does not altogether reflect a full and fair picture of the best talents in Lithuanian poetry. One could easily add quite a few names to the present list; let us hope this can be accomplished in some future project.

# About the Poets

## JONAS AISTIS

Jonas Aistis (b. 1904; d. 1973) is the pen name of Jonas Kossu-Aleksandravičius, a poet and essayist, who studied in Kaunas and Grenoble, France and taught in Nice and Paris. After 1956 he lived in the United States. He published eight collections of poems and three essay collections. Volume One of his collected poetry came out in 1988.

## ALBINAS BERNOTAS

Albinas Bernotas (b. 1934) is a poet who was graduated from Vilnius Pedagogical Institute and worked as a high school teacher and editor for several literary journals. Since 1960 he has published more than seven collections of poems. He also has translated from Russian and Polish prose and poetry.

## KAZYS BORUTA

Kazys Boruta (b. 1905 in Kūlokai, Lithuania; d. 1956) was a poet, prose writer, and translator. He studied in Kaunas and Vienna, was jailed for political opposition to the Lithuanian government, and was sent to Siberia by the Soviets after World War II. He has published four collections of poems and four pieces of prose, and has translated Henrik Ibsen, Friedrich Schiller, Lev Tolstoy, and others. Boruta is known for his rebellious spirit, for his modernistic, expressionistic style in poetry, and for his complex and creative handling of verbal folklore heritage in his tales.

## BERNARDAS BRAZDŽIONIS

Bernardas Brazdžionis (b. 1907 in Stebeikėliai, Lithuania), is a poet and free-lance journalist. He studied at the University of Kaunas and worked as a journalist. Having moved to the West in 1944, he now lives in the

United States. He has published nearly twenty volumes of poems, among which are works of poetry for children. He is known for his romantic, patriotic, rhetorical poetry, permeated with his love of homeland and with Catholic religious spirit. Occasionally he likes to dabble in experiments with style and diction.

## JANINA DEGUTYTĖ

Janina Degutytė (b. 1928 in Kaunas, Lithuania; d. 1990) graduated from the University of Vilnius and taught in secondary schools. She has published eleven collections of verse (among which are poems for children), has translated Valerij, Brjusov, Émile Verhaeren, Rainer Maria Rilke, and others, and has written for the puppet theater.

## SIGITASS GEDA

Sigitass Geda (b. 1943 in Pateral, Lithuania) is a poet, playwright, essayist, and translator. A graduate of the University of Vilnius, he worked on the editorial boards of the periodical press and has published seven books of poetry, plays and poems for children, film scripts, librettos, and articles about literary criticism. He has translated poetry from Polish, German, Hungarian, and other languages.

## JONAS JUŠKAITIS

Jonas Juškaitis (b. 1933 in Kuturiai, Lithuania) is a poet and translator. He graduated from the University of Vilnius and worked on the editorial board of the weekly publication *Literature and Art*. He has published seven collections of poems, translated works by Mixail Lermontov, Sergej Esenin, Ossip Mandel'stam, Johann Wolfgang von Goethe, Rainer Maria Rilke, and others, as well as Russian prose and plays.

## JUOZAS KĖKŠAS

Juozas Kėkštas (b. 1915 in Tashkent, Uzbekistan; d. 1981) studied journalism in Warsaw, was imprisoned for his leftist views, joined the Anderson Polish Forces during World War II, and later lived in Argentina and, since 1959, in Poland. The author of seven collections of poems and translator of Polish and Spanish poetry, he belonged to the "Earth" group of poets and prose writers (so named after a 1951 anthology of their works) as one of its most important members.

## ALGIMANTAS MACKUS

Algimantas Mackus (b. 1932 in Pagėgiai, Lithuania; d. 1964) was a poet and essayist. He emigrated in 1944, studied in Chicago, and worked in

Lithuanian-language broadcasting. Six collections of his poems have been published. Mackus has the reputation of a bitter and honest poet of the exile.

## MARCELIJUS MARTINAITIS

Marcelijus Martinaitis (b. 1936 in Paserbentis, Lithuania) is a poet and literary critic. Trained in engineering and journalism, he held a number of jobs in these professions. Since 1979, he has been teaching at the University of Vilnius. He has published eight books of poetry and one of literary criticism and has also written for the puppet theater. Martinaitis is one of the strongest "village" poets in Lithuania, mixing myth and humor with rustic diction and highly refined thought.

## VINCAS MYKOLAITIS-PUTINAS

Vincas Mykolaitis-Putinas (b. 1893; d. 1967) was a poet, prose writer, playwright, and literary critic. He attended the Seinai Seminary and studied in Freiburg and Munich. In addition to several poetry collections, two novels, and two plays, he is the author of works on literary criticism and history.

## JONAS MEKAS

Jonas Mekas (b. 1922 in Semeniškiai, Lithuania) is a poet, filmmaker, and film critic. He left Lithuania in 1944, studied at the University of Mainz, and has lived in the United States since 1949. While serving as editor of the journal *Film Culture*, Mekas has published seven collections of poems. He has also made several films that pioneered the "underground cinema" movement.

## HENRIKAS NAGYS

Henrikas Nagys (b. 1920 in Mažeikiai, Lithuania) is a poet and literary commentator. He studied at the University of Vilnius and later, having withdrawn to the West, at the Universities of Innsbruck and Freiburg; he now lives in Canada. He has published seven collections of poems and a number of works of literary criticism. His poetry tends to the romantic and has inner connections with Rilke and Georg Trakl.

## ALFONSAS NYKA-NILIŪNAS

Alfonsas Nyka-Niliūnas (b. 1919 in Nemeikščiai, Lithuania) is a poet, translator, and essayist. He studied at the Universities of Kaunas and Vilnius, as well as in German universities after leaving Lithuania in 1944. He worked at the Library of Congress in Washington, D.C., and was one of the leading members of the "Earth" collective. He has published five books of poetry, as well as translations from William Shakespeare, T. S. Eliot, Saint-John Perse, Dante, and Virgil. A poet of deep and broad humanistic education in literature, music, and the arts, Niliūnas is counted among the most profound Lithuanian poets who have an existential slant.

## HENRIKAS RADAUSKAS

Henrikas Radauskas (b. 1910 in Krakow, Poland; d. 1970) was a poet and translator. He studied at the University of Kaunas and worked first at the Klaipėda radio station and then in the book-publishing commission of the Ministry of Education in Lithuania. He moved to the West in 1944, did manual labor for a while, and later joined the staff of the Library of Congress in Washington, D.C. He has published six books of poems, as well as translations from the works of Thomas Mann, Stefan Zveig, Paul Verlaine, Heinrich Heine, Johann Wolfgang von Goethe, Anna Axmatova, and others. Radauskas is known as the most sophisticated, cosmopolitan, intellectual Lithuanian poet.

## JUDITA VAIČIŪNAITĖ

Judita Vaičiūnaitė (b. 1937 in Kaunas, Lithuania) is a poet and translator. A graduate of Vilnius University, she worked in an editorial capacity for several newspapers, and she has published eleven collections of poems and plays in verse. She is known to Lithuanian readers for both her urban and her mythological styles of poetry.

## TOMAS VENCLOVA

Tomas Venclova (b. in Klaipėda, Lithuania) is a poet, translator, essayist, and literary theorist. He taught at the University of Vilnius and then emigrated to the United States in 1977. He has published two collections of poetry, as well as translations from Anna Axmatova, T. S. Eliot, Ossip Mandel'stam, Oscar Milosz, and others. Venclova is a sparse, intellectual poet, a great master of the pensive word.

## ALBINAS ŽUKAUSKAS

Albinas Žukauskas (b. 1919 in Bubeliai, a Lithuanian region in Poland; d. 1990) was a poet, prose writer, and translator. He studied in Warsaw and Vilnius and worked as an editor, in belles lettres publishing, and in the cinema. He has published eight books of poetry, several collections of stories in prose, and has translated from Polish, Russian, Belorussian, and Estonian prose and poetry. Žukauskas was a strong-minded, often pastoral poet of old proletarian convictions.

# Lithuanian Poems

## THE ROADSIDE CHRIST
### Vincas Mykolaitis-Putinas

My dearest Lord, how luminous the night!
How high the widespread vault of heaven!
And, oh the stars, the stars! Both large and small,
They shine so, make me want to weep, dear Lord!

And I said to myself, I'll go upon the even road:
The even road stretched out to joyful freedom,
The even road, and shining, boundless night,
Just made for me, young man with spacious dreams.

But why this vigil, tell me, dearest Lord,
By distant roadside, mute, with pensive brow,
By distant roadside, where uncounted sorrows
Walk past and draw their breath in pain.

Pray tell, my Lord, if our troubled dreams
Have prayed you down to us from distant heavens,
Or maybe just these irridescent Autumn nights
Have dreamed you up from darkness of the earth?

Do fold me in, my vigilant dear Lord,
Here by the road, amidst the night's long dreams—
Oh, but the stars, so bright in distant heavens,
They shine so, make me want to weep, dear Lord!

Translated by Rimvydas Šilbajoris

## JUODKRANTĖ (THE BLACK SHORE)
### Judita Vaičiūnaitė

It smells here of the sweat of ancient Courlanders, and
of the heat, and of the pine tree.
And on the sand there are the chronicles of wind . . .
How shall I know thee,
tiny amber god,
        all covered up with sand and ashes,
dead in the sound of words, dissolved in winds,
forgotten? . . .
Only the sun—as it was then, when forests were becoming amber,
The sun keeps turning like the grindstone of some ancient
    mother . . .

*

The circles of the sun adorn the crosses and the ancient
    spindles.
I shall turn over a sun-warmed piece of sod.
And there will be decayed pine trees
and bees embalmed within the resin pieces.
But there shall be the luminosity of ancient honey—
to spread its own aroma in the village street . . .

*

A bell in a waxen tower.
The ring of fairy tales that we can't hear.
The sun shall glitter like a misty piece of gold—
thus I shall start the ancient hearth.
And from the distant air of our childhood
You took and threw upon my arms
some strands of mist
(their yellow color comes from apple rinds).
And now—there is the heat and night.
And I can smell again the old wild apples.
The bell sounds softly, yes, its voice is sweet.
Preserve and hold all this in your remembrance.

Translated by Rimvydas Šilbajoris

## OLD IS THE HUSH OF RAIN
### Jonas Mekas

Old is the hush of rain on underbrush branches,
the black cock's caws in crimson summer dawn—
old is this our speech:

of oats and barley, amber in the fields,
of shepherds' fires blowing in autumn's wet aloneness,
of potato harvests, the sultriness of summer,
white glister of winter, sleighs on roads without end,
the wagons heavy with logs, the fallow fields—with stones—
the red clay ovens, the gypsum in pastures;
and evenings by lamplight, in the graying of fall fields,
of wagons for tomorrow's market,
of October's roadways submerged and washed away,
the potato harvest, soggy.
Old is this, our life—these fields that were trodden
by long generations, their paces set in dark soil,
each measure of earth still talking and breathing fathers;
they dug yellow clay from these same pits
and golden sand from these same fields.
And when we too must go,
others will come to pause at these boundary stones;
they will scythe down meadows and plough the fields,
and when they sit at their table—their workday over—
each table, each pitcher of clay, and each cottage beam
will speak to them and recall
the yellow sand in the gravel pits,
the rye that billows within the wind,
our women's melancholy songs at the flax field's edge—
and this scent, first breathed in a brand-new cottage!—
the smell of fresh moss.

Old is the flowering of clover;
the whinnying of horses summer nights;
the chime of harrows, rollers, and ploughs;
the heavy groan, in the mill, of the grindstone;
the white gleam of the garden weeder's kerchiefs.

Old is the hush of rain on underbrush branches,
the black cock's caw in crimson summer dawn—
old is this, our speech.

Translated by Demie Jonaitis


## LATERNA OBSCURA
### Henrikas Nagys

Two of us draw the child's face in the first snow.
Beneath wild raspberry branches, my sister rocks her doll.
Last night the workmen laid light snow on the hard earth
and now they tar the wooden bridge over the Bartuva.
—The new-born snow, light as my sister's hair.

Through the crouched, empty town of Samogitia
the cossacks ride. They slash with naked swords
white, breathless winter moonlight.

We sketch our brother's face in the first snow.
The epileptic daughter of the watchman
crumbles dry bread, scatters it into the ditch
for the coffin. Snow drifts over the waxen face
of the peasant woman and her pillow of pleated paper.
And through the snowstorm echo
the hoarse chant and the breathless bells.

Through the white soundless town of Samogitia asleep
the cossacks ride. And their long whips cut
blue winter moonlight shimmering in the trees.

No one kissed you goodnight. And no one wept
with you for your dead mother. No one came to bury
your father, hanged. Your land, empty and naked.
Your earth, a peasant's palm. For you were not admitted
into the kingdom. Gray garments fluttered
like shrouds of long forgotten funerals
—the vestments of a plague.

Through the poor town of Samogitia ride the cossacks
who bear on their long lances, cut in pieces,
the blue moonlight of winter.

On a bright Sunday morning in a radiant land
the workmen tar the wooden bridge over the Bartuva.
Deep under ice, and slow, the river flows into the sea.
Under the raspberry branches, covered with snow,
my sister's doll sleeps. Two of us trace
our brother's face, asleep in the blue snow.

Translated by Clark Mills


## MY LIMBS ARE ACHING . . .
### Janina Degutytė

My limbs are aching from the cold lake's water,
My mouth is dry in blowing wind, my eyes are full of tears
And yet my hands cannot my brothers' dried-up blood,
My hands cannot wash out these shirts . . .

What will I tell my mother back at home?
The shirts are blooming, blooming tulips red . . .
And how am I to wash these set-in stains,

With my own life made barren by the northern wind?

So, in this lake, with the nine rivers flowing,
So, in the morning, when nine red dawns are rising.

Translated by Rimvydas Šilbajoris


## FROM "CHAPEL B"
### Algimantas Mackus

Death is an old and cooled
sunset above a Lithuanian landscape:
in the spring the dear sun was wedded
to the moon, who wooed her in an alien tongue.
Death is the crooked windmills
that face the biting wind for a piece of gold:
at midnight a girl sneaked out
secretly to grind the grain of her labor.

Death is fanatical plowmen,
the blind sacrament of blood and earth:
like wounded beasts they arise from their beds
and shatter against the cement in the evening.
Death is cynical and angry decorated soldiers
returned to the front:
a starving girl plunged into lead,
bereft of tears to cry her heart out over her lot.

Death is yellowed manuscripts,
the title pages of ancient books:
a grey-haired antiquarian of Vilnius collected them
into the chronicle of decay and the date of disappearance.

Translated by Mirga Girnius

## MAIOLI BLOOMS WITH POPPIES
### Juozas Kėkštas

Maioli flowers with death and blood, Maioli blossoms
with blood-red poppies. Mountains, meadows bloom with blood.
Corpses in long rows. In this common place of rest
lie Frenchman, Englishman, Hindu, Greek, Italian, Pole.

(The fallen have forgotten all; aware of nothing
and lucky, do not hear the friend's moans—crash of shells.
San Angelo, Monte Cassino, Albanetta, Cairo
perished ephemeral as dreams, as they themselves.)

Bridges down, markers gone, the roads we march
to Rome burst into rubble, smoke and dust
that choke the nightingales and cherry-flowering orchards.
Your tired legs buckle and the nights weigh black,
but friend, luckless as I, do not trip, do not fall!

We do not need cantatas, anthems, pathos, lies.
Our deaths, our lives are shoddy. We could no longer wait
—no longer bear, our errant leisure. Night's Pompeii
requires another end. Thus not to live, but to die here,
we bear the lava of the war Vesuvius on tank and rifle.

With death and blood Maioli flowers, and with poppies.
In blood red as the poppies we inscribe strange history
and in our dreams of freedom, shout: *Libertá vedi e muori.*

*Translated by Clark Mills*

## WHEN WILL YOU TAKE ME TO ZARASAI
### Sigitas Gada

When will you take me to Zarasai,
Where the lakes are blue and grasses high?

I am a child of the lakes, too,
Gently lapping, sleepy and blue.

My father hewed some stones,
The hedgehogs made hay.
My mother baked scones,
I was born on one such day.

Ten brothers drank sweet milk,
There were crayfish in the lake.
Horses scampered on a hill,
A cow scratched on a stake.

Our folk here in the past
The corvée served, with birch rods paid,
And of an evening shoes out of bast
Plaited, and oat soup ate.

And many, many corpses were
Here found after the great war.

*Translated by S. Roy*

## THE SUNDIALS
### Henrikas Nagys

I was awakened by the whistling sound of pigeons' wings
and the flood of sunshine rising in my eyes.
Old grandma's spinning wheel is humming evenly in the light-filled
   room,

and swarms of bees, invisible, are humming in the neighbor's
blooming linden tree. The wind is rocking in the fragile patterns
of blue and wavy window curtains.

The trains in the railroad station catch their breath after their long
    journey.
The stationmaster's whistle blends with chirping crickets' song.
I run out barefoot over the white stones
into the garden full of cooling shadows. There I drown
amidst the fragrance of sunflowers, earth, and cherry blossoms.
I see there slumbering on the whitewashed brick wall
my little lizard with the half-closed eyes.
The sparrows bathe and chatter in the roadside dust.

I fall to the grass; I hear how slow my heart is beating.
How ringing clouds have touched the boughs of the apple tree.
How little ray of light that ripened in the midday sun
has fallen on my face, how it burns my eyelids. . . .

The wind is sleeping in the grass. I hear how the dull stone
of the ragged artisan is sharpening the scissors and the knives.
The crickets and the whistle of the train are chirping. Chirping sound
    of blade.
I hear it all in summer's humming and enormous house.
I open, then, my eyes—and all the blue with its warm clouds
is falling drop by drop into my sleeping palms.

                              Translated by Rimvydas Šilbajoris


                        GIFTS OF AUTUMN
                        Albinas Žukauskas

The wind, in the stubble rustling, announces Autumn.
The fields have turned grey, and in hollows the oxen are lowing.
The gossamer's flying. The summer wheat's reaped and brought in.
The winter-wheat, also, the farmers have finished sowing.
Bloom, dahlias! Ground frosts will come down and scorch you.
Turn yellow, bend down by the road, Lithuanian birchtree!

The sun's getting lazy. Blue pinewoods are nodding, sleepy.
Make haste, o you cranes, before twilight, don't wait till the night!
You'll get lost if you stray. It is late, but the Milky Way's keeping
The chain of its beacons across the dark sky-vault alight.
Fall silent, green grasshopper! Autumn is here with his treasure.
Come, Father, pour beer in our mugs, let us drink it at leisure.

There's plenty of everything! Apples roll down from the hill.
And bread! For the greediest there'd be enough and to spare.
The rowan-tree burns. In the mud big fat porkers lie still.
Grey geese raise their clamour. The blackbirds on treebranches bare
Sit noisy and gay as young boys in a mischievous band.
Big carts in a caravan lined, at the cellar-door stand.

We sit down together to drink to the bountiful year,
Inviting our friends and our neighbours to feast with us too.
There's piles of brown meat-pies and juicy green cucumbers here,
And honey smells sweet, and good beer foams and flows: here's to you!

We drink, then we eat, drink anew, and then songs start to sound
Of the bounty that gladdens our hearts, that our labours has crowned.

To you, poet, Autumn brings new inspiration as well.
Go, praise with your rhymes the green rye-shoots that sprout in the
fields.
And the stubbly loam left for winter; harsh frosts our old peasants
foretell.
Sing of hard-working peasants rejoicing, of Autumn's rich yields,
Of the blessings and gifts of our fertile and bountiful land,
And your song will not rust while her birches and appletrees stand.

Translated by Dorian Rottenberg

## SUNDAY
### Jonas Juškaitis

Green Sunday.
Crimson peonies.

Silence and sunshine. The cottage
Filled with a bumblebee's drone,
Old, like happiness making you drunk
With an odor of jasmine and wax.

O beautiful langor! Only the shadows are wheeling,
The treetops swaying.

Green Sunday.

The cry of a steamer
Returns as a cry.

Crimson peonies.

The horizon touches your ear.
On the banks of dykes
Guileless wild flowers
Are restful. And ah! those rustles,
those rustles of northern grass!

Translated by Dorian Rottenberg

## I WILL WAIT
### Albinas Bernotas

We're watering cows. The chain hits the weeds
Like a pike. On the pond water wrinkles crawl.
Wrinkles . . . Can wrinkles be felt indeed
On one's face, like on water? It isn't yet Fall,

It's Summer. Waiting for grain and fruit.
Not today will nests show, but when last leaves fall.
Summer. It draws towards September's feast.
I'm waiting for apples. But who waits for Fall?

Still, still I wait for the first trip to school,
For the years to pass, for my beard to show,
For the cows to drink, for my first grey hair.
Waiting's the essence of life, I know.

Like a pikefish, the chain drops into the weeds.
Soon no wrinkles again is the water wearing.
Can you feel the wrinkles vanishing too
From your face? Is Fall really so wary?

Run the tips of your fingers over your face.
The gossamer clings to your hands. Sticky stuff!
Again? Oh well, we'll water our cows
And wait all our life till they drink enough.

Translated by Dorian Rottenberg

## THOUGHTS ABOUT ETERNITY
### Kazys Boruta

After an unsuccessful trip to eternity
I returned to old Vilnius, my native city,
and put up in a flat built not long ago,
which looked like a coffin—its ceiling was so low,
while into the window like ghosts, eyes agog,
crept shadows from the ruins of an old sinagogue.

On that first of a long line of a long line of sleepless nights
I fancied—the eeriest of nightmarish sights!—
that the blocks of old houses had come alive
and the ruined old sinagogue rose, revived,
and on its balcony, coloured blue,
rabbi Gaon was sitting anew.

"Rebe Gaon", I addressed the man,
"Accept my apologies if you can
for interrupting your thoughts on eternity,
but I'd very much like, from the standpoint of modernity,
to talk of philosopher Maimonides' ideas
which have long been upsetting my mental peace.

"I first came across them right after the war
when I met with a Jew who was old, tired and sore, having
gone through all deathcamps in Poland and Germany
and now flown as smoke from a crematorium chimney.
Facing a corner, in a cellar he sat,
plaintively chanting a prayer,
for he thought that, by some miracle,
he was the last Jew left anywhere,
and bemoaned the plight of his people.

"Then we started talking
about Maimonides' philosophy
according to which a man suffers
not for any fault of his own
but for all his people
and all its history.
I myself more than once thought the same
But dismissed it as quite impossible.
Be so kind, o rebe Gaon,
—for you are a pillar of wisdom—
tell me, can this really be true?"

Falling into thought, Gaon made no reply,
only, digging into a fat talmud,
sorrowfully wagged his head,
returning to his eternity,
while I again found myself sighing and coughing
in a new flat, low-ceilinged like a coffin,
with the unsolved puzzle:
for what do men,
peoples,
and all mankind
suffer terrible torments
which never cease?

When spring came,
I wanted to talk again
with rabbi Gaon about the same subject,
but there, in the place where the ruins had stood

I saw children at play.
But after all, maybe so it should be,
maybe they are eternity,
and through them, life will come back to the old city?

Translated by Dorian Rottenberg


## SAINT SEBASTIAN
### Jonas Aistis

I trembled; eyes uplifted, I deplored
That agony might break my will at last—
One arrow here, the first to strike, O Lord,
And all that dread anxiety has passed.

I feel the fall of warmth and gentleness,
Drop after drop on me; my joints melt, while
Upon my vigil falls the far-off smile
Of my Redeemer coming, luminous.

Almighty, gloried be! I thought, so long,
This moment I would need a will that's strong.
Instead, You come towards me . . . O light, your light—.

I cannot look, I'm blinded like the dead.
The vaults ring, jubilant with gentle might.
—I cannot lift my sinking, leaden head.

Translated by Demie Jonaitis


## LIFE'S NOSTALGIA
### Bernardas Brazdžionis

Processions of the morning stars shall pass us by,
Shall pass us by, and nobody will know,
If there be evening, if the silver stars will shine there,
Will there resound the prayer of the bells, the way it used to in the
    mountains.

I feel a gentle breath of wind against my face,
Also His voice upon the beating shore—
It is not wind, nor is it river running down the mountain,
O Lord, could it indeed be You . . .

I know the lonely traveler's bleak road,
I heard in darkness his complaints and prayers—
He cursed the fairy tale, his joy, the sun, and also You,
And he kept shouting "Never!" and he kept shouting "Never!"

You never, but the morning sun will rise again,
You never, but a thousand flowers will bloom.
You never . . . and this one sad voice
Has touched the earth, the flowers, and the stars and made them cry.

And if You are a brook that flows through valleys and through
     mountains
And carries little boats, the down of swans, and pine needles; little
     boats—
We will be boats and will be feathers of white swans, and fishes—oh,
     we
     shall no more be people,
But only take us, Lord, and carry us away.

And if You are the gentle breath of wind
That lulls to sleep a tulip in the prayer of the evening bells,
Do lead us, too, where the procession has departed,
Don't let the earth, the stars, and blossoms cry.

I feel a good and gentle breeze against my face,
Also His voice upon the beating shore—
It is not wind, nor is it river running down the mountain,
O Lord, it is You calling, You . . .

                              Translated by Rimvy das Šilbajoris

## IF I AM A TREE SOMEDAY TO BE CHOPPED DOWN
### Marcelijus Martinaitis

If I'm a tree, some day to be chopped down,
Don't make a stable out of me,
Don't saw me into firewood.

Make me into a bridge across a river,
A door or doorstep
Over which men greet each other.

Translated by Dorian Rottenberg


## ARROW IN THE SKY
### Henrikas Radauskas

I am an arrow that a child shot through
An apple tree in bloom beside the sea;
A cloud of apple blossoms, like a swan,
Has shimmered down and landed on a wave;
The child is wondering, he cannot tell
    The blossoms from the foam.

I am an arrow that a hunter shot
To hit an eagle that was flying by;
For all his strength and youth, he missed the bird,
Wounding instead the old enormous sun
And flooding all the twilight with its blood;
    And now the day has died.

I am an arrow that was shot at night
By a crazed soldier from a fort besieged
To plead for help from mighty heaven, but
Not having spotted God, the arrow still
Wanders among the frigid constellations,
    Not daring to return.

Translated by Theodore Melnechuk

## THE WINTER'S TALE
### Henrikas Radauskas

Guess what smells so . . . You didn't guess.
Lilies? Lindens? No. Winds? No.
But princes and barbers smell so,
The evening smells so, in a dream.

Look: a line goes through the glass
Bending quietly; and the hushed
Light, in the tender mist,
Is gurgling like a brook of milk.

Look: it's snowing, it's snowing, it's snowing.
Look: the white orchard is falling asleep.
The earth has sunk into the past.
Guess who's coming . . . You didn't guess.
Princes and barbers are coming,
White kings and bakers,
And the trees murmur, covered with snow.

Translated by Randall Jarell

## THE LAND OF THE LOTUS-EATERS
### Henrikas Radauskas

Careless nannies tell them cradle tales about the sweet land of
the Lotus-Eaters, and they spend their childhood as if in dreams,
waiting for the hour when they will be able to make that distant
journey.

The ship rocks them like a cradle in the gentle hands of the
Nereids (the gods are well disposed toward such journeys), and
camels rock like cradles walking from oasis to oasis.

When they reach the land of the Lotus-Eaters, they start
eating the lotus fruit and are soon sated, but they don't stop eating
and forget their homeland. And, having spent a hundred or a
thousand years in the Lotus land (the sun never sets there and no
one keeps the time), they grow weak with age and can no longer
raise their hands to pick the fruit and fall on the sand near the lotus
trees.

The Lotus-Eaters carry them out of the lotus forests and lay them down, dying, in the sun, and they scream barely audibly, tortured by hunger and thirst, and never die (the sun never sets in the land of the Lotus-Eaters, and no one there keeps the time).

Translated by Jonas Zdanys

## MADONNA AND FLY
### Henrikas Radauskas

Beyond her shoulders—a moon river falling golden from heaven, near which curly-headed trees run from the hill like a herd of green sheep and in which a miniature horseman waters a steed the size of a grasshopper.

Spreading a pearl and sapphire speckled blossoming purple robe, she gives the yellow babe a round red breast which he carelessly sucks while staring gloomily at a fly crawling on the marble balustrade.

"O, that man's mind, that his heart could understand her painfully mystical smile!"—wrote von Bock. (The child's fingers, which pinch his mother's flesh like pliers, are hidden by his right shoulder.)

In the middle of the night, after the lone light on the ceiling has squeaked and burned out, the madonna steps out of the frame, walks past the drunken Rubens and the savage Goya, walks down the stairs to the cellar and puts the child in a polished Assyrian basalt bathtub. Feeling the stone's cold, he begins to cry, but in front of her the complaisant door begins to open, and she, led by the buzzing fly, walks out into the neon lighted swimming, melting, disappearing street.

Translated by Jonas Zdanys

## INFERNO
### Alfonsas Nyka-Niliūnas

*Leave all despair, who enter here.*
*(Comte de Lautréamont)*

To J. G.

Through dark streams of the cerebral complex I penetrate a season
    that was not in the world
gray-horizoned, with ardent trees
(like ours, their roots more powerful than their trunks),
where my friend Hermes, the Aurora Gate in his eyes, sings the
    sheen of your hair,
and the sun—the scarlet domino of the carnival of our time—
    fixed in green polar ice, listens to him.

The bells of the Virgin's month that toll (under the earth);
the Mystical Rose, my Mystical Rose, Queen of Immaculate Time
    (under the earth), meet us.
Wild birds that would each autumn wrench us from dark-haired
    shadowy places;
fatherly errant parabolas of the familiar shadows of the rooms of
    youth
and of the closing wooden doors,
parabolas that filled the evenings of the departed, meet us (under
    the earth).
Thus my arrival at a melancholy town.
A saint, his hand somewhat corroded, stops me, cries: "You know
    —here's Inferno!"
Yes! This journey's not my first. And in my mind's eye rises
The First Circle: Shannon, the waiter from Perpignan, and the
    doomed, with ciphers on their faces.
But I go forward. I do not turn back.
A street of dust under my feet,
I see this woman, joyous—it may be, my mother.
At the rotten parapet of the bridge I find again, as in the mirror
    in my native home, Yvonne de Galais who waits, her hair
    mournfully fair;
she tells me like that *The Memory of Mortefontaine*, in velvet dark-
    ness, sleeps like a pearl that glimmers
—the full red moon drowned in the veins of a tree.

Wrapped close about the house, but dry already lies the river.
Only the lake has grown still more, both from sorrow and rain.
With a keener glance, one glimpses in the water the outline
of a church, like a drowned man, snail-and weed-bedecked.
I put my ear to the earth. I listen.
Clad in their small white shirts, the choir of moles con-
tinue with their singing;
In your world only the ironic forms of recollections live
—Eumenides, the world has died, your God exists no more.
Beside the yellow churchyard gate, in a Soutine-red jacket,
stands a young drummer.
Girls, their breasts quite hidden,
their bodies formless, and as if they had been mothers long before,
lead forth a faceless bride, in whose still childlike flesh we see a
    numerous family and a wooden table.
This is the Last Supper. The last bread and water.
A dry Garden of Gethsemane rustles beyond the pane.
In small white shirts, alas, the moles' choir sings the hitherto
    joyless *Epithalamium.*
Faces. Bells. Faces. Bells.
And a beggar bird, his cap on his knees.

He would stand up as we approach, but leaves, wind-driven, close
    our eyes, and he vanishes without a word.
In her body we find the silhouette of a ruined house.
Diligent as a little shepherd, a gray worm, that has constructed
    something with great care in the antechamber, starts.
He opens the door and, his face covered with tears, leads me into
    the room. There in the middle of the floor lies in pieces in
    a broken mirror my face.
Behind the table sit the brothers. But they no longer know me.
Across the floor scurries the mouse from Gorki's book,
the one that we would once have raised into a horse
to ride into more light. That, God did not allow.
Thus we remained, our hope of liberation smothered
in wretchedness—to us senseless, to others, sanctified.
Mother sits by the wall and thinks, perhaps, how every spring my
    father dreamed of sailing-ships and winds.
Then suddenly she lifts her eyes, and says,
"You didn't bring us God?"
No. I could not find Him anywhere.

Still, my wish is to console them (you will rise again);
but the worm outside the door resumes the song,
and I, who understand that the joy of oblivion has been, for them,
still greater than their hope for eternal being,
I burn for a long time with a bizarre illusion,
that, dead, I shall call up my sleeping angels from the sand, and
in time's distant reaches overtake the angel of Bellini
who bears on his enormous wings their bodies up to God,
and thus after a hard struggle, bring lost paradise to them
—heavens that open simply to the key of iron, and the footprint's
echo upon the earth.

Translated by Clark Mills

## DIALOGUE IN WINTER
### Tomas Venclova

Step into this landscape. It is still dark.
On the far side of the dunes drones the empty road.
The continent wars with the seas—
It is invisible, but brimming with voices.
A traveler or an angel left
This light snow-dusted track,
And the shore's reflection in the black window
Reminds us of the sterile Antarctic.

The deep sea still foams, is not yet frozen.
The sands have blown for more than just a mile.
Here the bridge becomes distinct, here obscure
As the severe cavity of winter grows and spreads.
There are no telegrams, no letters,
Only photographs. The transistor doesn't work.
It is as if a candle, dripping wax,
Stamped and sealed this dangerous time.

How damp the air, how steep the rock,
How powerful the roentgen of daybreak!
Straining your eyes you can see how the walls clear,
The church tower, and the figure of a man.
Only the foggy contours of trees stand out
Against the white background. Through the bark,
Even shut-eyed, you can almost see
The last, narrow resistent ring.

"That habit tires the eyes,
After an hour, it's not hard to get lost."
"Prophecy does not waste its whispers on us."
The hoarfrost-covered axis tilts,
And it seems that at the edge of the horizon,
Where ships blacken and sound stiffens,
In the sluggish ocean sky
Flare the planets Jupiter and Mars.

The emptiness spreads to the Atlantic.
The fields are bare—like unlocked halls.
February hides beneath January's layers,
The plains cower from the wet wind.
Beyond the seas, mountains bare themselves,
In the depths the dissolving snowdrift
Dwindles and blackens. "And what is that?"
"Again, river mouths, bays, and harbors."

Beneath the heavy net of clouds
Cramped clearings glitter like fish.
"Do you remember what the stars said?"
"This century rolls into being without signs,
That's the fact." "Death's attraction
Fetters man, plant, and thing,
That's why grains sprout and offerings burn,
And that's why I think not everything is finished."

"Where is the witness? I don't understand,
Who divides the truth from the lies:
Perhaps the two of us are alone in the world."
"And it seems to me you are the only one"
"And the third speaker? You say
No one hears this discussion?"
"There is heaven and the snow-covered fields,
And sometimes the voice outlives the heart."

Midday darkens the trees.
In broad daylight, you are conscious only
Of small things, scratched from nothing an hour ago,
Which stand in place of the words:

A broken chip of an ice chunk,
A skeleton of branches, a crumbled brickhouse
Near the bend in the road . . . Later—stillness
On this side of the sea, and on the other side of the sea.

Translated by Jonas Zdanys

# Part 2
# Poetry of the Central Eastern States

# Bulgaria, compiled by
# Ludmilla Popova-Wightman

## Bulgarian Poetry in the Eighties
## by Ludmilla Popova-Wightman

*The twilight of the dwarfs,* the eighties in Bulgaria, was a time of crass materialism, corruption, and cynicism, of economic stagnation and decline. That was not true for poetry.

*Spaces,* a book of poetry by Blaga Dimitrova, appeared in 1980. It contains a remarkable poem "Almost a Prophecy" dedicated to Konstantin Pavlov, a poet who was silenced after the publication of *Satires* (1960) and *Poems* (1966).

"Almost a Prophecy" is a desperate cry for truth, a deeply felt yearning for freedom of speech and print, a prophecy full of hope and tolerance, and a wise program for the future: "And for all crimes, and for all lies,/ a retribution will be asked.// And this retribution will not be a bloodletting,/ but a blood transfusion/ through the Word." The history of this poem deserves to be told. In its first version it contained a "subversive" stanza: "The graves will open,/ and the skulls with bullet holes/ will toll like Easter bells." The troublesome stanza was cut out. The poem was left out of the *Collected Works,* published in 1983, altogether. The uncut original poem appeared for the first time in a new magazine, *Bat,* in an issue dedicated to Konstantin Pavlov.

In the poem "The Great Wall," written in 1966, and in the "Bee Lesson" (1975), both included in *Spaces,* Blaga Dimitrova expressed the poet's inner struggle to overcome self-censorship, a necessity for survival and publication in a totalitarian society. In *Voice* (1985) and in *Labyrinth* (1987), she continued her thinly veiled resistance to the totalitarian regime.

Another important literary event in the eighties was the publication in 1981 of the almanac, *Sea,* in Burgas, a port on the Black Sea. It was the reappearance in print of Konstantin Pavlov after fifteen years of silence, strictly enforced by the government (with an official document, as Konstantin Pavlov says[1]).

In 1983, on his fiftieth anniversary, a celebration was organized by a courageous poet, Mikhail Nedialkov—naturally not in Sofia, but in a very small provincial town Pernik, not far from his birthplace,—and the publication of a book of poetry, *Old Things,* was finally approved.

In addition to selected poems from his first two books *Satires* and *Poems, Old Things* contained nine new poems. These poems introduce us to an original world of ideas and images and confirm our opinion of Konstantin Pavlov as "the classic of Bulgarian contemporary modernism."[2]

In the second part of the book, Konstantin Pavlov's screen plays, written during the seventies, appeared. Films had even made from some of them through the efforts of movie directors who admired Konstantin Pavlov's work. This provided him with some means of existence.

One wonders why the *nomenclatura* should forbid a poet to write poetry (literally!) and permit him to write screenplays, and even let some of them be filmed? The explanation could be a perceptive remark by Atanas Slavov[3] that the *nomenclatura* aimed at two things: first, to stop all gifted poets and literary critics from writing poetry and literary criticism; and second, to give them another opportunity to earn a living, in order not to create martyrs, by steering them to work in fields that were not the ones in which they were interested or best qualified. In this way, the victims were kept out of abject poverty and quite busy, so that they didn't have time or energy to write original poetry or prose. In the case of Konstantin Pavlov, this strategy didn't work: Konstantin Pavlov became a remarkable screenplay writer. The films for which he wrote screenplays were very successful not only in Bulgaria, but also in the West. He also continued to write poetry, although it is quite possible that he would have been much more productive if the ties to his reading public had not been severed so early.

In 1989, at the very beginning of the new era of freedom, his latest volume of poetry, *Reappearance*, was published by *Profizdat*, the publishing house of the Trade Unions.

In the six years since the publication of *Old Things*, Konstantin Pavlov had undergone one more transformation: death has become a close companion. Death was already present in his early poems ("Funeral" and "Poem without an End"), but in *Reappearance*, its presence is felt strongly. The closeness to death has permitted him to contemplate the future of the universe with cosmic eye: "It Was the Twentieth Century," "The Angel Scratched . . ."

In the eighties there appeared also some remarkable poetry by Radoi Ralin, a famous satirist, whose two-liners, making fun of the rulers, had brought a lot of pleasure to Bulgarians as well as a lot of unpleasantness to Radoi Ralin.

Ivan Radoev published a volume of his selected works, and new books by the younger poets Nikolai Kantchev, Ivan Tsanev, Boris Hristov, Georgi Belev, and Liubomir Nikolov appeared.

Valentina Radinska, a poet from Sliven, a provincial town, published two volumes of poetry of desperation—a deep pessimism that would have been quite unpublishable in the old times of socialist realism when reality had to be always optimistic, and the future always bright!

BULGARIAN POETRY IN THE EIGHTIES 149

Rumen Leonidov, who follows the tradition of originality in language and form of both Blaga Dimitrova and Konstantin Pavlov, published *Big and Small* in 1990. Edvin Sugarev's and Danila Stoianova's books also came out in 1990, after the fall of Todor Zhivkov. (Several of Edvin Sugarev's books had already appeared in samizdat.)

Danila Stoianova holds a special place in Bulgarian poetry. She was the daughter of Tzvetan Stoianov, a charismatic, gifted literary critic who had brought to Bulgaria the best of Western literature in translation and had written imaginative literary criticism. He died young after an unsuccessful operation. Danila, herself, fell sick of cancer at 18 and lived with death for several years, all the while writing remarkable poetry.

She suffered the most cruelly from the mediocre, brutal censorship of the time: she never saw her poetry in print—her book of poems, *Memory of a Dream*, was published only in 1990, many years after her death. During Stoianova's lifetime, Orlin Orlinov, one of the official poets, found it necessary to criticize Blaga Dimitrova for her praise of the poetry of this new, young, talented poet—despite the fact that it was well known that she was on her deathbed! What the official critics couldn't stomach was her modernism, her fresh poetic voice, her authentic poetic gift.

The end of the decade gave us a charming book by Stefan Getchev, a poet older than Blaga Dimitrova and Radoi Ralin and a well known translator from modern Greek (of Cavafy's poetry in particular) who was unable to publish any poetry for more than twenty years.

I would like to remark on the role that courageous editors played in the literary life of Bulgaria in the seventies (after the invasion of the Soviet army in Czechoslovakia—a bad time for literature) and in the eighties. Quite often when the official publishers like *Bulgarian Writer,* the publishing house of the Union of Bulgarian Writers (Konstantin Pavlov was finally admitted to membership not as a poet, but as a screenwriter), refused the publication of an interesting work, the poets had to look for a different publisher to place their work. Here the nonconformist editors (some of them poets and writers themselves), working for smaller provincial publishers, such as "Georgi Bakalov" in Varna, "Hristo G. Danov" in Plovdiv, or publishers in Sofia who didn't have literature as their main topic, played an important role in giving good literature to Bulgarian society. In Sofia, *Profizdat* published books by Radoi Ralin and Konstantin Pavlov. Blaga Dimitrova's *Forbidden Sea* was published in Varna. Her novel, *Face,* which immediately after its publication was "arrested" and "imprisoned" in the special "prison" for books in Sliven together with Konstantin Pavlov's *Poems,* was published by "Hristo G. Danov" in Plovdiv.

A new generation of poets, Ani Ilkov, Boris Rokanov, and Georgi Rupchev, are now publishing their first books, finding their poetic voice in a time when they can write the way they want to, without having to fight to tear down "their inner Great Wall!"

# Notes

1. Letter to Svetozar Igov, *Bat, a Literary Magazine,* 1990, no. 1: 9.
2. Rumen Leonidov, *Literaturen Forum,* 40 (4 Oct. 1990).
3. Atanas Slavov, *The Partisan Review,* 44 (1977): 594.

# About the Poets

## STEFAN GETCHEV

Stefan Getchev (b. 1912), novelist, literary historian, and translator of Cavafy, published his first book of poetry, *Belezhnik (Notebook)* in 1967, at the end of Khrushchev's thaw. The book was criticized as formalistic, and the poet was silenced until 1983, when his novel, *The Bridge,* appeared in a provincial press. His second book of poetry *Poezia (Poetry)* was published only in the spring of 1990.

## BLAGA DIMITROVA

Blaga Dimitrova (b. 1922), vice president of Bulgaria, holds a unique position in Bulgarian life and literature. Poet, novelist, playwright, and translator, with over thirty volumes to her credit, her books have been translated into more than twenty-five languages. In the last three years she has become the heroine of the opposition movement for democracy and the living conscience of Bulgaria.

## RADOI RALIN

Radoi Ralin (b. 1923) is a satirist, essayist, and active participant in the democratic movement in Bulgaria. "Ballad of Art" appeared in the book of poetry *Posleden ponedelnik (The Last Monday,* 1988).

## IVAN RADOEV

Ivan Radoev (b. 1927), poet and playwright, studied slavic languages and read law at Sofia University. He has worked as an editor on several literary magazines and in the theater and has published five volumes of poetry. *Greshni sunishta (Sinful Dreams)* appeared in 1987. His poetry and plays have been translated into several languages.

## KONSTANTIN PAVLOV

Konstatin Pavlov (b. 1933) came to Sofia from a small village Vitoshko by means of a sport scholarship. He read law at Sofia University. His first book *Satiri (Satires)* appeared in 1960; his second book *Stikhove (Poems)* was published in 1966, but reached the public only in samizdat—the printed copies were "arrested." After 17 years of silence, his third book, *Stari Neshta (Old Things)* appeared in 1983. His latest two books, *Poiaviavane (Reappearance)* and *Agonio sladka (Agony, Oh Sweet)* appeared in 1990 and 1991.

## NIKOLAI KANTCHEV

Nikolai Kantchev (b. 1936) graduated from Sofia University. His first volume of poetry *Prisustvie (Presence)* appeared in 1965. He has published seven volumes of poetry. His poetry has been translated into several languages. He translates poetry from Russian and French.

## IVAN TSANEV

Ivan Tsanev (b. 1941) studied Russian language and literature at Sofia University. His book of poetry *Sedmodnev* appeared in 1987.

## BORIS HRISTOV

Boris Hristov (b. 1945 in Pernik) is a teacher, journalist, editor, poet, novelist, and scriptwriter. His volumes of poetry, *Vecheren Trompet (Evening Trumpet)* and *Chesten krust (Cross My Heart)*, appeared in 1977 and in 1982, respectively. He was a participant in the International Writing Program at the University of Iowa.

## VALENTINA RADINSKA

Valentina Radinska (b. 1951 in Sliven) works as an editor for Bulgarian Cinematography. She has published two volumes of poetry. *Noshtna kniga (Night Book)* appeared in 1983 and *Ne (No)* in 1988.

## EDVIN SUGAREV

Edvin Sugarev (b. 1953) received a Ph.D. in Bulgarian language and literature from Sofia University in 1989. A Research Associate at the Institute for Literature at the Bulgarian Academy of Sciences, he published several volumes of poetry in samizdat. He is one of the main speakers of the democratic opposition, and he won a seat in the Bulgarian Parliament in the elections of 1990, after the fall of Todor Zhivkov.

## RUMEN LEONIDOV

Rumen Leonidov (b. 1953) has a B.A. in Bulgarian language and literature from the University of Plovdiv. His first book of poetry, *Preduprezhdenie*

*(Warning),* appeared in 1977, his second, *I oguniat si spomnia za iskrata (And the Fire Remembers the Spark),* in 1982, and his third, *Goliam i maluk (Big and Small),* in 1990.

## DANILA STOIANOVA

Danila Stoianova (1961–84) died of cancer at the age of 23. The fatal disease did not protect her poetry from brutal criticism by Party dogmatists who disapproved of the "pessimism" of her verse! What they couldn't stomach was her modernism, freshness, and real poetic gift. The volume of her poetry *Spomen za sun (Memory of a Dream)* was published only in 1990.

# Bulgarian Poems

### [UNTITLED]
Stefan Getchev

\* \* \*

I lay down on the hill to die.

The Sun, a priest in golden vestments,
gives me the last sacrament:
blue, sparkling, heavenly wine
and bread—a morsel of summer cloud.

Around me a choir of insects sing
a joyful requiem.
And the grasses slowly cover me
with a green, aromatic, living shroud.

Translated by Ludmilla Popova-Wightman

### BALLAD OF ART
Radoi Ralin

They imprisoned the sculptor
to deprive him of art, society and sun—
these permissible human joys,
to kill his feelings and thoughts.

Forced into idleness,
the prisoner was subdued for a while,
then suddenly burst into action:
the daily portion of bread
fed his fingers
and quickly became a face—
so like his own, the other prisoners, impressed,
handed him their portions of bread too.

The bas-relief was astonishing:
all prisoners were portrayed,
their faces crowded behind bars—
an enormous bunch of grapes,
ripe for the wine of freedom.

The sculptor smiled at his sitters,
"Isn't art invincible!"

But before dusk, before the bunch
of grapes lost its elliptical fullness,
a hungry hand reached
and broke off its own bread image,
followed immediately by other hands.
The prisoners munched bits
of the bas-relief's memory with zest.
Deeply moved, the sculptor finished eating
his own face. He was so hungry,
the bread didn't even stick in his throat.

Translated by Ludmilla Popova-Wightman

## ALMOST A PROPHECY
*To Konstantin Pavlov*
### Blaga Dimitrova

The hour of the Word will strike
when you don't expect it at all.

The truth will thunder like spring rain
on a roof of corrugated iron.

The rivers of words will flow upstream,
upstream, back to their sources.

The rocks will move
and find their true places.

The trees will cry and touch the stars
with severed fingers.

The graves will open,
and the skulls with bullet holes
will toll like Easter bells.

And for all crimes, and for all lies,
a retribution
will be asked.

And this retribution will not be a bloodletting,
                    but a blood transfusion
through the Word.

                              Translated by Ludmilla Popova-Wightman

NIGHT-LIGHT—
A NIGHT-BIRD'S EYE
Blaga Dimitrova

At midnight, I steal in on sorrow
                    like a thief on tiptoe.
Through her nostrils, an ancient kettle whistles,
                    boiling over.

I wake her up from last century
                    to give her medicine.
With her eyelids, she barely lifts
                    the stone shaft of light.

And looks at me with troubled eyes.
                    Who are you? she asks me.
I shudder. Mother, don't you know your own
                    daughter?

Don't you at least remember the face,
                repeating your own face?
On whom can I rely then, in these times
                of general amnesia?

Without batting an eye, my country is ready
                to forget me too,
as soon as I try to shake it lightly
                out of its sleep.

And mother nature with a night bird's eye
                will ask me too,
when I beg for a breath of air,
                Who are you?

Forgive me, mother, without wanting to,
                I thought of myself again.
Recognize me by my egotism,
                and let me tuck you in!

Translated by Ludmilla Popova-Wightman

## THE GREAT WALL
Blaga Dimitrova

I recognized it at first sight,
and it recognized me too.
I climbed, step by step,
straight up,
the thousand-year-old crenellated wall.
I didn't need a guide
or a language of misunderstandings.
The primeval umbilical led me
        blindly.

        I peeked through its embrasures
        and on the other side of the wall, I saw
        the same innocent grass,
        and mountain, and forest, and sky,
        the same, but quite different:
        foreign, forbidden, dangerous—
        haunts of horrors.

The wall traced
the ridge of fear.

I walked a long time on its dinosaur back,
stretched high from horizon to horizon,
from epoch to epoch,
shutting out the air,
dampening the echo.
Only time—a grass snake—
wriggles through it unimpeded,
instant by instant,
twist by twist,
century by century.

I patted its stones intimately
and silently talked to it:
You were raised in my cells
even before I was born.
Your embrasures,
staring suspiciously,
are my eyes
to the outside world.
Your stones are bonded
with my blood, and sweat, and tears
stone on stone,
fear on fear,
silence on silence.

How many millenia will I need
to tear my inner Great Wall down?

*1966, Peking*

Translated by Ludmilla Popova-Wightman

AMNESIA IN REVERSE
Blaga Dimitrova

She invites the dead into her room
for a chat, for laughs, for gossip.
She treats them to fig preserves
in little bowls; all gone long ago.

And uses a dead vocabulary, words
like "parlous," "bosom," "pimekan,"
"distractious," "draught," "baken" . . . .
This style speaks of a vanished world.

And she pets a dead cat on her lap,
and catnaps under her purring.
From her former garden, she picks
bunches of withered flowers. A dead mutt,

she chases away with caressing banter.
In the night, she listens to a dead grasshopper.
And a deceased mailman calls on her,
bringing a letter from my *dead* father.

Through that town, also dead long ago,
the dead horses pull the bridal carriage
and the white veil flutters in the wind
by the dry jet of the dry fountain.

For her the past is more alive, more
piercing than the stinging of a wasp.
To me it offers dead secrets,
smelling of moth balls.

Translated by Ludmilla Popova-Wightman


BEE LESSON
Blaga Dimitrova

If you want to spin a word
            of the wind,
            of the sun,
            and of a stamen's secret,
a word like thick honey,
sticking to your memory,
with a bitter taste of sweet suffering.
                    (why do you want it so much?)

you must have a sting,
a sting of bile,
swallowed all your life,
             tear by tear,
             silence by silence,
and to know that you can use it
only once.
                    (Do you really want it?)

Only once,
and revenged, to drop in the dust
like a bee, its honey not gathered,
             its little flower cup of the day not drunk
             its hither and thither not flown,
             its buzz-buzz not sung,
a bee with wings of air
and a breast of sunny,
fluttering fluff.
                    (Eh, do you still want it?)

                    Translated by Ludmilla Popova-Wightman


## THE SHADOWS OF THE TREES
### Blaga Dimitrova

They are cutting down the trees
in my town,
they are cutting down their shadows.

             First they break off
             the tongues of their leaves,
             to silence their voices.
             Then they cut off
             the branches from the shoulder,
             amputate them one by one—
             to quell their resistance.
The tree crown bristles—
a black fist without fingers.
             So it's easier
             to fell
             the defenceless trunk.

Birds, do not return
to my town,
you won't find your nests.
            Souths winds,
            blow around my town,
            your breath will remain barren here—
            can you crack open the buds of sidewalks,
            or dislodge the stone
            blocking my throat?
Thirsty rain,
do not grow tender
over my town—
there are no green lips
to drink your kiss,
there are no open hands
to catch your tears.

The trees are lying
stretched along
their summer shadows.
            They have no branches
            to embrace us,
            they have no wind
            to take leave of us,
            they have not a drop of rain
            to mourn for us,
            they have no sound
            to whisper
            a parting word to us.
Their roots remain buried
deep in the earth,
and their shadows—in our dreams.

                    Translated by Ludmilla Popova-Wightman

## OVERSTEPPING ONE'S RIGHTS
### Blaga Dimitrova

I arrest the stars with my eyes
    and ask them:
    Am I permitted
    to love
    without a body?

I rest my cheek on the earth
    and ask it:
    Do I have the right
    to love
    without a body?

I know incorporeal shame—
    to compare it
    with the shame of the body,
    this innocent shame,
    is a sacrilege.

Not to touch each other—
    separates us more inevitably
    than time and distance,
    draws us apart more unavoidably
    than being together.

And as soon as I touch you in my dream
    with so much thirsty tenderness,
    cast out of my sleep,
    I wake up suddenly
    at the very edge of your lips.

In such disembodiment,
    eery,
    without touch or pain
    as in timelessness,
    instants dissolve all at once.

And I cannot even retain one of them—
    wounded,
    sinful,
    made innocent
    by the miracle of touch.

Oh, Lord, it is a sin to choose me,
    the disrespectful,
    the unrepentant,
    the innocent—
    to be a saint.

                Translated by Ludmilla Popova-Wightman


## FROST
### Blaga Dimitrova

*To Todor Borov*

The day-prisoner
peeks through bars of frost.

Not a sparrow dares to fly
through the barbed wire of the air.

An ice lump has stopped
the gurgling throat of the water.

And our steps in the snow
jangle with shackles.

The only possible escape
from the white prison of winter is


    *to be your own freedom.*

*Boiana, 1986*

                Translated by Ludmilla Popova-Wightman

## DEAR MOTHER OF MINE
### Ivan Radoev

Bulgarian mothers!
You who for one thousand years
have been waiting for
your poor children
to come back from nowhere,
on dusty feet to return
from defeated rebellions'
dark recesses,
to take off their childish thin necks
those horrible necklaces—hemp and death twined,
to wash off their white shirts
the scarlet poppies of their proud executions,
and their homecoming's loud laughter
to light again the red peonies in the gardens,
where they used to play at future deaths—
Bulgarian mothers,
take off your mourning!
Your children will return soon!

Bulgarian mothers,
open your heavy trunks,
put on your best Sunday dresses—
blue,
and gold
and scarlet,
braid your dark hair again,
cut as a votive offering,
pick gentians and geraniums,
come out in the village squares,
wake up the fogs,
the Slavs,
the Thracians,
the Roman roads,
lift high over your heads blossoming apple twigs—
these white banners of spring rebirth
and sing,
      Our children are coming,   dear Bulgaria,
      our dear mother,   ours and theirs!
      Our children are coming!

Up there on the Balkan,   magic will flare up,
eagles will tear apart the memory of yore,
the flying militias,
wrapped in old legends,
will emerge from the children's readers
and will trample over our skulls.

Is there anyone
who doesn't believe in our return?

Who had forgotten the hard bread,
dear mother of mine?

Is there a handful of gun powder in our heads,
a lion in our hearts,
a fist,
a caress,
a word—
is there?
Is there?

Bulgarian mothers, your children are coming!
Lift high over your heads blossoming apple twigs—
these white banners of spring rebirth!
Bulgarian mothers!
Your children are coming!
They are coming!

Translated by Ludmilla Popova-Wightman

## SINGING COMPETITION
### (a fragment)
### Konstantin Pavlov

Immediately before
t h a t,
I want to test my voice one more time,
I want to rehearse my mime again,
and make sure of my fingers' dexterity.

I overdo it out of love
and respect for you.

As that architect, that genius,
because he empathized with the dead,
and was very demanding of himself,
delayed, delayed
the prepaid design for a tomb.
The dead however . . .
And so on . . .

The topic—a  c a t.
The feeling—t e n d e r n e s s:
(Is there any doubt that I could be tender!)

—My cat.
A white cat.
—My cat, despising death,
lies, looking dead now.
But only pretends to be dead.
Ah, sparrows land and rats roam
next to its very mouth.
My cat continues to lie, looking dead.
It will lie like that a long time.
But . . .

. . . but o n    a    m o o n l e s s    n i g h t
(a time for murder and remorse)
t h e    f a t h e r,    u n b u t t o n e d,
(more out of habit, less of necessity;
linen nightshirt and feet in clogs)
w e n t    o u t    t o    t h e    b a c k y a r d,

(a rock garden, rhododendrons, cypresses, a lake;
in the rock garden—a machine gun,
semiautomatic rifles (6), and a radio transmitter;
in the lake—a couple of swans, beers (6) to go with the
                        semiautomatic rifles, a rubber crocodile)
t h e    c a t    t h e n . .   .   .   .   .   .   .   .   .   .   .   .   .   .   .

Stop.

I only wanted to test my voice,
I wanted to rehearse my mime,
I wanted to make sure of my fingers' dexterity.
I'm all right.

That's how a singing practice
made all cats immortal
and equal to the sacred Cows,
and to the sacred Ibis.

Why do you glorify cats!
                    (a dog questions.)

And,
"Why? Why?"

Because people like animals.
That's why!

And because,
a squirrel
rolls a pine cone
up and down my throat.

Up and down.
And down and up.
That's why!

But because it isn't my turn yet,
let the person whose turn it is,
come onto the stage and start singing.

                    Translated by Ludmilla Popova-Wightman


## A KISS AS LIGHT AS AIR...
### Konstantin Pavlov

   ... And when the Ururungels are exhausted,
   I measure out a distance of one foot,
   and heap tacks in two small piles
   (with their sharp points up.)
   I kneel on the tacks, and imploring,
   I lift my arms and murmur
   with deeply felt sincerity,

---

(NOTE: The difference between "Urungels" and "Ururungels" is the same as the
difference between angels and archangels.)

"Let's love each other . . .
Let-us l-o-v-e each other . . ."
And I pick the scarlet roses blooming on my face,
plucking them with fingers—
fingers, whose nails have been pulled out.

. . . And when, to seal my vocal cords,
The Ururungels scoop lead
and pour it into my unreasonable throat,
I touch my burnt lips with the palm of my hand.
and lifting it, I blow a kiss to them.
It floats lightly through the air
(that's why I call it "a kiss as light as air")
and touches their foreheads gently,
but before reaching them,
like an ethereal caress,
it furrows the molten lead in the cauldrons
gently, very gently . . . .

Translated by Ludmilla Popova-Wightman

## A LITTLE MORE . . . A LITTLE MORE . . .
### Konstantin Pavlov

If electric bulbs started to torture me,
and I sensed that THAT was coming closer,
I would think of electric fuses.
I would have to think in images.
The images would have to be unnatural
and offensive to the fuses.
Time flies imperceptibly, and sooner or later
the electric fuses blow out.

In the dark, tranquillity sets in.

And THAT appears again.
I hurry to overtake it.
I grab two cats, a male and a female,
and start to rub the back of the male
against the back of the female.
Fast as a boy shining shoes.
And their vertebrae rattle.

Electric sparks disperse.
I enjoy their erratic flight.
The male sparks are clumsy.
The female—nervous and careful.

Platonic explosions follow the accidental bumps.
And when I sense THAT again,
I am not horrified,
I think about the back yard of hell,
and how funny it is. . . .
Palms stretch their slender trunks,
fountains spray fragrance,
chorales sound in perfect harmony.
Little devils jump with devilish lightness
from palm to palm,
pick big coconuts,
drink some of the milk
and give the rest to the birds.

And when I say "hello" to a little devil
and we shake hands,
our covered with coconut milk palms stick together,
and we laugh.

And then in the dark, I think—
when does this cuckoo bird
lay her eggs in my wristwatch, and how?
When and how so that I never see it?
The eggs hatch by the heat of my pulse
and look—every sixty seconds
a fledgling, a nightmare, flies out.
It is such a nightmare
that even THAT,
even THAT pulls back frightened.
That's how I profit from the happening.

Or I press a marble in my fist.
And I think about the marble.
But perhaps THAT has succeeded
in touching the marble briefly
because it starts to grow in my fist—
more and more.
It swells to the size of a planet.
But my hand remains the same.

And I don't feel pain, I feel acrid lust,
my fist so out of proportion with the marble-planet.
At the last moment, I realize what is happening
and loudly announce something naive,
something very familiar, something like,
See there, do what you can, so that no one will know
that he fell down and broke his head. . . .
The stupidity of the phrase, its irony
push THAT with the strength of coiled springs.
An IT pulls back in disgust,
understanding that it was too hasty,
that I am not ready yet, that. . . .
Before I had the marble,
I held a girl in my arms,
a slender girl with big breasts and thin shoulders.
And the result was the same.
But THAT. . . .

The words, I have invented, often help me out.
For instance—Perciphedron.
Each repetition brings a new meaning.
Perciphedron—a comet tail.
Perciphedron—the murder of an ancient Greek.
Perciphedron—a blow in the solar plexus,
which the moment the blow fell,
stopped being a solar plexus,
and became a plexus of reptiles.
Perciphedron, Perciphedron, Perciphedron. . . .
Until I exhaust each meaning
and I feel a taste of metal in my mouth.
In this case, a taste of bronze.
My bronze tongue hits my bronze palate
like the tongue of a bell.
And a deafening ringing echoes.
I am the only one who hears it.
If I used the word Iolanta
(Iolanta, Iolanta, Iolanta . . .)
I would get a silver bell.

Usually that would be the time needed
for a deceitful sadist
to replace the electric fuses.
And when the electric bulbs light up again,
I am ashamed to look at the things in the room—

I know I have corrupted each of them
in a way alien to their essence,
even if I have done so in the name of my struggle with
                                        THAT.

If they could blush,
I would transfer some of my guilt to them.


NEVERTHELESS I am comforted by the thought
that I defeated THAT today as well.


I only wish I didn't hear that shrill little voice
coming from who knows where,
"A little more . . . A little more . . ."
as sensible and comforting,
as Iolanta and Perciphedron.


Or Fresco,
or Freshti,
or Fritoli,
or Freton,
or Gigue.
Most of all Gigue!
AND NEVERTHELESS!
AND NEVERTHELESS!

Translated by Ludmilla Popova-Wrightman


## ADAPTATION
### Konstantin Pavlov


Quickly!
We must go to the square,
to the square with the powerful fountains,
the powerful fountains, spouting
rose fragrance and benzaldehyde.
We must be there at exactly half past five.
Exactly as it stands in the invitation—
at half past five!
(The circles were painted that very night.
I saw them.)
We shall start at exactly half past five.
Exactly as it stands in the invitation—

exactly at half past five.
Gentle music will melt our bones,
a gentle voice will urge us softly,
"Relax . . .
relax completely . . .
Everyone will walk in one of the painted circles,
everyone will hit himself gently.
And softened to suicide,
we'll tell each other
of our past crimes.
Exactly at the center,
at the very center exactly,
virgins dressed in white tunics
will dance, my dear, will dance
as a symbol of absolution.
Afterwards it will turn out (surely),
surely it will turn out (afterwards)
that they are men in women's clothes
not maidens.
But is the sex really important—
the symbol!—
the symbol is important, my dear.
And softened, we shall tell each other
of our past crimes;
relieved, we shall confess
our most terrible thoughts.

No one will listen to anyone—
everyone will talk only to himself.
And we shall relax,
we shall relax completely.
The procession will continue to move in a circle
up to the moment,
up to the moment, when we feel
that we don't need words any more,
that we don't have double-thoughts any more,
that our thoughts don't torment us,
and that we have only two or three wishes.

It will be enough for me then,
if you say to me, "Boo-boo-boo . . ."
It will be enough for you then,
if I say to you, "Voo-voo-voo . . ."
And a happy cow's moo

will best express
the thing t h a t has troubled us
for twenty centuries or so.

And now—
let us lie on the square
and have a nap
for two or three or five or six centuries.
Even dreams are already superfluous.
Someone else will dream in my name . . .
Someone else will have my nightmares . . .
And explain them to the world.
And misinterpret them.

Translated by Ludmilla Popova-Wightman

## CRUEL FERTILITY
### Konstantin Pavlov

Mushroom next to mushroom.
Tree next to tree.
Sun next to Sun.
Moon next to Moon.
(Jaws, teats,
bellies, fists,
space sondes,
tiresome poets.)
And more, and more.
And more, and more!

And—
in the middle of all this—
multiplied to eternity—
only one.
Someone—
survived by chance—
doomed like a wafer
destined for the billion-headed dragon.

Translated by Ludmilla Popova-Wightman

## FAREWELL, SAVIOR
### Konstantin Pavlov

Next to my step
I sensed another step,
I sensed,
but didn't hear it.

A tiny, black and brown speckled puppy,
coming from nowhere,
whining shrilly,
pounced.

Not upon me,
it pounced upon the other,
the one with the Different step,
whom I had only sensed.

The struggle was brief.
The puppy's agony was short too—
it squealed
and stretched its legs.

And then I heard the steps.
And then I saw—
victorious Death running away,
running away—
limping.

Translated by Ludmilla Popova-Wightman


## REHEARSAL FOR A GALA DANCE
### Konstantin Pavlov

Miss Death! Madam,
Madam!
My dance is a little old.
A little old.
And you are always so young.
So young!
Hop! Two small steps to the left?
To the left!

Why do you pull me to the right?
To the right!
Do I lead the dance, you little slut!
A little slut!
Or will you lead me, my little Sun?
My little Sun . . .
But why does your dance erect my . . . You know . . .

How should I call it? . . . How should I call it? . . .
And why do your bones blush?
Your bones?
Oh, my sweet,
such an unexpected morsel!
Oh, oh, oh!
And oh again!
Kick, rattle, little miss!

Translated by Ludmilla Popova-Wightman

## THERE IS ALWAYS A WAY OUT
### Konstantin Pavlov

If I went suddenly mad . . .
If suddenly my brain
faced the Great Absurdity
of its own existence . . .
If it disowned itself. . . .

If my own consciousness rebelled,
if it declared my skull
a cell for solitary confinement.
If it escaped. . . .

If my senses grew dull,
humiliated
by my wretched career. . . .

If I went suddenly mad,
if, imperceptibly, I became Someone else?
and this Someone, my double, turned out to be a
                              traitor?

If I went suddenly mad!
What could I hope for?

That,
a moment before That—
like a scorpion,
my instinct for self-preservation
would direct its sting
towards its own little belly. . . .

Perhaps,
this is the only way
I could save
*It,* the thing I wanted to be,
and to a certain degree
*I was.*

Translated by Ludmilla Popova-Wightman


## HUNGER STRIKE
### Nikolai Kantchev

Workers, strain your legendary muscles.
Thinkers, give freedom to your thoughts.
Girls, show your pretty bodies.
Women in child birth, push out your children.
Bakers, you won't be bread for others any more.
Pilots, fly out in space without a hurry.

Go calmly about your business, every body.
        The cannibals are on a hunger strike.

Translated by Ludmilla Popova-Wightman

## SONNET FOR AN OLD WOMAN

*"... and there is nothing more*
*pleasant than the gift of a second*
*life ..."*
Ivan Tsanev

She has lost all her relatives, lived longer
than her contemporaries, sons, and even her grandchildren.

She remembers each devastating parting
and can tell everything there is to tell about pain.

Look at her now, standing under the pear tree in blossom
(the neighbour's children playing round her)
and with half-closed eyes listening, listening
to the monotonous song of the oriole.

What does she hear? That a miracle has occurred,
that there is no old age, sadness, and decay. . . .
And in an instant the sun, the way it madly shines,

will turn her silver hair to gold
and the stick in her dry hand
will blossom no later than tomorrow.

Translated by Ludmilla Popova-Wightman


## ARCHEOLOGICAL EXCAVATIONS
Ivan Tsanev

In the middle of this town,
on the small square in front of the mosque,
some unceremonious moment brandished its picks,
eviscerated eternity, wrestled out of its recesses
stone rostra, steps of a Roman stadium (or amphitheater).
Surprised, we stared, bothered by the memory
of the gladiators' blood spilled here, on these stones,
centuries ago. Thoughtful, we stood
contemplating them the whole afternoon.

But how quickly our curiosity was sated,
and habit took hold of us again.
The little square is once more the arena of our daily,
shrill provincial life, undisturbed by history's ghosts.
So passes fame, would have said with irony,
that disguised goddess, the blond archeologist.
Little fountains of cotton candy spray pink,
crowds buzz joyfully, babies' rattles clatter
with youthful disrespect for the ancients.
It seems, only the present day is eternal
(should the living feel guilty,
if breathing intoxicates them?).
By the stadium's august ruins,
baby carriages move in a slow procession again,
the blue day glitters, and how many cooing soldiers
came, saw may be, and perhaps, conquered.

Translated by Ludmilla Popova-Wightman

## SCAFFOLD
### Boris Hristov

He died from fear on his way to the scaffold.
When they carried him away, the henchmen took off his hood
and we saw, he was without a head.

Translated by Ludmilla Popova-Wrightman

## INSCRIPTION
### Boris Hristov

What a slavery—
to think incessantly
of freedom.

Translated by Ludmilla Popova-Wrightman

## MEMORY
### Boris Hristov

The pain came back and circled a long time
over
the healed wound.

Translated by Ludmilla Popova-Wrightman

## CASUS
### Boris Hristov

The thief refused to steal.
The murderer threw away his knife.
What shall I do with the word?

Translated by Ludmilla Popova-Wrightman

## POSTMORTEM
### Valentina Radinska

Last night two fat spiders wove thin webs
and black mildew spread on the wet walls.
A sickly morning barely opens its eyes.
Move your stiff body and get up.

Get up and chase away the greedy gull
tearing into carrion on the dirty balcony.
Warm yourself, boil tea in the old kettle,
wash, and pull on your old coat again.

And here is your plan—go to the putrid beach,
to pubs full of thick smoke, soak up
everything, and soaked through,
take the road back to the old hotel . . .

Climb the creaking staircase in the darkness,
throw off your coat in the cold room,
hop into the bed, full of last night's nightmares
and don't turn on the fly-flecked light.

And listen how above your head
those same fat spiders spin webs again,
how the gull comes back and clumsily hops and
tears into the carrion in the overflowing garbage bin.

Translated by Ludmilla Popova-Wightman

## FEAR
### Edvin Sugarev

I am afraid of people, who think the world
stands on a turtle's back.

I am afraid of people, who imagine the world
to be a whipping-top.

I am afraid of the secret agreement
between them—
I am afraid of a turtle
with a whipping-top on its back.

Translated by Ludmilla Popova-Wightman

## INVASION
### Rumen Leonidov

Under the mantle of faith,
it's safe, warm and dry.
They say.
As in a sanitarium for people
sickened by fanaticism. I don't believe it
but I have seen it with my own eyes,
I've seen how this mantle moves by itself,
creeping along the ground.
It would not surprise me
if it fits dwarfs
best.

Translated by Ludmilla Popova-Wightman

## THE HOUSE OF DREAMS
### Rumen Leonidov

The house of dreams
burns
and dreams dream of visions
                    visions
                    visions
see horrible dreams
and the dreams see themselves in their dreams
and the visions visualize themselves
and the one who saw and the one who dreamt
don't believe their eyes
they rub their unbelieving eyes
and the house burns burns burns
and the smoke peacefully curls up
like the smoke of the peace pipe
pressed between a general's
smiling babyish lips.

Translated by Ludmilla Popova-Wightman


## [UNTITLED]
### Danila Stoianova

\*   \*   \*

I know that I won't have a funeral.
Because it is difficult to bury
the one who equates
death to life
and lives in both.

Translated by Ludmilla Popova-Wightman

## [UNTITLED]
### Danila Stoianova

\* \* \*

All year long, I've been waiting
for my tulip to open its bud,
enfolded in colours of spring madness,
to spurt cool freshness from its sealed pores,
sleepily unfurl reluctant petals,
and shivering sweetly—to be a flower at last,
not always a full-of-promise bud.
I am fed up with changing
the water in the glass,
where it shakes its naked,
green and round leg,
today I couldn't stand it any more,
I reached and opened it.

And only with my touch, I understood
the lips, pressed together,
the breath, held inside its folded petals—
not to let go; in its bud,
with fierce vanity
my little flower
was hiding
its death.

Translated by Ludmilla Popova-Wightman

## RAIN I
### Danila Stoianova

It smells of rain.
Oh, Lord—it smells of rain!
Wind blows, carrying the feel of rain.
A crazy spring.
Crystal drops
on green, excited trees.
Night, neon lights,
cars, glistening road.
Soaking streets, full of unknown notions.

Oh, my Lord—
loneliness is happiness!
Loneliness is communion with truth.
Specially, when it smells of rain.
I feel the rain.
I want the rain.
I know the rain.
Rain.
And crazy spring.
In this hot summer—
rain.

Translated by Ludmilla Popova-Wightman

## RAIN II
Danila Stoianova

There is irrelevant rain.
Dry and inscrutable.
When you feel bad.
When you search for something
you want, and it eludes you.
The air is crystal and cold.
And the rain is irrelevant.
Your desire is irrelevant.
Wind and drizzling rain.
Anguish is my consolation.

Translated by Ludmilla Popova-Wightman

## [UNTITLED]
Danila Stoianova

\* \* \*

In fall
when honey tears roll
from the black forest's bristles
and blue madonnas swing
on God's beard's sunny strands,

hand pink crutches of frost
to my lame mood,
crown it with a wreath of freezing flies
and it will leave
my empty body—
and enter an imaginary temple
to atone for our blind suffering's
sacred shame.

Translated by Ludmilla Popova-Wightman


## [UNTITLED]
Danila Stoianova

\* \* \*

The senses, the senses,
the senses become dull,
the senses grew jaded,
the senses are worn down
by their own playfulness.
They lie on the grass
and death covers them gently.
And when we say,
they are gone, dead,
they suddenly erupt
into bees, rain, plums,
trees, air, flowers, sea,
                    flies, daisies,
they burst forth with such violence,
they simply push us aside,
and we huddle and admit frightened:
the senses are eternally alive.

Translated by Ludmilla Popova-Wightman

## [UNTITLED]
### Danila Stoianova

\* \* \*

I heard music
and the blood streamed down my throat,
my torn cords vibrated,
the wind howled in my intestines,
my eyebrows curved from stress and surprise,
the sun moved into my head,
my eyes pulsated in their white orbs
and didn't see anything but sounds,
while my eardrums
cracked with thunder,
the music, surged into my cells, boomed
and then I felt how the atoms flew apart,
and I was no longer in one place,
to tell you . . .

Translated by Ludmilla Popova-Wightman

## [UNTITLED]
### Danila Stoianova

\* \* \*

I found the bees at the beehive
in conversation with a flaming sunset.
The lilacs' evening fragrance
surged in the deep-blue sky.
The caressing silence buzzed,
a bee—
a bee—
fluttered, facing the tired sun
and goldenly, serenely
kissed it

I felt with my skin
how the afternoon was sliding
into the glass full of its tears—
how sorrow was running,
I heard my loneliness,
shrieking like a leper,
fall into the fiery grandeur
of the sun's pyre.

Translated by Ludmilla Popova-Wightman

[UNTITLED]
Danila Stoianova

\* \* \*

The sun is restless
the wind—sick
the moon—dead
the river—drunk
only because
someone is not here.

Translated by Ludmilla Popova-Wightman

[UNTITLED]
Danila Stoianova

\* \* \*

Today I looked straight
into a bee's eye;
what color is
this world,
what color is
this world?
We stared at each other
stupidly
and she flew away.

Translated by Ludmilla Popova-Wightman

## LONELY FALLING IN LOVE
### Danila Stoianova

A dull sunset
through dirty window panes
in the studio
smells of quince
and oil paints.

This evening I invented
The color of your eyes.
Tomorrow I will give you a face.

The wind rustles
in the yellow curtains.
High up
the sky is alight
with bats
and early evening stars.

Translated by Ludmilla Popova-Wightman


## POEM OF BLINDNESS
### Danila Stoianova

Don't go away!

Now when I am asleep,
when I cannot see any more,
when I've become blind,
and the wind
outlines the shape
of my grey house,
when my visions are
only black blots,
when I cannot do anything,
even cry, but I still feel,
tell me, do you love me—
tell me with your touch,
not with your eyes,
do you want me,
stay.

I cannot see if you are smiling
or laughing at me,
are you silent
or already gone?

Don't go away!

My voice is strong,
at least my voice is
strong,
and you said, you were chilled
by its icy song.

By its dry rasping.
The dry rasping of dry snow
on dry paper.

They spread a frog to dissect it,
and its dry eyes
scraped against the dry paper,
and they dropped adrenalin
into its open heart,
and it started to beat–
fast, and strong, and painful,
unable to stop to feel pain,
to throb
to palpitate,
and the eyes—
to scrape against
the dry paper.

And have you seen
how frog's eyes
pop
when they blow up.

Don't go away!

I want you to hear!

The trees become deaf and mute.
The stone I carry
is of granite.
The light smashes into it,
and is covered with blood.
A drop of congealed light,
I saw myself mirrored in it,
before I was covered with blood,
and before I became blind.
The colours of the world
are gone.
A world without colour.
What colour is this world?

Dust gathers
on tree leaves.
Dust gathers
on my child's head.

How slowly I descend
into my own self.
Still I will plow through
the silted layers
of forgetfulness
and self-forgetfulness.
Concentrate.
Forget your considerations.
Listen to your own voice.
Forget what others think.

My child is crying
far away from me
in the bog of
that abandoned room,
it is not an orphan,
and its mother
cannot set it free.
From the dust.
From the dryness.
From the blindness.

The embryo, black and slippery,
sways in the brackish water
of the frog pond,
under the cracked walls
of the cave's wet mouth,
With their crooked fingers,
its hands
look like roots
pulled out
of the muddy earth.
And the eyes, full of water,
look dead.
The rain gives my embryo.
a bath.

Who speaks of death
before birth?
Who speaks of love
without copulation?

I sipped tea
from a Chinese bowl.
It smelled of live fish.
I was told the smell came
from the dragons on its bottom.

Translated by Ludmilla Popova-Wightman

# The Czech Republic and Slovakia, compiled by E. J. Czerwinski and Stana Dolezal

## Contemporary Czech and Slovak Poetry
## by E. J. Czerwinski and Stana Dolezal

Unlike contemporary Polish poets who unashamedly explore man's political and human condition, Czech and Slovak poets seem more reluctant to bare their own or their countrymen's psyche. The poets of the eighties seldom posed eschatological questions as did their Polish counterparts (e. g., Ewa Lipska, Ryszard Krynicki, Adam Zagajewski, etc.): "Why does man have to suffer?" "What is my place in the grand scheme of creation?" "Where do I fit in and why was I born?"—these are questions seldom raised. Instead Czech and Slovak poets seem to have been more preoccupied with the highly personal minutiae of existence—love of country, love for a mother, love for someone dear to them, love for something lost, and so forth. This is not to say that they were not concerned with universal problems, such as the future of mankind (Kántorová-Baliková), or did not question and criticize the devastating state of affairs that result from benign neglect associated with the country's ineffectual Socialist system (Žáček, Skácel, etc.). The point is that their voices were less strident than those of their Slavic neighbors.

It is true that the poetry published in *Petlice* (Padlock), the Czech-Slovak equivalent of samizdat, was far more direct and contentious, resembling the tongue-in-cheek wit of Václav Havel's poetry written during the sixties, prior to his incarceration. Unfortunately, few outstanding talents emerged during the period of artistic repression, which lasted until 1990. Poetry written during those two decades of enforced silence—of necessity relegated to drawer-literature—will, one hopes, be published—if money can be found to support these ventures. In the Czech-Slovak Republics, as in the other countries of eastern Europe, there is a need to fill in the lacunae resulting from forty-five years of cultural repression. Poetry, unfortunately, is often at the bottom of the list of priorities drawn up by politicians and bureaucrats. Introducing a free market does not necessarily equal freeing the arts from financial worry. The battle will continue: only the enemy will change.

The selection of poets presented here is, admittedly, subjective and represents a very small sampling of the community of Czech and Slovak poets. Others could have been included: Lumír Čivrný, Ivan Diviš, Peter Kabeš, Iva Kotrlá, Petr Král, Karel Šiktanc, and Pavel Šrůt.

In our evaluation, poetry, and not the poet, was the main consideration. It is true that some of these poets were "official" poets and, as such, often composed tendentious verse. We refuse to pronounce sentence on them: they must make peace with themselves. We can only be thankful that the muse refused to abandon them and that Czech-Slovak poetry is richer for it.

The presence of a persona and a predominantly lyrical base are the chief features of the poetry included here. In many cases the personal note is transmuted into a collective preoccupation, as in Mikulášek's "My Anatomy," in which he commiserates with a nation that is "guilty of guilt's guilts./ everything that's in our miserable life." Žáček, too, speaks for others, avowing that man is "Alone Against Himself" and that "Only dead people are not alone against themselves." In the long run, however, the poets voice their own personal agony, like Mikulášek, who answers his own question "Why?": "Mostly alone by myself."

Within the lyrical core of each poem is a note of sadness. Žáček complains that "Life and death both share [him]" ("At the Dentist"). Skácel admits that "In this world everything's for sale" ("Song About the Heart"). And Mikulášek, seldom sanguine in his verses, proposes "bitter wine—for everything, that's hard to forget" ("Goblets"). But within the framework of these poems is a gleam of hope, as if each poet, in his or her own way, were "trying to express love" (Florián's "Nouns"). In fact, love is the word most employed by most of these poets, and it is love that permeates all their works—love that forty-five years of repression could not extinguish or diminish.

# About the Poets

## VALENTIN BENIAK

Valentin Beniak (b. 1894 in Chynorany, Slovakia) has translated numerous works from Hungarian. His collections of poetry include the following: *Medalions and Little Medalions, Sonnets, Crying Amor, Home and Distances.*

## EVA BERNARDINOVÁ

Eva Bernardinová (b. 1931 in Prague) graduated from Charles University with a doctoral degree in Czech and Czech literature. She made her literary debut with *Solistice* in 1969. Her other collections of poems included *Tree from Paradise* and *Good Word.* When she became a mother in

1961, she began concentrating on children's prose. She has been a librarian, an editor at a radio station, and a free-lancer.

## MIROSLAV FLORIÁN

Miroslav Florián (b. 1931 in Kutna Horá) graduated as a librarian but did not pursue his profession. He worked for a radio station and in a publishing house, *Česoslovenský Spisovatel*. Later he devoted himself only to literature and translations from Russian. He made his literary debut with *Way to the Sun* in 1953. His collections of poetry include the following: *Ebb at Night* (1980), *Lighting Up Flowers* (1980), *Tomorrow's Snow,* (1981), *To See a Neapol* (1982), *Prague's Selection* (1982), and *Selected Works I–III* (1983)

## JOSEF KAINAR

Josef Kainar (b. 1917 in Přerov) made his literary debut with *Story and Smaller Poems* (1940). He has also written dramas, and humorous stories and has translated Mayakovsky and Rilke. His verses were published in several periodicals and collections of poems: *Czech dream, Poems and Blues, Thirteen Guitars,* and *Royal Evening.*

## JANA KANTOROVÁ-BÁLIKOVÁ

Jana Kantorová-Báliková (b. 1951 in Bratislava, Slovakia) is author of a collection of poetry, *Thirst and Elation* She also translates from English (Blake, Browning, and Poe).

## OLDŘICH MIKULÁŠEK

Oldřich Mikulášek (b. 1910 in Přerov) is perhaps the most important poet of this century. He was an editor of *People's Newspaper* and the journal *Guest in the House*. Since 1964 he has devoted his time strictly to poetry. He has strongly influenced the young generation of poets. His poetry is quite intellectual in spite of its concrete sensuality. He made his literary debut with *Futile Lovemaking* in 1940. In the last decade he has published the following collections of poetry: *Big Black Fish and Long White Greyhound* (1981), *Adam's Rib* (1981), *Solo for Two Breaths* (1983), *A Seagull's Cry* (1984), and *Other Pictures* (1986).

## JANA MORAVCOVÁ

Jana Moravcová (b. 1937 in Černice) graduated with a degree in Russian language and literature from Charles University, Prague. She taught in Cuba, did editorial work, and is presently an editor at *Československý Spisova-*

*tel* (Czech-Slovak Writers publishing house). In addition to her poetry for adults, *Circle in the Snow, Birth,* and *I am Coming from the Sea,* she has written poetry and prose for children and has translated literature from Russian.

# MILAN RÚFUS

Milan Rúfus (b. 1928 in Závažná Poruba, Slovakia) made his literary debut with *When We Will See* (1956). His various collections include the following: *Ode for Happiness, Joyful Chat, Stay with Us* (1985), *Little Well* (1986), *Severe Bread* (1987), and *Attempt for a Song* (1988). He is also a literary critic and translates from Russian, Czech, German, and Italian. In his poems he leads disputes with contemporary man who, according to him, enjoys materialistic things more than creative work.

# JAN SKÁCEL

Jan Skácel (b. 1922 in Vnorovy in Moravian Slovakia) belongs among the great Czech poets of this century and is especially well known for his lyrical poetry. He made his debut atypically when he was thirty-five with *How Many Opportunities Has A Rose?,* which established him as a mature poet. During the 1970s he was not allowed to publish, but his poems were circulated in a Padlock edition (a Czech samizdat). In the 1980s his *Ancient Millet* was published in Czechoslovakia and also in the West by a Czech publisher. Translations of his poetry have appeared in West Germany and Italy. *Hope with the Wings of the Beech* followed in 1983 and *Pouring into the Lost Wax* in 1984. He died one month before the Velvet Revolution in 1989.

# VILIAM TURČANY

Viliam Turčany (b. 1928 in Suchá, Slovakia) has published the following collections of poetry: *Spring in the Country, In the Flow, By the Anchor, Olive,* and *I Am A Bridge* He has translated the poetry of Dante, Michelangelo, Ovidius, Ronsard, and others. He has also compiled an anthology of old Italian and French poetry.

# JIŘÍ ŽÁČEK

Jiří Žáček (b. 1945 in Chomutov) graduated with a degree in engineering from Charles University in 1970. Since 1974 he has been employed at the publishing house *Československý Spisovatel.* His work was influenced by his various trips to Italy, France, the USSR, Germany, and Yugoslavia. He made his debut with *Green Fireflies* in 1972. During the past decade he published the following collections of poetry: *Cucumber Season* (1982), *Three Years of Vacation* (1982), *Rhymes for a Cat* (1984), *Text-appeal* (1986), *Paper*

*Roses* (1987), and *Little Things* (1988). He also writes for children and for television and movies. Žáček, probably the most popular contemporary poet, has proved that poetry can be a bestseller in Czechoslovakia.

# Czech and Slovak Poems

### THE POET IS TALKING . . .
### Valentin Beniak

Without you I am nothing, a switched off lantern,
a lost coin, a cracked jug.

Little boat anchored on the shore:
please, let me afloat again.

Let it be like a coin, from hand to hand,
I have a lively jingle and my stakes are high.

So that I might fulfill my mission—
before the wind comes that will blow me away.

Translated by E. J. Czerwinski and Stana Dolezal

### HAPPY END
### Eva Bernardinová

I cannot tolerate poetry
he said
But poetry cannot be blamed
for your being fed up with me

It's not your fault
that I dream about you.

Take to your heels
cries frustrated love

that's what the book of dreams says

It's not your fault.
that I dream about you.

Translated by E. J. Czerwinski and Stana Dolezal

## A STORY FROM MY DECAMERON
Eva Bernardinová

I started to go steady with him
without a chambermaid without a servant
married with two children

The moon was choking
the only one, only one
and the darkness was putting on
ruby necklaces.

Who are you and who am I
We were nameless
You were crazy about me
I was crazy about you

Exquisite madness
my third time.

Translated by E. J. Czerwinski and Stana Dolezal

## I ALREADY KNOW
Miroslav Florian

I already know where the turtle-doves nest . . .
In your throat
or under your eyelids.

And I also know what they are pecking at:
the tears,
when they don't have enough.

They fly with you like guardians
in the night
they cover you—

Warm me, my love. The crows
are flying
into my hands.

Translated by E. J. Czerwinski and Stana Dolezal

## GOODIES
Miroslav Florian

When I went off to work
you used to put
bread and an apple
into my winter-coat's pocket.

I'll share the bread
with the sparrow-mafia
which is quite generous
and takes only half

But the apple
with its cross-core
I secretly hug and draw close
like your hand.

Translated by E. J. Czerwinski and Stana Dolezal


## THE POSTCARD FROM THE SPA
Miroslav Florian

I could take a walk; I don't feel like it.
I could drink from the hot spring—but let it fall to earth.
I know, the white steam washing the roses
will hardly help me today.

I already miss the smog and the bustle,
and Prague, her volcanic breath,
the rain, which has dirt under its nails
Believe me, Ida, you will cure me!

Translated by E. J. Czerwinski and Stana Dolezal


## NOUNS
Miroslav Florian

When bird touches water with his belly
I carry it to my mouth
June the word June that garden's strawberry

June and evening and again June
parole of honeymoon and sacrilege
bordering an embankment with the secret of cypresses

My bitter mother tongue
thanks for allowing me to wave again the word Vltava
I an old spider spin silver thread

not my Golgotha not my cross and loneliness
but finally again like bread
I am trying to express love.

Translated by E. J. Czerwinski and Stana Dolezal

## UNFAITHFUL
### Josef Kainar

Where did I leave my eyes,
what bewitched my soul,
that I ever liked him,
that I allowed him to embrace me!

Now I tear the dandelion's petals:
loves me, loves me not, is close to me,
does he or does he not want to hear about me?
Actually, why waste dandelions.

He has slanted eyes, like a wolf,
eyebrows like bushes
he stubbornly and clearly says nothing
it's frightening to come near him.

Dry like a shingle, freckled,
one rarely sees anything like it.

Perhaps
if he would come back to me from her
he would be beautiful again, that monster!

Translated by E. J. Czerwinski and Stana Dolezal

## SYBIL'S PROPHESY
### Jana Kantorová-Báliková

Again somewhere they are shooting—even at children.
And Sybil's prophesy will indeed be fulfilled
like an enormous chalice.
Enough poison for the whole world.
Meanwhile I am preparing the soup very deliberately
as if the future of mankind depended
on a little spoonful of farina.

Translated by E. J. Czerwinski and Stana Dolezal

## GOBLETS
### Oldřich Mikulášek

We poured wine
from goblet to goblet—
from one to another.

Did you love someone else
or did I?

You drank from my goblet
or did I from yours?
Grapes ask the grapevine—
or the grapevine asks grapes in old age?
She was so quiet and somber,
suddenly without him.
And his hand didn't even quiver,
when he poured into her goblet
bitter wine—
for everything, that's hard to forget.

Translated by E. J. Czerwinski and Stana Dolezal

## WHY?
### Oldřich Mikulášek

Mostly alone by myself

like a flower with its fragrance;
like water with its depth;

like the moon in nova,
like murder in a racoon's lair,
why do I perish embraced

by the loop of your sweet arms,
why am I dying from blissful love
unhumiliated—
and why do I live by silent grief?

Translated by E. J. Czerwinski and Stana Dolezal


## MY ANATOMY
### Oldřich Mikulášek

All scars and all bruises
on my body and my soul.
The heart—one beam to four rafters—
barely carrying itself,
but must.

Must carry love, must the wine
must the verse, and futility—smoke
Never guilty of anything
guilty of guilt's guilts,

everything that's in our miserable life,
everything that's royal.

Translated by E. J. Czerwinski and Stana Dolezal

## LITTLE FISH
### Oldřich Mikulášek

Little fish jump up above the water's surface
on a necklace of water beads.
And fall again into the clearing
of the river, and I feel sadder.

You will see, just close your eyes.

Little fish jump up above the water's surface
and some will get caught,
The fish is silent like the spring air in the tree
it does not cry, it only sparkles.

I saw one little fish
as it swallowed water
Little fish, you mute face
wrap me in a wasted gill
I will drink your water.

Translated by E. J. Czerwinski and Stana Dolezal

## PROXIMITIES
### Oldřich Mikulášek

On the naked prairie
of autumn
a patch of grass exists.

Like the thin hair
on the head
spending its old age silently.

I in the autumn's sun almost blind
lean over the patch of autumn's grass.
Not far from here is Palava.
The patch nourishes me; and the grapevine saves me.

Translated by E. J. Czerwinski and Stana Dolezal

## NUDITY
### Oldřich Mikulášek

I will create you to your image
and to my own. And still—
and after that still for the applause
of sudden summer rain.
As if slowed down lightning
reluctantly slipping down on you,
I will create you in your image—
and yet lightning from my eyes.

You will be naked up to your soul
and the soul to the very truth.
And the truth will be naked down to your blood,
which I will down like wine,
oh, wine from those black cocoons.
Then I will thirst for you.
Like the last time. Like the first time.

Translated by E. J. Czerwinski and Stana Dolezal

## ARS POETICA II
### Oldřich Mikulášek

Lord in heaven!
Woman on Earth!
Men in a woman!

Wine's delight on my palate,
love's delight unguarded!
The delight of every verse
which sleeps with everyone
in one poem!

Liberty of liberties! Cruel yoke
of a pelican pecking
on his chest!

Translated by E. J. Czerwinski and Stana Dolezal

## THIS GLASS OF WINE BEDEWED
### Oldřich Mikulášek

This glass of wine bedewed
cools our hot palm.
And being lovingly embraced
yearns to pour out its whole inside

until blood beats in the temple.
Who was alone, is not lonely,
has the wine glass, even a full pitcher

rocking the red wine
and will float far away

as if rocked by an ocean

Translated by E. J. Czerwinski and Stana Dolezal


## YOU SLEEP
### Oldřich Mikulášek

You sleep lost in your dreams—
where I cannot go.

You sleep alive in your dreams—
where I do not want.

You sleep beautiful in your dreams—
where I do not dare.

You sleep heavy on my heart,
I pound on you—
Don't wake up!

Translated by E. J. Czerwinski and Stana Dolezal

## SECLUSION WITH A POEM
### Jana Moravcová

A movement light as a feather from the depth of dusk
and knocking.
Then silence
perfidious like betrayal.
And suddenly clashing
sounds like crossed swords . . .
A click of a poem with closed eyes
spurts forth
from the ballpoint pen.

Translated by E. J. Czerwinski and Stana Dolezal

## MICHELANGELO
### Milan Rúfus

To carry a burden and sing.
You knew
who carries beauty for christening.
We no longer do.

We do not know, we only are getting to know.
How to wind up a watch.
How many bones a whale has. And a poem.
Oh, every little hair, counted three times
on beauty's body. So what, so what?

With wisdom grows futility
like in a daze—and a poet,
the knocked down rider, wants to create a horse
from the imprint of a horseshoe.

Anguish, weariness . . .
Like children in the forest we lost our way many times.

And the beauty which was close to God,
today talks to itself
about confused, strange things.

Translated by E. J. Czerwinski and Stana Dolezal

## THE SNOWDROP
### Milan Rúfus

Greetings to you, arrogance of the innocent.

From the underground depths up to the meadow
crawl through the first pore of the ground.
To lodge in the little open door
not a leg—
but a tiny neck.
And to laugh: "Just try,
you won't close these doors anymore!"

Always feminine strength in fragility,
where does it come from?
The courage to be . . . .

Translated by E. J. Czerwinski and Stana Dolezal

## DO NOT ASK
### Milan Rúfus

Do not ask, my daughter,
who has keys from the lake.

Where earth gets its spring?
Who made a cut-out swallow?

Who up there on Martin's peak
cuts off heads of wild geese

and then from their bodies after that
strips cold and silent feathers?

Do not ask your father
who is singing in the spinning wheel,

who wakes up bees in the morning.
Do not ask. He is big already.

He would only feel pain.
Do not ask, tell him that.

Translated by E. J. Czerwinski and Stana Dolezal

## SECOND POEM FOR THE MOON AND THE MAN
### Jan Skácel

Don't be afraid
and sweep that little sadness off your lap
because we are children no longer
And still, my tenderness
I would like to fall asleep
under the black lilac
until one day from my childhood
would seize me.

Don't be afraid
and sweep that little sadness off your lap
because we have been man and woman for a long time.
We are night and day and into our night
the moon falls like a cut rose.

Don't be afraid when I'll be falling asleep by your side,
under the black lilac sinking into the past
which will trap
one day from my childhood,
so that I might return
and hold a rose in my hand,
so that you would meet me dreaming again.

Don't be afraid, there are such nights
made to order, to Beethoven's gesture,
when soldiers put violins to their cheeks
and a stricken rose falls from the sky.

And a clean, clear rain falls from the sky
on human hearts blackened a bit,
and you, don't be sad
that we are not children anymore
that I am a man and that you are a woman.

Translated by E. J. Czerwinski and Stana Dolezal


## SONNET ABOUT LOVE AND POETS
### Jan Skácel

From the skein of time at least one thread
into the needle to sew a wound in the heart
that's what the poet would want
And to salt bread with coarse-grained salt.

He would like to give sad Pierrot a rose
which blossomed when the shadow in the river matured
and which has no thorns
and he himself would hide his eyes in the flowers

Suddenly all the salt turned black overnight
from the skein of time
desire entangles a tangle

the rose's somersault killed Pierrot
and the proud poet celebrates on his knees
the old loves which will not fade

Translated by E. J. Czerwinski and Stana Dolezal

## TOAST
Jan Skácel

Let's toast once more
and drink it silently.
We won't tell anyone
what wine knows about us.

And a star will fall.
Thin as tin
And the water near bridges
will be silver.

Translated by E. J. Czerwinski and Stana Dolezal


## A SONNET INSTEAD OF A ROSE
Jan Skácel

It is possible to steal the public rose in the park
during a summer night. A rose in the vase
is wounded and sheds the petals by morning
like everything like human glory

There are roses placed on a coffin
white roses for brides
there is the rose picked up out of revenge
and a rose out of rebellion dark as blood

From those flowers none. We will go together
to pick the rose for you on the meadow
where you leaned your elbow on heaven

when we divided the past from the recent
And the Milky Way was suddenly navigable
and the rafts of love could float on it

Translated by E. J. Czerwinski and Stana Dolezal

## SONG ABOUT THE HEART
### Jan Skácel

In a little shop where time dozes
a graceful salesgirl said
good day, sir, how can I help you
her voice was silky
and when I said that I wanted her heart
she protested quietly: is it permitted?

A heart, dear sir, is not for sale
the heart is, after all, worth more than a diamond
it is given only as a gift sir
I don't intend to sell mine.
I took off my hat, left the shop
and was on the street alone.

But the girl came after me
and called me with her velvet voice
forgive my acting proud
I did not mean to be unkind
For love I will give my heart to you
for love I would gladly give it.

In this world everything's for sale
even honor and glory everyone knows it
Only the pure heart, the beautiful pure heart
cannot be bought in any market.

Translated by E. J. Czerwinski and Stana Dolezal

## A DIALOGUE
### Jan Skácel

How are you doing, my darling?
    I feel like a little tree
    to which a little lamb has been tied
    So as not to go astray in the black forest
    Where a bad wolf might follow it.

And how are you doing, my lovely?
    Like a white birch
    that bows to the wind
    bows, bows.

Translated by E. J. Czerwinski and Stana Dolezal


## THE SONNET AS TALISMAN
### Jan Skácel

To protect you from any harm
(that's how the world is)
I give you an amulet
and wear it all the time

It shields from hard times
it drives away hunger in the soul
and protects the one who loves
from any curse

Perhaps that rare magic formula
fell from heaven down to earth
In the light of the shooting stars

I engraved in silver
SINE AMORE NIHIL
without love there is nothing

Translated by E. J. Czerwinski and Stana Dolezal

## SORRENTO
Viliam Turčany

When the sea is calm,
when it only has wrinkles,
it looks like a mother,
who is embracing you.

Gone are the waves—the anguish.
Every grief passes.

High above the wrinkles is
the delicate fabric.
The deepest sea—
that mother's face.

Translated by E. J. Czerwinski and Stana Dolezal

## ALONE AGAINST HIMSELF
Jiří Žáček

Everyone writes along against himself
But through the fault of others
Nicanor Parra

Anyone who breathes is against himself
life is in general very unhealthy
even though we are well equipped for it:
Look the hydraulics of veins and sex
Computer of the brain counts and commands
and motor of the heart turns the mechanism
And that is a perfect and brilliant feat

And still with everything you love and what you cling to
second after second
you are again an inch closer to death
Alone against yourself but through your own fault

What are you afraid of? What else could you want
than be burnt as a fire which gives warmth
To scorch the darkness, that crude oil of hopelessness
to change into heat light and a handful of ashes
To burn—even though standing one foot in the grave

Only dead people are not alone against themselves

Translated by E. J. Czerwinski and Stana Dolezal

## AT THE DENTIST
### Jiří Žáček

Number four down on the left: another cavity
What are the touch-ups good for when my whole body is falling
apart
Oh God—But never mind. I'm simply aging
Life and death both share me.

Translated by E. J. Czerwinski and Stana Dolezal

## IN THE MIRROR
### Jiří Žáček

The older you are the more you cling to life
even though now only remnants of pleasures await you
You no longer want to look into the abysses
Your mask smile would unglue

In a few years you'll be reproaching young men
for their lovely proud, contemptuous scepticism
You always wanted to wrestle with life like a wolf—
today you silently prefer howling with dogs

Translated by E. J. Czerwinski and Stana Dolezal

## THREE YEARS
### Jiří Žáček

Three years
poems elude me   Who knows
perhaps they go after younger, greener
poets

Three vacation years
without a lyrical sore throat
Where are my verses
my golden fishes?

Three years of chases
of successes and phrases
Ocean of time
is what I forever lack

And after three years
waiting, waiting again
Come poems
be my most faithful widow

Translated by E. J. Czerwinski and Stana Dolezal

## REASON FOR OPTIMISM
### Jiří Žáček

There are all kinds of people
There are even people
who still earn a living

Translated by E. J. Czerwinski and Stana Dolezal

## EPITAPH OF CONTEMPORARY MAN
### Jiří Žáček

He was born.
Died.
Meanwhile
they threatened to kill him.

Translated by E. J. Czerwinski and Stana Dolezal

## BEFORE FALLING ASLEEP
### Jiří Žáček

The best poems come by themselves
a moment before sleep comes
in gaps between seconds

and get lost in the dawn
like the woman I spent the night with
who silently disappears from my room in the morning

without a goodbye
without a sound
and doesn't even leave me her address

Translated by E. J. Czerwinski and Stana Dolezal

## LA MODE MEDITERRANÉE
### Jiří Žáček

Voluptuous bosom, tiny waists
long legs, rounded buttocks
simply no imperfections
are fashionable at the seashore this year
But men's
bald heads, humps and pot bellies are pardoned
if they are rolling in money.

Translated by E. J. Czerwinski and Stana Dolezal

## SPRING'S NEUROSIS
### Jiří Žáček

The month May grins provocatively at my face
Fulfilled dreams restrict the same way as a period oppresses a
sentence
Spring opens its festival altars
My love survived my first cigarette

Translated by E. J. Czerwinski and Stana Dolezal


## THE RESCUER OF ICARUSES
### Jiří Žáček

The proper wife will teach you
to exchange a pair of wings
for a pair of slippers
Then you will not be afraid
to take a fall like Icarus

Translated by E. J. Czerwinski and Stana Dolezal


## FOR TRUTH
### Jiří Žáček

There are different rewards for truth
at one time a monument
at another a prison
If someone reveals truth before its time
it will break his neck

Translated by E. J. Czerwinski and Stana Dolezal

## POCKETBOOK
### Jiří Žáček

To survive on a salary that would be wonderful!
But what if you pay everything with your blood?
Barely born the creditors are here
Death has become too cheap and life too expensive

Translated by E. J. Czerwinski and Stana Dolezal

## READING THE NEWSPAPER
### Jiří Žáček

With your morning coffee bite into
a bloody steak of fresh news
How do you feel today my dear world?
Are you still alive and well?

Translated by E. J. Czerwinski and Stana Dolezal

# Hungary, compiled by Bruce Berlind

## Hungarian Poetry
### by Bruce Berlind

Hungarian poetry is at a crossroads, as, to some degree, is poetry in all the countries which once formed the Soviet bloc. Much of what is original and exciting about eastern European poetry since World War II was a direct consequence of the strategies poets were forced to develop in order to express the inexpressible in totalitarian regimes. Not all poets, to be sure, courted the inexpressible; Sándor Weöres, mystical, visionary, and endlessly inventive, would have written as he did under any conditions—although he too, for precisely those "unpatriotic" qualities, was for years prohibited from publishing. But it is difficult to imagine what the poetry of Ágnes Nemes Nagy would have been like had she not, after the proscription of her publishing activities had been lifted, insisted on responding to the moral and political world in which she lived—notwithstanding the fact of her husband's imprisonment following the revolution of 1956.

The most outspokenly political poem in the following selection is Gyula Illyés's "One Sentence on Tyranny," an exception that proves the rule of "strategies." The poem was written in 1950, when it could not, of course, be published, and first appeared in a Budapest newspaper on 2 November 1956—that is, two days before Soviet tanks crushed the revolution. It was not published again until 1986, when it appeared in a posthumous collection of Illyés's poems, although it had achieved underground currency in the intervening years. So the poem is typical in its provenance of samizdat publications, with the important exception that Illyés was no typical dissident writer, but Hungary's preeminent man of letters, a popular and populist writer who, because of his peasant background, exemplified an ideal of which the establishment approved. Had he not been so, he might well have suffered under the Kádár regime.

But Illyés's poem *was* an exception. For the most part, poets who found it possible to continue writing found their possibilities in one or another form of ulteriority. "You get from here to here," one writer once told me, pinpointing two spots on the table between us, "by going this way"—and his hand made a circuitous excursion across the table. A critical study of those excursions ought to be written; it would make fascinating reading. Meanwhile, we contemplate the discursive ironies of László Nagy's "Cognition, Language, Poetry," the hallucinatory landscape of Ágnes Nemes

215

Nagy's "The Statues," and the silences surrounding János Pilinszky's minimal, barely audible, utterances, and, as radically different as they are one from another, we perceive a common subtext. And as difficult as that subtext is to articulate in language other than that which the poems use, we acknowledge it and recognize it as something dangerous, in some elusive way subversive, and, at the same time, life sustaining. One is reminded of the dying Pablo Neruda when Pinochet's goons invaded his home in search of weapons and other evidence of insurgent activity. The officer in charge explained that they were acting on information that there was something dangerous in the house. "Very dangerous indeed," Neruda is reputed to have replied, "it's called poetry."

But it seems that the days—the decades—that required such strategies are thankfully past. The poetic legacy of that half-century is as extraordinary as that of any comparable historical period. Consider, for example, what is surely the central generation of that era, poets who came to maturity during World War II and whose lives and writing careers were, until recently, conducted entirely under oppressive regimes. In addition to Nemes, Nagy, and Pilinszky in Hungary, the following poets were all born between 1920 and 1924: Zbigniew Herbert, Tadeusz Różewicz, and Wysława Szymborska in Poland, Vasko Popa in Yugoslavia, Stefan Aug. Doinas, Nina Cassian, and Ion Caraion in Romania, Miroslav Holub and Antonin Bartušek in Czechoslovakia, and Blaga Dimitrova in Bulgaria.[1] Older poets like Gyula Illyés, Sándor Weöres, and István Vas had begun writing well before the war, and their adjustments to the new postwar dispensation were, at least in part, of a different kind. The destruction of the old way of life—that is, the assault on central European culture—must, for them, have been a more crucial consequence of the war and its aftermath than it was for poets who had had less firsthand experience of that life. A prevailing sense, in many of the poems of the older poets, is of deprivation.

But what now? The experience of war and the police state will not, of course, be forgotten by those poets whose lives were most affected by it— even if they do not choose to deal with it explicitly. But what of younger poets, who were not subject to the same constraints as their elders and who have the prospect of futures which their elders, at their ages, could not imagine? One answer at least was in the wind long before the recent momentous changes. Younger poets, for some years past, have seemed less challenged by their political environment than have their elders. For whatever reason, one does not find in the work of Imre Oravecz (b. 1943)—the youngest poet represented in this selection—the sort of political dimension that is everywhere evident in the works of what I have called the central generation. As unique as Oravecz is as a poet, he is typical in that respect of many of his generation. Ottó Orbán (b. 1936) and Dezső Tandori (b. 1938) exhibit tensions that may be reflective of the broader historical situation, but those tensions are privatized in ways that deflect attention from the purely political condition of Hungary and Central Europe. In the case or Orbán, it is his childhood in war-ravaged Budapest and the death of his Jewish father on a forced march between concentration camps that are paramount experiences, while for Tandori the formative obsessions seem to be rooted in early familial relationships that are never made explicit. Sándor Csoóri (b. 1930) is the youngest of those poets for whom the experience of political oppression was clearly a major factor; he was, in fact, muzzled as late as 1983 for speaking in print of the Romanian persecution of ethnic Hungarians, and he has been prominently active in the political restructuring of the new Hungary.

What I am suggesting is that whatever the directions Hungarian poetry will take in the future, we can expect it to be significantly different from the important achievements of the Communist years. That does not mean that it will be less "Hungarian"; the Hungarian poet's consciousness of ethnic identity has always been particularly strong—a cultural feature which has rendered certain poets virtually inaccessible to the West.[2] Some poets, in fact, are using this consciousness as subject matter. Imre Oravecz, for example, is embarked on an epic-length sequence of poems (in this case, highly accessible) rooted in the vanished village of his birth and childhood. And many of Ottó Orbán's poems that proceed from his sojourns and travels in foreign countries—most notably the United States, where he has lived for extended periods—serve as epiphanous recognitions of his inescapable Magyar identity.

Still, such poems are not purely "personal" in the sense that has characterized lyric poetry in the West. Hungarian lyric poetry—and this is true in some measure of other central and eastern European literatures—has almost always echoed with an historical resonance that is rare in the West, and especially rare, perhaps, in America.[3] It is the quality which Miroslav Holub had in mind when he remarked, during an interview with Daniel Weissbort,[4] that "[t]he more I learn about American poetry . . . the more I feel, my God, they are so good and yet they are missing something, something from my household, something more concrete, beyond the personal. . . ." Holub's "household" is more than the sum of crockery and bedsteads; it is the lived context under pressure of the political, historical, and moral weather that gives shape and character to a nation's culture. From its beginnings, Hungarian poetry has had its own weather, usually turbulent, to which it has been especially sensitive. Whatever forms it takes in the future, that sensitivity will prevail.

# Notes

1. While the terms of their experiences are substantially different, it is worth noting that Paul Celan and Yehuda Amichai are also of that generation.

2. The chief instance in twentieth-century literature is Endre Ady (1877–1919), generally regarded by Hungarians as their greatest twentieth-century poet. His work is in large measure untranslatable.

3. A recent remark of Yehuda Amichai suggests his central European roots: "I come from a part of our world where history is so dominant and so dynamic that even a very private love poem is or becomes engaged with the world." Yehuda Amichai, "Literature as Celebration, The Joy of Writing," *Graham House Review,* 12 (Spring 1989): 111.

4. Daniel Weissbort, "Interview with Mireslav Holub," *Poetry East,* 29 (Spring 1990): 109.

# About the Poets

## SÁNDOR CSOÓRI

Sándor Csoóri (b. 1930) came of a peasant family in western Hungary and studied at a language academy (the now defunct Lenin Institute) in Budapest. In addition to his many collections of poems, he has been a prolific journalist, has served on the staffs of various magazines, and has written several filmscripts. Since the demise of communism, he has been active in the Hungarian Democratic Forum. A selection of his poems in English, translated by several hands, appeared from Corvina in 1989.

## GYULA ILLYÉS

Gyula Illyés (1902–83) was Hungary's preeminent man of letters for decades before his death. From a peasant family in western Hungary and largely self-educated, he was forced, by political events following World War I, to flee the country and lived in Paris from 1921 to 1926. A popular and populist poet, he was also novelist, playwright, editor, translator, and cultural historian. *People of the Puszta,* his socio-autobiographical account of life in a peasant village, has been widely translated. A selection of poems in English, translated by various hands, appeared in England in 1971.

## LÁSZLÓ NAGY

László Nagy (1925–81) was born to a peasant family in western Hungary, studied painting, and, while in his twenties, lived for several years in Bulgaria. His poems and translations—notably of folk poetry from the Balkan countries—appeared in four volumes in 1975. He also translated Robert Burns, Dylan Thomas, and Garcia Lorca. A selection in English, *Love of the Scorching Wind,* translated by Tony Connor and Kenneth McRobbie, was published by Corvina and Oxford University Press in 1973. He is survived by his wife, the poet Margit Szécsi.

## ÁGNES NEMES NAGY

Ágnes Nemes Nagy (1922–1991) studied Hungarian, Latin, and art history at Budapest University. A critic and essayist, as well as the most important woman poet Hungary has produced, she edited, with her husband the critic Balázs Lengyel, the revived *Újhold (New Moon)*, a major literary journal originally published from 1945 to 1948, when it was suppressed by the Stalinist regime. Her many translations include works by Corneille, Racine, Molière, Brecht, and Rilke. There are two volumes of her poems in English: *Selected Poems*, translated by Bruce Berlind (University of Iowa Press, 1980), and *Between*, translated by Hugh Maxton (Corvina and Dedalus, 1988).

## IMRE ORAVEZ

Imre Oravecz (b. 1943) graduated from Kossuth Lajos University in Debrecen with specialties in English and German and pursued graduate work in linguistics at the University of Illinois at Chicago Circle. He has been a Visiting Fellow at the University of Iowa and a Fulbright Lecturer at the University of California at Santa Barbara. He has published five collections of poems and translated, among others, Paul Celan, Reiner Kunze, John Ashbey, Robert Creeley, and Gary Snyder.

## OTTÓ ORBÁN

Ottó Orbán (b. 1936 in Budapest) was the son of a well-to-do Jewish father who was clubbed to death on a forced march between concentration camps and a peasant mother "from the poverty that is found in fairy tales." He attended Budapest University, studying Hungarian and English, but left without a degree. He has published a dozen collections of poems, in addition to collections of travel notes, essays, and translations (among them a selection of Robert Lowell's poems and plays), and has served as visiting professor at the University of Minnesota in 1987.

## JÁNOS PILINSZKY

János Pilinszky (1921–81) was born in Budapest, attended the university there, and worked as an editor until he was drafted into the Hungarian army in 1944. Taken to Germany with the retreating Nazi forces, he was interred as a prisoner of war following the German surrender—an experience which, along with his meditations on the death camps, proved crucial to his thinking and his poetry. A Catholic who was influenced by Simone Weil and for whom God revealed himself in the holocaust, his poetry grew more and more spare. There are selections in English by Ted Hughes and János Csokits and by Peter Jay.

## DEZSŐ TANDORI

Dezső Tandori (b. 1938 in Budapest) graduated from Budapest University and is a poet, playwright, novelist, memoirist, exhibiting graphic artist, and translator from a score of literatures (among his translations from American being selections of Wallace Stevens and Sylvia Plath). A selection of his poems in English, *Birds and Other Relations*, translated by Bruce Berlind, was published by Princeton University Press in 1987.

## ISTVÁN VAS

István Vas (1910–1991) came from a Jewish merchant family and studied business in Vienna as a young man. Notwithstanding his conversion to Roman Catholicism in 1938, he was subsequently incarcerated in a forced labor camp, where he attempted suicide. A prolific translator—of Shakespeare, Molière, O'Neill, and Thackeray, among others—his three-volume *Collected Poems* (1977) was succeeded by several further collections. A selection in English, *Through the Smoke*, edited by Miklós Vajda and translated by several hands, appeared from Corvina in 1989. He is survived by his wife, the painter Piroska Szántó.

## SÁNDOR WEÖRES

Sándor Weöres (1913–89) was born in western Hungary, studied geography, history, and law, and earned a doctorate in philosophy and aesthetics at the University of Pécs. His collected works include three volumes of poetry, three of translations (Shakespeare, Mallarmé, etc.), a volume of verse plays and plays for children, and a two-volume anthology of early Hungarian poetry, annotated and introduced by him—almost six thousand pages in all. A selection in English, *Eternal Moment*, edited by Miklós Vajda and translated by several hands, was published by Corvina in association with Anvil and New Rivers in 1988.

# Hungarian Poems

## ONE SENTENCE ON TYRANNY
Gyula Illyés

Where there's tyranny
there is tyranny,
not just in gun barrels,
not just in jails,

interrogation cells,
the sentry's calls
challenging the night,
there is tyranny not

just in the smoke-dark burnt
flaming prosecutor's indictment,
not just in confessions,
in Morse wall-taps in prisons,

not only in the chilly
verdict: the judge's "guilty,"
there is tyranny
not only in the soldierly,

crackling, "tens-hut!"
in "fire!", in the drumbeat,
in the way that
they drag corpses to the pit,

not only in the news
in fearful whispers
passed through furtively
half-opened doors, not only

in the hushing finger
dropped on the mouth,
there's tyranny not only
in the sturdy

bar-solid faces, the
wordless shrieks of woe
struggling in those bars,
in the mute tears'

torrents magnifying
the silence,
in the glassy pupils,

there's tyranny not just in
the standing ovation
of roared hurrahs,
of songs and cheers,

where there's tyranny
there is tyranny
not just in the unremitting
booms of palms applauding,

in the trumpet, the opera house,
the lying, strident, sonorous
stones of statues,
in colors, galleries of pictures,

in each separate frame,
it's in the brush and paint,
not only in the soft glide
of car noises at night

and the way
it stops at the door;

where there's tyranny
it's everywhere,
in everything as
not even your old god was;

there's tyranny in
the kindergartens,
in the fatherly counsel,
the mother's smile,

in the way the child
answers a stranger;

not only in barbed wire,
in book-phrases more
deadly stupid-making
than barbed wire; it's there

in the good-bye kiss
as the wife says
when will you be home dear,
it's there

in the street, the customary
how-are-you's, the abruptly
softer grip, the slack
of the handshake,

there as your lover's face
turns suddenly to ice,
because it's with you
in the rendezvous,

not just the interrogation,
it's in the declaration,
in the rapturous moan,
like the fly in the wine,

because even in your dreams
you're not alone; it's even
in the marriage bed, and earlier
in the desire,

because what you think lovely
*he's* had already; it's he
who lay with you in bed
when you thought you loved,

on the plate, in the glass,
the mouth, the nose,
in cold, in twilight,
indoors and out,

as if the window were open
and a dead-flesh stink blew in,
as if somewhere gas
were escaping into the house,

if you talk to yourself it's he
who puts the question to you,
you're not free even
in your own imagination,

and the Milky Way: a zone
where border searchlights pan,
a whole fieldful of mines;
every star a spy hole,

the teeming celestial tent:
a single labor camp;
because tyranny speaks
from fever, the torture rack,

the priest who hears your confession,
the ringing of bells, the sermon,
from parliament, from church:
all those theatrical stages;

you shut your lashes, open them,
you're under observation;
like illness, like memory,
it keeps you company;

the rumbling train wheels whisper
a prisoner, you're a prisoner,
beside the sea, on the mountain,
it's this that you breathe in;

lightning flashes, it's there
in each unexpected murmur,
it's there in the light,
the jolt of the heart;

in tranquility, in this
shackled tediousness,
in the pelting downpour,
these sky-high bars,

the incarcerating snowfall
white as a cell wall,
that eyes you through the eyes
of your dog, and because

it's in all you aspire to,
it's in your tomorrow,
in all that you think,
every move you make,

as a river bed is cut,
you follow it, create it;
it's you spy from this circle?
*he's* in the mirror, watchful,

he sees you, escape's absurd,
you're the prisoner, also the guard;
it seeps into the fabrics
of your clothes, your tobacco's

aroma, it eats into
your marrow bones; you'd
have ideas, but those
that come to you are his,

you'd look, but what you see
he's conjured up for you,
and a forest fire, lit
since you didn't stomp it out

when you tossed a match to the ground,
flames up now all around;
so his eyes are on you, sleepless,
in factory, field, and house,

and you don't feel anymore
what even bread and meat are,
what it is to desire, to love,
to open your arms, to live,

so the servant himself forges
and wears his own manacles;
if you eat, you're feeding him;
it's for him you beget children,

where there's tyranny everyone
is a link in the same chain;
it flows and festers from you,
you yourself are tyranny;

like moles in the sun, we walk
blind in the pitch-dark,
as restless in the closet
as we are in a desert;

because where there's tyranny
everything's vanity,
song, like this one faithful,
any art at all,

because from the beginning
he's been standing at your grave,
it's he who says who you've been,
even your dust serves him.

*Translated by Bruce Berlind with Mária Kőrösy*


SEVENTH SYMPHONY
The Assumption of Mary

Sándor Weöres

*To my mother's memory*


Shadow, stone, linen, lime,
the pillow under the skull's vault,
iron padlock, swaddling clothes,
the knocking sundering clod,
do not see ascend the dark of the body
over the final flame, the world pried open
by the smoldering chaplet of sweat.

Foot protrudes from the brindled shroud,
its clotted veins coated with wax,
a violet beam on the nail.

Shins, ensheathed, are sleeping,
the tendon straight, the knee relaxed;
olive trees line the path.

Hail to you, shrivelled womb!
An armored insect in the wall's fissure
scratches the lip of the blind abyss,
lowers its ensigns, its arms.

Hail to you, prayer-locked hands,
plunging arches of a shrine,
two rows of casketed tapers,
ten swans' wings immersed in dew,
enfolded night-blooming flowers.

Hail to you, seven-pained heart!
The scream, from the start its neck weighted with stone,
falls down a bottomless well, fails of its journey.

Narrow neck, tilted head, sticky hair,
lead-coin of the final ransom on the pale face,
around the mouthhole and sunken eyes
the senses' cooled-off scatter of wrinkles,
twig-knots of trampled-down acanthus,
spoors of galloped-off steeds.

2

Shadow, night,
silence, cold,
crack, crackle,
clay flies,
beam cleaves,
dust sings—
Two newmoons in
the sky culminate,
blazing mesh
descends,
spider-legged
glowing coals race
up, wings hover on
gleaming roof,
flock of lambs,
harps, flutes,
violin screeches,
bell peals,
horn replies—
For long faceless,
ashy ancestor,
face of gold,
assembles bones,

leans on an elbow,
rears up,
gives ear—
*Chorus*
Wailing, wailing, wailing
for her own at the edge of dark!
We saw her with her child in starlight;
we were grazing our plump sheep,
with the coming of spring we sheared the fleece,
when winter came we flayed the hide;
slowly, cloud-like, we drafted
on the mirror of water filled with fleecy hills,
      our boat
      came ashore,
      she saw
      who we were,
      brambles tore
      our thin shoes,
      earth
      painted our brows.
We're shepherds, also sheep.
Now for the shearing,
now for the skinning,
strew it in her path.
Wailing, wailing, wailing
for her own at the edge of dark.

3

*Alternate choruses*
The drone of oars infuses
the infinite clear stillness,
the curly breath-hue, faintly purplish,
churns in the glistening white,
a maelstrom of mast a whirlpool of sails
looms through,
ferry of flame, bridge of haze, golden ark,
fever's nether side on a diamond mirror,
circles, in the distance ripples,
the rush and scurry of small ones,
on the rainbow a smiling tear,
veiny swish of milk-foliage,
the woman's festival alive in the world . . .
      (But we always cried.

We were starving.
What else could we do?
We always cried.)
. . . her skiff sparkling in the rush of spume,
on the lusterless yellow sickle of heaven,
on the giant azure scales of the eye,
on the red wheel of the war-car,
on the crest of the green monster,
on the black mouthhole of cold,
and at night she turns down your white bed,
through every inferno she follows you,
though the nest be razed she summons you back . . .
    (Bottom-up stumps
    with our roots upwards,
    earth cast us out.
    Nobody stoops for us.)
. . . she kneels within you, my dear, and you become her,
forsaking your chaplet whence
color comes to the rose and light to the eye,
and you feel her as you cover your chalice
which the vagrant foggy shapes of the chasm
and the numbered centuries of years
with frenzied omens on their foreheads,
impassioned, drank from . . .
    (Flowers crawling with worms,
    who wants the tattered petal
    while the spring dawn rains down?)
. . . from the crusty dark ascending
the distending moons shimmers,
aroma that under the rind
gathers to flame in secret veins,
under the heart a regal star-crowned dream
in the shade of a warm bower,
falling clusters of grapes, red wine,
the flame of the mother ablaze in the world . . .
    (Whom have I killed? Myself.
    Whom does it pain? Me.
    Leave me alone in her lap.)
. . . the lovely hands close-clasped in prayer,
clinging columns of kindness,
a hazy roof-row of fingers,
ten mother-wings of live silence,
naked fingers in a sea of petals,
the tenfold soundless ringing

gleams, dispensing its brightness,
its light, beamlessly, pathless as a kiss . . .
     (The salt of sweat in our bread.
     The taste of death in our meat.
     Around us the coffin-wall.)
. . . she who stood under the cross
unbroken by misery, stares
with a child's scared blue eyes
at the frothing world on the cross,
sobs at the sill of hell;
in festering dens the dead
wrapped in closely watched night
wink at the wounding light . . .
     (Take from our hearts the dripping poison,
     take from our hearts the black maggot,
     take the ember from our hearts,
     take from our hearts the dark.)
. . . the gleam of the pure blue eyes
pierces through all the circuits
mirrored in the curving hoop of space
and the hundred-tunneled race of time;
like a sweet drop on the nodding sedge,
a sparkling bead on mutability,
it is always replenished, always rolls off,
the peace of the Virgin flows over the world . . .
     (We shiver, draw close our cloaks,
     have mercy on us, Blessed Virgin,
     pray for us, have
     mercy on us.)

4

     Over the spring
     down spins off
     from fanning wings;
     light snow falls;
     young wine makes
     in big basins;
     on a thousand balconies
     a thousand armies;
     the shackled rage of
     the earth is still,
     everything fills
     with the clamor of wings:

*Chorus*
Through flame, through light
wings the dark earth's virgin,
never are shadow and night
more violently flung open,
valley and peak, by the looking-dance,
assault-waves of mazes of flowers
setting the grayness ablaze.

Vein of rose, blood of dove,
brimming chalice of wine,
where the mountain-shadow plunges
faith harvested the vines;
blood-pearl of chamois in snow
calls the hunter, where he climbs
the trail is narrow, the space wide.

Dear mother, bashful bride,
our blushing tender maid,
our wings billow toward you,
their thick combs quake like the sea;
are you flying toward us, do you see us?
we are rugs laid in your path,
dear mother, be our spring.

*Mary*
I glorify him I conceived in my womb
who raised to the sky my sickle of moon
and set on my forehead a string of stars
who made my cloak to be borne on the milky path
who made my veil to be blown by the storm of sweetness
who made my triumphant car to be flown by the living fires
who peoples with armies my victorious progress
who raises around me towers of endless song,
as it pleases him; and it cannot be explained
by the fiery armies, the misty generations
turning under the furrows where I walk.
My father from the beginning, I brought him forth
who towers, three-headed pillar,
with his triple forehead's glory
over the far-flung void, above
the glistening crystal of silence
surfacing from the wake of creations,
like a roof of lightning he covers me.

*Chorus*
Queen of flowerbells,
assembled before you, welded around you,
bell-hearts beat in a thousand bodies,
a cupola of rays wavering,
a tower of haze quavering,
they peal for you, appeal to you:
when our bell-metal chips,
silence it out of your power.

*Mary*
It is not mine to judge; the scales, the sword
are someone else's; I never learned to strike,
only to stroke; nor to starve, only to feed;
to be hurt, but not to hurt; nor to take, only to ask.
In the resonant silence, the anonymous silence,
larvae and wedding-gowns blossom alike on me,
the lion lies down with the lamb in my bosom.
The babe defiles me, no stain is left,
he scratches my breast, a necklace of blood flows out,
the heaving sea has more and will not miss it.
The killer spatters me with blood, I wipe it off;
revile me, I do not turn away my face.
I am no stone wall returning caresses and blows
measure for measure;
I am no clay road returning steps and turnings
measure for measure;
I am no fountain of fire that exposes body and space
as they manifest before it;
I am only a nest that sheds what warmth there is.
You who see me shining forth in glory,
think for a moment: it does not come from me;
a tear in my only treasure; so with you;
my son's wound my immeasurable possession
and the agony of this world my gateless garden.
The luxuriant tree of life lies in my lap,
and if, torn off, you fall down under it,
your powerful fist clutches my apron, you fell
your head's log on my knee. Do not fear:
you are watched over by silence, tears, and me.

*Chorus*
There where there is no light,
my heart is born among thorns,
down where the nightingale nests,
in the jungle of numberless moans;
new threats buffet the planets,
but the blest sleep on in peace,
nectar-drops on their lips.

Down there a rose-tree blooms,
dawn spreads out on the hill,
fingers—weak and strong—
proffer a feast; debris
of ashes litters the hearth,
but a purple flood in the depth
proclaims eternal dawn.
Field of roses swaying,
wisps of flame in the wind,
bewitched by her bright eyes;
she comes, turns slowly again,
a rose-sea of waving babes
clutches, clutches at her hem;
death and time stand still.

Mutability, wire-like,
grows taut;
cooled-off ancestral coal
glows hot;
patriarch
from tomb's dark
hums to himself
fulfilled words;
the clod is quiet,
lips stuck together;
the sound of wings
outspread forever.

CODA

Lady of orbits, Mary,
protect Mary my mother,
lest, torn from my sight,
sorrow befall her.

You who have heard this song,
a fragment only of the song
that wrung the world's heart:
you who have heard this song:
wake up from your sluggish dragons.

Translated by Bruce Berlind with Mária Kőrösy


## WE AND THEY
János Pilinszky

That we should suffer damnation
is fair enough, but fairer still
for the barefoot beasts. Since they
bear, nurse, nurture
the helpless God, and
hiding him even from Mary,
the Son freed from the cross,
lug him around everywhere.

Translated by Bruce Berlind with Mária Kőrösy


## DECEMBER 22, 1970
János Pilinszky

Mangy dogs, we bleed on the pillow.
We are beautiful.
Afterwards only clumsy
and immortal.

Translated by Bruce Berlind with Mária Kőrösy

## VEIL
János Pilinszky

No sun. No Moon.
And no childhood.
And chiefly no earth, mother-earth.

No coffin and no country.
No cradle and no turned-down bed,
death shaped to our heads.

To live is to spin on a pin-point,
and our peace—it's nothing more
than a sagging wing that swoons,
as a bride's veil—slipped off or
still on—swoons, on the nail.

It's hanging loose.
We're hanging loose.
We have no graveyard either.

Translated by Bruce Berlind with Mária Kőrösy

## FOR LIFE
János Pilinszky

The bed is communal.
Not the pillow.

Translated by Bruce Berlind with Mária Kőrösy

## HERE AND NOW
János Pilinszky

I look at the lawn, maybe the lawn.
The grass moves. Wind or shower maybe,
or simply the fact that you are
moves the world, here, now.

Translated by Bruce Berlind with Mária Kőrösy

## TREES
### Ágnes Nemes Nagy

What must be studied. The winter trees.
How they're shrouded with frost to the footpads.
Immovable curtains.

What must be learned is that streak,
where the crystal is already steaming,
and the tree swims into mist,
like a body in the memory drifting.

And the river behind the trees,
the wild duck's muted wings,
and the blind-white blue night
where hooded objects loom,
what must be learned in this place
are the trees' inexpressible acts.

Translated by Bruce Berlind

## BUT TO LOOK
### Ágnes Nemes Nagy

But to look, to look, she said, the instant
the smoke-screen dissolves, in that split-second interval
the moment between the smoke, the acid, the lye, the onslaughts
to look, you know, like a table whose form is decomposing
to see simultaneously its profile and surface

And to act, to act, you know, I'm continuously acting
my body is acting history, biology
and to meditate, you know, my head seems so queer to me
          so interminable
I don't even know why I love
          spherical forms
eyeball, skull, globe, such
          limited endlessness
but they are shredded spheres these, coconuts
matted fibers with the hair of mortality
          edged in a circle

And to look from above, from below, from every angle
to finger all round the thing with all my eyes
to carve out contours with them, to scrub, to knock down
while they're opening, closing, opening with uneven
                    sea-swells
and also the many slow glimpses outward from things
gigantic glimpses of the hollows in imperceptible
unmoving pools and stones
shooting out arrows of splintered light-signals

Although it's no good, she said, these far-flung hundred thousand eyes
though it's no good the biosphere's rustling
                    broom-of-an-eyelash around me
foliage, scraggly branches of cedars
the revolving season's scratches
                    night and day
                    rising, falling above me
though it does no good, but to look, to look

To look, you know
as a scar looks, she said, at the tree

Translated by Bruce Berlind


## STATUTES
### Ágnes Nemes Nagy

Bitter.
            It was bitter, the sea, when
I rolled through the rock-throat down
a spiral staircase. A shingle, I spun,
behind me the hum of snail-shell
like memory in an abandoned house,
I rattled
like a skullful of shrapnel.

Then I rumbled out onto the beach.
And there were the statues.

On a pedestal
a leather-covered tortoise-egg:
my skull boiled boiled in the sun,
my white helmet rolled away
a bubble on the sand,
I was lying down, my shoulder against a rock,
in filthy filthy white array.

       Whose is this hunk?
       Who was it, from a mountainous shale-chunk
       with monstrous passion hacked
       this indifference out?

And the plates of sheet-iron on me, the sheer-iron.
Banged-up boxes,
as they reflected their stammering light,
—a plane-wreck glitters like this,
but inside what stirs still lives,
a smatter of blood on the watchstrap,—
I lay smeared out on the rock,
life—the filth of it—on a stone.

       Nothing more stubborn, more stubborn,
       you fling yourself into a stone,
       fling into a thing, fling into a stone
       your living neck,
       it's already a stone season,
       its switched-off life half-blind,
       who sculpted this indifference?
       who was it, from a mountainous shale-chunk
       chiseled your living neck?

Salt and sand and above them the rock-hunk,
gouged out cave-like in the sky,
this relative eternity,
this half-light of minerals—

the water murmurs, murmurs, its bed an Earth:
bitterness in a stone cask.

Translated by Bruce Berlind

## DEFEND IT
### Ágnes Nemes Nagy

Defend it if you can, admit: it was worth it,
it was worth it, admit that it's good like this,
it was worth every uphill scramble,
the wise resolve, the striving,
the slow switch-blade knife,
that instructor of treachery,
admit, admit that it was worth it, the mind's
candy-striped flashy love
that slices into a dark room,
it was worth this choking
gasp of breath, this illusion
of reason, this mute word,
abstraction, distinction,
the heart that convulsively bursts into flame,
the heart in pot-bellied snow-clouds,
as if inside, while the snow stabs down,
a town were burning endlessly,
say to the moment it was worth it,
while unremittingly on the two shoulders,
on the two wrists, on the two feet
of the indefensible terror's
torn wounds they ooze open
spilling black blood—

Translated by Bruce Berlind

## CRIME
### Ágnes Nemes Nagy

The punished who were innocent of crimes
have lost their senses, their minds
like a blind window. Still,
was the sentence sufficient?
Is one who has lived innocent?
Minerals are innocent.
The eunuch is innocent.
And the one whose flames burned to the sky
is the blindest splinter of all
and does not know why.

Translated by Bruce Berlind

## LIKE SOMEONE
### Ágnes Nemes Nagy

Like someone who came with a message from far away
and then forgot it completely,
and of all of the grainy light only a handful
stayed in him, tied in a bundle—

so wanders the forgetful one
in his body's rumpled coat.

Translated by Bruce Berlind

## A DROP OF BLOOD ON THE GROUND
### Sándor Csoóri

The cat crunches the pigeon's bones,
    he's lustfully crunching, then turning his head,
but his eyes stare fixedly into nothingness
even from above the bloody shreds.
Only predatory Autumn can stare at us this way,
        with such a yellow lynx-gaze.

And look there: there's a drop of blood on the ground, too,
    a little purple leaf plopping from a tree,
and in a moment another one, a third, and further, there,
under the horizon, the red block of an entire butcher's woods.
It's best for us to slip away from here,
        to give no evidence about the cat, nor the blood.

Besides, there are too many signs of death in our lives,
    too many memories of breaking
and of mangled chests. Come, maybe the destroying angels
don't know the secret lovers' way yet;
October's infantryman-crickets carouse thereabout,
        and honey, nut, and blackthorn offer themselves to those
            in exile.

Translated by Len Roberts

## POSTPONED NIGHTMARE
### Sándor Csoóri

I'm sitting in the sunshine,
    getting warm as the rocks
        after a rough, rheumatic winter.
    At my ankle a small wind stirs in the grass,
your breath from down below, perhaps.

They say I wept months for you.
    That may be; I can't recollect.
        On either side of me the nights blackened
    and horses reared with blood-frothed mouths,
as they do when a shell bursts among them.

And trains and cities and a flock
    of crows plummeting headfirst
        and the skidding, burning wrecks after
    midnight on America's roads,
where I waited, mid-dream, for a crash.

I yelled to you: come, there is a renewal
    in my madness, my pain that is
        greater than pain: the severed
    head, the arm, fly toward you
and our eyes meet again—

I'm sitting in the sunshine,
    getting warm as the rocks.
        A winter's postponed nightmare cries out in my bones.
    At my ankle a small wind stirs in the grass,
your breath from down below, perhaps.

        Translated by Len Roberts and László Vértes


## QUESTIONS, TO CARRIERS OF THE DEAD
### Sándor Csoóri

Who are you? What are you dragging?
Are you hauling the Unknown Dead toward the cemetery?
The untimely victim of speeding?

I saw the dent of the man's body that had clapped
against the stone wall in the nightfall,
I saw his blood and time's blood stream together.
So simple was this haphazard, clumsy last judgement,
as when a dew-drenched calf is killed.

And what is that wreck you have left?
The car's knotted dream of itself?
Hell's junk? iron-trash?
I feel an itchiness beginning slowly under my skin,
the unswingable hand's eternity here on the ditch-bank,
and among the stones the silence of butterflies and excrement.

Translated by Len Roberts and László Vértes


## YOU WEREN'T A TOTAL
### Imre Oravecz

stranger to me, I'd noticed you in the public areas of the apartment
house, fitted out as it was with every convenience, coffee shop, TV
room, gymnasium, sauna, swimming pool, where I always saw you in
the company of men, but I didn't even know your name when one
evening you knocked at my door, walked into my flat, and asked me
whether I knew what you wanted, and you came straight to the point,
the purpose of your coming, in one single movement you slipped out
of your long denim skirt, it was clear you were sure of yourself because
you had no panties on, and I found out what you wanted, and you
sure enough wanted it, with no shame and no inhibitions, only *that*,
that and nothing else, both then and afterwards, any time and any
place, and I felt that you only *used* me, as, when I came to see you, you
used that handy wooden frame mounted over the center of your bed,
which you always parked your legs on so as not to waste energy
holding them up while we were making out, and that's why I got sick
of you so soon, because you were not what you pretended to be, a
strong-minded, brainy, educated, self-respecting feminist rebelling
against the traditional woman's role, but a self-centered, small-time,
shameless slut out only for sensual enjoyment.

Translated by Bruce Berlind and Mária Kőrösy

## IT WAS ALREADY LATE EVENING
Imre Oravecz

It was already late evening when we left the restaurant,
where we'd sat for hours drinking tea, and decided to go
up the hill, so we got into the car we'd left in the nearby
parking lot and started up the steeply winding serpentine
street between the houses, the district was quiet, hardly
any traffic, only once in a while a solitary taxi passed
us or approached us, and only an occasional person was
standing at the bus stops, there were still leaves in the
trees, but a slight fog was already descending, and the smell
of rotten leaves permeated the autumn air and occasionally
drifted into the car, TV screens still gleamed in the flats,
but where the curtains weren't drawn we could see that the
film had come to an end, and people were already in pyjamas
and nightgowns and were getting ready for bed, reaching the
top we took in the panorama, hurriedly identified a few
far-off shining points, and, after cruising around a bit,
dispelling in each other all doubts about the object of our
coming here, we stopped in a badly lit side street, the
neighborhood was sparsely populated and deserted, the nearby
tiny park with its monument was abandoned, we chatted for a
while about something, several times we raked with our eyes
the nearby bushes, checked if there were voyeurs between
them or behind them, but since nothing moved the spot seemed
to be satisfactory, and the window, steamy because of the
great difference in temperature, veiled us, we felt safe and
set about doing what we were tacitly allied for, and, as
if on signal, we turned to each other, we grabbed each other,
and, freed of our clothes, quickly, like two experienced
lovers, satisfied each other, and, when we'd finished, we
drew apart, wiped ourselves dry with kleenex, and, like two
empty bottles on the return counter, motionlessly continued
to stay beside each other, and, in spite of our strangeness,
were just beginning to feel something like a sort of
affection for each other when, reaching out, we suddenly
bumped into each other's bodies, which until then had been
assets, but now towered like insurmountable barriers before
us, and this unforeseen development nipped that feeling in
the bud.

Translated by Bruce Berlind with Mária Kőrösy

## AIR GRANMA
Ottó Orbán

She, though, had grown up among a better class of people. She
boasted of that, even if her father was a peddler in Bacska. Once
when she was holding court for "family," she threw herself down
on her back and, tearing at the chaise longue's dustcover, began
to bay like a dog at the moon: "My son . . .! Those awful . . . ! Those
    miserable . . . !" Soap tragedy, audience in tears. The tin box was
full of colorful crocodiles—her hoarded candy. Early in '18, she
blew the family fortune on some broom business. In '44, she lived
in woodsheds, behind stacks of wood. When she was alone she
talked out loud to her dead son, whom she had not sent to school
because it cost too much, whom she'd once disowned. As long as
she could still walk, she'd dash for the door—it might not be just
the mailman with the pension check. Dead, she lay on the chaise
longue as if she were flying without wings. The family loon tore
away her down comforter: "Take a good look at what a human being amounts to!" I looked: a bloated pair of white tits, and pro-
fanely-vivid curls on the Mount of Venus—a woman's body
wildly alive; except, it's chin was sagging. Minutes passed, or
years, I dont know. "He's crazy . . . ! Right in front of the child . . . ?"
And Earth brought me to. The sun was drowning the room in gold.
Cars, milk cans: Szondy Street's clamorous life. The clock had not
stood still; the wind was throbbing in Spring's breast.

Translated by Jascha Kessler with Mária Kőrösy

## EARTH GRANMA
Ottó Orbán

She never said she was Hungarian. She was Julianna Gasko, 176
lbs., daughter of the homeless. Among her people, the name of god
was worshipped like the railroad. Pension—the name of the ut-
termost star to be seen from her village. Finally, god's only begot-
ten son, Trolley, came down to earth for her: for years they lived
next to the carbarn, the four surviving children out of six growing
up in unlubricated screeching. Later on, she often took care of

(NOTE: *Bacska* [pronounced "Batchka"] is a county in southern Hungary.)
(NOTES: *Ganca* [pronounced "gansa"] is a flour-and-potato cake; Kelenföld is an
industrial district in Pest with a train station; a "snotty sea," i.e., of runny noses.)

me. We ate *ganca* and garlic-fried bread in the kitchen—her
imagination's delectable poems. Her kind cake-face glowed like
the moon. The destiny of the poor slowly drowned her, the water
rising gradually to her knees, to her heart. Then her clay-and-
wattle lungs collapse, some odd items drift on the surface of the
rattling flood. Including her invention, "open bloomers," a lin-
gerie-mastodon born from the marriage of a pair of men's socks to
a pair of flannel underpants, a palm's-width opening at the bottom of the latter, so they didn't have to be dropped even then—
the first time I saw panty hose . . . in that hovel in Kelenföld. The
smell of the poor lived on; a cold iron stove. And autumn sneezed
in the bristly yard; a snotty sea.

Translated by Jascha Kessler with Mária Kőrösy

## THE USES OF POETRY
### Ottó Orbán

For a miraculous child, I was pretty ordinary. If anything at all oozed
from me, it wasn't Mozart's grace, but the siege. The miracle was—I
was alive. Our building caught three bombs—all duds. Between
two raids I whistled the American radio's theme song in the hallway
    over
the heads of the SS—*Yankee Doodle went to town* . . . —and they
didn't waste me: they were tone deaf (back in our apartment my
mother nearly cracked my skull). All the buildings around us were
burned out—except for ours. Miracle, miracle, and miracle. The poet
in me, however, was appreciated by adult society. I was taken to the
radio station; no tape recorder then: my recitation was put on wax. I
got on the nerves of the sensitive producer: "What a neurotic little baboon!" Emil Grandpierre looked at me with his seablue eyes as though
I was a sparrow that could count. But no one knew my secret: I had
two pockets full of pumpkin seeds. The Poet's Prize—pumpkin seed
pleasure the reward for orphanhood, for beatings, for the baboon, for
a radio interview. Gasping, I climbed Shady Street back to the Home,
my mouth full of pumpkin seeds. Poor Orphan: I grunted and
    chewed.
Of course, I couldn't make out that cunning jigsaw puzzle right on the
spot. That bubble burst, too, somewhere, and sometime else. But when

(NOTES: In Hungarian a prodigy is called "a miraculous child"; Emil Grandpierre
is a contemporary novelist; "Shady Street" is in the Buda Hills.)

it did, and wherever it was that it happened, tears parted from laughter in me like a ship leaving shore; I was the widening gap, and I was the person waving from them both. The tender landscape of that private pastoral masque was broken up by a murderous humor like a clod by the rays of the sun, and a mirror-like abyss of blood opened before my eyes just where the mind's fissure splits into poetry.

Translated by Jascha Kessler with Mária Kőrösy

## ANCESTORS
### Ottó Orbán

They preserved their reputation by a sort of emotional swagger. In the beginning it belonged to the Orthodox ironmonger who delivered cannons to Kossuth, for which he earned a majestic scolding from the Emperor; in Bach's day he was jailed, so they said. Then Fate the sculptor fashioned my great-grandmother's breasts. For years that handsome woman gazed at me from a Budapest wall, courtesy of some brush imitating Miklós Barabas. "Beautiful Adele"—her entry in the oral encyclopedia. A fact: even on canvas her doe-face blushed—lust and neurosis. No portraits of the babuskha'd ladies of ancient history however, who knows why; at best, they may have been browned by summer's sun-brush. One of them, as lip-service would have it, knelt in the dust of the village street to kiss the young priest's hand even when she was gone in years. That's about all that's come down to us. Not even that much about their husbands: their history's been ground to dust in the dragon's belly of earth's clods. Only one of them is identifiable: the lord of history, a Bujak swineherd. Black finger, white breast—a lust for revenge already conceived in the cells. A reeking sty and grandiose gossip—their blood's fiery soup boiling in an earthen pot, their love salting the taste of time's grave.

Translated by Jascha Kessler with Mária Kőlösy

(NOTES: Miklós Barabas [pronounced "Barabash"] is a 19th Century portrait painter; Bujak [pronounced "Booyak"] is a hamlet.)

## THE BRIDGE
*(University of Minnesota, Twin Cities Campus, East Bank)*
Ottó Orbán

Here's where John Berryman jumped into the Mississippi
but missed it (strictly speaking) and crashed on the embankment
    stones—
you can see the whole scene from the roof garden:
the two-level bridge between intellect and emotion,
and down underneath the darkly rolling alcohol . . .
We must risk our lives near a downed transmission line;
it's bad news if high voltage doesn't arc between two words . . .
Charged myself, I too totter dizzily on the bridge between continents,
my highest ambition to think what I think
and not my position or, more precisely, not only that.
The desire for objectivity is the craziest of passions, especially if
we're from a community that heats up easily but is capricious—
I've often seen this whirl heady with icy drunkenness,
in the underworld Charon paddles on it, here the crew-cut canoers.

Translated by Bruce Berlind with Mária Kőrösy

## WHAT BECAME OF THE SIXTIES?
(San Francisco)
Ottó Orbán

We report everything in good shape in Union Square
ideas financial institutions tourists all doing their business
a black boy practices karate on the green grass
the imaginary jawbone breaks
COME TO JESUS FOR HE IS THE KING
and the French don't keep shouting out of malice
but because here they are the Americans
LOOK AT THIS PROPHET JANINE

on this sunny Wednesday or Friday
the face of the Earth is markedly spherical
and the red juice that trickles down both sides
perhaps isn't blood but some exotic sauce
war and earthquake dwarf beside the latest news
that in Palo Alto two whorehouses
disguised as massage parlors have been closed

THE PUBLIC FINALLY COULD NOT TOLERATE IT ANY
    LONGER
the recapture of the city is on the agenda
THE CITY BELONGS TO ITS INHABITANTS
only the feeling of proprietorship must be rekindled
which elbows the unseemly element off the vehicle
and the citizen may now travel peacefully
to Berkeley toward the moral
that the revolution jolted the family
but not the banks
and that the Fast Train in the Bay Area
is the last underground poet
who has no gas pump or property

so here we are (on Fisherman's Wharf)
but what's the significance for the capital-strong present
of a future with questionable interest
we squander the pixie moment while we still can
to the left the Golden Gate Bridge
to the right the two-level Oakland Bridge
straight ahead the blue water yachts swooping gulls
and to the rear under the trees
the Shore Patrol's squad car armed with a machine gun

Translated by Bruce Berlind with Mária Kőrösy

## THERE IS NO SOUTHERN ISLAND
László Nagy

The soul was cold, too; we headed south
like swallows flashing off,
tossing boiled wine down our gullets
from the mirror-well of our chromed bottle
against the going-blue; but icicled locomotives
rattled up from the South to confront us: we couldn't believe
the treachery of tomorrow's Southern Island;
shivering, we teased each other: what
machinery, what brandy-stills
could be scavenged from them, all those copper
pipes and rings—but finally
we saw the palms fettered with ice,
men wearing old women's scarves

to protect their ears, and the bird
of poets, the albatross, staggering towards us
in galoshes . . . and our souls simply turned back,
back into the sword blades of the North,
where winter's natural.

Translated by Jascha Kessler with Mária Kőrösy


## COGNITION, LANGUAGE, POETRY
Lázló Nagy

Let's not be ruthless to ourselves: we must
not condemn humanity to the infinite. Full
cognition is in itself infinite.—If I
thought I was arguing against action, I'd
be praying through livid lips; in fact,
it's from the very first that I went after
this agony, the essentially human. Creature
of action even then, from the moment the
first word was shaped, a poet and scientist
both.

Heisenberg's formula for the world is lovely,
because radiating at me from it are the
strikers of fire, casters of bronze,
seafarers, stargazers, and bloodypinioned
Icaruses too, fierytongued heretics,
mouthcrushed singers.

They chatter on about describing the world,
expressing it. I don't believe the goal
is happiness. Science was here in the very
act of cognition even before the human word.
Still, poets haven't just clambered down
out of the trees either. Eddington's
dinnertable, the apparent one and the real
one, is made by the poet. And the woman
in Attila Jozséf's "Ode" isn't just an

(NOTES: Attila Jozséf, the most famous poet of the 1930s. The "Ode" imaged a
woman in terms of machinery, somewhat in the manner, one might say, of a Leger
painting.

anatomical marvel in verse form. Without
the word, nothing occurs. Thinking, they
say, the act of imaging and of equating
originates in the brain linguistically.

The abuse of words is no modern conceit,
but it's more spectacular and distressing
than ever before. We see language being
used for eyewash, for lies. No wonder
people turn away from the vital questions;
all right if it's towards amusement; but
if toward wordlessness, then it hurts. The
philosophy of silence wasn't made up yesterday.
Csokonai was also wounded by its barb, though
in vain; Rimbaud was whisked off forever
by its blackness. Silence is a comfortable
condition for me: a dead quiet. Bombast's
comfortable too, though immoral. What I'd
like is being the world's true champion.
If the Impossible's out of reach, let our
Fall at least be festive.

I'm grown up now and even the least of my
cells knows that the word and I are one
and the same thing. I think the poet's
revealed by his language. (Just as work,
even table manners, usually reveals the
Human.)

If the poet can be judged objectively, it
is by his poem. This certainty comforts
me: I believe in the word. My duty's
paying attention to the word. Handling
the word with care, devotion. I also believe
that it carries me beyond the locks to where
secrets wait for me alone. It takes me
to where the nonexistent begins. It leads
me along the edge of the bluff, always on
the lip of death.

Translated by Jascha Kessler

## OCTOBER NIGHT IN THE GARDEN
### István Vas

They've left. A success. You held out.
You didn't let yourself be swept away
Again into fruitless
Fuss. It's pure profit
This dreary, chilly twilight.
Put it to use. Go about your business.
Wrap yourself up in your dark cape.
Look, the purple cactus-dahlias
Droop toward the ground, frost-stricken.
Six wretched roses still hang on.
A pallidly anguished medley of colors
On stunted shivering sunflowers
And frost-bitten zinnias and asters.
But the two pinetrees darken upwards
Formidably. Two exclamation
Marks advise: do your business!
Get ready for what the garden around you
Gets ready for. *Philosopher,*
*C' est apprendre à mourir,* said Montaigne.
The garden too has its philosophy.
Shouldn't you have one? Minute by minute
It gets darker. The lights have gone on
Outside, past the railing, and in the house.
Two pines, two soft knots of shade
Blacker in the blackness.
Do you hear? They whisper the secret to each other:
The two of them survive in this garden.
Stretching upward. They too have
Philosophy. Should only you not have?
You sit wrapped in your cape.

Translated by Bruce Berlind


## IN THE ROMAN FORUM
### István Vas

The stones no longer interest me
Neither does history
These days it's hard for
My eyes to make out

The Latin texts on the stones
Nothing interests me any more
Only what I can credit
When it happens to come along
Yet I only vacillate alone
On the way I started
Where have the Romans gone

Translated by Bruce Berlind


## I PUT THE FELT PEN DOWN
### István Vas


I

You lived within me sixty days.
You walked within me light of foot.
I was your Jerusalem, your Galilee.
The whip that lashed you cut through me.
The nails of your cross pierced my palms
And my two feet, one lapped on the other.
The rude spear stabbed my cooling side.
Doubting Thomas fingered my wound.
You flew to heaven then to your Father.
I put a period at the story's end
And put the felt pen down.


2

Eli, Eli, lama sabachthani?
Why am I empty since then?
I look for your footprints in vain:
Even in the desert I cannot find them.
Where are the hillocks, the gardens?
Have the figtrees all shrivelled?
Without you the world is no world.
I don't see where your cross stood.
It's nearly twenty days since you spoke in me.
Your words branded my heart.
My Lord, why have you forsaken me?
Why did you leave me filled with midnight?

3

The wind of resurrection, forever fresh,
Blows on the earth—blow then through me,
Blow into my desert's emptiness,
Clear the confusion of doubt away.
What's withered will be a Beginning then:
Let the palmtrees send forth shoots again!
Thou who didst not cast out Thomas,
Though blessed is he who believes in faith,
Will you vouchsafe me to see once more
The faith-making beam of your beautiful face?
Patience pitches its tent in me,
And devotion and doubt are twin beseechers:
Resurrect in me, now, eternal Easter!

Translated by Bruce Berlind

## THE CHRISTMAS OF LONG WALKS
Dezső Tandori

In March we began the longer and longer walks,
in populated areas, and what with the diversity
of houses and street we walked out of ourselves the
desire to get away, which however would have been only
a so-called trip, but we did not dare leave
the birds here, then we discovered—while a number of
routes were still childhood systems, in the hilly region
neglected for years, neglected only by us of course,
walks of the old days, not for me the most successful
ones, due perhaps to my chronic lack of self-confidence,
first with my parents, later in friendships, and who knows
how each side remembers it now; the phases came to an end,
changes in the structure took place on an even larger
scale; what would the material of even more sweeping changes
be composed of, and so on, of the most central defects of
material and of innumerable possibilities—, then we discovered
how good it was to stay home, walks, grasses, weeds, in the
world of almost passionately gathered greens, not however
for their own sake, but brought home in their natural setting
to our birds; for someone who died at the end of the period
of walks, we "brought home," or rather kept home,
his natural setting: to wit, ourselves, we were here

with him, and so for him it was as if life had jolted back
into its, for him accustomed, "ruts," before jolting out.
On his last birthday he did not say, as on others,
"I've had enough," and that he wished this were his last; this too
is the sign of a personality change. We spoke little
to him about the birds, or rather he wouldn't have known "what
to say," finally; he would have taken collecting grass
as "overdoing it"; then we came out of the hospital with the
green plastic bag, crossed a weedy area, one could leave there
only a—mentioned elsewhere also—walking stick
in the brush of one of the sparrows' favorite kinds of grasses,
in the empty lot, where the stripped-down Christmas trees would
also end up (in the other poem: where perhaps there'll be a park
some day, and new generations of sparrows will
return; Tradoni's remark), after the new year, in times
not always conducive to walks; nevertheless, these too
must surely have their reason for existence, at least we
felt, with our for-the-time-being, one hopes, only half-lived time,
which of course has no sum-total, that
man in the temperate zone lives only half-years, and
belying everything not after all a half-life. (But
a quarter, or two-thirds, because he sleeps through
a good part of the rest as well; Tradoni's remark;
therefore we can speak of our lives only as so-called.)

Translated by Bruce Berlind


## TRADONI,
## STRESS ON AN ABANDONED PLACE
### Dezső Tandori

So much change comes about easily, you just have to deal
with the subject, the stress is displaced, something else
takes the place of the vanished element: so much of the poem.
A room is something else. Tradoni sits in a room, writes the poem,
and it's not about being conscious of writing: that he's writing
about writing; but writing is part of the room, a way
of investigating a subject, and the bird custodian now begins
to investigate when he looks up at a shelf where a vase stands
which was once occupied by a bird who took it from another bird,
but then he died, and the other bird, whose vase it was, whose
twigs it was, who is still alive, is not roosting on that vase,

has not gone back up to the vase, below the vase, since then the shelf
is abandoned, nobody is gardening on the potted plants,
that bird died, and Tradoni knows those who are to blame.
The two themselves, the custodian and his wife, and two others; and
about whom, says the custodian, I can now say something concerning
this subject, I am saying something concerning this subject,
I am speaking about those who are to blame, owing to
some degree of indifference, for the death of this bird;
I keep repeating things, which I never liked to do. Furthermore, I
believed not so long ago that I had my own dead, but one's own dead,
I now understand, are only those who lives I could have
saved; and do these two, my good friends, have their own
dead because of this bird, do they know that they have their own
dead. And what I discovered, Tradoni relates to somebody
from whom they once received a poppy stalk for that vase, what
I discovered is that it's more bearable to speak of others (another),
to reprimand anyone, it hurts less, ten minutes and we're over it,
it's less intolerable than just looking at a place on the shelf which
promises to be deserted in the near future too; whether there is or
there isn't any piety in sparrows, our surviving bird, I say,
he writes, and doesn't look up, doesn't look back from
the chair, doesn't go up there, and when the two of us here
mention it it's almost unbearable, and this explains why people
deal so often with each other, why they reprimand even me,
the poor bird investigator, they're not strong enough to look
at their own unoccupied places, and let's admit, writes Tradoni,
it's easier for us too to reprimand someone, and really no one
can wish us to do any harm to ourselves, of course places
even so become empty, and Tradoni deals with criminal cases not
to credit such clear motivations for his fellow man's backbiting;
but this is the better working hypothesis, and he wants to work,
while a tape is playing, from the musical material of former mornings,
which the bird still listened to, those tunes, but by now
he would have forgotten them, even if he were alive. We're no
different with each other either, writes the bird custodian,
we can begin forgetting while we're still alive. Now, for just
this reason, he turns around, and examines those twigs,
the abandoned plants, the bookshelf, the vase. For something.

Translated by Bruce Berlind

## WHAT GETS LOST IN THE LIGHT
Dezső Tandori

When I climb higher and higher up the mountain,
without stopping, through crumbling walls of stone,
thirty years ago, at age fourteen,
having no reason to do it, no motivation:
        on account of the debt I have to pay
all reasons and motives are mine outright,
because I'm a part under the sky
of the picture that's lost in this earthly light.

No sound echoes from the water's surface,
and I too silently withdraw,
but the chipped circle reimburses
times past in my downward path:
        what can I do? the sun's empty,
yet my share is barely a shadow's bite,
because I'm a part under the sky
of the picture that's lost in this earthly light.

What is this vaulting torrent of rain,
shelter even from its own self,
although it's needed? While I'm sustained
by the blind spots of the blink of an eye,
        why does the lookout tower grow higher?
And yet I'm convinced I'll reach its height,
because I'm a part under the sky
of the picture that's lost in this earthly light.

It gets lost, stands there in its glorious place,
while I, the live one, am staggering,
trampling on figs, on bunches of grapes,
rotten pears, nuts cracking:
        all that is left gets lost,
so all that's left is not left half undone.
Exploding, extravagant instant! I exist
because what I need not live through is still to come.

Translated by Bruce Berlind

## THE NO-HAND
### Dezső Tandori

A blind bird believes he's had a dream,
though all that happened was I stroked his back,
    normally not routine.
And this one pair of birdfeet, in point of fact,
never touches our hands if it has its way
    —though this too will come one day,
when fading away with a few of our own souls,
this one body, he'll lie there in our palms.
A down payment for death!—what kind was that,
that it proved possible to stroke his back?

He flung out a gray feather at his wing
as he stood still in total darkness there.
    I knew somewhere we had our being,
not on the floor, the stubby floorboards, where
there's a tiny heat at the point where his soles press
    —and endless night's is even less,
which I must come to know, though two blind pits
transmit it, filtered, to our consciousness:
a down payment for absolute oblivion,
which we ourselves will come to in the end.

I was only as much, as little, as the No-Hand,
that points neither to this side nor the other,
    that's neither lost nor found,
as if time, between here and there, could pass and hover.
The pattern on his back still felt unruffled
    under my finger, as if invisible.
Slowly, but not panting, he opened his bill;
he seemed to want to dip into something cool,
because the heat of that unexpected hand
entered, re-entered, the body of thirty grams.

And a voice spoke to him, familiar, mine,
the voice forever unanswerable; instead
    of a traced three-sparrow line,
he stood there silent with his sightless head

like an answer to questions we never thought to guess,
   for which to be oneself is best.
Slowly my hand moved sideways in the cage,
it blended with the imperceptible waves;
and the minute's miracle, until now never seen,
became good reason enough for him to preen.

                              Translated by Bruce Berlind

# Poland, compiled by Daniel Bourne

## Polish Poetry
## By Daniel Bourne

A major figure in pre-Christian Polish mythology is Światowid or Świę-towit—god of war, fortune-telling, and harvest. In the village where the center of the Światowid cult was located, the god was represented by a four-faced statue who could see in all directions. The story goes that at the very beginning of the *Drang nach Osten*—the movement of Germans towards points east of the Elbe River, which began in the early tenth century and continued through the next thousand years—a certain German bishop with a contingent of armed troops appeared in the village early one morning and announced a challenge to the four-faced god.

Światowid had until noon to strike the bishop down. If the god gave no sign, the bishop would have his men topple the statue, and force the people to convert to Christianity. Noon came and went; nothing happened. (Of course, the bishop had not offered his challenge one-on-one and had spent the entire time safely ringed by his troops). The victorious bishop there-upon ordered that the wooden statue with its four faces be tossed into the nearby river, commanding that anyone who should find the statue downstream was—under pain of death if he did otherwise—to cast the image of the fallen god back out into the current until it was lost to human sight permanently, its memory erased.

I like the story of Światowid for many reasons, but above all my fascina-tion with the story has to do with the ending: how a thousand years ago there was already a war of image and interpretation going on in the Polish experience. I could add also how the image of a four-faced God—a god of harvest as well as of war, a synthetic rather than analytic god, if you will—also coincides with what originally drew me to Polish poetry, the ability to combine the personal and social dimension within one poem. But, ulti-mately, it's that crafty bishop and the supposedly helpless god that attract me the most: the battle between authority and the free word that has continued up until the very recent past.

The first written Polish text, the Bogurodzica (literally, "she who gave birth to God"), shows the connection between literary and political history. Dating from the thirteenth century, it was a hymn sung by soldiers on their way into battle. But it was later—after the partitions of Poland at the hands of Russia, Austria, and Prussia towards the end of the eighteenth century— that Polish literature was to play its most crucial role in the preservation of a Polish historical and cultural identity. Indeed, from 1795 until the regaining of independence after World War I, the Polish homeland existed only to the extent that the language and literature preserved it. The Romantic poets Adam Mickiewicz, Julian Słowacki, Zygmunt Krasiński, and Cyprian Norwid were especially important in keeping both literature and national consciousness afloat. Mickiewicz (1798–1855) is perhaps the most significant figure of all. A visionary of national independence, he spent a good part of his life in exile, eventually dying of cholera during a journey to Constantinople to solicit aid for the Polish soldiers fighting against Russia in the Crimean War.

Then came the twentieth century: the brief interval of Polish independence from 1915 to 1939, then the outbreak of World War II, the German occupation, and the postwar experience under the domination of the Soviet Union, including the Stalinist stranglehold of the early-to-mid-fifties and the Martial Law Period of the early eighties. I would like to concentrate on one single event in the postwar period, however, and see how it serves as a focal point for the experience of Polish poetry in the past several decades—how history intertwines with the present. In 1968, a Warsaw University production of Mickiewicz's epic drama, *Forefathers' Eve,* a distinctly anti-Russian play that had been banned during the nineteenth century by the Czarist powers, now found itself closed by the twentieth-century Soviet authorities as well. Two things occurred after the play's suppression. It sparked several student disturbances nationwide, and it also served as the catalyst for the recreation of the underground press in Poland, reminiscent of the clandestine presses at work during the German occupation.

These presses tapped into the tradition of exile, or cultural diaspora, that had been a facet of Polish literature since the partitions. Indeed, later sojournors abroad (Czesław Miłosz, Stanisław Barańczak, and Adam Zagajewski, to name only a few) now found themselves resonating with a paradigm of literary activity in exile that had been forged by the Romantic poets. Thus, for two centuries, poets living in Paris or London, or, later, in New York or Boston, although severed from day-to-day life in Poland, nevertheless continued to participate in the unfolding literature.

The experience of exile was also a metaphor for those still living within the Polish lands—in internal exile, divorced from the alien government that was in control of their lives. Both of these groups—poets writing abroad as well as those in Poland writing "for the drawer—" found an audience in the underground Polish press of the last two decades. Such presses were indeed able to take advantage of a wider range of voices than were at the disposal of the official Polish literature culture. Indeed, "the second circulation" (to translate literally the term favored in the eighties, when this unofficial print culture was at its most vibrant) could publish the work of Czesław Miłosz, Stanisław Barańczak, Zbigniew Herbert, or Jan Polkowski while still publishing the work of poets whose work appeared in official places, such as Wisława Szymborska (though she too kept a great distance between herself and most of the official publishing world).

The interaction between the official and unofficial publishing worlds was indeed a fascinating and complicated situation. Some poets such as Tomasz Jastrun published the same poems in both underground and official publications. A poet like Bronisław Maj would have the same poems printed by an underground publisher, by the quasi-official (at least there was less censorship control) Catholic publishing house Znak, and by the London emigré press Puls, all editions appearing within a year or two of each other. At the same time, Jan Polkowski steadfastly refused to be published in any official publication, although he too had a book published abroad by Puls which was then smuggled back into the country. Meanwhile, to avoid the problems of legal responsibility for literature being published underground, books would mention that the work was printed without the knowledge and agreement of the author; yet, often, there would be a copyright notice given right below in the author's name.

In discussing Polish poetry, it is indeed difficult to disregard the interweaving of history and literature, to ignore the pressures the word and the sword put on each other. What happened five years, fifty years, or five hundred years ago forms an unwritten part of the poems, that proverbial "reading between the lines" for which eastern European literatures are famed, but which, undoubtedly, can be found in any literature. Polish literature abounds in codes and icons, and often the dialogue between poet and reader may seem unfathomable to the outside audience.

What strikes me about Polish literature, however, is how much of it *is* translatable, even though the historical context might seem exotic. For example, in Tomasz Jastrun's poem, "The Captive Dream" (p. 303), in which the poet's dream-reality mixes the worlds of czarist as well as Soviet-dominated Poland, it is the rare American reader who would be able to follow everything: that Mickiewicz (although not his *Forefathers' Eve*, of course) had become appropriated by official Poland as being a "safe" writer, that the two-headed eagle was the imperial insignia of Russia, that Szucha Boulevard was the site of the central Gestapo post in Warsaw during World War II, that in Poland's turbulent eighties, May 1st and 3rd marked regular clashes between official and unofficial Poland over the observance of International Workers Day (May 1st) and the May 3rd commemoration of the late eighteenth century Polish constitution, and that frequently, during this period in early May, opposition figures (including writers such as Jastrun) were rounded up by the police and *legally* held up to forty-eight hours *without* official charges. But, with this background information supplied, the poem emerges with its intense focus on a moment that is both dream-

state and essential reality, an ironic and frenzied layering of the intercon-
nections between different historical periods in the Polish experience.

Similarly the prose-poems in Krystyna Lars's *Those Who Come to Me in
Dreams* not only contain a subtext of patriotic legend, literary history, and
biography, but also rework this cultural legacy—Lars's personal rewrite of
a history that has often been retouched for dubious aims. For example, in
Lars's hypothetical fictions, an esteemed figure such as Mickiewicz, long
taught by government and underground alike to be a symbol of courage
and selflessness, chooses the easy way out: collaboration, retreat into one's
own private affairs ("internal emigration," as it was called in Poland of the
1980s), empty Romanticism, and hedonism. What emerges is a parallel
universe in which—to shift the names and situations to our own cultural
history—Thoreau dines at the home of a local dignitary to petition for a
job, Paul Revere decides he cannot leave his engraver's business to deliver
a message, and Clara Barton joins New York society. The intention is not
so much satire as reevaluation, an attempt to glimpse these historical creatures and their effect on the Polish human comedy afresh by seeing them
as they were not.

Child of William Carlos Williams that I am ("No ideas but in things"), I
am nevertheless drawn to Polish poetry's attempt to deal with social and
metaphysical obsessions through rhetoric as well as image. But always at
play in Polish poetry's "telling, not showing" is information from a crucial
sixth sense—irony. From Adam Zagajewski's "Poems on Poland" to Wisława
Szymborska's "Hitler's First Photograph," this irony—capable of being
gentle as well as caustic and of being directed towards the sacred cow as well
as the obvious evil—shows a very dexterous grappling with the surrounding
cultural iconography. It is not just the echoes of their cultural and historical
backgrounds that these poets present that is important, but it is the often
iconoclastic variations that they create out of this raw material.

Perhaps now it is time to say a few words about the poets themselves. Let
me start at the end and work backwards. For one thing, this selection is
heavily weighted in favor of writers who have come of age as poets during
Poland's turbulent eighties. Some of them, Tomasz Jastrun, Antoni Pawlak,
and Jan Polkowski, for example, were interned during Martial Law. Others,
such as Bronisław Maj, have been instrumental as coordinators of uncen-
sored literary readings. It would be a mistake, however, to reduce this generation's achievement to the confines of a "literature engagée." Even the
most pointed political poems (if they are successful) work because of the
intersection between language and experience. At the same time, the work
of Bronisław Maj and Mira Kuś stands out as being more obsessed with
the purity of knowing: they explore our ability to apprehend and grasp
the world. Their questions are epistemological ones—while, at the same
time, it could be said that their poems are "political" since their quest
for an integrity of knowing resonates against the background of a system

dependent on distortion. Meanwhile, other poets have turned their gaze to the small ironies and surrealities of culture—e.g., the devil-infested childhoods of Katarzyna Boruń-Jagodzińska's "Exorcist" and Stanisław Esden-Tempski's Rat poems.

These younger poets, however, had a "tough act to follow." Immediately preceding them is the so-called *Nowa Fala*—the New Wave generation of poets instrumental in the creation of the underground press. Two poets from this generation are already well known to American readers—Stanisław Barańczak and Adam Zagajewski—while two others, Ewa Lipska and Ryszard Krynicki, are beginning to attract attention. There are many, indeed, who would argue the younger poets are very much still in the shadow of the New Wave, and owe much of their own poetic concerns and obsessions to the New Wave's exploration of contaminated political language, of the ironic minutiae of existence in a totalitarian regime, and of the re-mythologizing of cultural and historical figures.

Before the New Wave came such writers as Czesław Miłosz (the Nobel Prize Laureate for Literature in 1980), Zbigniew Herbert, Wisława Szymborska, Tadeusz Różewicz, and Miron Białoszewski (a poet as yet less known to American readers because his work is heavily dependent on what we currently call language poetry—thus, what he is doing is virtually impossible to translate). Each of these poets deserves a book of introduction, but it may suffice to say that in their work too the tensions between icon and iconoclasm, between communication and distortion, between the individual and authority, and between the lyric and the metaphysical are very much in evidence.

And what of Polish literature in the future? In the foreward to his 1926 *Antologia wspólczesnej poezji polskiej (Anthology of Contemporary Polish Poetry)*, literary critic Edward Słoński celebrated the freeing up of Polish poetry, given the independence of the country itself after World War I, a period perhaps analogous to the post-Soviet situation in Poland today:

> many of those currently writing in a Poland reborn and free . . . will create a new direction, more suited to the conditions of a new political life, that these new writers will find in themselves a new tone for a new way of singing, which will not be just a call outward to the whole world that "we are still alive and we will continue to be alive—" for we already have our own ministries and bayonets to do this for us [p. 5, translation my own].

Is this déjà vu? It might be true that, given the new state of affairs in eastern Europe, Poland can now turn to other matters—but I should also mention that Słoński was wrong. Poland's bayonets and ministries weren't any better at defending Poland than was its literature. Indeed, thirteen years after Słoński wrote these words, the Polish cavalry was charging German panzers—an act more representative of the grand symbol than military strategy.

At the same time, I believe that Polish poetry talks about more than just what has happened in Poland, that it will continue to bear witness to the ongoing war between the armed and the unarmed still very much alive in other parts of the globe. Indeed, reading the poetry of Poland's martial law years evokes the same clashes between bone and steel continuing in other areas—China, the West Bank, the Balkans. To echo Machiavelli in the preface to his play *Mandragola:* "This time it may be Florence. The next time it may be Pisa or Rome."

Also, in regards to younger voices, such as Katarzyna Boruń-Jagodzińska, Mira Kuś, Bronisław Maj, and Krystyna Lars, we will see poets develop in paths that will diverge even further from the "political poem," although I do expect their work to continue to be marked with the previously mentioned concern with integrity—the exploration of the difficulties involved in perceiving and interacting with the world and other people in a nondistortive way.

A source of great anxiety to many, however, is the place of poetry in the "dog-eat-dog" world of current Poland—part Klondike gold rush and part Hooverville—as the country tries to shrug off years of mismanagement. For literature, the times are tough. Many of the journals and presses that helped to bring about social change in the country find themselves in bankruptcy because either they are no longer needed or their readership cannot afford to buy books and journals. The government itself has no money to help out, while the general public consensus is that Poland needs more entrepreneurs, not poets. Sounds familiar, doesn't it?

Perhaps even more disturbing is the absence of support for newer writers, currently in their twenties and early thirties. Even less in this area is being done than previously, and this lack of either publishing opportunities or fellowships for younger writers threatens to be more successful in hampering Polish creativity than decades and decades of censorship. A final troubling note is that the Catholic Church in Poland is beginning to ask for repayment of its previous loans of support, expecting loyalty to its current social and aesthetic agenda. Instrumental in serving as an umbrella for independent culture in the eighties as well as a bastion of Polish identity during the partitions, the German occupation, and postwar Soviet domination, the Church—to many writers and intellectuals—has begun to play a disturbing role in the social and political life of post-Communist Poland.

Still, it is very difficult to succumb to the temptation to complain too much. Many of the editors and publishers involved in the "second circulation" have assumed positions of responsibility in the established publishing houses, and many writers who suffered harassment or persecution find themselves able to work and travel freely. It is hoped that support for the arts will return in a few years. In any case, the four heads of Światowid remain in sight, bobbing up and down in the current.

NOTE: I would like to thank the translators for bringing these poems to life in English. Almost all established and newly emerging translators are represented here. One excellent translator, Renata Gorczyński, is not, however; I would like to mention her fine translations (often with Robert Hass) of Adam Zagajewski, especially.

—Daniel Bourne

# About the Poets

## STANISŁAW BARAŃCZAK

Stanisław Barańczak (b. 1946 in Poznań), prominent critic and translator, as well one of the major poets of the New Wave generation, is currently Professor of Slavic Languages and Literatures at Harvard University. Leaving Poland in 1980, after having been removed from his teaching position at Adam Mickiewicz University in Poznań, his early books included *Korekta twarzy* (*Proofreading of a Face*, 1968), *Jednym tchem* (*With One Breath*, 1970), *Dziennik poranny* (*Morning Diary*, 1972), *Sztuczne oddychanie* (*Artificial Respiration*, 1974) and *Ja wiem, że to niesłuszne* (*I Know It Isn't Right*, 1977), many of which remained in print in Poland during the 1980s in the underground press. His later books, also circulated in Poland through the underground, include *Tryptyk z betonu, zmęczeniu i śniegu* (*Triptych of Concrete, Weariness and Snow*, 1981). In English translation, his most recent collection is *The Weight of the Body* (TriQuarterly Books, 1989). He is also the author of *A Fugitive from Utopia: The Poetry of Zbigniew Herbert* (Harvard University Press, 1987).

## MIRON BIAŁOSZEWSKI

Miron Białoszewski (1922–83) born in Warsaw, grew up during the Nazi Occupation, graduating from an underground high school and studying literature at the underground wing of Warsaw University. His *Pamiętnik z powstania warszawskiego* (*Memoir from the Warsaw Uprising*, 1970) is a classic in Polish prose, while his extensive body of poetry, starting with *Obroty rzeczy* (*The Revolutions of Things*, 1956), earned him the reputation as one of Poland's major twentieth-century poets. His work, virtually impossible to translate, is roughly analogous to American projectivist verse or language poetry.

## MAREK BIEŃKOWSKI

Marek Bieńkowski (b. 1953 in Gdańsk) taught philosophy at the Medical Academy of Gdańsk and published several books of poems, including *Ogród dłoni* (*The Garden of the Hand*, 1980) and *Trzeci Znak* (The Third Sign, 1983).

He spent 1984–85 on a Kościuszko Foundation fellowship to the United States, where he remained, working as a social worker in the New York City area.

## KATARZYNA BORUŃ-JAGODZIŃSKA

Katarzyna Boruń-Jagodzińska (b. 1956) is the author of five volumes of poetry, including *Życie codzienne w Państwie Środka* (*Everyday Life in the Middle Kingdom*, 1983), *Muzeum automatów* (The Museum of the Automatons, 1985), from which the poems here were selected, and *Ostatnia fotografia* (*The Last Photograph*, 1989). She participated in the International Writers Workshop at the University of Iowa in Autumn 1989. She lives in Warsaw.

## ERNEST BRYLL

Ernest Bryll (b. 1935) has been, within Poland, a prolific and controversial writer of poetry, prose, and drama. Despite his publication of several volumes of underground poetry during the Martial Law era and afterward—including *Wiersze (Poems)*, in which "A Scene by the Fire" appeared—he has continued to be dismissed in some circles for his previous collaboration with the government.

## STANISŁAW ESDEN-TEMPSKI

Stanisław Esden-Tempski (b. 1952 in Gdańsk) began his university studies quite late—after working as a plumber, lab technician and Pepsi-Cola plant foreman. His first full collection of poems, *Wytrwale rozwijam swe złe sklonności* (*Perversely I Develop All Bad Tendencies*, 1978), received the first-place award for first book at the Warsaw Poetry Festival in 1979. His other books include the novella *Człowiek, który udawał psa* (*The Man Who Acted Like a Dog*, 1980) and *Szmaciane lata* (*The Raggedy Years*, 1985). He also published an underground chapbook in 1984, entitled *Organy Rosji pracują nocą* (*The Organs of Russia Work through the Night*), about his culture shock in returning to his mother's Belorussian village.

## JERZY GORZAŃSKI

Jerzy Gorzański (b. 1938) is a poet whose books include *Próba z przestrzenią* (*Experiment with Space*, 1963), *Czynnosci* (*Functions*, 1967), *Kontrabanda* (Contraband, 1973), *Małpi Zamek* (*Monkey Lock*, 1975), and *Młode lata bezsenności* (*The Early Years of Sleeplessness*, 1977).

## ZBIGNIEW HERBERT

Zbigniew Herbert (b. 1924 in Lvov) published his first poems in the underground press during the Nazi Occupation and also fought in the

Polish Home Army resistance movement. His books include *Struna światła* (*A String of Light*, 1956), *Hermes, pieś i gwiazda* (*Hermes, a Dog, and a Star*, 1957), *Studium przedmiotu* (*The Study of an Object*, 1961) and *Pan Cogito* (*Mr. Cogito*, 1974), together with a book of literary essays, *Barbarzyńca w ogrodzie* (*The Barbarian in the Garden*, 1962). Increasingly alienated from official literary publishing in Poland, during the eighties he was printed almost solely in the underground press or abroad, including his *Raport z oblężonego miasta* (*Report from the Besieged City*, Instytut Literacki, Paris, 1983). Widely translated into English as well as other languages, he is recognized as a poet equal to the stature of Nobel Laureate Czesław Miłosz. Ecco Press has published *Report from the Besieged City* in English (1983) and is scheduled to offer his collection of essays and "apocrypha" on the Golden Age of Holland, *Still Life With Bridle*.

## RYSZARD HOLZER

Ryszard Holzer (b. 1955 in Warsaw) is the editor for a former underground news magazine that has gone "above ground," *Przegląd wiadomości agencyjnych* (*News Agency Review*). His books of poetry include the officially appearing *Życioris* (*Life History*, 1982) as well as the underground *Kilkanaście wierszy* (*Ten or Twenty Poems*, 1984) and *Powrót barbarzyńców* (*The Return of the Barbarians*), published in the late 1980s. He is also the author of a collection of short stories, *Twarze* (*Faces*), published in the underground in 1986, and a book of stories for children. In the spring of 1987, he traveled to the U.S. on a Kościuszko Foundation fellowship.

## TOMASZ JASTRUN

Tomasz Jastrun (b. 1950 in Warsaw) is the son of another major Polish poet Mieczysław Jastrun. The winner of the 1981 Polish PEN Club's Robert Graves Award for his book of poetry *Promienie błędnego koła* (*Pulsations from a Vicious Circle*), Jastrun was scheduled to be arrested at the beginning of Martial Law for his activities as a Solidarity journalist. Not at home when the police came for him, he went into hiding where he wrote most of the poems for his first underground book of poetry, *Na skrzyżowaniu Azji i Europy* (*On the Crossroads of Asia and Europe*, 1982). Finally apprehended in October 1982, he spent two months in detention in the Białołęka Prison Camp, where he wrote the poems for *Biała łąka, dziennik poetycki* (*The White Meadow Prison Diary*, 1983), several of which appear here. In April 1983, he received the cultural prize "S" from Underground Solidarity. Afterwards he published several more books of poetry and essays both openly and covertly and was an editor for *Res Publica*, the new independent Polish cultural journal organized in the late 1980s. In the post-communist Poland,

Jastrun has been named cultural attaché to the Polish Embassy in Stockholm.

## WIESŁAW KAZANECKI

Wiesław Kazanecki (b. 1939 in Białystok) is a poet whose books include *Kamień na kamieniu* (*Stone upon Stone*, 1964), *Portret z nagonką* (*Portrait with Closing Trap*, 1969), and *Pejzaże sumienne* (*Scrupulous Landscapes*, 1974)

## KRZYSZTOF KARASEK

Krzysztof Karasek (b. 1937 in Warsaw) became a poetry editor during the 1980s for the official literary journal *Literatura* (*Literature*). From 1967 to 1971, he was an editor for the journal *Orientacja* (*Orientations*). His books include *Godzina jastrzębi* (*Hour of the Hawk*, 1970), *Drozd i inne wiersze* (*The Thrush and Other Poems*, 1972) and *Prywatna historia ludzkości* (*A Private History of Humanity*, 1972–76), the latter of which caused him to be classified at times with the New Wave poets.

## RYSZARD KRYNICKI

Ryszard Krynicki (b. in 1943 in Sank Valentin, Austria) is a prominent poet of the New Wave generation whose work deserves more attention in English translation. Only his first two books, *Akt urodzenia* (*Birth Certificate*, 1969) and *Organizm zbiorowy* (*Collective Organism*, 1975), appeared in the official press, the latter already heavily censored, and his subsquent works appeared only in the underground press: *Nasze życie rośnie* (*Our Life Grows*, 1978), *Niewiele więcej* (*Not Much More*, 1980) and *Jeżeli w jakimś kraju* (*If in Some Country*, 1983). He also was the editor for *Zapis*, Poland's first underground literary journal in Poland, which existed from 1976 to 1981. In 1985, Mr. Cogito Press published a chapbook of Krynicki's poems in English translation, *Citizen R. K. Does Not Live.*

## MIRA KUŚ

Mira Kuś (b. 1948 in Gorlice), a physicist by education, currently lives in Kraków with her son. Her first book of poetry was *Gdzieś jest ta oaza* (*That Oasis Is around Here Somewhere*), published in 1981. A second book, *Natura daje mi tajemme znaki* (*Nature Sends Me Mysterious Signs*), came out in 1989. In the United States, translations of her work appear in *Crosscurrents*, *Artful Dodge*, and *Hawaii Review.*

## KRYSTYNA LARS

Krystyna Lars (b. in 1950 in Ełk) has been a recipient of the prestigious Sęp-Szarpiński Award for Younger Polish Poets and is also the author of three books of poetry, including *Chirugia mistyczna (Mystical Surgery)* and *Kraina pamiętek (The Land of Souvenirs)*, from which the prose-poem cycles included here were taken. She lives in Gdańsk.

## EWA LIPSKA

Ewa Lipska (b. 1945, in Kraków) is a major voice of the New Wave generation; work is just now beginning to get attention in English translation. Her five collections of poetry published during the late sixties and seventies carried the titles of *Wiersze (Poems)*, *Drugi zbiór wierszy (Second Collection of Poems)*, *Trzeci zbiór wierszy (Third Collection of Poems)*, etc. In 1982 she published *Nie o śmierć tutaj chodzi, lecz o biały kordonek (It's Not a Matter of Death We Have Here, Rather a Small White Thread)*, and her collected poems, *Utwory wybrane*, appeared in 1986.

## BRONISŁAW MAJ

Bronisław Maj (b. in 1953 in Łódź) teaches in the Department of Polish Philology at Jagiełłonian University in Kraków. In 1983 he received the Sęp-Szarpiński Prize for Younger Polish Poets, and in 1984 he was awarded the Kościelski Literary Prize, given each year by the Geneva-based Kościelski Foundation in recognition of outstanding younger Polish writers. His books include the officially printed *Wspólne powietrze (The Air We Share between Us, 1981)*, *Album rodzinny (Family Album, 1986)* published in the underground, and *Zmęczenie (Weariness)*, appearing that same year from the Kraków Catholic publishing house *Znak*. At that same time, *Puls*, a London-based emigré press, also issued an edition of Maj's poetry collected from both his official and underground books. During the eighties, Maj was also the editor and director of *Na Głos (Out Loud)*, a reading series that served as one of the few "legal" literary forums available to the many Polish writers who chose not to belong to the government-controlled Polish Writers Union. Now, *Na Głos* has become a leading literary print journal.

## JAN MARTY

Jan Marty is the pseudonym for Warsaw poet and painter Jarosław Markiewicz, who also was head of the prominent 1980s underground publishing house Przedświt.

## CZESŁAW MIŁOSZ

Czesław Miłosz (b. 1911 in Lithuania), the 1980 Nobel Laureate for Literature, published his first poem in 1930 and his first book in 1933: *Poemat o czasie zastygłym (Poem on Frozen Time)*. He soon forged a reputation as a member of the Catastrophists centered around the literary review *Zagary* *(Glowing Brushwood)*, whose 1930 apocalyptic visions became all too true. During World War II he edited an anthology of anti-Nazi poetry, and his book of poems *Ocalenie (Rescue)* was one of the first books published after the War. Miłosz was a cultural diplomat for People's Poland until 1951, when he sought political asylum in the West, eventually becoming professor of Slavic languages and literatures at the University of California at Berkeley until his retirement. In addition to the Nobel Prize for Literature, he has also received the Prix Littéraire Européen and the Neustadt International Prize. Several volumes of his verse are available for the American reader, including *Bells in Winter, Selected Poems,* and *Separate Notebooks,* all from Ecco Press. His prose available in English includes *The Captive Mind* (Random), *Emperor of the Earth* (University of California Press), *Visions from San Francisco Bay* (Farrar Straus), *Native Realm* (University of California Press), and *The History of Polish Literature* (University of California Press).

## GRZEGORZ MUSIAŁ

Grzegorz Musiał (b. 1952 in Bydgoszcz) has published several books of poetry, including *Przypadkowi świadkowie zdarzeń (Accidental Witnesses to the Events,* 1986), two novels, and has translated Allen Ginsberg's *Howl and Other Poems* (1984) and *Kaddish and Other Poems* (1989). A medical doctor, he is also an editor for *Res Publica,* the first major "private" yet nonunderground cultural journal in 1980s Poland. He has been a Fulbright fellow to the United States for work on an anthology of twentieth century American poets and has also been a member of the International Writers' Workshop at the University of Iowa. He was interned for a short period during Martial Law.

## ANTONI PAWLAK

Antoni Pawlak (b. 1952) was interned for several months during Martial Law because of his satirical reporting on the life of a Polish army conscript, *Książeczka wojskowa (A Little War Book),* published in 1981. His book of underground poems *Zmierzch i grypsy (Dusk and Smuggled Messages)* appeared in 1984. He is currently an editor for the newspaper *Gazeta wyborcza,* which sprang up during the 1989 Polish elections and has since emerged as the country's leading newspaper.

## JAN POLKOWSKI

Jan Polkowski (b. 1953) is thought by many to be the major poet of the post-New Wave generation. Along with a poetry that combines elements of the linguistic poetry of a Białoszewski or Celan with the Romantic and nationalist fervor of a Mickiewicz or Byron, Polkowski's presence on the 1980s Polish literary scene was marked by a total rejection of the official literary world. His books include *Oddychaj głęboko* (*Take a Deep Breath*, 1981), *Ogień* (*Fire*, 1983) and *Drzewa (Trees)*, all published in the underground press, as well as a collected works, *Wiersze (Poems)*, published in London in 1986 by the emigré press Puls. He has also been the editor of the underground journal *Arka*.

## TADEUSZ RÓŻEWICZ

Tadeusz Różewicz (b. 1921), a member of the Home Army resistance movement during the Nazi Occupation, appeared on the Polish literary scene right after the War with such books as *Niepokój* (*Anxiety*, 1947) and *Czerwona rękawiczka* (*The Red Glove*, 1948), both known for their fiercely ironic juxtaposition of the war experience with the background of European humanistic culture. Since then, Różewicz's poetry has continued to draw great attention as has his drama, including *Białe małżeństwo* (White Marriage) and *Kartoteka (The Card Catalogue)*.

## WISŁAWA SZYMBORSKA

Wisława Szymborska (b. 1923), one of the major postwar Polish poets, debuted in 1952 with *Dlatego żyjemy (Why We Live)*. Along with several collected works, her other volumes include *Pytania zadawane sobie* (*Questions Given to Oneself*, 1954), *Wołanie do Yeti* (*Call to the Yeti*, 1957), *Sól* (*Salt,1 1962*), *Sto pociech* (*A Hundred Satisfactions*, 1967), *Wszelki wypadek* (*Any Event*, 1972), *Tarsjusz i inne wiersze* (*Tarseus and Other Poems*, 1976), *Wielka liczba* (*The Big Number*, 1976), and *Ludzie na moście* (*People on the Bridge*, 1986). A booklength collection of her work appears in English in *Quarterly Review of Literature IV*, translated by Grażyna Drabik, Austin Flint, and Sharon Olds.

## ZBIGNIEW ŚMIGIELSKI

Zbigniew Śmigielski (b. 1952) has taught at the University of Wrocław and has published several books of poetry, including *Słowem ptakiem* (*Bird Word*, 1982), where "A Visit to the Department of Miracle-Works" appeared.

## MAREK WAWRZYKIEWICZ

Marek Wawrzykiewicz (b. 1937 in Warsaw) is a poet and theater critic whose books of poetry include *Malowanie na piasku* (*Writing on the Sand*,

1960), *Orzech i nimfa*, (*Walnut and Nymph*, 1963), *Ultima Thule*, 1967, *Jeszcze dalej* (*Further Yet*, 1968), and *Przed sobą* (*In Front of Oneself*), 1973.

## ADAM ZAGAJEWSKI

Adam Zagajewski (b. 1945 in Lvov) is a prominent poet from the New Wave generation. He currently divides his time between Paris and the University of Houston. His books include his first collection of poetry, *Komunikat* (*Communiqué*, 1972), and a volume of critical essays co-authored with poet Julian Kornhauser, *Świat nieprzedstawiony* (*The Undescribed World*, 1974). His most recent works are *Drugi oddech* (*Second Breath*, 1978), *Cienka kreska* (The Thin Line, 1983), *Jechać do Lwowa* (*Going to Lvov*, 1985), and *Płotno* (*Canvas*, 1990). His latest collection in English translation is *Tremor* (Farrar Straus, 1985).

# Polish Poems

### THEY WILL PLACE THERE TELESCREENS
#### Czesław Miłosz

They will place telescreens there and our life
will be appearing from end to end
with everything we have managed to forget, as it seemed, forever,
and with dresses of our time, which would be laughable and piteous
had we not been wearing them because we knew nothing better.
Armageddon of men and women. It is no use to cry; I loved them,
every one seemed to me a child, greedy and in need of caresses.
I liked beaches, swimming pools, and clinics
for there they were the bone of my bone, the flesh of my flesh.
I pitied them and myself, but this will not protect me.
The word and the thought are over, a shifting of a glass,
an averting of one's eyes, fingers unbuttoning a blouse, foolishness,
a cheating gesture, contemplation of clouds,
a convenient dispatch; only that.
And what if they march out, tinkling bells
at their ankles, if slowly they enter the flame
which has taken them as well as me? Bite your (if you have any) fingers
and again look at everything from end to end.

*Berkeley, 1964*

Translated by the author

## THE TREE
### Tadeusz Różewicz

Happy were
the poets of the past.
The world was like a tree
and they like children.

What should I hang
from the branch of a tree
on which
iron rain has fallen?

Happy were
the poets of the past.
Around the tree
they danced like children.

What should I hang
from the branch of a tree
which is scorched to the roots
and will not sing again?

Happy were
the poets of the past.
Beneath oak leaves
they sang like children.

But our tree
creaks in the night
from the weight
of a person despised.

Translated by Karen Karleski

## THE GRASS
### Tadeusz Różewicz

I grow
in the seams of stone in a wall
there, where they are joined,
there, where they meet,
there, where they are vaulted.

There I penetrate—
a blind seed
scattered by the wind.

Patiently, I multiply
in cracks of silence.
I wait for the wall to fall
and return to the earth,

then I will cover
the faces and the names.

*1962*

Translated by Karen Karleski


## INSTINCTIVE SELF-PORTRAIT
### Miron Białoszewski

They stare at me
so I may have face.
Of all familiar faces
I remember mine least.
Sometimes my hands
live quite separately.
Maybe they don't add up to me?
— — —

Where are my borders?
— — —

I am after all coated with
motion and apparent life.
Yet it always
steals inside me
full or empty,
but still a kind of life.
I carry in me
my own indefinite
place.
When I lose it,
it means, I don't exist.
— — —

I don't exist,
therefore I don't doubt.

Translated by Peter Harris and Danuta Łoposzko


## YOUNG FAUSTUS VISITS THE INSTITUTE OF ONCOLOGY AND DOES RESEARCH ON EXPERIENCE
### Jerzy Gorzański

I enter.
The girl is sitting on the bed.
She is bald.
The right side of her face and eye
is marked off with indelible ink—
areas for radiation.
—You've promised, doctor, I'll be fine.—
I don't know what to reply.
The beauty of the past melts away in the nuances of words.
I take a photo of her.
At the door they take the film away.
—Why?—I ask.
—Your illusions are laughable. This sort of contraband . . .
I have already read this somewhere.
I leave.

She's standing at the window.
Through all her lines a cry.
And a whisper:—Faustus . . .

Translated by Peter Harris and Danuta Łoposzko


## HITLER'S FIRST PHOTOGRAPH
### Wisława Szymborska

Who ever is this sweet little baby in his sleeper?
This is tiny Adölfchen, son of the Hitlers!
Maybe he'll grow up to be a lawyer?
Or maybe a tenor in the Viennese Opera?
Whose little handkin is this, whose ear, whose tiny eye, tiny nose?
Whose tummy full of milk it's too early to tell:

maybe a printer's, a surgeon's, a merchant's, a priest's?
Where are these funny little legs going to take him, where?
To the garden, to school, to the office, to the altar maybe
with the mayor's daughter?

Little angel, lambie, crumbcake, tyke,
when a year ago he came into this world,
there were signs in the heavens and on earth:
spring sunshine, geraniums in the windowbox,
hurdygurdy music from the courtyard,
a favorable omen done up in pink tissue,
just before his birth his mother's prophetic dream:
if you see a dove in your sleep—joyful tidings;
if you catch it—a long-awaited guest will arrive.
Knock knock, who's there, it's the pitter of tiny Adolf's heart.

Teething ring, diaper, blankie, rattle,
a baby boy, thank God, and touch wood, healthy,
looks like his parents, like a cat in a cradle,
like children in family albums everywhere.
No, we're not gonna cry, are we?
Look, the man in the black cloth is going to go flash.

The Atelier Klinger, Grabenstrasse, Braunen,
Braunen is a small but proper city,
prosperous shops, friendly neighbors,
the aroma of yeast cake and gray soap—
sway from the howling dogs and the footfalls of destiny.
The history teacher loosens his collar
and yawns over his notebooks.

Translated by Karen Kovacik

## A SCENE BY THE FIRE
### Ernest Bryll

My city frozen into silence. The tanks
stand in the shadows like chunks of coal.
Soldiers so uncertain of what is what
they bend their heads down close to the flame.

They're cold. And there's ice in our throats too.
No one knows if we still speak
the same language any more. The silence wells
as if we were at a wake for the dead.

A small fire with smoke. A man on duty
puts his head in his hands. Do his eyes hurt?
Has he scorched himself? Is he crying?

We don't know. They are standing too far way.

Translated by Daniel Bourne

## A JOURNEY
### Zbigniew Herbert

1

If you set out on a journey let it be long
a wandering that seems to have no aim groping your way blindly
so you learn the roughness of the earth not only with your eyes but by
    touch
so you confront the world with your whole skin

2

Befriend the Greek from Ephesus the Jew from Alexandria
they will lead you through sleeping bazaars
cities of treaties hidden entrances
there on an emerald tablet above an extinguished *athanor*
are swaying Basileos Valens Zosima Geber Filalet
(the gold evaporated wisdom remained)
through a half-open veil of Isis
corridors like mirrors framed by darkness
silent initiations and innocent orgies
through deserted tunnels of myths and religions
you will reach the naked gods without symbols
dead that is immortal in their monsters' shadows

3

When you come to know keep your knowledge silent
learn the world anew like an Ionian philosopher
taste water and fire air and earth
because they will remain when everything passes away
and the journey will remain though no longer yours

4

Then your native land will seem small
a cradle a boat tied to a branch with your mother's hair
when you mention its name no one at the campfire
will know which mountain it lies behind
what kind of trees it bears
when really it needs so little tenderness
repeat the funny sounds of its speech before going to sleep
*ze—czy—sie*
smile at the blind icon before sleep
at burdocks at the brook the brood of chicks
home has gone
there is a cloud over the world

5

Discover the insignificance of speech the royal power of gesture
uselessness of concepts the purity of vowels
with which everything can be expressed sorrow joy rapture anger
but do not hold anger
accept everything

6

What city is this what bay what street river
the rock that grows in the sea does not ask for a name
the earth is like sky
signposts of winds lights high and low
inscriptions crumbled to dust
memories worn by sand rain and grass
names are like music transparent and with no meaning
Kalambaka Orchomenos Kavalla Levadia
the clock stops and from now on hours are black white or blue
they absorb the thought that you lose the lines of your face
when the sky puts a seal on your head

what answer can an eroded inscription give to thistles
give back the empty saddle with no regret
give the air back to another

7

So if it is to be a journey let it be long
a true journey from which you do not return
the repetition of the world elementary journey
conversation with elements question without answer
a pact forced after struggle
                great reconciliation

                                    Translated by John and Bogdana Carpenter

## THE DEATH OF LEV
### Zbigniew Herbert

1

With great bounds
across an immense field
under a sky heavy
with December clouds
Lev flees
from Yasnaya Polana
to the dark woods

behind him a thick
line of hunters

with great bounds
his beard streaming behind
face inspired
by the fires of anger
Lev flees like a lion
to the forest on the horizon

behind him
Lord have mercy

an unrelenting line of beaters
moves ahead
hunters beating for Lev

in front
Sofia Andreyevna
drenched completely
after the morning suicide
she lures him
—Lovochka
in a voice
that could shatter stones

behind her
sons daughters
servants hangers-on
policemen Orthodox priests
bluestockings
moderates anarchists
Christians illiterates
Tolstoyans
Cossacks
and every possible kind of riffraff

old women squeal
peasants bellow

hello

2

the finale
at the small station of Astapovo
a wooden knocker
near the railway

a merciful train worker
put Lev in bed

now he is safe

above the small station
the lights of history go on

Lev closes his eyes
no longer curious about the world

only the bold
priest Pimen
who has vowed
he will drag Lev's soul
to paradise
bends over him
and shouting above
the hoarse breathing
the terrible noises of the chest
slyly asks
—And what now
—I must run away
says Lev
and repeats once more
—I must run away

—Where to—asks Pimen
—Where to O Christian soul

Lev fell silent
he hid in eternal shadow
eternal silence

no one understood the prophecy
as if the words of Scripture were not known

"nation shall rise against nation
and kingdom against kingdom
some shall fall by the sword
and others be chased into slavery
among all the nations
for these will be days of vengeance
so all that is written
will be fulfilled"
so arrives the time

of abandoning homes
of wandering in jungles
of frantic sea voyages
circlings in the darkness
crawling in dust

the time of the hunted

the time of the Great Beast

Translated by John and Bogdana Carpenter
(Reprinted by permission; © John and Bogdana
Carpenter. Originally in *The New Yorker.*)

## HOW WE WERE INTRODUCED
### Zbigniew Herbert

—for perfidious protectors

I was playing in the street
no one paid any attention to me
as I made forms out of sand
mumbling Rimbaud under my breath

once an elderly gentleman overheard it
—little boy you are a poet
just now we are organizing
a grass-roots literary movement

he stroked my dirty head
gave me a large lollypop
and even bought clothes
in the protective coloring of youth

I didn't have such a splendid suit
since first communion
short trousers and a wide
sailor's collar

black patent leather shoes with a buckle
white knee-high socks
the elderly gentleman took me by the hand
and led the way to the ball

other boys were there
also in short trousers
carefully shaven
shuffling their feet

—well boys now it's time to play
why are you standing in the corners
asked the elderly gentlemen
—make a circle holding hands

but we didn't want tag
or blind man's buff
we had enough of the elderly gentlemen
we were very hungry

so we were promptly seated
around a large table
given lemonade
and pieces of cake

now disguised as adults
with deep voices
the boys got up they praised us
or slapped us on the hands

we didn't hear anything
we didn't feel anything
staring with great eyes
at the piece of cake
which kept melting
in our hot hands
and this sweet taste the first in our lives
disappeared inside our dark sleeves

Translated by John and Bogdana Carpenter

## AFTER GLORIA WAS GONE
### Stanisław Barańczak

After several hours' showing off, the hurricane figured out
that it makes no sense to perform on three channels at once
as a whistling background for interviews with a local mayor
from another disaster area, disrupted by dog-food commercials,
and, at the same time, to put on a live show in our street.
So much work for nothing? Behind our windowpane, crossed aslant
with tape, we waited for the wind to get disheartened,
to go on strike, to leave for the north, toward New Hampshire.
The door opens to the smell of ozone, wet leaves, and safe adventure.
We stop by the knocked-down maple tree that snapped the electric line
while falling across the street in front of Mrs. Aaron's house.
Tapping her cane and still looking not that old,
almost like the time when, because she was blond,
the nuns were willing to hide her, Mrs. Aaron walks around and
    calculates
the repair costs. On the nearby sidewalk, Mr. Vitulaitis
examines the tree trunk thoughtfully, volunteers his help
and electric saw for tomorrow, those years of practice in the taiga
will come in handy, he jokes. Crushing sticks that lie on the asphalt,
here comes the pickup truck of the new neighbor, what's his name,
is it Nhu or Ngu, who brakes close to the tree and gets out,
surely without recalling the moment when, on the twenty-ninth day,
their overcrowded boat was found by the Norwegian freighter.
In something like a picnic mood, we all share comments and jokes
about the disaster. After all, it wasn't so fierce
as the forecasts had warned, no big deal, no big scars;
the harm it did to us is a reparable one, and tomorrow,
first thing in the morning, there'll be another expert visit
from the electrician, the sunrise, the insurance inspector.
It's time to go back home, remove the crosses
of tape from our windows, though we can't do the same
to our pasts or futures which have been crossed out
so many times. "The so-called pranks of nature,"
Mrs. Aaron sums up disdainfully, and she adds
that whoever is interested may inspect the devastation—
as far as she's concerned, she's going in to make some coffee.

Translated by the author

## SETTING THE HAND BRAKE
### Stanisław Barańczak

In an empty surburban parking lot, setting the hand brake,
he wonders what it actually was that brought him here
and why on earth he was never able not to succumb
to the cliches of sorrow, familiar to all who practice
the invisible craft of exile. There always will be a homeland
of asphalt under the chilly streetlamps, a homeland of rusty cross-ties
under a pair of rails, which likewise can count on meeting
in infinity only; a homeland that comes along and apart,
that rushes forward with him in the canyons of floorboard cracks
and lights in strangers' windows, and his veins, and trajectories
of galactic explosion. What is it that still holds him here,
pins him down, encloses him in the circumference
of this and not another skin, planet, suburban parking lot.
And whence this arrogated, arrogant right to exile,
as if it weren't true that no one will fall asleep tonight
on his own Earth. There will be a homeland somewhere: an
    involuntarily chosen
second of awakening in motion, in the middle of a breathless whisper
a comma placed by chance, by mistake, for the time being, forever.

Translated by the author

## IN MAY
### Adam Zagajewski

As I walked into the forest
at dawn in May,
I asked where are you,
souls of the dead.
Where are you, the young ones
who are missing, where are you,
the entirely transformed?
Great silence reigned in the forest
and I heard the green leaves dream,
I heard the dream of the bark,
from which boats, ships and sails will be formed.
Then the birds slowly joined in,
gold-finches, thrushes and blackbirds
hidden in the balconies of branches;

each spoke differently in his own voice,
requesting nothing,
with no bitterness or regret.
And then I realized that you are inside singing,
as unseizable as music,
as impartial as musical notes,
as far from us
as we are from ourselves.

Translated by Karen Karleski

## POEMS ON POLAND
Adam Zagajewski

I read poems on Poland written
by foreign poets. Germans and Russians
not only have guns, but also
ink, pens, a little heart and a lot
of imagination. Poland in their poems
resembles a reckless unicorn feeding
on wool tapestries, it is
beautiful, weak and imprudent.
I don't know what the mechanism
of illusion is based on, but
even I, a sober reader, am enchanted
by that legendary, defenseless country,
on which black eagles feed, hungry
emperors, the Third Reich and the Third Rome.

Translated by Karen Karleski

## THERE ARE WORDS
Ryszard Krynicki

There are words, which spreading in our mouths
thirst only for our blood

Translated by Bogusław Rostworowski

## TONGUE; THIS WILD MEAT
Ryszard Krynicki

For Zbigniew Herbert and Mr. Cogito

Tongue, that wild meat growing in a wound,
in an open wound of the mouth, the mouth that feeds on
    deceitful truth,
tongue, this bared heart beating outside, this naked edge
that is a defenseless weapon, this gag suffocating
the defeated uprisings of words, this beast day by day tamed
by human teeth, this inhuman thing growing in us and
surpassing us, this beast fed with the poisoned meat of a body,
this red flag which we swallow and spit out with blood, this
divided something that encircles us, this real lie that seduces,

this child that learning the truth, truthfully lies

Translated by Grażyna Drabik

## MUCH SIMPLER
Ryszard Krynicki

Your heart broadcasts and receives signals
from not yet and no longer existing civilizations

your brain is an extinct city of the distant future
grave-looters are building new tombs

your fingerprints circulate in unknown regions
your files were in a fire, recycled, or merely misplaced

your "you" is perplexed by your "I"

"nothing is certain" went down the elevator
at the same time that "everything is possible"
went up the stairs

you'll get used to all this
it's much simpler than it may have seemed

Translated by Frank Kujawinski

# HONEY
## Ewa Lipska

This honey is the product of the empire.
Above the empire
the sun rises.
Blue uniforms swarm.

Fifteen thousand workers
move out
to three thousand flowers.

In the empire, there's a struggle
for the throne. It tumbles down
sting by sting.

The drones distribute placards:
For one kilo of honey
twenty thousand flights.

Those who flee the empire
live alone in patches of clover.
Sometimes they stop in exotic hotels,
light on the sleeves of premiers
or on The Last Supper
in a Milanese monastery.

Sometimes they die
in history textbooks
slammed violently shut.

Sometimes
in a pale jar of honey
in the liquid empire of greed.

Translated by Karen Kovacik

## A COURTESAN CONFESSES
### Ewa Lipska

"Most of all, they fear light," she says,
fastening a black garter. "They fear the people,"
(she opens a cigarette case) "and their own associates."
She props a leg on the side-rail of the bed:
"They're paranoid. They peer behind the curtains.
They invite me to parachute jumps,
for bulletproof cocktails in secluded bars.
When there's an emergency, they summon.
I have a bunch of mementos.
Photos. Awards. Clippings.
That one on the left is dead. They shot him.
Officially I run a wedding gown rental.
These dresses survived many revolutions,
witnessed many reversals of love.
In some, you can still hear the flutter
of hearts. Cages of white frills,"
—she keeps saying, touching up the rouge on one cheek.
"Over the years, they lose their sheen
and sag around the shoulders." She lights
a cigarette. "To amuse me, a certain general
once ate all the insignia off his uniform
and remained till morning.
We appreciate such clients
in these indifferent times
when the sight of a black swan
is a bad omen."

Translated by Karen Kovacik

## FROM A LETTER OF BERTOLT BRECHT TO HIS SON
### Krzysztof Karasek

When is the word blood not present in a poem?
The word blood is absent from poetry when blood is suspended in
the air. When it turns into rain. When the veins in the burning tin
can of the body can no longer hold it back and it throbs out toward
freedom and the future.

The word blood is absent when real blood is spilled on the streets. At such a moment blood is mentioned only reluctantly. The word blood vanishes from encyclopedias and dictionaries. Textbooks turn pale. Newspapers sicken from anemia. Pages of history disappear under mysterious circumstances. Syntax becomes the object of derision.

The word blood becomes non-aesthetic. Does not respond to the requirements of convention and poetics, of lexicon and grammar. Does not respond to the obvious needs of a language. Meanwhile the guy next door can't tell a flower from a rifle shot. (At such moments it might be said the poppies have bloomed out of season, in the dead of winter. Or, that tomato juice has washed up on the beaches of the port city—because at the end of summer the water from the bay always takes on a reddish color.)

The word blood is absent when those who have spilled blood no longer talk of its price, only the benefits that it will buy.

Learn to sniff out the flecks of blood scattered from page to page of your textbooks of history and grammar, in the cracks between the lines of irregular verse, in the cracks between the words. Learn to read from their presence or non-presence the tracks behind the wheel of history. The crack of a bone breaking, the scream of a tortured sentence, a sentence once filled with the flow of blood.

Translated by Daniel Bourne

## ORPHEUS IN THE DINER
### Krzysztos Karasek

Orpheus in the diner eats his eggs hard-boiled. Eurydice scrubs the floor. Under the wet rag's slap the slopwater moves between the cracks of the linoleum tile. Stream spirals as the cool floor feels the boiling water of Hades.

Eurydice is on her way to the underground. First there is a numbness in her hands and feet, a slight murmur
in her heart. Her knees are puffy. The unseen wrinkles wrap around her body like the tiny threads of a net. With desperate gestures, the captive still tries to protect herself, hunching lower and lower, her backbone bending as the Furies' scouring pads go to work on the back of her thighs.

Eurydice's face grows more and more gray. Gray as a board
pressed flat on the floor of the Mediterranean. Orpheus cracks his
eggs. He follows the bent arc of Eurydice's back around the room.
Meanwhile the universe blinks, trying hard to rethread the needle
with a broken myth. The road which could have ended among the
dark gullies of the body, in a wail of pleasure, the sharp brightness
of pain, ends instead with an exchange of glances. His meaningless
look of sympathy. Her dumb appeal of faith.

Thus they both fall victim to the age-old disease of a myth un-
fulfilled. He finishes his eggs. She slips through the lit doors to the
hell-hole kitchen, from which no champion hand nor secret charm
will ever draw her back. Only the thin threads of myth remain, like
the tatters of an old sheet hung up in the overheated diner, swayed
by the draft blowing in the foyer to hell. Nothing remains of
the first sentence they never managed to utter. Nothing except the
bare thread of a myth. The small change left on the table by
mistake.

In public, Orpheus our contemporary only talks to himself. The
words on his lips smear like the dark grease of breakfast. Eurydice
has had two coat-hanger abortions. As in Berkeley's philosophy, their
hells stretch parallel, simultaneous but separate. Orpheus's hell
begins at home. The room he rents from a dermatologist's widow.
Blind Oedipus pounds and pounds on the door. Meanwhile at
Eurydice's, crazy Niobe is once again wailing about the loss of her
children, her face a red, swollen bowl. Ancient tragedy just can't
handle the strain. Myth freezes during its exam before the world,
while the world gets tired of all these sentimental games, wants
to put the failure of the myth behind it.

Could it be better this way? At least Orpheus's body won't be
shredded by the Furies, though his words will never fly off in song,
mounting the dirty wave after wave of the Mediterranean streets.
All he needs is the forgotten sound of his voice. The private tongue
that calls out his death day by day.

Translated by Daniel Bourne

## LITTLE FEARS, BIG FEARS
### Krzysztos Karasek

Sit down, rest yourself, don't move a muscle. Soon they will be
here. The little fears on spider-feet. They will skitter in quickly and
infest everything. They will approach you on their knees. But later,
they will sit on your shoulder and whisper. Such things that your
skin starts to crawl. Your teeth start gritting. Your hair stands up on
your head. No way you can beat them back once they are here.
And then later the big fears come. On the flat feet of geese. They
dance around in a circle, counting each and every hour you have
left, and you will bring the ring of their dancing, and in this
spot you will remain.

                                        Translated by Daniel Bourne


## WHAT IS IT LIKE IN PARADISE?
### Ryszard Holzer

In paradise the chosen sleep on feathery clouds. Sometimes they
dream they've awakened. They find that they're horribly sleepy.
They can't raise their legs. Their heads keep nodding. Their eyelids
burn. Their jaws wrench open as they yawn. Ah, to sleep, sleep,
once again to fall asleep.
They dream they have fallen off to sleep and are dreaming of life.
But this time their mistakes are obvious, easily corrected. Lost
money returns to their wallets. The glassware never shatters.
Unnecessary words are stopped at the border of their tongues.
Ah, to dream, dream, dream through life as if through a movie
with a happy ending.

                                        Translated by Daniel Bourne


## A PRE-CHRISTMAS TOAST
### Marek Bieńkowski

We raised up a toast to the dead
The table before us like a casket
and we the gravediggers
threw on clods of solemn words

Someone grabbed a bottle
an instrument to fortify our voices
and our silence

The crying of my mother shook
the pot before her on the burner
Father still hadn't come home
We knew quite well
that in the city around us
people were dying

Meanwhile a helicopter worked overtime
even casting a glance downward
into the window of my room
We were dressed to go out
but stayed
Like a group of altar boys
celebrating the mystery of our lack of power
we sang over the corpse of our bottle
My father didn't die
He forced his way home through the crowd
smelling of smoke
as if he had been out camping
Fires were kindled
among the trees of the inner city
and around these fires went
the dance of death
That night stars lit the sky
and lit the shoulders of the uniforms
Searchlights with their crisscrossing beams
looked like gold sleeves raised in supplication
the blood host gripped tightly in their hands
And with the first strains of Christmas carols
We draped the tree with chains

O sacred wafer
You take away the sins of the world
Now break apart as we do

Translated by Daniel Bourne

## THE WORD AND THE FLESH
Marek Bieńkowski

I try to find you
at the point where the word struggles
into flesh

Because you were the word
teaching that man consists
of the edge
between one type of love and another
as you yourself became flesh
to prove that even God must live
with the decision
between two types of suffering
two types of fear

I try to find you
at the point where the word struggles
into a full-blown cry
wrenched from the throat
with the glowing tongs of pain

I try to find you
as I sit here alone
at the moment of my own struggle
word into flesh

Translated by Daniel Bourne

## I, PETER
Marek Bieńkowski

From the time of my last denial
there have passed several . . . .
The date I don't exactly recall.

I denied myself
with my thoughts
my speech
and my actions.

Deep in my heart
I wanted truly to be someone else.

For penance I will keep repeating
that I must be courageous.
I will hear my own lips
whispering denial.

Still I will keep trying.
The cock crows every day.


## ICARUS DESCENDING
### Marek Bieńkowski

Before I hit earth
victim of the wind's broken wing
slip into my hand
the heat from your own hand
& thrust in my pocket
a smile from your face
Only this will give me the surety
you were not just something I dreamed

Translated by Daniel Bourne


## THE PAIN
### Marek Wawrzykiewicz

I don't remember that pain. I don't understand it.
I remember it like a book read long ago.
Like a gallery, now closed, which I once visited.

But I know it exists and will return.
As if it had no choice.
As if it could not choose just any passerby.

It will come and take me. One spring morning,
One December evening, in the elevator between floors,
Between two sips of tea, in silence or with screams

I own it, I am faithful to it. Or
it owns me. An intimate
Possession, inseparable from my heart,
My head, my existence.

The streets grow deserted. The forest paths vanish
Into black underbrush. Trains lose light.

The pain arrives. My property,
My identity card and trademark,
Curse and expectation.

So make yourself at home inside me.

Translated by Danuta Łoposzko and Peter Harris


## NO SMOKING
Wiesław Kazanecki

The earth drenched in gasoline.
The continents and oceans drenched in gasoline.
Cities and highways drenched in gasoline.
Government buildings and computers drenched in gasoline.
Human hearts and tanks drenched in gasoline.

Dreams and statistics drenched in gasoline.
Automobile plants and apartments drenched in gasoline.
From the poles to the equator
The world drenched in gasoline.

Insane Alexander the Great.
Insane Julius Caesar.
Insane Karol the Great.

Insane builder of the tower reaching to the feet of God.
Insane builder of the ladder reaching to the lips of God.
Insane ravager who burned the city so the smoke could reach the tears
of God.

Insane viewers in front of the TV screen.
Insane shoppers in front of store windows.
Insane scholars bent over unread books.
Insane pilots at the controls of airplanes.
Insane mechanics in the engine rooms of submarines.
Insane map-gazers staring at flammable rectangles, the world's cities.

Translated by Danuta Łoposzko and Peter Harris

## POEM FOR ALLEN GINSBERG
### Grzegorz Musiał

Allen it's not for you
a thousand year old rabbi in the plush embrace of the armchair
on the third floor on Chłodna Street
under the lamp the grandmothers remember

we talk our lips move
English French you who wrote about your true mensch father
are you the old Jewish woman from the Bronx the old Jewish woman
from Warsaw we drink help yourself to a sandwich the familiar
decor the grit scream fingers scratching the flame
the beautiful green flame holding a gun to your head
O Allen what right do we have to savage youth?

we plunge into dream
I see the Jewish boy in his billed cap
it's only you with your hands raised
the New York gentleman with a little dog
the beautiful athletes rob at night
in Central Park where Naomi died
on one of the moon-swamped meadows we walk
dreaming of bridges and stone towers
hugging the boy in the cap repeating
"someday even you will be a flame";

O Allen Allen poetry
not in everyone dwells the Tasmanian native
the little charcoal nut of earth
thousand year old Svul Awrum from Odessa or Lvov
not everyone's hand like yours
feels for matches on the tablecloth

not every eye is smaller than the other
not everyone recites for hours
the poems of his dead *chasidim*

Kerouac Cassady
the most beautiful fall
it's evening Allen under the cold ghetto rain
we will monitor the bones the stones
pressing our hands together trembling
under the fierce spotlights of the sky

Translated by Richard Chetwynd

## AN EVENING IN VENERATION OF THE WARSAW PACT
### Antoni Pawlak

Warsaw in October 1980 the first days
of Solidarity and we were all sitting
in an empty room the ballads of Karel Kryl
playing on the tape deck and I still don't know
if it was due to atmospheric pressure
or several shots of vodka but in one big
gust of wind Warsaw disappeared and
it was Prague in the declining days of August 1968
Polish tanks formed into a wedge
plowing through Hradec Králové's sleeping little streets
our national disgrace but at least Polish boots
were not the ones squeezing the windpipes of the Czechs

"history repeats itself like a bad joke"
Tomek quoted from a book and I envisioned
pot-bellied tanks on every corner of
Warsaw's Constitution Square but this aroused
sudden pangs of fear in no one instead
a swelling urge that something would happen

and meanwhile our talk was all up in the air
flitting like swallows above the rain-slicked streets
as night advanced without missing a step.

Translated by Daniel Bourne

## VISITATION RIGHTS
### Antoni Pawlak

*to Dorota*

you tell me about the gang
how they drink to my health
to my return
you say that thanks to them
you're not so alone

I know—everyone gets together more
everyone wants to help
with the fears you face everyday
the hopes and joys
they see your new dress
when it is still new

every time you visit me
my friends whom I love so much
are my mortal enemies
they pull themselves
like curtains between our eyes
right now I could swear
I'd like to rip them down.

Translated by Daniel Bourne

## IN THIS CHIMNEY THEY ARE BURNING BOOKS
### Antoni Pawlak

Knowing nothing of this
we raise our frozen fingers
to the warm tiles

Translated by Daniel Bourne

## CHASM
### Tomasz Jastrun

The first day of spring
And life goes on almost normal
The second channel back on radio
And with Frank Sinatra crooning
Life goes on almost normal
There are fewer patrols
And even curfew has its merits
And despite the layers of dialectic
I am still almost always free
While prisoners swarm in their jail cells
Like termites in a chunk of wood
And surely you've heard that in the provinces
Officers are drinking themselves to an early grave
And at a police station in Katowice
They beat somebody up and in Poznań
This guy just got through dying
While next to a wall in the Wujek coal mine
A cross just sprouted its first buds
But nothing strange in that since it's March
A month almost free
And between the words
*Almost* and *free*
Is this chasm
If you want to jump over
Try flying head first

Translated by Daniel Bourne

## PROSE
Tomasz Jastrun

*When they lock me up*
I used to say
*I'm going to write poems*
Well they locked me up
but the words
just won't lie down in a line
Everyone here just talks prose
a few simple hard-headed words
repeated over and over again

Translated by Daniel Bourne

## SILENCE
Tomasz Jastrun

They have already said everything
Polish poets of the nineteenth century
The only thing remaining is the silence
We fill with the content of our stomachs

Translated by Daniel Bourne

## POWER
Tomasz Jastrun

They have no more idea
Than we do
Of the power
That makes us walk unarmed
Into the barrel of their crimes

Translated by Daniel Bourne

## FIRE
Tomasz Jastrun

Ripping sausage from its skin
Krzyś is ruthless
The furnaces burn
In his mill around the clock
But another fire sputters
He wants to get away
Toss himself on
As one more sliver

Translated by Daniel Bourne


## FATHERLAND
Tomasz Jastrun

He has been here a year
His wife a bag of tears
His father dies slowly
His own soldiers
Have shot his brother
Beat his son unconscious
And should a truth flare up
They take care of it
With a shot of phenobarbital

And the fatherland
Has anyone word
From the fatherland

Translated by Daniel Bourne

## A SINGLE DROP
### Tomasz Jastrun

They busted the freedom from our mouths
Just so someday they
Will have a place to lay flowers
So freshly cut
The stems glisten
With a drop of a neighbor's blood.

Translated by Daniel Bourne


## THE CAPTIVE DREAM
### Tomasz Jastrun

And once again before dawn a police search
This time the Czar's gendarmes
I thought the place was clean
But they sling down my Mickiewicz
I yell it's published after World War II
But the two-headed eagles on their shoulders shrug
"time like Siberia has no borders"
only the ring of the telephone scatters them
And they start circling
In the flock of crows above our building

On the line is a friend
*Did you hear*
*They're running people in*
*Get the hell out of your apartment right away*

But where am I to go
On Szucha Street the SS pull fingernails
A block away is the KGB
The 80s slope down like flatlands
Into the depths of God knows what
But this is familiar terrain I've been here before
Where I hide my books in panic
And hide myself the First and Third of May
Yet I always return
Where I tiptoe from room to room
Afraid to turn on the lights

A lit match in my hand until
I find Poland curled in my bed asleep
With the shoelaces removed from its shoes
The crows still circle above the building
And as if to toy with me the crowbar rifle fist
Pauses before knocking on the door

Translated by Daniel Bourne


## A VISIT TO THE DEPARTMENT OF MIRACLE-WORKS
### Zbigniew W. Śmigielski

they seized my long disturbing fingers
my physical resemblance to an angel
and curtly ushered me in through the door

I was surrounded by sterilized hands and fingers
busy peeling every layer of my identity
they unswaddled the dummy's bandage
till the last strip of skin slipped away
the scissors of the dedicated staff kept snipping
at every landmark on my body

during my operation
they slapped poultice after poultice
on every small crack that sprang up
and spilled on water smelling of fungus

and when they escorted me out to the snow
I looked like a reform school graduate

it sure was cold between my ears

Translated by Daniel Bourne

## A LITTLE BATTLE HYMN
### Jan Marty

Nothing will happen
You stand here near the wall
And I take five steps away
To keep an eye on you
We Poles have to work together
I have a gun and you have a back.

Translated by Daniel Bourne

## AMONG US, THE UNCLEAN
### Jan Polkowski

At the table they play cards. An old man, skinny,
and a young man with a beard. The third
lies on a bed, reading. Dark window,
low hum of talk, it is peaceful.
From a photo glued to the wall, a young woman
watches the three men, holding in her lap
a small boy. The child watches closely, but still
doesn't recognize his father. Instead he raises up his hand
(the photo in this place is blurred)
as if giving benedictions to the three prisoners
(and to the Jews, the Greeks,
and the world world).

Translated by Daniel Bourne

## BY THE FIRE
### Jan Polkowski

The simplest allegories
depict our even simpler lives.
A story, in which you play the sheep,
the hand, the wine, the sign burned
on the forehead or doorpost of the condemned.
A tale in which by deceit you kill your brother.
Fate and word so equally brief.

Deeds like small branches, words like fire.
Shriek on top of laughter.

Behold both woman and your son.
Kneeling by the fire, begin
to recount the world
in the dialect of extinction.

Translated by Daniel Bourne

## [UNTITLED]
Jan Polkowski

*   *   *

Abiding with us—the fear and laughter,
and the anemic, loveless horizon, tightening
like skin no longer desiring
to carry anyone within.
We will live, sister grass,
like dust standing in sunlight
after the last wall of the house
has collapsed.

Translated by Daniel Bourne

## [UNTITLED]
Bronisław Maj

An afternoon in August. This far away we can hear
the rush of the sunlit Raba. We can see the mountains,
my mother and I. Such clear air.
Each black spruce on Mt. Lubon stands out
as if it grows in our own garden.
Such an overwhelming sight. It surprises my mother
as it does me. I am four years old. I don't know
what it means to be four years old. I'm happy
and I don't know what the word *happy* or *to be* means.
I just know my mother is here with me.
She experiences what I experience. And I know for a fact

that this evening
as with every evening, we will go
for a long walk in the woods. Any moment now
and we will start.

Translated by Daniel Bourne


[UNTITLED]
Bronsław Maj

Rain ourside the window, on the table a glass of tea,
a lamp glowing. Naive, but that's how I see you
in five, twenty, a hundred-twenty years as you read
this poem and think about me, from a generation
or a century ago. You wonder how it was
I lived. My life and times, the bottomless
weariness of people. A few names and dates, a few
fields of defeat, all the magic formulas
repeated with the childlike hope of the living,
lacking the wisdom time has given you
who live after us and everything we know. I have
so little to pass down, so little
just as everyone else. But I know
I lived and I don't want to be completely erased—
to become for you another statistic
for pity or scorn. What I was, what
could have been me and nothing else, remains
on the outside of history. And I can only speak
the language accessible to us both—the smell of rain
settling the dust of the city (yes,
it is raining here, too), the pain in my elbow
cracking the edge of the table, the ticking clock,
the taste of hot tea, and the light, glaring in my eyes,
as I write this poem in the common language
of our five
immortal senses.

Translated by Daniel Bourne

## GDAŃSK IS DEAD
### Stanisław Esden-Tempski

In the jaws of the city my own house rots
between the gaps of broken down walls
oozes the stickiness of bad gums
beyond repair the city touches the tongue of its streets
to the gray clouds at the roof of the mouth
no word makes its way through the lips untouched
the syllables of semi trailer trucks wrench to a stop
braked at the edge of the Motlawksi Canal
the scrape of metal on metal throughout the hospital
ward of Pomerania where the sun ducks in and out of clouds
where they keep the most dangerous obsessions
Gdańsk is not breathing it grips the edge
of its sills crumbling from the sky
with the soot of worn out sea gulls
Gdańsk is dead
its coated tongue my own blind body
my own arms yanked away from my sides like the brightly
colored wings of a letter my own lips
zippered shut on the tracks of a passing streetcar
the screaming postage stamp of the sun searing through my skin
Is this the spring I've been waiting for
its stomach weighted with my body
I can still taste the dead flesh of August
while the freezer meat from June
spoils in the ditches of a private drive

Translated by Daniel Bourne

## TESTAMENT
### Stanisław Esden-Tempski

his rat tongue licks and his tears swell
he doesn't blame you if you hold your nose

doesn't care if the experiment is electrical
he'll twirl in all the drums of the world

only he endures
of all creatures his heart suffers most

inwardly hoards the strength of nuns
who owe their purity to him

he has wandered the basement and in his fur
sleeps the eternal darkness of the Bible

the most wise of all he eats while his food
is as tiny as a seed although

his mouth bleeds and his teeth know agony
like nails in the wooden cross

debauching himself he is our saviour
I believe in him our father and creator of the heavens

Our Lord and God
The Rat

Translated by Daniel Bourne

EXORCIST
Katarzyna Boruń-Jagodzińska

In salacious pictures the color of sepia
black stockings are gartered above the knee,
the torso squeezed by corset till the palms sweat.
In salacious pictures a bronze fog
tightens around languorous thighs and smudged eyelids
with a shadowy promise of pleasure.
The brewed tea is weak.
Boys in uniforms buttoned crooked in haste
gulp the bitter brew. To spite their professors
they still believe in pleasure.
That one in glasses
unclasps his hands and notes in his journal

that the threshold has been crossed—
though it's only a chalky line
drawn on the sidewalk.
At tea time the girls in rose-colored skirts
play hopscotch. During each leap,
in a rustle of lace,
the devil winks.

Translated by Karen Kovacik

## MUSEUM OF THE AUTOMATONS
### Katarzyna Boruń-Jagodzińska

Watch her
dancing alone in a room
crammed with furniture.
The windows blaring light,
the doors under lock.
She wakes up earlier than she has to
to atone for her sins.
Once again her body
tenses for the show:
gorillas dance in her veins,
a cat arches in the crook of her arm,
raising her knee she feeds a snake
from her bare hand.
Warm dew collects on her lips
as she flashes you a smile.
But don't get too close
in this world of windup toys.
Undo the top two buttons at her throat
and the metallic scent of her breasts will engulf you.
You will die from the bite
of her poisoning springs.

Translated by Karen Kovacik

[UNTITLED]
Mira Kuś

\* \* \*

In the kitchen it's quiet.
The moon flickers over
the glasses in the credenza.
I creep in on tiptoe,
in my nightshirt, in my bare feet.
But nothing doing.
—Someday for sure I'll catch prose
on its way into poetry.

Translated by Karen Kovacik


[UNTITLED]
Mira Kuś

\* \* \*

This bald little chickie
opens a blue eye—
oh, cuz he smells milky

and milky
ah, milky—is his whole world
this big wide river
filled with milky

far far
on the opposite bank
the first sprouts
of a mustache

Translated by Karen Kovacik

## SEVEN SCENES FROM THE LIFE OF MEN
### Krystyna Lars

**(#1) Kosciuszko**

Over Petersburg comes the wind. The scent of grain. At times the
dawn sky is red and white, at times like the blue of a swordblade, at times
it bursts forth like a burning bush. He is free to take his time, to smoke
and read. The ink in its well ages like black wine. The snow-covered
peaks of Switzerland glisten above the Peter-Paul Fortress. The Neva
River like a looking glass. Just one step. The earth turns slowly, balanced
on the edge of an officer's saber. He is free to take his time, to write.
Beyond the walls, the Winter Palace. It might as well be the Himalayas.
The broken ribbon of the Vistula. The Cossacks outside the window. On
the table a freshly-prepared quill. Blotter, a few pencils, a piece of white
paper nearby. His first words: "It is most obvious that I lost my way."
The messenger—a young man from Bobrujsko—has arrived from the
printer. Puffing on raw tobacco, he waits patiently, in love with his new
job. This is easier, more interesting, than his time with the Russians at
Modlin. Besides, just yesterday he had his first reading lesson.

Heaven opens and the spilled drawers of type fall like snow on the
white steppe.

**(#2) Prince Jozef**

Upon your wounded chest, the red-purple amaranth and gilding
dazzle. A brush smoothes out the swirling river of lost memory. Your
sword, freshly polished, knocked out of your hand, slowly revolves in the
cold air. Its whistling flight across the water will last forever. We listen to
your words. They are so beautiful, so full of truth.

But it is your horse which captures our eyes. His swollen nostrils, his
main breaking out under your white gloves like a black flame, the taut
glistening of his leg muscles. He is so beautiful. But we know that he is
strong as well, that he will swim to the other side.

**(#3) Ordon**

No illusions. In a moment they will strike. Already you can make out
their black helmets. They are coming. Unsuspecting, they are coming.
Their pink necks are cleanly shaven, their hair as yellow as steppe grass.
In their pockets are their mobilization cards. They can already feel the
bullets from their officer's revolver in their backs. They know that if they
are careful, tomorrow they will return to the village. So they are careful.

They quiet the clinking of their medals. They speed up their pace. In a moment they will be here.

You look down at your hands. You see nothing in them of shame, a mother's anger. At hand is the powder. At the rain barrel's bottom, a reflection of the sun's bald head. An ant creeps up your sleeve. It climbs to your soldier's stripes, to the insignia "for you as well as for us." The ant still has a few seconds to live. The phosphorous match does not want to light. Your only thought: will you succeed?

Then the earth changes into a white shudder. Then you watch it turn black. From the kicked-up cloud looms your mother's face. Naples and gray Vesuvius. The small village near Borodino. The red rowan in the birch trees. The crimson.

### (#4) Wallenrod

Paper helmets, plumes of chicken feathers, wooden swords. The Grand Master is a boy who lives on the edge of town. His movements are certain, planned in advance. He never cries, keeps his fingernails black, enforces peace and order. They are ready to march. The army will soon cross the paved bottom of the Niemen. By noon they will have reached Lida and Berlin. Everyone stands at his post. The armored-plates of tinfoil glisten.

Only the role of the Lithuanians remains to be settled. A wooden pike lies on the sidewalk, abandoned by the redhead across the street. There he is sitting against the wall, the sweat from his fingers rubbing off as he turns the pages of a comic book. On its blue-purplish cover, you can see your iron breast. Your hands jut from steel sleeves. The great sword. Your lover Aldona is nowhere in sight. Only a white kerchief hangs from the tower.

Everyone knows that the redhead is the milkman's son, that he has trouble throwing a knife into the black back of a tree.

### (#5) Ark of the Covenant

The bunkers in Marienburg stand gaping, o Wallenrod. The wind kicks up through the burnt towers. Snow falls on the charcoal of stumps. Everyone knows it was Grandfather Frost and not you who did your cohorts in. In the illustrated weeklies we see your picture reproduced. The face of an inept leader (stupidly you pick your battle during winter), the drinking, the self-inflected death by morning. Kerosene, the broken lamp, your beard bursting into flame. The fire spreads to your heavy coat, to the lake of vodka on the table.

We still think our enemy is as stupid as he is strong.

The apprehension of Halban a few days after your accident. He had on him a dirty wad of manuscripts. One cannot deny the poems were lofty. Clumsily written. Maybe it is better no one will read them.

Now Halban works on Black Street. A copyist for the Tsarist police. They keep him busy on the minutes of Traugutt's investigation. He has given up poetry. Only in the evenings will he read a little. For the most part he keeps silent and studies foreign languages.

### (#6) Slowacki

The mirror fogs over. In the depths of the room a glassy shimmer. A clearing filled with snow. The emptiness birched by the whips of shadows. The red couplets of rowan berry.

In the washbowl a damp towel. The flash of the sun on a silver spoon left on the sill. At the bottom of a glass the black sludge of light. The flame gone cold in the crimson fire. The glow of spilled wine thickens.

The city sky flushed with fire. Scarlet. A cry rings out resonant as gold. Wave after wave of swallows erase and rewrite the first light of dawn. The black wreaths of cyprus tap slowly on the window. A vegetable cart in the courtyard. The chopped-off heads. Wet, slippery hands. The setting in of cold and rain.

The luminous body keeps throbbing in its sky-blue bedsheets.

The fever mounts on the forehead of earth.

Page after page the sun puts the sky to the fire.

### (#7) Witkacy

The rain plunges into the deep water of dawn.

Greenery fills the compartment. Its swollen stream like thick strands of hair filled with nightingales and will-o'-the-wisps emptying out of a large mirror. It splashes onto my hands. Beyond the window a great silver lake suddenly opens itself up to view. Like red apples, Cossack heads bob on the glassy surface amidst the metal leaves of sweet flag. The comet's tail glistens.

A heavy pistol pokes out from behind the clouds and bangs out its white corrections on the typescript of night. In the corner by the door to the compartment a black overcoat rocks without hands. We are already there. The light bursts out purple in the nickel-plating around us. The plush headrest quickly overgrows with slimy moss. Wet print runs down the side of the newspaper. A still burning stub sizzles dead inside the mirror. Giant dew-covered ferns cut through the glass and make their way inside. The sun gushes through the cracks in the forest canopy. The train cars rumble like a bomber in the fog.

A pale razorblade slips from your hands and into the water. The quick reflection. The murky startled fish vanish beneath the night skin. Slanted eyes open and close among the black rocks of the bottom. The cavalry pounds beneath the ice. The steppe rocks in the cold riverbed of darkness. The roar of tunnels.

The blade creeps about the bottom. Gropes through the twisted scarlet weeds. Glistens. Then it approaches my naked feet. The toenails' blue enamel. Near my ankle pulses a pink gash. The upholstery on your seat puckers up like the arched spine of a frightened wave. The throb and quiver. The plunk of coins lost to view.

Steel glistens like a blue shard of mirror. Changes color as it refracts every light from the sky. While above the forest the deep purple dawn rattles its wings above the unsheathed sharp edge of blackness.

### (#8) Irony, Mr Dear Sister

Irony, my dear sister . . . Black ivy crawls the high buildings. Diseased reptiles chase their tails in the elevator shafts. A charred pigeon alights on the windowsill and shakes ash from his feathers. The shadows slowly sag from the walls and onto the cracked pavement. They look like the baggy clothes of an invisible body. Black water scrubs the smelly underbellies of the stopped trams. The town looks deserted.

You are the only one around, walking the rows of shop windows. In the tinted panes you see your wreath of white roses reflected. In each glass sarcophagus there lies a paper casket stuffed with letters. The pages hand each other twigs of laurel. The lines of poetry weave themselves into garlands. They mimic the morning glories that twist through their images. Dry rivers start to gurgle. Someone's voice. Someone's crying.

This then is Fire. The fire which writes its alexandrines of breath on the tips of its own tongues. The perfectly-transparent hand which forges the white shape of each Letter.

Admit, my sister, your perspective has been wrong.

We have no higher calling than to express with our own lives the Written Word.

Translated by Daniel Bourne

---

(NOTES: Tadeusz Kościuszko (1746–1817) is the well-known Polish hero of the American Revolution. In his own country he led several unsuccessful military campaigns aimed at preserving Polish independence from Russia at the end of the eighteenth century. In 1795 he was taken prisoner by the Tsarist forces and incarcerated in the infamous Peter-Paul Fortress in St. Petersburg from December of that year until the end of 1796, when he was released under an amnesty given by the new Tsar. At that time Kościuszko resolved to emigrate. During the rest of his life, he strove through diplomatic means in America, France, Switzerland, and Vienna to improve the deteriorating situation of his homeland. Modlin was the site of a huge Russian military enclave in Poland.

Prince Jozef Poniatowski (1763–1813) was the leader of the Polish Legions fighting with Napoleon against Russia in the Campaign of 1812. Unlike his fellow Austrian and Prussian officers, Marshal Poniatowski did not abandon the French side during its disastrous winter retreat from Moscow. At the Battle of the Nations at Leipzig in the autumn of 1813, he was mortally wounded and while continuing to receive bullet wounds spurred his horse into the Elster River and was lost from view.

In Romantic poet Adam Mickiewicz's verse drama, *Ordon's Redoubt*, Ordon sacrifices his life for the Polish cause by stationing himself with some explosives in a redoubt abandoned by the Polish side. He waits for the Russian troops to occupy the small fort before he detonates the blast. The insignia on Ordon's shoulder refers to a slogan used by the Poles during several rebellions that called for the citizens of Russia to join them in overthrowing the yoke of Tsarist autocracy.

The Grand Master was the title of the leader of the Teutonic Knights, whose presence along the Baltic Coast during the Late Middle Ages (ostensibly to do battle against the Lithuanian and Latvian pagans) plagued Poland and newly-Christianized Lithuania. Konrad Wallenrod, hero of the romantic epic by Adam Mickiewicz, was a Lithuanian, Germanized from birth, who rose to great power in the service of the Grand Master. But, when informed by his Lithuanian tutor of his true identity and heritage, he resolved to work against the Teutonic order as a spy, setting up an ambush of the very army he was to lead and dying in the ensuing battle without anyone realizing his true sympathies. Lida was a fortified city in Lithuania hotly contested between the Teutonic Knights and the Polish-Lithuanian allies.)

Wallenrodism, the scheming for the ruin of an enemy under a mask of loyalty, was a subject of great debate in Poland during the years of partition from 1795–1918. For many people, any conspiracy against the authorities was doomed to failure from the very beginning. But for others, clandestine activities and organizations—and even the ability to read between the lines of the newspaper—became an essential part of Polish life that has continued to this day.

The prose-poem "Ark of the Covenant" combines a nineteenth-century setting with characters stemming from Mickiewicz's *Konrad Wallenrod*. Marienburg was the headquarters for the Teutonic order, while Halban was the Lithuanian poet and tutor who revealed Wallenrod's true background and persuaded him to fight secretly on its behalf. Romuald Traugutt was the leader of the 1863 uprising against the Russians. He headed a shadow Polish government that functioned under the noses of the Tsarist authorities for several months until Traugutt's arrest and execution.

Juliusz Słowacki (1809–49), along with Adam Mickiewicz and Zygmunt Krasiński, was a major poet of the Polish Romantic period. His poetry, which tended toward a mystical vision of Poland as the sufferer and redeemer of all nations, was also filled with a sense of the interconnectedness of all things through metaphor.

Witkacy (Stanisław Ignacy Witkiewicz, 1885–1939), painter, novelist, and dramatist, became, with such plays as *The Shoemakers*, one of the pioneers of the Theater of the Absurd. The themes of his work often involved a catastrophic vision of the coming totalitarian state, while he filled his artistic language with the stresses and metaphorical explosions he saw in the world around him. Fleeing by train towards the east during the Nazi invasion of Poland in September 1939, Witkacy committed suicide upon learning that the Soviets had also invaded. It is rumored that a female companion witnessed his death.

## THOSE WHO COME TO ME IN DREAMS
Krystyna Lars

### Children

On the day the cavalry units stretch through the streets with their drums of triumph, children line the road for hours with eyes dark and shrewd. Carefully they count each piece of artillery, the wagons and field kitchens. The slick cobblestone steams in the rain. Above the Citadel, a red sun floats in mist. The bronze trumpets glisten.

At noon a Cherkes officer passes on a squat, long-haired pony. He is young and full of laughter. He wears a black Hungarian coat covered with brocaded loops and carries a silver-tipped whip. He rummages for a second in the bag strapped to his saddle then throws out little cubes of sugar. The children respond with a flash of teeth as they skillfully snatch the little white pieces crumbling in their hands.

The defeated are no longer visible. Faraway in the peaceful City of the North, they await the convoy to the mines. They are dirty. Their eyes red from the ice and cold. They chew their bread slowly, stare out the guarded doors of the carriage house at the snow-packed road.

In front of a neighboring Orthodox Church lurks a mischievous blond-haired boy. He startles women in flowered babushkas by rearing up a straw man in their faces. They think it is a rebel from the Western Province.

### A Country Gentleman Stands at the Window, September 24, 1863

Always you repeat: not just yet. The time is not yet ripe. Everything so paltry, twisted and unclean.

Where is that longed-for death in a burst of scarlet? The great fiery dahlia that blooms on the earthworks? Let your gesture be suicide, but let it be grand.

Thoughts, but never action. The dahlia frozen in its bud.

Beyond the window, in the darkened yard in front of your verandah, a freezing courier in a dirty frockcoat lights a cigarette in the cup of his

(NOTE: The Citadel, a Warsaw fortress built by the Russians in the wake of the 1830 Uprising to garrison troops in the Polish capital, was paid for by funds the city itself had to raise. Political prisoners were housed in Pavilion 10. The City of the North refers to St. Petersburg. The Catholic Poles and Orthodox Russians have always been divided by religion.)

fingers. He has traveled far. In his bag he has an old shirt, a small fragment of canvas and a short knife. A fistful of printed leaflets.

In a few hours he will die on the muddy road by your pond. Already the ravens hunch on the limbs of the willow trees, morosely count the peasant wagons passing in fog.

Right now he is hungry. No place to sleep.

He waits.

### Emilia Plater

Your hair is pinned up. Hot beads of sweat glisten on your uncovered neck. With closed eyes you lie in the porcelain bathtub. You shiver. Purple dahlias like the color of dark blood in the vase in the window. The clouds pink from the blood red windrose.

A delicate light seeps into the interior. The wings of doves beat on the milky windowpane. You hear the light brush of their feathers. You close your eyes even tighter. In the depths of the room, on a white chair by the window, hangs your black dress. Its hands are constantly in motion, but it sleeps. You won't turn to look at it, for you know it is faking.

Underneath the mirror, an iron ring lies next to a cross of cyprus.

On the terracotta floortile your discarded sword. A trace of lipstick on its naked blade.

### Rejtan

Don't look at me like that. With the black wound on your chest. The night flares up through the open doors behind you. The ceiling shakes. The pounding trains laden with their human cargo travel through the black coal basins of clouds. The crystal chandeliers jingle. The glow intensifies beyond the window. Haze. The windows drip with the silver afterglow of letters. The whisper of crumbling bones. Flags like giant written messages flow across the dew-heavy grounds of the park. White statues exchange their secret notes of marble. Slowly the town of Grodno flounders. On the dark face of the pond two long thin scars appear. You must get away. . . .

---

(NOTE: In January of 1863 an armed insurrection against the Czar rose up in the Polish lands. The immediate cause was a planned conscription of 30,000 Polish young men into the Russian army. By spring the rebellion spread eastward toward Russia. But, by autumn, after a series of defeats and costly battles, the revolt retreated from the field and took the form of a shadow government that functioned until the capture of its leader Romuald Traugutt in April 1864. All through the uprising the rebels' military cause was severely damaged by factional strife, poor communication, and haphazard logistics.)
(NOTE: Emilia Plater (1806–31) was the "virgin leader" of a partisan band active in eastern Poland during the 1830 uprising. She died in battle.)

At this moment a young woman comes to life in your mirror. Her eyes sharply outlined with pencil. Her green make-up speckled with silver. Her hair pulled back above her ears to a tight ponytail beckons with a golden light.

On her pale temple sits a butterfly. It looks like a small tin ornament with sharp edges. The picture of a large bird almost rubbed from its face.

### Soiree at the Czar's Plenipotentiary

You see his face before you, and realize you exaggerated, making of him a fiend in the grip of other devils. He is weary. The soiled cuffs of his white shirt. The dandruff on his white collar.

On the table before you, beside the champagne and pink roasted slabs of wild boars, lies the great sin of your youth: a dog-earned copy of reckless poems. They once stirred the hearts of Lithuanian students and chambermaids. Your companion smiles at you indulgently. A glass with a few drops of wine balances on the tips of his spread out fingers.

You have decided to stay. The Niemen rolls undisturbed by the foot of the palace. Clover sways in the warm breeze. Cries of merchants and women hawking vegetables waft from the city. In Paris the rent for an attic apartment has gone up again, the price for anything has gone up. Nothing else is new. The same old quarrels, stupidity and filth. You look out the window. Above Castle Heights the sun with the Czar's emblem etched into its face. You have learned to hold your tongue.

You know your task is a great one, devoid of the easy pathos that attracts minds unsettled and shallow. A friend of yours just finished his epic on the planting of peas. You are at ease, confident you can write it better.

At home your shredded manuscript about an over-sensitive youth with a weakness for thunderbolts, priests and symbolic numbers. It lies in tatters on your mahogany desk. Beside it a white page and fresh-sharpened quill.

---

(NOTE: Tadeusz Rejtan (1746–80), a representative from Grodno on the eastern frontier to the Parliament of 1773, protested the governing body's acquiescence to the first partition of Poland. The scene, made familiar to every Polish child by a frequently reproduced painting by Jan Matejko, shows Rejtan lying on the floor in front of the meeting-chamber doors. He exposes his breast and calls for the other members to kill him with a sword rather than murder Poland through the words of the treaty. Rejtan later died insane.)

(NOTE: In 1823, the Czar's authorities, headed by one Count Novosiltov, clamped down on the various secret societies, including school organizations, flourishing in Polish Lithuania. It was through this police action that Adam Mickiewicz, the twenty-four year old author of *Ballads and Romances* (1822), a book of poems that heralded the beginning of the Romantic Period in Poland, was sent into exile to Moscow. Other Lithuanian schoolboys were not so lucky, convoyed to Siberia or the Russian army. After several years of a fairly easy life as a school teacher in Russia, in 1829 Mickiewicz left the Empire for permanent exile in the West. In Mickiewicz's

## The Military Governor Contemplates the Statue of Adam M.

Buttoned waistcoat and combed hair. Not a wrinkle in his pants. His face tranquil, yet fraught with concentration, the burden of reason and responsibility. A gold gaze, but not brazen. No carved angels or classical poets. No scrolls with goosequills or unclothed symbolic ladies. Any palm leaves would be a waste of stone.

The pedestal done in good taste as well. There are ornaments, but none of them too gaudy. Flowerbeds line the wrought-iron fence. No chains to rope them off. The best touch of all are the exuberant floral arrangements hiding allusions to Crimean plant-life.

On the bronze plaque this short note: "Author of the narrative work *Comrade Thaddeus* and a verse drama in several parts, the most-noted of which describes various dreams of the author and expresses his hope for a better morrow."

Any gate in the fence would be a waste of time.

Translated by Daniel Bourne

---

subsequent epic play *Forefathers Eve,* printed in Dresden in 1832, the character Novosiltov reappears as the host of a magnificent debauchery. Afterwards he is carried off by devils.

In Lars's portrait, however, Mickiewicz has not only stayed in Russia, but he has torn up his manuscript of *Forefathers Eve* and joined in the feast at Novosiltov's—whose own portrait is recast into that of a modern day *apparachik*. Mickiewicz in turn has become a party hack. Castle Heights dominates Wilno, the capital city of Lithuania.)

(NOTE: In rather gentile exile in Russia during the early 1820s, the historical Adam Mickiewicz, through the help of acquaintances, wrangled a post in a prep school in the resort city of Odessa. While there he travelled to the Crimea in the company of the chief military commander in southern Russian, General Witt. His travels occasioned the poems entitled *Crimean Sonnets,* which appeared in Moscow in 1826 and were quickly translated into Russian, enjoying great popularity and further entrenching Mickiewicz in favored circles until his unexpected flight to the West in 1829. The inscription on the plaque in memory of Lars's "anti-Mickiewicz" involves an ironic reference both to Mickiewicz's epic poem published in 1834 (*Pan Tadeusz;* or, *Count Thaddeus*) and to the third part of *Forefathers' Eve,* published in Dresden in 1832. Both of these works were strongly anti-Russian in character, and their publication burned any bridge that might still have connected Mickiewicz with the Czarist regime. In Lars's piece though, the contents of these books are most certainly innocuous. Their author has stayed within the bounds of Mother Russia, becoming institutionalized just as the real Mickiewicz was appropriated by Socialist hagiography in Poland's postwar period.)

# Romania, compiled by Stavros Deligiorgis

## Poets of Romania
## by Stavros Deligiorgis

An appalling fact emerges from even the most superficial reading of the present gathering, namely, the number of Romanian poets who died within the last decade—and not all of hoary old age. Indeed, it is to them that this entire section ought to be dedicated, in remembrance of their grace in life and in death.

In a sense, all of Romania's poets and artists have good reasons—to this day—to see themselves as martyrs, victims, and dissidents under the policies and practices of their country. Yet an examination of the background against which much of the poetry was written must take into account the sizable numbers of writers who first toyed with the promises of the communist utopia and then found themselves summarily coopted into the service of the state, the purveyor of ideology, instead of the other way round, as they had hoped it would be. For every benefit at the hand of the centralized system (generous print runs, cheap editions, the security of government supervised writers' unions, etc.) a price was paid. At no point during the Ceauşescu years did the official organs of the writers' unions ever fail to devote a good 25 percent of the space in each issue to propaganda or lack the writers to fill it. The sanctimonious, sycophantic slaver of the literature-and-culture magazines was not just the reinforcement of the jargon and the authority of the masters, it was the outright source of it. Perversely, it looks as if there was a price even for bowing and scraping, and the price took the form of censorship and the ever-present commissars in every publishing house and in every apartment building.

In many respects, the poets in this anthology are men and women who often chose not to create rather than lose their self-respect, and who often silenced themselves rather than suit themselves to opportunities constantly waved before them. They fought alignment with the mindless state, but they also fostered the new voices that would learn how to stand up to it from their first tottering steps. The present generation may receive considerable satisfaction at the thought that the new artists coming to the fore will not need to repeat their elders' history, who, at some point in their early careers, had to prostitute their talent in order to get underway, by publishing partriotic or "philosophical" bilge.

A measure of the diversity and quality in the anthologized poets' work coupled with their public stance during the Ceauşescu years has determined their inclusion in the present gathering, although it is important to keep in mind that the poets included could be said to have had a more complex relationship to their environment than those excluded. The latter would be prone, during the period of the dictatorship, either to have written allegories of their plight or, often on the same day, paeans to their "socialist" uniqueness. Those represented here understand that to write programmatic poetry is to forget that exploitation and injustice are not exclusively east European traits. Had these poets written "poetry in response" to their circumstances, they would be doing little beyond making use of the same "reformist" language the despots were using, thus blurring the difference between the oppressor and the oppressed.

On a very general level—and if one read, indiscriminately, only texts by the poets included here as well as by the poets who were not—one might find it hard to distinguish between the ones with a conscience and those without. Taken together they would appear to have one pressing agenda, the loving preservation of every nuance of every major European literary movement from symbolism and surrealism to hermeticism and expressionism. It would seem that they are all agreed to serve the republic of letters and to desist from alluding, even obliquely, to the oppression over them. Compliance, then, was the process by which the writers obtained small loans, pensions, and minimal medical care (through the mediation of the writers union, which also shielded them from being redrafted or forced to work in factory assembly lines). But the Romanian writers soon found out that they provided legitimacy to a police state (one in which the secret police governs) with its paranoia and brutality. The writers could offer no opinion on restrictions to travel, universal indoctrination, the requirement of political clearance for access to libraries, harassment for attending a visiting writer's reading, the absence of the foreign press, the appointment of illiterate Education and Culture secretaries, or the unavailability of typewriter ribbons or carbon paper in a country awash in Soviet vodka and Czech beer.

Yet the insistence of the creative community to be there at all costs was so strong—and lasted for so long—that when it found out it was of no genuine use to the cynical state, it could not change itself. Nor could it distance itself from the literary texts it created under these conditions. It is obvious that these texts were part of the conditions.

In all likelihood the poems selected here would not be the ones Romanian readers or Romanian translators into English would select, for they would tend to look for the face of their suffering and betrayal in the texts that were circulating at the time of the crisis. Selection (and translation) would be guided by the projection, and by the wish that outsiders see it also.

It is rather improbable that a Romanian reader of poetry would be drawn to Gellu Naum's piece that, in the course of a few spare paragraphs, brings together Catherine Mahoney (hardly a Romanian name), a dog called Raphael, a second non-Romanian name (Abend), and two English hairdressers! The coda, however, de-insularizes everything by bringing up, quietly, the same two forces that animate the European tradition since the Renaissance, namely history and melancholy.

Romanian anthologists might definitely respond to Ion Caraion's "Logos" and its fulminating "those were strange seasons," which Caraion also, wisely, underlines with when "people rotted alive." The English version has a strong taste of finality in the evenness of the double beats in the three words and the two pauses between them. Just wonderful congruence between two languages that are only indirectly related.

In exactly the same vein, but with a different inflection, Maria Banuş sets out to work with the tones of police interrogations, with the suspicions and hostility towards intellectuals and dreamers. It is the daily nightmare few tourists or journalists ever experience. The accomplishment of her poetry lies less in the chronicle and the speaker's reaction and more in the regime of the terrorized childhood clinging protectively to a photograph album that could stand for all Romania in the imagination of the latter quarter of the twentieth century. The poem may be illustrating also the closing in of the poet who is speaking to herself so as not to lose strength and not to be engulfed.

Not too deeply underneath Ştefan Augustin Doinaş' classical allusions— "Pythia;" "Mycenae"—is the attestation of the bewilderment at the reversal of codes, the perverting, the enfeeblement of identity and of myth the speaker sees around him. Friezes, temples, and chariots are references to the ideals of the classical past, but, lest they degenerate into caricature, also to its utterly problematical aristocracy and the civilizations it created, from oracles and games, to the dusty, democratic agoras.

Ana Blandiana situates the reading—and it is explicitly alluded to in the reading of omens—in the poet's own territory about which few things can be said. It is an agony of too much, or not enough, drought or flooding. Resignation and defeat—not dreaminess—might begin to describe the sickening struggle in "wars begun by others" that Romania finds herself in for such a long time. Blandiana's "Children's Crusade" allows the interpretation that Romania is the original "unconsulted," mangled mother, conceiving a nation of fetuses, "condemned to birth."

Should lyrics of intimacy and not so subtle amatory antagonism have a place in the present anthology? Marin Sorescu's "Moveable Feasts" overhears the playful and arch lovers' interruptions set against eclipses, sea tides, and conflict over personal territory; in other words, a world, in just two poems, from which Aesop, Shakespeare, and Heraclitus have not fled. Should Nina Cassian who, like Sorescu, has written almost every kind of political poem, be represented by a text of erotic, almost mystical promise of initiation to all knowledge and all time? Alcaeus, Ovid, and Dante would earnestly concur.

Smooth, urbane language—conceivably the medium favored by most Romanians—describe both Florin Mugur's persona and its language in the face of ordeals (such as walking on fire) that were designed not to be survived. The terms of endearment, the deliberateness in the organization of Mugur's apostrophe clearly implying that, contrary to a well-known Romanian proverb, the survival was not due to "luck." Deliberateness of a different kind can be found in Ion Mircea's verse, in which Cheops' daughter plans a pyramid that is taller than her father's and, in order to achieve that end, proceeds to sell her body "a cube of stone at a time." The darkest state of the soul is linked to the loftiest in a single proposition; stone upon stone, precept upon precept, Isaiah would have said, is the body unbuilt.

Similar devolutions are in Nicolae Prelipceanu's woods in which Troy—Vergil's, Ronsard's, or Blake's—is still on fire and to which fortunate dead are being added daily. Prelipceanu is not evoking events long past or some beatific fantasy that stands, in effect, for evasion. The elegiac ending on wood for "coffin boards, old homes, and cities for a future Trojan horse" does not leave much room for comfort to the bane of his country and the support that it received from the older modernist artists of the left. Prelipceanu is not—nor is he interested in being known as—a political writer. At this particular time, however, and in the present company of fellow poets, he could not avoid being read also for probity and vision.

Petru Romoşan's railing loses track of cultured proprieties and makes violent transitions between medieval plays on saints' lives (Paphnutius) and contemporary, iconoclastic allusions (Rosa canina). In his addressing Constantine Cavafy on the progress of his Alcibiades poem, Romoşan brings in not only Plato's ideal lover of the wise, but also Thucydides' destroyer of his homeland. In a nonrealist mode, the acclamations to stupidity, combined with the response that the "mountain be with the people always," does not only—narrowly—reverse the injunctions in the Book of Zechariah and the Gospel of Mark towards the removal of mountains, it also casts the manipulated/manipulating populace into a pose of shocking passivity and fatalism.

The rage at the legion of official abuses suffered for a quarter of a century could not fail to surface in the dissociative vocabularies of other young writers as well, such as Daniel Turcea's who overflies "vales, circuses, dice" of words, and wishes for a passage "from the outside to the outside"; or Virgil Mazilescu's, observing the four-thousand-year-old visitant who is "cooped up with officious parrots" returning to the sad site of disaster and creeping oblivion.

Dorin Tudoran, Mircea Dinescu, Ioana Ieronim: writers who have suffered gag orders, house arrest, and personal persecution offer statements covering not just other writers who could not speak for themselves, but also the tormented and the hounded everywhere. They communicate the vehemence of the repressed and the despairing of resistance and integrity.

Mariana Marin, who eerily predicted the December 1989 revolution in a poem of hers written in 1984 (". . . we have all been waiting for the revolution . . . all of us Decembrists . . ."), should have the last word, since in it she epitomizes the simple-mindedness of any expectation of circumstantial and topical reflection in Romania's better poetry: "such a waste . . . the exit from the crisis. What a joke!" Those who felt well grounded in "reflecting" the times are having the ground removed from under their feet. The writing of poetry by numbers is accommodation, and little else. The socialist east's famed support of the arts—the wax-museum arts we should call them—is exploded in just one sentence of Marin's: "Proletarian emperors of the whole world unite, at last; for you then will give the world the most solid dynastic tyrannies, for the mind, for the heart, and for literature."

# About the Poets

## CEZAR BALTAG

Cezar Baltag (b. 1937) studied literature and has worked for various literary journals. *Vis planetar* (*Planetary Dream*, 1964), *Odihna în ţipăt* (*Rest in the Shout*, 1969), and *Unicorn in oglindă* (*Unicorn in the Looking Glass*, 1975) are among his books of poetry. Cezar Baltag has also written criticism and has done numerous translations from English and French into Romanian.

## MARIA BANUŞ

Maria Banuş (b. 1914) studied law and literature and was one of the youngest contributors to the famed avant-garde "newspaper" *Bilete de papagal* under the editorship of Tudor Arghezi. *Ţara fetelor* (*The Land of Young Women*, 1937), *Bucurie* (*Joy*, 1949), *Ţie-ţi vorbesc, America* (*I'm Talking to You, America*, 1955), *Portretul din Fayum* (*The Fayum Portrait*, 1970), and *Oricine şi ceva* (*Anybody or So*, 1972) are among her books of poetry. She has written for the theater and translated Goethe, Pushkin, Rilke, Pablo Neruda, Mayakovsky, and Strindberg, among others.

## ANA BLANDIANA

Ana Blandiana (b. 1942) studied literature and has worked as a librarian as well as an editor. Some of her books of poetry are *Câlciul vulnerabil* (*The*

*Vulnerable Heel,* 1967), *A treia taină* (*The Third Sacrament,* 1970), and *Octombrie, noiembrie, decembrie* (*October, November, December,* 1972). She has also written poetic prose and travelogues.

## CONSTANȚA BUZEA

Constanța Buzea (b. 1941) studied literature and has worked as magazine editor. *De pe pămînt* (*From the Earth,* 1963), *Norii* (*The Clouds,* 1968), and *Coline* (*Hills,* 1970) are some of her collections of poetry. She has written children's literature also.

## ION CARAION

Ion Caraion (1923–86) studied literature and held jobs as a magazine and book editor. *Panopticum,* an early book of his, was confiscated by Nazi authorities in 1943. Other books by Caraion are *Cîntece negre* (*Black Songs,* 1974), *Dimineața nimănui* (*Nobody's Morning,* 1967), *Munții de os* (*Mountains of Bone,* 1972), and *Frunzele din Galaad* (*The Leaves of Gilead,* 1973). He wrote books for children and translated, among others, Defoe, Sherwood Anderson, Marcel Aymé, Dumas the Elder, Saint-Exupéry, Baudelaire, Valéry, Whitman, Emily Dickinson, Sandburg, Edgar Lee Masters, and Ezra Pound.

## NINA CASSIAN

Nina Cassian (b. 1924) first studied the dramatic and visual arts, then music and musical composition. An early poem of hers is entitled "Am fost un poet decadent" ("I was a decadent poet," 1945). An important book of poems is entitled *La scara 1/1* (*On the Scale 1 to 1,* 1947); *Florile patriei* (*The Flowers of Our Homeland,* 1954), *Sîngele* (*The Blood,* 1967), and *Marea conjugare* (*The Great Conjugation,* 1970) are some of her other titles. She has written children's literature and translated Christian Morgenstern and Paul Celan into Romanian

## LEONID DIMOV

Leonid Dimov (1926–87) got his early education in literature, but continued study in the areas of theology, philosophy, and biology. His books of poetry include *Pe malul Stixului* (*On the Shores of the Styx,* 1988), *Carte de vise* (*Book of Dreams,* 1969), *Semne cerești* (*Heavenly Signs,* 1970), *Eleusis* (1972), and *La capăt* (*To the End*, 1974). He translated R. M. Alberes, M. Raymond, A. Belyi, and C. Malaparte.

## MIRCEA DINESCU

Mircea Dinescu (b. 1950) has worked as an employee of the Bucharest Writers Association. He was first published in 1967. *Invocație nimănui* (*Invoking Nobody*, 1971), *Elegii de cînd eram mai tînar* (*Elegies from the Time When I Was Younger*, 1973), and *Proprietarul de poduri* (*The Owner of Bridges*, 1976) are among his works.

## ȘTEFAN AUGUSTIN DOINAȘ

Ștefan Augustin Doinaș (b. 1922) studied letters and philosophy. He taught Romanian in his native village for a number of years. Some of his books of poetry are *Ipostaze* (*Hypostases*, 1968), *Alter ego* (1970), *Ce mi s-a întîmplat cu două cuvinte* (*What Happened to Me in Two Words*, 1972), and *Cai in ploaie* (*Horses in the Rain*, 1974). He has published several collections of essays on contemporary Romanian poetry, as well as translations of Hölderlin, Mallarmé, and Paul Valéry.

## IOANA IERONIM

Ioana Ieronim (b. 1947) has six books of poetry to her credit, one of the earliest being her *Vara timpurie* (*Early Summer*, 1979), followed by *Proiect de mitologie* (*Mythology Project*, 1981), *Cortina* (*Curtain*, 1983), and *Luni dimineața* (*Monday Morning*, 1987), among others. She translates from the French, Swedish, English, and German.

## ILEANA MĂLĂNCIOIU

Ileana Mălăncioiu (b. 1940) studied philosophy and was first published in 1964. *Pasărea tăiată* (*The Butchered Bird*, 1967), *Inima reginei* (*The Queen's Heart*, 1971), and *Ardere de tot* (*Burnt Offering*, 1976) are among her books of poetry.

## MARIANA MARIN

Mariana Marin's (b. 1956) first book of poems was *Un război de o sută de ani* (*A One-Hundred Year War*, 1981). Twelve texts of hers appeared in the anthology *Cinci* (*Five*, 1981); these were the nucleus of her *Atelierele, 1980–*

*84 (The Workshops, 1980–84,* which could only appear in 1990) and *Aripa secretă (The Secret Wing,* 1986).

## VIRGIL MAZILESCU

Virgil Mazilescu (1942–82) studied Romanian language and literature, taught, for a time, in secondary education, and worked as an editor. *Versuri (Verses,* 1968) and *Fragmente din regiunea de odinioară (Fragments from the Late Region,* 1970) are two of his books of poetry.

## ION MIRCEA

Ion Mircea (b. 1947) studied literature and, for a time, worked in a museum. His poetry has appeared under the following titlle: *Istm (Isthmus,* 1971) and *Piramida împădurită (Pyramid Wooded Over,* 1989).

## FLORIN MUGUR

Florin Mugur (1934–91) studied literature and worked as an editor. His first publication was in 1948. Among his works: *Cîntecul lui Philipp Müller (The Song of Philipp Müller,* 1953), *Romantism,* (1956), *Mituri (Myths,* 1967), *Cartea regilor (The Book of Kings,* 1970), and *Carta prinţului (The Book of the Prince,* 1973).

## GELLU NAUM

Gellu Naum (b. 1915) studied literature and philosophy in Romania and in Paris. His earliest publication dates from 1934. *Documentul incendiar (The Incendiary Document,* 1936), *Vasco de Gama* (1940), *Medium* (1945), *Culuarul somnului (The Corridor of Sleep,* 1946), *Athanor,* (1963), *Copacul animal (The Animal Tree,* 1971), *Poetizaţi, poetizaţi . . . (Poeticize, Poeticize . . . ,* 1970), and *Tatăl meu obosit (My Tired Father,* 1972) together with numerous books for children are among his credits. He has adapted Diderot's *Rameau's Nephew* for the theater, and he has also translated Stendhal, Hugo, Kafka, Prevert, René Char, Samuel Beckett, J. Gracq, and Jules Verne.

## NICOLAE PRELIPCEANU

Nicolae Prelipceanu (b. 1942) studied literature and worked as an editor. His poetry titles include *Turnul inclinat (Leaning Tower,* 1967), *Antu* (1968),

*131 iluzii* (*131 Illusions*, 1971), *Arheopterix* (*Archaeopteryx*, 1973), and *Intrebaţi fumul* (*Ask the Smoke*, 1975).

## PETRU ROMOŞAN

Petru Romoşan (b. 1957) has published a gathering of his poems under the title *Rosa canina* (1982).

## MARIN SORESCU

Marin Sorescu (b. 1936) studied literature and has been working as editor and editor-in-chief of a number of publications. His first poem was published in 1957 and his first book, *Singur printre poeţi* (*Alone Among the Poets*), in 1963. Among his other titles mention should be made of *Tinereţea lui Don Quijote* (*Don Quijote's Tender Years*, 1968), *Unghi* (*Angles*, 1970), *Astfel* (*Thus*, 1973), and *Fîntîni în mare* (*Fountains in the Sea*, 1982). He has written novels, plays, criticism, and books for children.

## NICHITA STĂNESCU

Nichita Stănescu (1933–83) studied literature and worked as an editor. His first book of poems was *Sensul iubirii* (*Love's Sense*, 1960). *11 Elegii* (*11 Elegies*, 1966), *Roşu vertical* (*Vertical Red*, 1967), *Necuvintele* (*Non-words*, 1969), and *Operele imperfecte* (*Unfinished Work*, 1978) are only a selection from his books of poetry. He also wrote critical essays and collaborated in the translation of poets from Yugoslavia into Romanian.

## DORIN TUDORAN

Dorin Tudoran (b. 1945) studied Romanian literature and has worked as an editor for several literary journals. Two of his books are entitled *Mic tratat de glorie* (*A Short Treatise on Glory*, 1973) and *Cîntec de trecut Akheronul* (*A Song for the Crossing of Acheron*, 1975).

## DANIEL TURCEA

Daniel Turcea (1945–79) studied architecture and published only two books of poetry: *Entropia* (*Entropy*, 1970) and *Epifania* (*The Epiphany*, 1978).

## GRIGORE VIERU

Grigore Vieru (b. 1935) is a citizen of the former Moldavian Republic of the Soviet Union. Grigore Vieru studied education and was published for the first time in 1957. His poems have been translated in Russian. Ukrainian, Latvian, Lithuanian, and Estonian. *Numele tău* (*Your Name*, 1969), *Un verde ne vede* (*One Green Sees Us*, 1976), *Steaua de vineri* (*Friday's Star*, 1978), and *Izvorul și clipa* (*The Spring and the Moment*, 1981) are among his books of poetry.

A note on the language of Vieru's poems: Since Bessarabia's (Vieru's native region) seizure in the 1940's by the USSR, the use of the Cyrillic script was mandatory on all publications. The Cyrillic look of Vieru's originals is only that. Contrary to USSR official descriptions, the language of the majority of Moldavians is not "Moldavian," but pure, unadulterated Romanian.

# Romanian Poems

### DREAM WITH ONE ANGEL
Maria Banuş

So everything is going according to the rules:
I cross the bridge, leave a copper coin
in the hand of the winged customs guard
as he begins to rifle through my luggage.
What's in this bag?
A book of pictures
What pictures, you've got grey hair.
And he looks at me suspiciously.

I feel terribly cold.

A memory,
an owl flies in
from the earth
and unlocks my chest with its claws.

I bet you anything they'll put me up
with the feeble-minded, those unfit for paradise.
Over the bridge
there is a gas chamber

for the insane and the sick.

I blurt out, It's not what you think,
I have permission,
I can be a child for as long as I like.
I can bathe in the twilight,

in blue gullies of forget-me-nots,
in nightly explosions like rain daggers;
I am free to;
can you hear me,
          I am a writer.

The sarcasm of that angel sizing me up!

What will they pick to take out of me,
out of the picture album?
I hug it closer to my chest as I sweat
and tremble
and wait
on the edge of waking.

Translated by Stavros Deligiorgis


## THE ECLIPSE
Gellu Naum

The old folks were coming from far away
all wrapped in their ragged exhaustion.

Someone would say: they came to see.

When they reached the river the water rose up into the air
and they crossed the dry river bed.

One step away from us they stopped,
took a quiet peaceful breath
and then sat on the ground.

Their backs covering bull's manes.

Translated by Stavros Deligiorgis

## [UNITILED]
### Gellu Naum

A couple of days later Catherine Mahoney dreamed of a man sitting at the table in her room; she described his appearance in such detail that those present identified me as the person dreamed.

May 25 I was in the neighborhood pharmacy and I asked the pharmacist if he still remembered who lived in the building that had burned down thirty-five years earlier. He answered, I remember perfectly.

And he showed me a photograph in which I saw myself with a big black dog called Raphael that I had at the time.

Infantile, adapted, and therefore hostile, I stood there.

The supremacy of the vocation was constant and the pharmacist wore it over pants.

Fear of premeditation made him believe that Abend and I might be one and the same person. Although Abend had married a girl from those same parts.

He wore on the forehead the sign of the others' remorse.

From here on, it was but one step to the miracle.

Anatomy as of two English hairdressers.

Next to him there was also a surgeon specializing in the plague.

They were in possession of a couple of unexceptionable rules (History and Melancholy).

Translated by Stavros Deligiorgis

## PYTHIA
Ștefan Augustin Doinaș

A glib page.
The nearsighted priestess
trying to decipher my writs
dreams of holding
on to the ball of air.
But the letters,
faster than her stained finger,
and just like the black waters
sharing in the moon's unmaking,
pass it around
from hand to hand
behind her back.

Then between the crazed lines,
like bruises on paper,
they laugh at the inverted name
and the point
of this terrorized game on verso.

Translated by Stavros Deligiorgis

## LIMITS
Ștefan Augustin Doinaș

Lion rampant
standing
on the way into the city
          on the way out
       its copy.

I wanted to conquer the agora.
its pavement beat
with chariots and dogma.

I wanted to make love
in slimy sheets.

I initiated
moldy gestures,
I wanted to speak my truths;
they turned away
shrugging.

In the beginning of every poem
        the name;
    at the end
        its pseudonym.

Translated by Starvos Deligiorgis

DELPHI
Ştefan Augustin Doinaş

Starting low with a gulf that can't be seen,
climbing a peak
another gift of vision
from the frontiers of Hellas;
        rising and falling, rising endlessly.


Green in spirit, not in grass
        is this place.

I sit on slabs and chase off the lizzard.
The cool seems like an embodiment of honey.
I feel that I am higher than myself.
The feeling
that I am but a scent in a green nostril
is stronger than the afternoon.

O for ballast stones to fasten to my feet
to redescend to a cool frieze:

I am picked up by the armpits
        by the buzz of a swarm of bees.

Translated by Stavros Deligiorgis

## MYCENAE
### Ştefan Augustin Doinaş

I go through the Gate of Lions
then I see the hawk
regally Archimedically circling
up there
           in its sphere of air.

About its shadow? Imagine the shadow:

A bat on the wall; a net in a tub;
a retching; a rat; a rag;
something that runs, then trembles, and falls;
elongated, at times indented, at times truncated;
passing, and, for a moment, returning:
pausing, and then, again, moving on
itself smelling of carrion, even.

No. The regicide, if it was ever that.
took place up there.
Here, it's just dirty lichens on the cyclopean blocks,
a tiny anthill, a plotting of frogs,
dampness, bugs,
        and worms.

Translated by Stavros Deligiorgis

## CONQUERED TREASURE
### Ion Caraion

Fingers may well keep their eyes open, it is hands
that preserve their memory, only the hands
of the unlikely moment.
Lips and tombs speeding skyward
           open and crying . . .

Right in the middle of the unforeseeable I have known a tree;
    All things born of you have loved you under it
these twenty years.

There is nothing more precious than a people's blood

Translated by Stavros Deligiorgis

## LOGOS
### Ion Caraion

The unhurried ones are coming.
Those who can wait will triumph.
Always is different. To know is to hurt.
Life flows after itself like running water.

You slept on wildflowers, the wind's blood dripping from trees,
And I was thinking of peasant women with gooseberries and soothing
   words.
We are departing from ourselves, from things, mists, and whispers,
for something to make sense, whose scent upsets us so.

I have seen sunrises and sunsets, seen the moon rise and set.
All is one of a kind. Always is different. Birds of paradox sang . . .
And I heard them, I heard them! Women made of fever hallucinating
   on men's chests.
I have known pallor and madness as I have known these arms tired of
   remembering.

Life has followed after itself like running water.
The relics of the moon are asking about us through the haze.
*Those were strange seasons* . . . . People rotted alive.
A mouth bent over to drink water from the night.

And from that moment you have been waiting for the end like a come-
   on.
Harmoniously tired, the summer was at its end.
The Jacobin moon was lifting itself
on the knees of the apocalypse. Nothing blooms more beautifully than
   a corollary:

Birds, water, trees were dear to you,
yet you had no birds, trees, or waters.

Translated by Stavros Deligiorgis

## BAIT
### Nina Cassian

I promise I will make you more alive than you ever were.
For the first time you will see your pores gaping
like fish mouths. You will hear
your blood rushing down pipes;
you will feel the light gliding
on your corneas like the train
of a dress;
for the first time you will feel
the stab of gravity
like a stickler in your heel.
Your shoulder blades will separate under the goad
of wings: I promise
I will make you so alive dust falling
on furniture will deafen you.
Your eyebrows will smart like open wounds.
Your memories will seem to you to begin
with the beginning of the world.

Translated by Stavros Deligiorgis

## SUAVE
### Nina Cassian

hills picking up the moonlight
like huge stone sheep

their sleeping heads
huddling in the hard freeze
and sparkle

the moon then comes to me
sets me up
plasters me up
it smashes my forehead

the moon

Translated by Stavros Deligiorgis

[UNTITLED]

*
* *

Nina Cassian

as the rain turns to snow
I get so scared I will die in my sleep
I spend the night slapping my heart
from one side of my chest
to the other
lest I should fall asleep

to keep my heels and palms awake
I drive my rusty nails deeper
into them
nails of no sainthood

then day comes
I look at the big white
and think that I survived in vain

Translated by Stavros Deligiorgis


## OF THIS WORLD
Leonid Dimov

We are not alone. The flocks of clouds
are lambing. From out the scrubbed floor
feasts are watching us; fluttering over
our left shoulder veils sown from grove
edges stalk on glass panels with Gauss' law,
with Balaam's ass, with piles of planks turning
lemon yellow in the sun, with machines
of grease and rubber also.
Let's leave the soonest
for the fair of the crocks. The acrobats
will be clogging it in the tortoise
night; we will do the whirly-
gigs, then, come morning, we will
carry pans for the fireplace.

Translated by Stavros Deligiorgis

## DESTINY IN THE BAOBAB
### Leonid Dimov

The graphboard city at the end of its wits
lived mostly in movie houses. Its streets
shouldered weights of whispers except
between the hours of seven and eight.
In the square of the celebrated Swabian
name a baobab tree grew as high as heaven
complete with house-sized fruit, taverns,
mother of pearl trains that sped through
the trees past blue depots where we sat,
sappy, looking through our glasses of clear absinth
spinning real-life yarns and laughing
at the fish eyeing us through the panes.
Those were evenings when sad clouds pained
themselves to mirror snarling dogs, chicks
and Swabian doctors made of snow-slabs,
lying by their sick inside the baobab.

Translated by Stavros Deligiorgis

## AFTER THE BATTLE
### Nichita Stănescu

I suffered my temple to lie on a walnut leaf
almost to travel the length of streams on it
toward the melancholy part of the day,
part of dipped flags, sunken boats,
cold dying lakes,
pressing my mouth on bitter bark
almost falling through the roots under the ground.
Like a swimmer of quick motions
pulling ahead in a river of tree sap
and on against an unseen enemy,
I bore my shoulder down on the moist shade
that was trying to flee all the time,
in love with the hare's paw, and after hares,
and away from me into a valley
filled with warriors down on their backs.

Translated by Stavros Deligiorgis

## FOOD STONES
Nichita Stănescu

Comes a beast
grabs a rock to eat;

comes a hound,
and takes a stone in its mouth;

comes a kind of nil,
and eats silt;

finally, I bring my ego
to eat this echo.

Echo of what?
I know not what of echo.

Translated by Stavros Deligiorgis


## FOOT RACE
Florin Mugur

Then men run on bare heels, they jump, they sail over the fire.
The fire grows tall, it flickers, the fire has long fingers.
Someone laughs: a boy just tripped awkwardly in the air
and fell near the fire.
Someone is pushing Valter from behind.
He walks ahead, just like that, towards the fire
and stands staring at it.
Fire, my son, where have you dropped form?
You scatter your seed senselessly into the wind.
What are you doing here in that torn shirt?
In your red hair, your beard a home for dozing gnats?
What are you doing here in your glorious hat,
bloodied plume snapping?

Valter thoughtfully steps onto the burning logs, walks
through the flames, then quietly

leaves.

Translated by Stavros Deligiorgis

## THE CLOUDS
### Florin Mugur

The clouds then, regally, withdraw and there you are, apathy, once more.
Valter is walking this way.
If you don't want to, all you have to do is not look.
He strokes his face and his beard falls off like ashes
               on his fingers.
He is going through the valley among the unseen blasts of the pods
               shooting their moist seed into the dust.
He is heavy, he is made of lead.
The earth would swallow him up were he to lie down.
Buried under old pillows some absurd clocks are ringing out calls.
The kings' tracks are nowhere to be seen.
My taut nerves are like fishing line that caught an ogre.
The chick is picking its way among forks and cauls,
       it drops its mediocre claw on the written word.
The clouds then, regally, withdraw and there you are, apathy, once more.

Translated by Stavros Deligiorgis

## FACING THE HILLS
### Grigore Vieru

How dare I curse the sun?
His rays will fall off.
Or the hills,
their houses will die.

The space I sing in undulates.
My soul, you're so much like
this place,
this spring which sings, hills
sweet wooded spheres.

May the light beam flourish.
May the houses live forever.

Hush, my soul,
it wouldn't be right to shout here;
outside maybe,
and if you called out a holy name,

like Anne's, for instance.

Translated by Stavros Deligiorgis


## YOU BIRD
Grigore Vieru

"I stop before a leaf
To ease its dying by looking at it."

The fall leaves are coming down,
the light cut off by them.

There is a sacred bird
tied to this place, like a tree.

The leaves of autumn
are falling from its song;

as it stops before a leaf
it peers into my soul.

Translated by Stavros Deligiorgis


## MOVEABLE FEASTS
Marin Sorescu

Eclipses are compounding eclipses.
We meet in the dark and think through felt cloth
(felt on the inside of windowpanes). How deep
the reflected angles breathe and swell like tides.
A sea of angles, waves of angles;
this is the image I have of you, nearing the shore.

Here, hold the nailpolish. It's very discreet;
skin hues.

Everything about you is skin hues, which explains
why I can't tell one thing from another. You will take on
anything.
Like my rights, for I too have my rights on you.
As far as I am concerned you might as well leave
your nails undone, although it certainly makes a man
proud to know that a woman is making herself ready
for him, making herself prettier.
getting the street decorations up as they say
for a feast.

All women being the sign of a moveable feast, or
of gardens hanging by one hair, like the sword of Damocles,
some of us observing them, some not, some of us simply
having a limited number of holidays
(Sundays counting as holidays).

With a fine brush has nature drawn you;

that has a Shakespearean ring to it. Let it ring,
I won't answer.

By the time nature's brush got to me it was all
crudded up. For a likeness done in broad strokes
I'm not bad, am I?

It's a pity the world doesn't know you.

You are slippery.

Saying you're sure of yourself you survive.

your words are slippery.

I don't agree.
If there ever was a firm man, that's me.

Why talk in the past tense? We
are in the present, and in the future.

You say present
and I'll say future.

Future.

Translated by Stavros Deligiorgis

## ITALICS OURS
### Marin Sorescu

Everything was made just for our benefit.
It seems we are the ultimate purpose of nature.
We inherit not only the family fortune,
But also the evolution of the species, from the apes onwards,
As well as the divine gene of the animal kingdom.

Shshshsh! No one must know;
We are the very heirs of the
*Entire* universe. (Italics ours).

Those estate taxes are killing us.

Translated by Adam Sorkin and Lidia Vianu

## A QUESTION
### Marin Sorescu

A question which kept worrying
The Greeks:
Is the soul dry,
Or is it a more refined form of water?

Being surrounded by so much sea,
From the beginning they could have supposed it
Dry:
A kind of wax tablet
On which is scratched, in fragmentary and indecipherable signs,
The secret cipher of man.

Translated by Adam Sorkin and Lidia Vianu

## IMAGO IGNOTA
### Cezar Baltag

there was snow inside of him
when he opened the book

Argonaut swimming . . .
Argonaut in his shell . . .
Tyrian purple mollusk . . .
first time in heaven
second time on the asphalt
third
deep inside the earth

the shadow then
understood
the heights angels fall from

Translated by Stavros Deligiorgis


## BEAR'S BLOOD
### Ileana Mălăncioiu

To heal you, Hieronymus, I brought you
bear's blood. I begged you,
whispering, have a taste, it will do you good.
I truly believed
that night you would be healed.

You wouldn't touch the blood.
I felt like forcing it down your throat;
it was thick, it stuck around your lips,
I would wipe it quietly and throw
it away, to bring then one more pitcher of it.

You'd spill it again and would scream my way.
You cannot know, Hieronymous, how bad I felt,
how I wanted that night to be different, even
if your broken bones gathered hastily in one spot,
the bear's blood could not heal or enliven.

Translated by Stavros Deligiorgis

## NOW THERE IS SO MUCH EARTH, ALAS, BETWEEN US
### Ileana Mălăncioiu

Now there is so much earth between us, beloved,
you'd say we were interred at two opposite poles
and have forgotten whether in truth we ate, for
three days and three nights, the same sickening greens.

Let's slowly start burrowing our way
towards the same place again,
though it's unlikely we will recognize each other,
considering the state our graves are in.

And since I believe the earth covering
us from the start so changes us that we are
never quite strangers to the lump
of clay from which we are all derived,

let us advance slowly towards the middle of the earth
and thus get nearer the instant in which
its angel will show himself to us at the same time
as proof that he is no mere make believe.

Translated by Stavros Deligiorgis

## I'M NOT HERE, NEVER WAS
### Constanţa Buzea

I am reminded of the vestments
I meant sometimes to throw
around the trees in winter.

My son's asleep
and his sister quietly paces
over runners so as not to awaken him.

At the other end of the world, I am torn
between the dusk at home
and the midnight all around.

My nightmare
is filled with pure sounds
as distinct as armed feuds.

All in vain.

I am not here, never was.
I am only sick and on this earth
like a twig stuck into a snowman.

Translated by Stavros Deligiorgis

## AFTER SNAKES
### Constanţa Buzea

Of a sudden I can't stand
this man who sicks his pain on me.
Featureless,
a hyena to his own shadow; he is
hunger itself in a stony desert
                where only madmen
barehanded
walk after snakes.

Translated by Stavros Deligiorgis

## IN THE SOUL OF THE LAND
### Ana Blandiana

In the soul of the land
it is forever yesterday.
The same fear
forever
that it will not rain
or that there will be too much rain.
The garden is hanging for dear life
on the mindless flight of the clouds
and on distracted winds.
I open up a grave to read,
as I would the entrails of birds,
what the future holds
for the next one thousand years.

Wars begun by others
          which we are fighting heroically
               mindlessly
silently
our eyes, all this time, on the clouds
on which the earth hangs.

Translated by Stavros Deligiorgis


## AMBER
### Ana Blandiana

All this light in the air,
All this honey in the sky;
All of space seems
An amber ball
In which
Fossil gods
And unfinished angels in the making
Can be glimpsed
Astonishingly exact
And nearly moving.

Translated by Marguerite Dorian


## CHILDREN'S CRUSADE
### Ana Blandiana

A whole nation
As yet unborn
But condemned to birth
In march formation before birth
Fetus next to fetus,
A whole nation
Not hearing, not seeing, not understanding,
But advancing
Through convulsed bodies of women,
Through blood of mothers
Unconsulted.

Translated by Marguerite Dorian

## POINT OF VIEW NR THREE
Virgil Mazilescu

blind as we were in our wanderings we ran into
an old man with a stone tied around his neck the old man

with the stone around his neck in the midst of his family
who knows how the watch on his left leg has been
doing lately well thank you it's working it tells me the century we're in
when I should eat and the moment of truth
when time is come to set out for a defensive war

Translated by Stavros Deligiorgis

## THAT WOMAN ALWAYS KEEPS COMING WHO NOT LONG AGO
Virgil Mazilescu

*your hands give me your hands give me your hands*
(George Seferis)

that woman always keeps coming who not long ago
was cooped up with our officious parrots
most likely in the small swept
and sprinkled court of the country grandparents
little do the petty clerks know
the optician uncle grandparents and neighbors
that she keeps coming back these four thousand years
and coming back next to the sign of an unfortunate
journey the board with the year and the name
of the sunken ship somewhere
close by
who would take an interest or be patient enough
to mumble and recall
nobody

on these sands
ground fine by blind sleepwalking foxes
come with that laughter of yours frantically
crossed by time through and through
and give me your hands give me your hands give me your hands

Translated by Stavros Deligiorgis

## THRICE HAPPY
### Nicolae Prelipceanu

happy those who have no questions
thrice happy people overly crazed overly joyous people
whose voice rings out
without fearing silence
thrice happy men women
thrice happy children
of another age

anyway
    I know a grove
    close to the city and beyond it
    where the circle does not roll
    where the square does not stand up straight
    a grove that shakes quietly
    with no winds blowing
    or maybe with the winds blowing
anyway
I know a grove

sad grove of question marks
wood of hard and bitter matter
that will go in the making of coffin boards
old homes
and cities for a future Trojan horse

Translated by Stavros Deligiorgis

## THE IRONICAL POET
### Nicolae Prelipceanu

The ironical poet stays in the kitchen and does the dishes
from which he has just eaten his ironical bread
it's there that he writes and thinks
the complex smell of the kitchen being nearer
the true smell of the world
it drives him away from roses
the ironical poet descends directly
from the court jesters

or as directly as the next person
from the apes
but nowadays the courts are gone
wherever they still last
the antics are his majesty's perquisite
and now even the apes are gone
they have withdrawn into humans and refuse to come out
it's not the devil that gets into people but an ape
the ironical poet keeps aloof and doesn't meddle
or is not called upon to meddle
people have learned that he isn't OK company
because he spoils their celebrations
five minutes before
they get spoiled all on their own
and the reveler starts wondering
what's so rotten in his Denmark
the ironical poet knows a lot of things about the world
and the world knows but a few things about him
life gentlemen what an irony the clear-sighted exlaims
irony what a life the ironical poet faintly murmurs
don't look for the ironical poet in this world
the ironical poet has withdrawn from it and converses only with himself
alone at home he sadly washes his clothes
have you noticed how ironically the beacons blink in estuaries
the ironical poet dies when he loses
the irony of living
the ironical poet respects his neighbors thinking they are ironical too
the neighbors respect him only as long as
they think he is scowling
he never shouts hooray long live irony
as others shout hooray long live life
the only eternal thing in this world is change
actually meaning that
the only eternal thing in this world is irony
it keeps us all alive
as we forgive those who trespass against us
so we trespass against those who forgive us
the ironical poet never lies in a bed of roses
on the rose proper he spies the only spines
he coins from a Spinoza the plural spy-noses

Translated by Adam Sorkin and Sergiu Celac

## POETRY TO THOSE WHO YES AND THOSE WHO NO
### Dorin Tudoran

whoever wants to hear me
may do nothing better than listen to his blood

whoever wants to see me
can look at the sea till he gets dizzy

whoever wants to touch me
need only walk
barefoot in the snow

whoever does not want to hear me
need only live in fear of himself

whoever does not want to see me
need only spend his nights and days
in the files of the history of sight

whoever does not want to touch me
had better put on gloves of human skin

whoever wants to get the better of me had
better wait until a deadly and transparent
weapon grows in his hand

like an idea

Translated by Stavros Deligiorgis

## SOMETHING WAS YELLOW SOMETHING ELSE WAS PURPLE
### Dorin Tudoran

something was yellow something else was purple
a rocker was there too
two lengths of dried up rope one cuckoo
or three or none extinguished
a barely discovered sun in their mouths
we carried a few words
piled up on the shoulder or in the knee cap
or hanged on to them
that is us or others then

Translated by Stavros Deligiorgis


## WELLSWEEP
### Dorin Tudoran

somebody stole the wellsweep
in its place was my brother
telling us what he saw under the water
then he screamed lighting up above us
and we saw we were covered by snow
(some of us had our stiff chests licked by horses
while my brother had his forehead split
into a long purplish mouth
each finger dripping sounds
like a beechwood flute
we listened to the music falling
drop by drop in the fountain)

Translated by Stavros Deligiorgis


## THE REST
### Dorin Tudoran

talk to me of the laws
of your outlaws I said to her
the mother of all dyspepias in this world
my insides burn and burn

talk to me about
tell me that nothing
really nothing
ever goes beyond
talk to me I implore you
and let me realize that we're talking
not about the sweet bird of youth
but about that infectious disease
of no cure
talk to me still you law of laws
and outlaws just you talk to me
as for the rest I know I have
enough worldly book lore
to know that the rest is silence
talk to me

Translated by Stavros Deligiorgis


## STRAIGHT LINE
Daniel Turcea

trying to use words that describe the action
of the Principle
amounts to dealing not with It but with Its contrary
words are vales circuses
dice

distance
therefore
it is all absorbent because it is
this arrangement of objects under the sign of proportion
of music therefore
derived from the antiquity of the air
trapeze and segments planes and cones of air
like an animal made of void
of the Ceremony of mineral blood where
a prince breathes and sleeps

his dream is the body of this Age
and of the scattered vowels
the Exile

Translated by Stavros Deligiorgis

## ZEN
### Daniel Turcea

my blood throttled into smoother flight
above then waited
for it to break up

down below I can't figure out how soft and cold forms
become one
the main point being one blinding door to burn
the main point being to cross to the other side
from the outside to the outside
through these lichen pores that have loved
they were live and livelier still
the red faded twilight
when they undulated
and the wind
went through the silences of a xylophone and hatred
led down a lazy vale

no other way out
except this only possible unending
in which the logical thing is to wrench yourself
from under the equations of all movement
so you may
thus
live countless
lives

Translated by Stavros Deligiorgis

## OATH OF ALLEGIANCE
### Ioana Ieronim

I swear to tell the truth and nothing but
to name that correspondence
that quality
that value, most candidly,
having thrown open the windows of signs
and seen the view they are connected to
by fine ropes, floating

to tell nothing but the truth
on this day when
there's hardly a whisper of wind
and dragon kites
plummet to the ground

Translated by Adam Sorkin and Sergiu Celac


## CERTAINTY
### Ioana Ieronim

the dodecahedron is the symbol of the World
the pyramid the most stable form

around every object from afar
the eye perceives a sphere of light

mad god: your paradise,
an impression of sugarsweet certainty
and only a shudder—sometimes
a question
with no answer under its wing

—a totally insignificant flicker
of your Savagery

Translated by Adam Sorkin and Sergiu Celac


## ADORATION
### Ion Mircea

I am beheaded and bathed in the same light.
From glittering swamps as far away as the stars
            ancient sleepless peoples sing my praises.
Place your foot upon my head, O my Queen,
this is the muck from beyond the city,
            which is dreaming that it's being carried
            cityward on your shoe soles.

Translated by Adam Sorkin and Liliana Ursu

## THE TRAVELER FROM MELBOURNE
### Ion Mircea

Logic-lilac.
I search for you by zigs and zags, through memory, in this tower.
I hear news from the one I once was who now comes straight to me,
the traveler from Melbourne.

It is night and I contemplate the difference.
Don't scold me for being more silent than both of us.
Your eye is green, your thought is a forest,
I, I am a beach with a mammoth's bones.

Translated by Adam Sorkin and Liliana Ursu

## [UNTITLED]
### Ion Mircea

Dreaming of a pyramid higher than her father's,
Cheops' daughter began to sell her body a cube of stone at a time.
Little by little the tale took the exact shape
of a unicorn in the presence of death.

Translated by Adam Sorkin and Liliana Ursu

## HE
### Ion Mircea

He loved so deeply
that at his death he left behind two bodies

Translated by Adam Sorkin and Liliana Ursu

## METAMORPHOSIS
### Mircea Dinescu

A rose may have no smell any more
but it will grind a pound of flesh
equally well.
Stuck under the tongue of the oceans
it will swim with an oil slick between its teeth.
And just as the latest anatomy
textbooks portray the heart as a tumor
in the contagious time of the twilight,
in exactly the same manner I will ask you
not to kiss me.
My blood is welling up,

cut my veins open instead
so I may breathe.

Translated by Stavros Deligiorgis


## GOAT OF OUR TIMES
### Mircea Dinescu

A goat that eats the roses in the park,
chews on cable cars like on raw carrots;
mornings, it doesn't leave for the office,
it doesn't read evening papers, it
strips telegraph poles like mulberry trees
and shamelessly ignores traffic lights.
It lusts after no luxury car, it
has not entered its patent on artificial grass yet,
though it may know a thing or two about the woods.

The whole city is rocking in a swirl of smoke;
gone, replaced, is the statue from downtown,
yet this one hardheaded goat
keeps giving milk without knowing how.

Translated by Stavros Deligiorgis

## SO?!
Mircea Dinescu

Let me have my own way with a small-town newspaper
and a wooden shack with just a stained sign-board
three days later the cities will reek of vanilla
and free ports.

Translated by Adam Sorkin and Sergiu Celac

## NOT TODAY
Mircea Dinescu

Reeling 'midst the empty glasses
over wine that's never there
I carouse with death—and so time passes
on this day for fast and prayer.

Worms come crawling on the lamp
doornails sizzle, the table thrashes
I breathe the perfume of that vamp
stripped naked of her robe of ashes.

Not today, perhaps tomorrow
(the devil knows what hour's mine)
young by moments snatched from sorrow
old all too soon in time's design.

Translated by Adam Sorkin and Sergiu Celac

## THE TALE OF PAPHNUTIUS
Petru Romoşan

on my way into the fair bearing that woman's name
an unholy name a sleepwalker's name
glory to stupidity I said glory to stupidity
and may the mountain be with you always
my beloved Rozalia Birch Blossom Rosa Canina
had just been delivered
I said to them this child will be named Paphnutius

he will have my dark eyes
one arm shorter than the other and one ear longer
he will be the last real man of the seas
and well may he die at thirty three
my child saying amen the blood half grinning off his face
the geraniums wilted in the windows
but for one small fleshy leaf that still glowed
the women and the children wept
one thousand men and one man turned grey
I took to my heels smiling
they sang glory to stupidity
and
may the mountain be with us always

Translated by Stavros Deligiorgis


## THE GREAT GREEK
### Petru Romoşan

behold the great Greek
cutting the lemon in four equal parts
his green earings shining
the juice dripping down his chin and onto
the white sheet of paper

I am asking you again Constantine P. Cavafy
your Alcibiades poem is it finished yet
has Alcibiades come out mad enough

you know all there is to know about beauty and wisdom
but that Alcibiades of yours

is he mad enough

is he

Translated by Stavros Deligiorgis

## [UNTITLED]
Mariana Marin

Without my friends—the young German poets from Romania—
    subjectivity
would even now be sucking its thumb before reality.

    Poetry would have never understood why
    it was overtaken by the smells of the slaughterhouses
    and the round-the-clock dissecting rooms.

Without them it would have been much harder.

Translated by Stavros Deligiorgis

## [UNTITLED]
Mariana Marin

    The revolution did not start this year either
    But we keep on waiting for it;
        We are, all of us, Decembrists;
        for this December we also lacked snow


    as we lacked everything else.

Translated by Stavros Deligiorgis

## LIKE THE NIGHT, DEATH HAS SET BETWEEN MY BREASTS
Mariana Marin

    Like the night, death has set between my breasts;
    and between you and me, it's being said,
    there will always be a Europe, or a Red Sea.
    The language in which I think the word death
    is not the language in which you think the word love.
    Whatever is separating us today, it's being said,
    will separate us even more tomorrow.
    This is why, with all the darkness of our past
    which we are unrolling like a scroll from ancient Egypt

I am asking that we run away towards the abyss
that has been given us.
Out there, your freckles and red hair
will certainly understand, certainly love
the language of my breasts

between which, like the night, death will be setting even then.

Translated by Stavros Deligiorgis

# Ukraine, Compiled by Larissa M. L. Z. Onyshkevych

## Ukrainian Literature in the 1980s
## by Larissa M. L. Z. Onyshkevych

Modern Ukrainian literature has had a very capricious fate. There were several periods when its sudden downward slides proved fatal to many poets and were almost just as fatal to Ukrainian literature as a whole. Such periods, however, were usually followed by generous growth. After many attempts to eradicate Ukrainian language and literature by foreign rulers in Ukraine, the first major blossoming in this century occurred in the 1920s with Pavlo Tychyna and Mykola Zerov representing it best in poetry. Yet, within a decade, in the central and eastern part of Ukraine (which was absorbed into the USSR), this generation was stifled, taking a toll of several hundred Ukrainian writers; the smothering was accompanied by the famine of 1933 with over 7 million Ukrainian victims. Several writers emigrated to the West, where, together with other Ukrainian poets living and writing in the westernmost part of Ukraine (not part of USSR at the time) or in surrounding countries, they kept Ukrainian literature alive.

World War II, Hitler, and Stalin created the second downward trend. Later, the Soviet "thaw" in the 1960s provided an opportunity for a new generation of writers to emerge in Ukraine. Lina Kostenko, Ivan Drach, Dmytro Pavlychko, Mykola Vinhranovskyi, Vasyl Holoborodko, Vasyl Symonenko, and Vitaliy Korotych came out with strong voices and an unmistakable identity and presence; they were referred to as "writers of the sixties." Yet, again, within a decade, during a new "freeze", many of them were silenced or died (Vasyl Symonenko), while others were barred from literature (Holoborodko). Poets Ihor Kalynets, Iryna Stasiv-Kalynets, and Vasyl Stus spent many years in prisons and harsh exile. By 1972, the continuity and the very existence of Ukrainian literature and culture was threatened again. There were, however, many Ukrainian poets living in the West who served as deputy spokesmen for the common concerns. One such poet, Wira Wowk, living in Brazil, poignantly depicted the situation in Ukraine in the 1970s, in her poem "Litany" (from *Triptych*, 1982):

*Pilgrims:*
cities without friends
villages with no bells
churches without crosses
fields with bitter smell
graves plowed over
banners defaced
icons blinded
ballads dead

candle extinguished
hearth smothered
key rusted
string silenced
song drowned
dance frozen
embroidery faded
fate withered

plead for us
o, eye of the sightless
bread of the hungry
cup of the thirsty
path of the lost
shelter of the homeless
dowery of the deprived
candle of the departed
tear of the innocent
*pysanka* of eternity
vessel of prayers
signet of ancestors
cincture of the faithful
chalice of the word
shore of grace:

o, language of our mothers!

Translated by L. Onyshkevych

While few good poets were able to write and publish in Ukraine, many of those who were in prison (e.g., both the Kalyntsis and Stepan Sapelak) were published in the West. Then in the 1980s, some poets made it back (both the Kalyntsis); others did not. One of the most outstanding Ukrainian

poets of the century, Vasyl Stus, died during his second term of imprisonment. Just as Symonenko's (1935–63) name had become a symbol of
strength and verity in poetry and life two decades earlier, so Stus came to
symbolise the fate of Ukrainian literature during the Brezhnev era.

And then the *glasnost* days rode in on the back of the terrifying after-
effects of the Chornobyl nuclear plant disaster.[1] Paradoxically, the period
of such immense misfortune coincided with a period of many opportunities for literature. As young or new poets felt free to seek their self-expres-
sion, former political prisoners and dissidents began to be tolerated and,
later, reinstated. At first they were being published on the pages of "unofficial" periodicals—and then also in state publications. This was the time
when many of those who had perished in the 1930s were posthumously
rehabilitated, and their works were allowed to be published again. In 1988,
during two months alone, the names of 359 Ukrainian writers were cleared
of charges by the government. Several former political prisoners are now
elected public officials (e.g., both the Kalyntsis).

Since 1986 there are more opportunities to publish daring works. Many
literary manuscripts that were kept hidden for several decades (giving rise
to the term "desk drawer literature") began to appear. Critic and poet,
Mykola Riabchuk observed that when poems and books by such poets as M.
Vorobiov, Viktor Kordun, V. Holoborodko, and others have been published
finally, "We see that this is a matter of a whole generation—of a lost generation; who knows how strong our literature would have been today had these
books appeared at the time that they were written?"[2]

While the poets of the 1960s were often concerned with intellectual,
artistic, and ethical issues, in the 1980s, ethical concerns and ecology (both
biological and cultural) predominated. Chornobyl, the fate of future generations, and the Ukrainian culture (often symbolised by Ukrainian language itself) are now among notable themes and imagery. Since for many
decades Ukrainian poets were not allowed to mention many of the ills that
befell Ukraine in this century (e.g., the 1933 famine), there is now a surge
of expressions of concern for their country. Poets openly protest now that
Ukraine, one of the largest European nations, has been politically manipu-
lated for decades—to the peripheries of cultural life (see N. Bilotserkivets's
poem "Untitled"). In addition to historical allusions, ever since the 1988
commemoration of the millennium of Christianity in Ukraine, religious
imagery has also reappeared in literature.

In the 1990s, numerous styles and trends coexist in Ukrainian poetry.
While several leading poets of the 1960s continue to provide a significant
contribution to literature with such major works as *Marusia Churai* and
*Garden of Unthawed Sculptures* (by Kostenko) or *The Chornobyl Madonna* (by
Drach), new poets assert themselves in their own manner. Some poets still
cling to realism and romanticism, while most of the younger generation
may be said to reflect postmodernistic trends with heavy reliance on inter-

textuality, fragmentation, irony, and scepticism. In contemporary poetry, gone are the stereotyped "role models" of collective farm workers and political leaders, and few contemporary heroic figures and situations are depicted. The average man and his daily problems predominate, but without the stress on conformity and didacticism. The quest for the truth, however, is everpresent, and the protagonists are often seen isolated and contemplative. The uniqueness of time and the present is felt.[3] And Chornobyl, with its multilevelled symbolisms, hovers above all.

In Ukrainian poetry there are now more first-rate poets than ever before. The 1980s have delivered a poetry that is rejuvenated, strong, and thriving,[4] and one that also provides inspiration to Ukrainian poets in the diaspora, living in Poland, Czechoslovakia, Romania, Western Europe, and the New World. This poetry also demonstrates that despite periods which have brought about an almost complete annihilation of Ukrainian literature, each new wave of poets was still able to build on the heritage of their predecessors.

(Note: The selection of translations, regrettably, does not represent all the leading Ukrainian contemporary poets and poems.)

# Notes

1. Mykola Riabchuk, "Chysta krynytsia," *Ukrayina*, 37 (Sept 1988): 11.
2. Since the town of Chornobyl is in Ukraine, the Ukrainian transliteration of the name is used here. For information on Ukrainian literature on Chornobyl, see: Larissa M. L. Zaleska Onyshkevych, "Echoes of Glasnost: Chornobyl in Soviet Ukrainian Literature," in *Echoes of Glasnost*, ed. Romana M. Bahry (North York: Captus Publications, 1989), pp. 151–70, or an abridged version in *Agni*, 29/30 (1990): 279–91.
3. For a review of recent Ukrainian poetry, see: Bohdan Rubchak, "Because We Have No Time: New Poetry in 1988," *Echoes of Glasnost*, pp. 130–50.
4. Ihor Rymaruk, ed., *Poets of the Eighties, An Anthology of New Ukrainian Poetry (in Ukrainian)*, (Edmonton: Canadian Institute of Ukrainian Studies, 1990).

# About the Poets

## NATALKA BILOTSERKIVETS

Natalka Bilotserkivets (b. 1954) is a poet and author of *Ballad of the Unvanquished* (1976), *In the Land of My Heart* (1979), *Underground Fire* (1984), and *November* (1989).

## IVAN DRACH

Ivan Drach (b. 1936) is a leading Ukrainian poet, head of the Ukrainian Writers Union, Member of Parliament of the Ukrainian Supreme Rada, and leader of *Rukh* (a democratic coalition). He is the author of the following books of poetry: *Sunflowers* (1962), *Roots and Crowns* (1964), *Protuberances of the Heart* (1965), *Poems* (1967), *Everyday Ballads* (1967), *To the Source* (1972), *Kievan Sky* (1976), *Duma about a Teacher* (1977), *A Sun Phoenix* (1978), *The Sun and the Word* (1979), *An American Notebook* (1980), *A Sword and a Scarf* (1981), *Dramatic Verses* (1982), *Kievan Harvest* (1983), and *Works in Two Volumes* (1986). He has also published a book of essays, *Spiritual Sword* (1983), and other works. Some of his works have been translated into English and appear in *Four Ukrainian Poets: Drach, Korotych, Kostenko, Symomenko* (New York: Quixote Press, 1969) and in *Orchard Lamps,* edited by Stanley Kunitz (New York: Sheep Meadow Press, 1978).

## VASYL HOLOBORODKO

Vasyl Holoborodko (b. 1946) is a poet, officially excluded from the literary life of the 1970s. His first books of poetry, *A Little Flying Window,* was published in France (1970), and his later work, *A Green Day* (1988), in Kiev.

## IHOR KALYNETS

Ihor Kalynets (b. 1939), a poet, spent ten years in prisons and camps. He has been elected now to the position in charge of cultural affairs in the Lviv area. Except for his first book of poetry, *Kupalo's Fire* (1966), all of his other works were published originally in the West (in the Ukrainian language): *Poetry from Ukraine* (1970), *Reassessing the Silence* (1971), and *Crowning of the Scarecrow* (1972). *Kupalo's Fire* was published in the West in 1975. *Crowning of the Scarecrow* has been translated into German (*Bilanz des Schweigens,* 1975) and into English (1990).

## LINA KOSTENKO

Lina Kostenko (b. 1930) is a leading Ukrainian poet and author of *Rays of the Earth* (1957), *Sails* (1958), *Wanderings of the Heart* (1961), *On the Shore of the Eternal River* (1977), *Originality* (1980), *Marusia Churai* (1979, 1982), *Garden of Unthawed Sculptures* (1987), *The King of Lilacs* (1987), and *Selected Works* (1989). Translations of her works into English can be found in *Four Ukrainian Poets: Drach, Korotych, Kostenko, Symomenko* (New York: Quixote Press, 1969) and in her *Selected Poetry,* translated by Michael Naydan (New York: Garland Press, 1990).

## RAISA LYSHA

Raisa Lysha (b. 1941) is a teacher, artist, and newly discovered poet. She lives in Dnipropetrovsk, and several selections of her poems were published recently in the Ukrainian periodicals *Porohy* and *Ukrayina* and in the United States, in *Suchasnist*.

## SOFIA MAIDANSKA

Sofia Maidanska (b. 1948) is a poet and violinist. She is the author of several books of poetry, *My Good World* (1977), *Palms of Continents* (1979), *In Praise of Earth* (1981), *Scales* (1986), *Coming of Age of Hope* (1988), *Love Poems* (1989), and *Admission of Love* (1990), as well as several books and an operetta for children.

## OKSANA PAKHLIOVSKA

Oksana Pakhliovska (b. 1956) is a poet, staff member at the Academy of Sciences in Kiev, and author of the book of poetry, *Valley of Cathedrals* (1988).

## MYKOLA RIABCHUK

Mykola Riabchuk (b. 1953), a poet and literary critic at the *Vsesvit*, a monthly journal of world literature, is the author of a collection of essays, *The Need for a Word* (1985) and of a book of poetry, *Winter in Lviv* (1989).

## IHOR RYMARUK

Ihor Rymaruk (b. 1958) is poetry editor at the Dnipro Press in Kiev and author of two books of poetry, *High Waters* (1984) and *Amidst a Snowstorm* (1988).

## VASYL STUS

Vasyl Stus (1938–85), a leading Ukrainian poet and translator, was arrested twice by the Soviets, spent a total of thirteen years in prison, and died there. His first books of poetry, *A Candle in a Candleholder* (1977) and *The Palimpsests* (1986), were published in the West. He was posthumously rehabilitated, accorded membership in the Ukrainian Writers Union (in 1990), and awarded several prizes. His first work published in Ukraine was *Path of Pain* (1990). His works have been translated into German by Anna-Halja Horbatch with the title *Du has dein Leben nur geträumt* (1989) and into English by Jaropolk Lassovskyj (*Selected Poems*, 1987).

# Ukrainian Poems

### [UNTITLED]
Vasyl Stus

How good it is that I do not fear death
and do not ask whether my cross is heavy,
that, evil judges, I don't bow to you
out of foreboding of distances unknown.
That I lived, loved and did not take on filth,
hatred, profanity, nor contrition.
My country! To you I will return
and so in death I shall turn facing life.
To you my fair and suffering face I'll bow
just like a son, low to the ground
and straight I'll gaze into your honest eyes
and become one with my own native land.

Translated by Volodymyr Hruszkewycz


### [UNTITLED]
Vasyl Stus

What love! A whole eternity has passed
since I did love and dream from day to day,
that all would merge and memory bypass
parting, to the last comma and contracting learned.
But once again I go into that cell, among
the melancholy willow's boughs. I will await
some kind of random and unknown feelings
which will turn virtue into shame.
And there will be parting enough for two,
and there as well will be a silent joy—
to feel with the whole heart the long debt
owed to a past with a white headboard,
where a pair of ebony braids still flow,
and a pair of long arms, drunk upon the dark,
and a pair of lips, with passion greedy,
suddenly send us headlong down the slope
of idiotic virtue. Beneath the sorrow and beneath
the wing of some most saintly sinner,

who gifted us with those kinds of rooms
where sleep is no disgrace and love—no shame,
where in the middle of the night can one exceed
the bounds of self.
                    . . . To friend, to wife, to mother,
leads you by the hand your generous and melancholy
lover.

Translated by Volodymyr Hruszkewycz

## [UNTITLED]
### Vasyl Stus

Come back to me, my memory!
May my land settle with heaviness on my heart
with quiet torment,
so the heart of the nightingale may descend with song
in the night grove. Memory, come back
from wild thyme, from the summer with scorching heat,
where apples of the autumn harvest lurk about
in my red-sided dreams.
Let Dnipro's bewitching current
flow for me at least in a distant vision.
And I will call out. And my land will hear me.
Come back to me, my memory!

Translated by Irena Eva Mostovych

## [UNTITLED]
### Vasyl Stus

Blessed is he who knows how to spend,
when comes a time of loss,
so that hope would remain
and grow a hundred fold.
A white world is always white
and always a good white world,
even though within it you are a timid son,
shivering all over.

For your entire life is in flight
and in this is your salvation.
Only a poet is your entire essence,
and the rest only humus
that nourishes the root. Come autumn
and apple orchard turns to gold.
Blessed is he who knows how to spend
when comes a time of loss.

Translated by Irene Eva Mostovych

## [UNTITLED]
### Vasyl Stus

Like fearful sleep—these days and nights here
drain me and fill me up
with endless strength. There's no other way,
but to thread sleep through my eyes by force. Visions appear—
remembered, careworn, foreboding,
tapping salty blood from my arteries,
and cry, like bloodstarved cuckoos.
Don't coo, you bloody birds,
above my poor head—
when haze shrouds my tiny window,
when it's unbearable to be without the earth,
to be suspended in a vertical coffin.
O, circling footsteps, stealthy, and soundless.

Translated by Larissa M. L. Z. Onyshkevych

## [UNTITLED]
### Vasyl Stus

Here sleep overcomes the weight of forgetfulness,
and, like a snake, toys with memories.
Here, on the stage of a bygone life,
sleep jests and twists and turns,
like a *commedia dell'arte* actor.
Here, the live hide in the dusk
and abide, smelling of death. The vault's lid

won't let us out of sight. Always—watching,
always—its eye on us. And into the stolen sleep,
my biggest enemy, a curse, shall enter,
sharp as knife, to twist and turn inside
the naked soul, and hasten
to wet the blade with my own blood,
so you too will become, as you must—hard.

Translated by Larissa M. L. Z. Onyshkevych

## [UNTITLED]
Vasyl Stus

A hundred mirrors glare at me,
into my loneliness and silence.
You are really here—here really?
                    But surely,
you are not really here. Not—really?
Where are you? Where? Where are you?
You haven't reached your full height yet?
And here it is, the long awaited rain (pouring as from a sieve)
flooding the soul that's all in tears.
Your hundred deaths . . . your births . . .
How hard it is for dried out eyes!
Who art thou? Alive or dead? Or, perhaps,
both alive and dead, and—all alone?

Translated by Larissa M. L. Z. Onyshkevych

## THE COPSE
Ihor Kalynets

The autumn copse, through children's eyes:
    so high and so translucent.
    Above, at night, among the leaves
    on rennets rock the autumn stars.
    Together with the dry Fall leaves
    they'll tumble to the yellow grass
    when in the heavens the tree branches
    suddenly argue with the wind.

And now the stars like crystal shatter
and spray their shards into the night.

The autumn copse stands so translucent
and so high . . .

Translated by Volodymyr Hruszkewycz


## A WOODEN HUTSUL CHURCH
Ihor Kalynets

Timeless beams ruptured
and shingles scattered like feathers;
the wooden miracle of toil and faith
was being savaged.

Quietly etched into the gentle mountains,
cupolas swayed for the last time,
dying clear-eyed and dignified,
the way only last survivors die.

Centuries were dying thus,
beauty was extinguished.
And from despair—golden clusters of the iconostasis
shattered into splinters.

And holy icons sought eternal rest
amidst the weeds;
cradled in the yet unruptured frame
quietly wept the Hutsul Madonna.

And St. George in an unbeknown battle
having lost his spear and his arm
with his head split open,
in a final farewell looked around

as long as the requiem lingered,
as long as it covered the ground,
the orphaned spruce trees,
with mourning thick, intransparent.

Translated by Larissa M. L. Z. Onyshkevych

## [UNTITLED]
### Lina Kostenko

A shady spot, twilight, a golden day.
White roses cry and pray.
Perhaps it's me, or someone, or you
over there sitting in a corner of the veranda.
   Perhaps he's crying, or waiting—
   he heard footsteps, or the wicket gate squeaked.
   Perhaps he'll get up, hang his head,
   there, on the veranda, pressed to the door post.
Where are you, people, who lived in this house?
My wide world, what flat lands lie here!
The sadness of posterity—like the dance of a bee,
the dance of a bee to the immortal field.
   Perhaps after a thousand years—
   I will not be me, but awakened anew in genes,
   here on the earth I will seek out the trace
   of my lineage in laments and legends!
Voice of the well, why have you grown silent?
Arms of mulberry trees, why have you grown stiff with cold?
Windows nailed shut, and the lock hanging—
a rusty ring above the claw of the knob.
   Rainy weather beats the white side of the building.
   Who wails there in this house in the nights?
   Perhaps loneliness lives there alone,
   stuffing the empty house in the oven with tongs.*
Perhaps this is our pain, perhaps our guilt,
perhaps a balsam for neglected souls—
memory of a well and memory of a window,
memory of a path and a wild pear . . .

Translated by Michael M. Naydan

---

(*NOTE: The underlying echo for this line in Ukrainian is *xata rohata*, literally, a "house with horns," i.e., a house where much work needs to be done.)

## [UNTITLED]
### Lina Kostenko

A terrifying kaleidescope:
> at this moment someone somewhere died.
At this moment. At this very moment. Each of every minute.
A ship has broken apart. The Galapagos Islands burn.
And the bitter star-wormwood* descends above the river Dnieper.

Somewhere an explosion. Somewhere a volcano. Ruin. Destruction.
Someone gets better. Someone falls. Someone begs: "Don't shoot!"

He doesn't know the tales of Sheherezade.
Lorelei doesn't sing above the Rhine.

A comet flies. A child plays.
Faces bloom, not effaced by fear.

Blessed is every minute of life
on these universal scythes of death!

Translated by Michael M. Naydan

## [UNTITLED]
### Lina Kostenko

I open the dawn with a squeaking key.
The blank night encrusted with tenderness.
With a crimson shoulder the horizon lifts
the day—
> like a musical note page of eternity.
What will be today?
> Which joyful piece
of my passionate fate?
Truth smiles with the eyes of legends
and freedom with the eyes of captivity.
Inimitable love
> is my French horn.

---

(*NOTE: In the Bible there is reference to *star-wormwood*, which in Ukrainian is *chornobyl*, the same as the name of the town in Ukraine.)

Parting paths—
           the first violin of sadness.
And I will beat like a drum
                     to the grey days.
It is very easy for me. And so very hard.

        The evolution of goose quill pens.
        The bespattered nimbus of philosophies.
        The word is the name of thought now,
        and more often its pseudonym.

So what do I seek and what gives me vitality?
The much-loved many-peopled world.
You, poetry, verse?
             Or only words?
The future's hearing is absolute.

                              Translated by Michael M. Naydan


### [UNTITLED]
### Lina Kostenko

In childhood I floated above dahlias,
and grew up, flying, for years.
Now I walk the paths and trails
and pave the way through swamps.
My heart has tired of rattling.
I endure and quietly pave the way.
I, who learned to fly in dreams . . .
I, who could have walked on spires . . .

                              Translated by Michael M. Naydan


### THE MYSTERY OF BEGINNING
### Ivan Drach

Is there a beginning in wailing? Or in a black piece of flint?
In the wind or in or in a gentle draft? In God? In a demon?
A thought is sliced open, the endeavor begins—
Where is that beginning?

Is it at the tip of a star above a rainbow tone?
This youthful butterfly once was Newton,
Today it only flutters its wings—
Where is that beginning?

Where is that star that gave birth to a star?
Where is that Einstein who takes the sphere of being
By the bridle like the mane of a horse,—
Where is that beginning?

To my screamed scream there is silent silence . . .
But I thirst to hear the wailing of beginning.
And I will place all the wisdom of the universe on watch—
At the beginning I want to begin the beginning . . .

Translated by Michael M. Naydan

## [UNTITLED]
### Ivan Drach

It is good for me in this sadness,
Although this instant pains me so.
Have I lain down my brazen wings,
Or does my scorched heart ache?

It is so hard to sweep
Silent wonder into my past,
For just now it really occurred,
Already it's passed—the moment's like a thief!

It is so sorrowful for me in this sorrow,
Yet in exchange for joy I will not give up
This sadness, that faces the truth,
Nor these tears, surrendered to the winds.

And the moment burns like a silent candle,
And wrings its hands like a widow,
And joy gazes into two eyes—
Jealousy slays with sobs . . .

—Translated by Michael M. Naydan

## [UNTITLED]
Ivan Drach

When the Serpent cores the apple
Before giving it to Eve,
He cuts away the skin in a spiral—
And a green coil flows from beneath his knife,
And this is called cognition . . .
The Serpent cuts the apple in two
And pulls out the core from both halves,
He husks the seeds from the insides—
And only then he presents it to Eve.
And Eve shares it with Adam . . .

Translated by Michael M. Naydan

## [UNTITLED]
Ivan Drach

Hornets began to strike the windows
And bumblebees to drone,
Souls that grievously died arose
In a dense swarm.
Why do they need to ask me,
And what good am I to them,
When I know not what to do
With my own life.
But they continue to ask me—
What's what and where to go,
Yet they don't breathe—they sob
With the voice of distress.
What counsel can I give myself?
For it is they,
it is they whom I ask most for advice
In my nocturnal doubts . . .

Translated by Michael M. Naydan

## MOTHER'S ETERNAL ELEGY
### Ivan Drach

*She passed through fields—*
*The green greening . . .*
*And Her Son's Disciples greeting:*
*Blessed You be, Maria!*
            *from Pavlo Tychyna's "Mother of Sorrow"*

Her Son's Disciples meet her,
Lead her by the arm.
That strange woman again!
"Don't you know me, Son?"

"Mother, why d'you keep coming back?
We have to drive you away from here.
And, frankly, I must confess,
You really can't fool me.

I'll take you to the City,
To the grandchildren, to die there."
And proudly she said:
"But I am the undying mother!"

Soldiers watched
The generals crying,
The old woman again
To her house hurrying.

To her stork and her well,
Her cat and her cow,
And her dreams
Without words or curses.

She bypassed the sentries,
And passed through the barriers.
Her roses were flaming,
Like roosters—stood the generals.

Everything as on a blade of a knife,
Ready for cutting.
And the mother kissed a flower
Smack into the cesium.

Everything under the sun shed tears,
Not wanting to die.
And the mother kissed a flower
Smack into the strontium.

Translated by Larissa M. L. Z. Onyshkevych

## SEEKERS OF GRAVES
### Vasyl Holoborodko

*For Ihor Kalynets*

We gaze into each other's eyes,
calling out most important words, as if
our existence was imperiled at this moment,
through the dense air
compressed into oppressive ocean waters,
but instead of words we hear mutual silence:
   —where is our voice—

We stand in front of narrow slits in prison gates
in endless lines, beg for brief visits,
a chance to bring a parcel—but we are told
that those for whom we search are not found here:
   —where are our poets?—

We roam through the world's cemeteries
pressing our ears to silent nameless
graves in forests, taigas, tundras
and strain to listen at the gravemounds of our dead brothers
ravaged in thirty-three by famine[1]
(perhaps we'll hear the sounds of flutes, reed pipes, dudkas,

_____

(NOTES: 1. artificial famine of 1933 enforced by Stalin, as a result of which 7–10 million perished.

floyarkas and sopilkas buried together with the perished)[2]
like divers we descend to ocean bottoms
until we reach the graveyard
of a barge sunken with the condemned,[3]
with horror we approach the lime-filled hole
barely covered with dirt:
   —where are the graves of our poets?—

(We light a candle
before the wasteland of the world
abloom in cherry blossoms)
                              * * *


                              Translated by Myrosia Stefaniuk




                    [UNTITLED]
                    Vasyl Holoborodko


          On rare occasions
          separated by many years
          when I return to Kiev
          with a few living friends
          I visit graves of dead ones
          at Baykiv Cemetery.

          Later we go
          handful of those remaining
          to an outdoor museum
          we walk among the windmills
          in which no one grinds grain
          among old cottages
          in which nobody lives
          to spring-wells
          from which no one draws water.


                    Translated by Myrosia Stefaniuk


2. series of reed-pipe folk instruments.
3. entire barge of sentenced poets, deliberately sunken during the purges of the 1930s.)

## FROM CHILDHOOD: RAIN
Vasyl Holoborodko

I am completely intertwined
in green tresses of rain,
entwined is the road that leads to my father's house,
entwined is the house that shimmers on the mountain,
    like a green bird
entwined is the tree, grown silent by the wayside,
entwined is the stream's blue ribbon laced in a maiden's hair
entwined is the herd of cows resting by the trough.

A cloud weaves and weaves
green tresses of rain,
cold tresses of rain.

But everyone is warm
they know—the rain will stop
and some will graze to their full
some will scurry about
some will sway to their full
some will sit on the mountain
some will lay in repose,
and some will return home
into the house that, like a nest,
    is filled with warmth.

Translated by Myrosia Stefaniuk

## A GIRL'S NAME
Vasyl Holoborodko

You asked me to guess your name,
but I simply could not.
 At first, I called you Water,
saying:
—To follow you
is to follow a river of no return.—
You said you were not water.
I said:
—Grass, then.—You laughed, and I explained:
like the last blade of grass out in a meadow,

you beckon me with a green lantern
so I may always find you.
Admit it, perhaps I should call you Bird
for when we kiss, it's as if my hands—were catching
a bird over your head!
Never will I guess your name
nor guess anything about you,
for I know only about water,
about grass,
and a bird.

Translated by Myrosia Stefaniuk

## PAINFUL MEMORY
### Vasyl Holoborodko

White feather of a bird
whose name people do not remember
lingers on green on the white wall of eyes

with eyes wide-open
silence sifts flowers
with mirror-petals
young girls glance into them with pain.

Translated by Myrosia Stefaniuk

## ROADS
### I.
### Sofia Maidanska

All roads
pass around me.
But still
I try to catch
at least one.
I seize a road
by the neck,
no matter that it

winds around my arm,
around my whole life.
I keep gripping it tighter
until
from its sharp teeth
drops of healing venom
drip down.

Translated by Larissa M. L. Z. Onyshkevych

## LETTER NO. 24
Sofia Maidanska

Condemned to faithfulness,
I'll wait for you
all of my life,
like a tamed fox,
and maybe
you'll fly in once again
from that far plane,
that belongs to you
and that capricious
            rose of yours.
I will accept a leash of crab grass
and with unseeing eyes,
filled to absurdity with dreaming,
I'll catch the final wedding dance
of short-lived May flies . . .
until you
rise on the horizon
and wave
your hand to me . . .
I'll start up then
            like a small pile

of dried up maple leaves,
and whirl together with a cloud of dust
and a piece
     of yellowed newsprint
from last March.
In my loneliness
I'll whirl so laughably
chasing
my own
     ruddy tail.

Translated by Volodymyr Hruszkewycz

## LETTER NO. 43
### Sofia Maidanska

On a deserted shore
I lifted a stone
it too was once
a heart
awaiting a wedding
and from deceit
o yes
from deceit
became forever hard . . .

I lifted the stone
and far away
on a deserted shore
you felt my palm
next to your heart
and you let out a heavy sigh
like the maple tree
that in bad weather
trashes about with its broken wing.

Translated by Larissa M. L. Z. Onyshkevych

## LETTER NO. 28.
### Sofia Maidanska

We descend from the heavens by the stairs.
They float under our feet
like the old swing
that our parents had tied
to a walnut tree.
You're out of breath,
I know . . .
I can feel it,
it is my own tear
that fell in the field, like a lark,
and then soared like a song . . .

Farewell.

Translated by Larissa M. L. Z. Onyshkevych

## LETTER NO. 27.
### Sofia Maidanska

Only once
does a clod of soil
fall on the grain
of our coffin . . .
But my dear one,
don't cry!
the time will come—
and my shoot will gently pierce through
the ceiling of my sarcophagus,
and I'll grow as a primrose,
through the palms held tightly for prayer . . .
And Father shall shout:
At last!
It's time to leave the Ark.
From Chornobyl
charred waters have receded
and a pigeon
has brought a branch of guelder-rose . . .

Translated by Larissa M. L. Z. Onyshkevych

## LETTER NO. 34
Sofia Maidanska

*Chornozem has risen
and looks in my eyes . . .*
                    *Pavlo Tychyna*

You'll always be able to find me
quite easily in the desert,
amidst hollyhocks,
guelder-roses and wells,
like a pillar of salt
I'll be standing there in a white scarf.
At the place where for three hundred years
*chornozem* will not rise,
will not rise
will not look in my eyes,
at the tomb of my own people,
who haven't yet died,
haven't died,
have not died! . . .
Cripples grow up!
Grow up deaf and dumb,
grow up blind,
leaning on crutches of a foreign tongue,
jumping frantically across a stage.
You'll always be able to find me
quite easily in the desert,
amidst hollyhocks,
guelder-roses and wells,
like a pillar of salt
I'll be standing there in a white scarf.

Translated by Larissa M. L. Z. Onyshkevych

## A HUNDRED YEARS OF YOUTH...
### Natalka Bilotserkivets

A hundred years of youth, and all beyond—a wasteland.

The neighborhoods of your old city
Do you not hear them, when you close your eyes?
Through the dead smoke of blazing leaves
Hounds of our childhood run
And the blood thickens . . . A hundred years

of youth, and all beyond—a wasteland.
Here nightingales, like spikes, are thrust
Into the hearts of fading blossoms;
September's parched-out rains
Are rinsed in sunlight, like linens
Between windows. And the snows!
Mammoth and violet . . . But you

you must come closer
To the hands, shoulders, skin and shirt
Torrid from heat. And to the walls,
Grown cold from fear and mosses.
Do you not hear it, when you shut your eyes,
Your own lost innocence?
Do you not want to melt into the rock,
And hide from those first kisses?

There, over there—into the stone and moss,
Into the timeworn brick, the tattered balls,
Into the nightingales! Into the gentle hounds
Of childhood, that creep behind us always
Through the dead smoke of blazing leaves,
Until blood rises on their spines.
Into the moss! And into fear!

. . . and all beyond—a wasteland.

Translated by Myrosia Stefaniuk

## [UNTITLED]
### Natalka Bilotserkivets

*I will die in Paris on Thursday evening.*
—*Cesar Vallejo*

Scents, colors, lines and hues fade
eyesight-hearing weakens and dims, simple joy passes
you'll lift your arms and face to your soul
but it's flight is high and out of reach

what's left is the depot—the last stop
the grey foam of goodbye churns and swells
washing over my vulnerable, unprotected palms
its hideous sweet warmth slithers to my lips
yes, love remains, but it would be better gone.

I cried myself stupid in my provincial bed
as an ugly rose lilac gazed through the window
the train moved steadily as spent lovers watched
the dirty shelf heaving under your flesh
outside, a depot's spring passes, quiets down.

we're not gonna die in Paris
this I now know for sure—
but in a tear- and sweat-soaked provincial bed
and no one will hand us our cognac,
I know
we won't be comforted by anyone's kiss
the circles of darkness won't disappear under the Pont Mirabeau
we cried too bitterly and abused nature too much

we loved excessively
thus shaming our lovers
we wrote too many poems
while disregarding the poets
never
they won't let us die in Paris
they'll encircle the water flowing under the Pont Mirabeau
        with heavy barricades.

Translated by Vera L. Kaczmarskyj

## TO MY WIFE
### Mykola Riabchuk

Finally, the trash has been picked up. The Snow
removed. The streets are empty . . . .
And we, night's forgotten travellers,
turn into narrow city side streets.

Because only here it's winter. Only here
the ragged Christmas trees still lie about,
broken toys and lemon rind,
carnival jumble of the holiday season.

Time moves slowly. It doesn't really move,
it lies, like snow, waiting for some sound,
not voice, not the clacking of footsteps,
nor the rustling of shoulders touching.

Feel and say the word,
let it shove time and snow like an avalanche,
this city is *ours,* it is the only one we have,
like love, and blood, and blood once more.

What a harsh and merciless sound!
How painful it will be in dreams to both of us!
Like a sharp nail, like dried needles of a fir tree,
which prick the hand and fall to the ground.

Translated by Asya Humesky with Estelle Titiev


### #1
### Mykola Riabchuk

At twilight this is quite a different city,
as heat departs, and noise subsides,
dust settles and your thoughts drift
homeward to the soft dwelling place,
the warm books and tremulous stillness,
to the coolness of old city streets
that trickless from doorways and cellars,
to that, as yet unknown something,
which frightens you, which you shun and reject, but

yearn for and desire—take courage!
Go, go there! In the light of the moon,
in the glow of street lights, when
accacia leaves seem theatrical,
and one feels theater drafts when
the curtain is raised in a stuffy auditorium.
As tardy owners of dogs
hasten to leave city parks and squares,
you hear the muttering, the squeeking, the elusive
summons of the future—why so soon?
Why such a pull, such fright?
Like life and death, and pain and love,
like cruel gentleness and tender cruelty?
Is it not because *this is* life
and death, love and pain, is it not because
this is life, this is life, this is life? . . .

Translated by Asya Humesky with Estelle Titiev

## NIGHT VOICES
### Ihor Rymaruk

These voices of the night,
    these duty-exacting officials flung into the fright,
will not forget your face,
    no matter how you plead:
you've brought them on yourself,
    sought them out in the universal chaos,
and now they descend in flight
    upon your solitary candle.

They're secretive—
    while you yearned to lay them out in quatrains
to spread them out neatly, sheet by sheet—
    o holy simplicity! . . .
And the voices of murderers
    insinuate themselves as those of the murdered,
while prophetic words
    slip out of insane lips.

And now you beg:
    "Grace me with a different calamity,

and not this night choir
    of proselytizers, murderers, rapists . . .
Their hymns and curses
    can they possibly be stuffed into anapaests?
After all, everyone has something he's concealed.

—Some confession, some lie
    which wraps itself 'round one's wrists, like shackles
You cannot shake them
    not even in the wide open meadows of Podillia
    nor the vast forests of the Carpathians . . . .

O, you voices of the night
    you'll pursue one even under ground!
Mute my hearing!—
    The voices of the night are drawing nearer.

They're great summoners—
    propositioning me with yet another interrogation?
Or have the sages seen fit to glorify
    yet some other rising star?
Whose voices are you, anyway?
    Dear God, why've they gotten so entangled?!—
I speak with all of them—
   As if knowing, what it is that I'm creating."

Translated by V. L. Kaczmarskyj

## WALK, WHILE IT'S STILL SNOWING
### Ihor Rymaruk

### *I.*

You truly did not imagine it
you did not find that horse-shoe in the forest.
You brushed it of the caked mud
trying to divine the colour of the mare,
discern the outlines of the night rider,
hear the whisperings of years past.
From those quaint old legends,
you might even have recognized
the smithy who shoed him.—

Perhaps you even gave him a name,
chose the cross-stitch pattern for his shirt . . .
Called into the forest for the woman
who embroidered it
her hair so fragrant
and lizards flickering under her feet
as she walked to the shop in the valley!
. . . It matters little that you lost
the horseshoe that very same day—
you nonetheless know
the very spot
on the doorpost
you would have nailed it
for luck

Translated by Vera L. Kaczmarskyj

[UNTITLED]
Ihor Rymaruk

Keep talking, keep talking.
You've managed to utter just one word—
while hundreds of words keep disappearing,
keep getting lost forever, with no return,
the eyes needlessly
leap over the cemetery gate.

Keep talking.
Why do you keep silent?
Perhaps for years you've shuddered
at every knock on the door?
Or, perhaps, like a movie camera,
glory closes in on you now—
for that one word?
And so—to ennoble the film,
you're scrubbing away everything else from your memory,
like blood from the floor.

(NOTE: Ustym Karmeluk (1787–1835) was a Ukrainian rebel leader who fought against social and national injustice. A wax figure of him is at the Kamianets-Podilsk fortress.)

Is this not why your spirit
is so silent and stubborn?
Just like the wax figure of Karmeluk
standing in a refurbished museum tower—
holding a sign: "Do not touch."

Translated by Larissa M. L. Z. Onyshkevych

[UNTITLED]
Ihor Rymaruk

*

And you'll remember . . .
You'll wonder:
   where is that
      autumnal woman?
And from the sinless walls
you'll walk into the night,
yet even in the darkness
     there is always someone ready to cast a stone.
And you'll get slapped in the face by the downpour,
and tears shall overtake and sting you . . . .

But you'll keep on walking.
And you'll spit over your left shoulder,
the shoulder awaiting the stone.

Translated by Larissa M. L. Z. Onsyhkevych

[UNTITLED]
Ihor Rymaruk

I don't know where you come from:
from the future or from a more distant past,
from the quiet December warmth

or from a river that frantically tears
the threads of centuries, I don't know . . . . You've vexed
hundreds of rivers—and inundated half the world!

I don't know who the person is
who falls into your frozen tracks
with lips as though into a stream,

and above the din of waters he bends
bare branches like arms to his brow:
where should he look?!

Thanks be to fate
I don't know where you come from.

Translated by Michael M. Naydan

## [UNTITLED]
### Oksana Pakhliovska

Once again branches of trees are broken.
Once again far off cities gleam.
Once again this flight. And the wind
whips my cape and scorches my lips.

Weariness from the road and the voice of pursuit.
Wind rips off the cape from my shoulders.
Once again invisible horses carry us
from the hollow morning to a starless night.

Perhaps we'll get there. Or perhaps we'll die.
The scarlet moon becomes linen.
In the morning forgotten goddesses will dream
Of two riders above a glass city.

Translated from Michael M. Naydan

## FORESTS NEAR PRYPYAT
### Oksana Pakhliovska

Forests near Prypyat flare.
Dry
    forests
        burn
           in May.

. . . Voices of your fowl
and your ancient stumps.

Age-old pine forests
now suddenly
            defenseless.
These burned-down trunks
and crowns reduced to ashes!

Smoke hovers above pines,
and you
        raving
           in the rain.
There will be neither years nor centuries for you,
but a hundred fires and scorched fields.

You don't have to grow here,
for what
        would you remember
               now?
You toss black pines
like crosses above the ashes.

The burnt horizon disappears
beyond grey
        winds.
. . . Your earth. Your river.
Your conflagration in May.

The last bird on a branch,
A tiny nest—
        like a live coal.
. . . You burn, pinned to the earth,
for your roots—are here.

Translated by Michael M. Naydan

(NOTE: Prypyat is the town closest to the Chornobyl disaster that occurred in April
1986.)

## CHORNOBYL'S VILLAGES
### Oksana Pakhliovska

*Ukraine grieved, for there was nowhere to live life*
*Traditional song*

I will not look. It never was—like this.
Beside the road the same old grasses grow.
But oh the dread—this new made village
And these towns—now lying empty for eternity.

New houses—with no boundary, nor end.
Where can I turn for consolation now?
The grove has no sapling—to call my own!
Nor even a small path into the grove.

Agitate, people, clouds and birds,
Songs, trees, the tongues and dialects!
Do you think storks returning from warm climes
Will find their way across these clones of roofs?

Where will the emerald-green grasses grow
Once all the living meadows are all gone?
Agitate, people, while you still live,—
Agitate, people, lest this come to pass!

About us hums the worldwide marketplace.
Belated realization wrings her hands.
Ancestral memory—like an ancient bard—
Goes to the people, staggering and blind.

Translated by Volodymyr Hruszkewycz


## MINIATURES
### Raisa Lysha

a house on green
lilac limbs
suspended
from the moon

a calf frolics about
arches
and motorcycles

the St. John's wort bows low
over the very heart

my father's world
still glimmers
we eat this bread
under the gaze of pain
and the white birch

Translated by Myrosia Stefaniuk

[UNTITLED]
Raisa Lysha

the pear tree carves
a cradle
in the sky
and sows poppy seeds
into a searing-yellow house
of red robins and colts

it rocks the sky
until it grows
a bird

*

I fear
the world
will hear my breathing
and find out where I am

Translated by Myrosia Stefaniuk

## [UNTITLED]
### Raisa Lysha

white calla lilies
two ears
in boundless space
two little snakes

path cracked through the shell
white, fragile

bull stepped on to it
contemplating the sea

obscure existence bellows

something sobs in the thicket

flowing green—green

stars sprout like seaweed

Translated by Myrosia Stefaniuk


## [UNTITLED]
### Raisa Lysha

God filled a dipper
of sky

with moon and stars
and comets

And said:
"Have a drink."

*

a river head
in the moon's lap
trees pass
feet glowing in the sand

precariously
foreshadowing a face

a sandgrain boat carries
a green twig
   to the wedding
and no one knows
where the translucent music
flees
hiding its face
in water

Translated by Myrosia Stefaniuk

## [UNTITLED]
### Raisa Lysha

dahlia lips
emit a fragrance of the sea
into the elongated eyes of an acacia
evening rolls in
a gypsy wagon
music glows
on thickets

high overhead a woman flies

light has no home

Translated by Myrosia Stefaniuk

# Part 3
# Poetry of the South Slavs

# Croatia, compiled by Aleš Debeljak

## Croatian Poetry in the Eighties
## by Aleš Debeljak
## With research assistance by Jadranka Pintarić

Croatian poets in the eighties do not rally around ideological banners or poetic manifestos. This is because they have none. In their first public appearances, these writers, born between 1950 and 1960, tried to command attention by throwing themselves into abortive attempts to forge new *isms* out of the modernist debris. From the mid-seventies on, there was hardly a new trend on the international *Kulturträger* circuit that passed unnoticed by young Croatian poets and critics such Branko Čegec, Branko Maleš, Neda Miranda Blažević, Jagoda Zamoda, and others. Appropriations of poststructuralism yielded a demand to stretch the language for its own sake, a trend called "semantic concretism," and prompted Anka Žagar, Sead Begović, and others to try their hands at it at least tangentially. More intimate "lyricism," advocated by Drago Štambuk, was generally reprimanded for its lack of cosmopolitan "zip." The exercises in textual style, however, soon proved their futility.

Subsequently *Quorum*, a literary magazine that, in the eighties, became a major forum for fledgling *literati* from all over Yugoslavia, was started. The editors and writers absorbed the failures of nationalist zealots as well as of orthodox Marxists to entertain quintessential dilemmas of human existence. The eighties writers then came to terms with hitherto publicly avoided reasons for the abrupt interruption of a vibrant literary life—advanced in the fifties and sixties by magazines like *Razlog* and *Krugovi*—which was brought to a halt in the seventies. At that time, a governmental intervention established a communist party line once again as the paramount cultural standard.

What set young Croatian poets apart from their Slovene peers, with whom they communicated regularly, was not just a routine rejection of ideological concerns. Croatian writers were anchored in experiments of European and—incidentally—Slovene avant-garde, especially Tomaž Šalamun's work. This rendered them resistant to the emerging literary relevance of meaning that dominated the Slovene scene in the eighties. Rather than entirely a drawback however, the modernist legacy proved a kind of boon.

Zvonko Maković's writing displays the potent nature of a modernist impulse in its "softened" or—for want of a better word—"postmodern" version. A poet of remarkable influence for the *Quorum* group, he was seen as a representative of experimentalist continuity. Having fashioned himself as a solitary voice, he nevertheless succeeded in putting forth a poetics of uncompromising descriptive method. This objective technique has allowed him to contemplate everyday life in the eerie tones of a dispassionate notetaker. His long narrative poems are haunting calls for a perpetuation of a modernist distinction between *things* and *words,* giving access to a moment of truth as it emerges out of a recognition of the unbridgeable gap between the two.

A paradox? Yes, but a very productive one because Maković has a keen ear and writes about simple, barely perceptible shifts of bodies, emotions, objects, and thoughts. He aims to figure out the ultimate source of nausea, which he poignantly presents as a fundamental trait of the human condition. Informed by the nonlinear works of Peter Handke and by the central European obsession with details, he proclaims the arbitrary and relative nature of words. Through his detached descriptions of the material underpinnings of existence, however, a larger sense of social bond is seen in the anxieties over different meanings for the same things. Hence his verse— "I am faithful since I know what it is like/to see oneself in the eye of another"—does not merely record a self-evident observation, it also succinctly encapsulates the author's poetic credo.

Maković's justified reluctance to give up the modernist strategies is shared by Anka Žgar. She came to maturity during the seventies when it was almost impossible to write against the grain of "semantic concretism." Anka Žagar, like so many other writers of her generation, duly paid the price. Although in her ascetic metaphors she remains indebted to the *ism* that stripped language down to its essentials, her lyrical imagination helped her gradually excavate the intimate dimensions of a highly personal cosmos. In her recent poems she has overcome the limitations of the cerebral linguistic tricks of her earlier works, thus creating an individual space within which fragile patches of dreams and sleepwalker's visions take pride of place.

The poetic priorities were reversed finally. In the seventies, Anka Žagar's poetry represented a series of buoyant masks that were meant to keep the flow of words going without ever arriving at an authentic image of self. In the eighties, linguistic bravado was replaced by the flauntings and vauntings of rich emotional imagery. This move away from the self-referential, sometimes even tedious, analyses of innovative quirks indicates her growing focus on metaphysical dimensions of her poetic world. Anka Žagar's hope to call human experiences of sorrow and joy to life in a magic manner is quite apparent.

In a broader sense, her shift of focus reflects that of her colleagues. The vapid experimental rhetoric of the seventies almost completely obscured bleak social reality outside the poem. It was precisely this social reality that young writers did not allow to lapse. In order to put poetry on a different footing from that of explicit political writing, two hurdles had to be jumped. First, human isolation and the fragility of identity had to be rescued from the disparaging label of "traditionalism" and the legitimacy of the self had to be restored. Second, correspondences between historical and social events and those of personal life had to be drawn.

Drago Štambuk's lyrical meandering through medical and other professional vocabularies maintains the tension between *words* and *things,* but he is using it to evoke deeply felt ethnic and individual traumas of exile. The efforts to reintroduce classical standards of beauty, truth, and good give his poetry a strangely beautiful undertow. His aesthetically rounded and harmonically composed poems bring us closer to the historical and social forces that drive and wreck our lives. Hence, exile becomes a temporary and personal condition, but a permanent and universal one in the (east European) societies in flux, especially in the times of displacement and migration. The acrimonious flavor of exile makes him all the more aware of how fruitless a contrived modernist "death of the subject" can be when carried out in shopworn linguistic escapades. Because of his carefully crafted tropes, one gets the feeling that Drago Štambuk attempts to articulate his hope for the renaissance of the subject—or else the act of writing is worth nothing at all.

Writers who chose to pursue that path before it became common practice in the late eighties, of course, gained less public exposure. This is not to say they have not had any clout. Božica Jelušić, for example, has never made a real splash, but was constantly respected for her poetic illumination of age-old topics. As she puts it: "(I write about) . . . let's say death and love, soul and the right to truth." The privileges accorded to these sentiments, not unlike those in the recent work of Sead Begović, cast sentient perceptions of the world and the concomitant pain of rendition as one, quietly defying a spiritless public arena in which there is not a word that would not fit on a billboard.

One thing is clear: the return to somewhat more traditional concerns has gained the upper hand. The fact that a poem written under past historical dispensation is, by definition, different from the "same" poem written under another now lies at the heart of much of contemporary writing. Croatian poetry in the eighties is, thus, not out to escape the censor's red pencil, but to humbly address itself to the perennial problems of human existence. This is less and at the same time more than we have grown accustomed to expect. Therefore, the challenge to answer Branko Miljković's question—"Will freedom know how to sing in the way slaves sang about it?"—remains ever more urgently with us. Political courage will no longer do in place of excellence of style and content.

# About the Poets

## SEAD BEGOVIĆ

Sead Begović (b. 1954) studied comparative literature and graduated from Zagreb University where he now works as a librarian. He published the following books of poetry: *Vodjenje pjesme* (*Governing the Poem*, 1979), *Nad pjesmama* (*Above Poems*, 1984), and *Ostavljam trag* (*Leaving Traces*, 1988). He is a frequent contributor of literary criticism to Croatian magazines.

## BOŽICA JELUŠIĆ

Božica Jelušić (b. 1951) studied English and Croatian at Zagreb University. In addition to her six books of poetry, she published a book of criticism and travelogues. Her poetry books include *Riječ kao lijepo stablo* (*A Word like A Beautiful Trunk*, 1973), *Golubica i pepeo* (*A Dove and Ashes*, 1974), *Cekaonica drugog razreda* (*Second Class Waiting Room*, 1979), *Kopernikovo poglavlje* (*Copernicus's Chapter*, 1983), *Meštri, meštrije* (*Masters, Masters*, 1985), and *Belladonna* (1988).

## ZVONKO MAKOVIĆ

Zvonko Maković (b. 1947) graduated in comparative literature from Zagreb University where he teaches art history. A winner of prestigious Nazor Award (Croatian Book Award), he published three books of art criticism and eight books of poetry, including *Činjenice* (*Facts*, 1983), *Strah* (*Fear*, 1985), *Ime* (*Name*, 1987), and *Točka bijega* (*Vanishing Point*, 1990). He frequently writes on art and literature for various Croatian magazines.

## DRAGO ŠTAMBUK

Drago Štambuk (b. 1950) received his M.D. from Zagreb University and now works at St Bartholomew's Hospital in London, England, where he has lived since 1983. He has edited two anthologies of Croatian poetry and published seven books of poetry of his own, including *Vapnena trupla* (*Lime Corpses*, 1987), *Brač* (1990) and *Croatian aeternam* (1990).

## ANKA ŽAGAR

Anka Žagar (b. 1954) graduated after studies in comparative literature from Zagreb University. Among other awards, she won the Seven Leaders Prize, an all-Yugoslav award for young writers. She has the following books of poetry to her credit: *Išla i sve zaboravila* (*She Went and Forgot Everything*,

1983), *Onaon* (*She-He*, 1984), *Zemunice u snu* (*Bunkers in Dreams*, 1987), and *Nebnice* (*Sky Poems*, 1990).

## DID I ASK FOR SOMETHING
### Zvonko Maković

Love was born but nobody had noticed
how terrible it was. They shower it with gifts
every day without understanding that it is ready for a pogrom.
Love is placed on the walls like a painting.
On the houses, like flags for the Day of the Republic.
It is a cold bowl at first, cold since
it is made out of porcelain, fragile and displaced.
Between the bed and the phone it finds
a tiny space that favors it,
that will protect it.
I drew it and it looked like an enclosed circle.
I engraved into it all the faces
I knew, I touched
and laughed at them. I am faithful since I know what it is like
to see oneself in the eye of another.

The hollow pupils are senseless.
They are marked by victims,
by trivial deals.
Love sneaks into the belly, into the meat—
than it echoes and we recognize it as words.
I stretched myself out on the floor and stared
at the spot on the ceiling.
The nuances have evaporated from that state,
that state is cruel and unscrupulous.
It should not be expected to yield some
particular desires, or complete unconcealments.
Did I ever ask for something?
There is a shadow on my face that feeds
on the blood vessels and leaves wrinkles around the eyes.

I know that here I can reach the ultimate
heights, transform myself into pure energy.
Now I feel that it is dawning,
although I am not yet able to see that.

But the time will come when we will
relax, get rid of the dreams.
When we will be as light as the scent.
I feel nameless and that apparently
liberates me from responsibility.
I would rather be a torrent which
floods indefinite motions,
which describes forebodings and devours fear.

I speak in the first person. Therefore I am not just
an instinct, an accidental voice.
And my sentences are keen like a heart of a flame.
I know that, I see and hear that.
I have read somewhere:
bread, silence, memory, zenith, eternity,
overwhelming unease. I knew that those are the words
that would not remain unspoken, that I would
take them up some day. That I would spill them
like a seed feeling then something more than
pleasure, more than a joy of spawning.
Now they still tremble, because I tremble.
Love trembles. Before it is spoken,
the word is only the air, the trembling air.

Do you want to?
I could again walk over
to the window,
and in the branches recognize the same aggression
that radiated from the skin I used to caress,
the skin that I can now hardly remember.
I can't sleep.
To watch, to watch in silence,
to remain without words,
without wonder.
Listening for the sounds which
represent perfectly nothing.
If they were only words
that I could take up,
and suck them into my body and
than resist clumsiness carelessly.
While I type
I sense the aimless incertitude
on my fingertips.
Do I really write with my body?

Or is that longing reaching out,
greedily looking for a place on
a piece of paper?
*Nothingness,*
*Emptiness,*
*Nightmare.*
The decision ground into tiny particles,
Unmelted sugar crystals
lost on the upper lip.

I got the scissors
and started cutting off the tips
of the leaves on my plant.
Suddenly I discovered the *uselessness*
which trickled across the leaves
in tiny jets
becoming a mere pile of dust.
I will lick that dusk,
push it into my nostrils,
and finally turn into something that
trembles in the faintest wind.
I may go out,
abandon myself to the unknown drives
just barely inscribed in my cornea
and strain my eyes looking for
some sharp contour on the horizon.
Or I will stay at my desk
and tremble from time to time
from newly found pleasure,
and sighing loudly write
a sentence which I avoided before—

*"In the past when I took every mistake*
*for a defeat,*
*I believed that it is very easy to love."*

Translated by Tomislav Longinović

## [UNTITLED]
Zvonko Maković

I have almost started this poem
with
"*Long time ago*".
With this displacement into indefinite past
I could easily commit an error.
Remain motionless,
free from the cracking of moments
which permeate the body with warm patience.
Without a blissful smile
that slowly matures.
That turns suffering into a smooth beauty.
That can be sipped straight from the lips,
then sucked in like a phantom
which offers a different outcome.
It is late.
From the window to the door there are
only a few steps.
When I pause
I am seized by panic,
I feel the barren time invading:
from the floor,
through the cracks of the walls,
the errors multiply,
the ones I was not aware before.
When I think about what I missed out on,
I tremble.
What do I feel? What do I give?
What can I receive?
"I write with my body,"
I used to say.
To be without scruples,
invading the void slowly.
Finally, I waved my head,
finally, I could recall.
I did not shout, I did not sigh,
I did not wave my hands.
I was sitting down.
Staring dully I tried to reach the rest
of the trifles.

I held that my desk was a machine
for the erasure of forgetfulness,
and the fine layer of dust on it
was the imprint of time.
From one of the photos applauses,
merriment caught in passing.
I want to tame that which you
could call unthinkable,
than turn it into a letter—
expected,
received,
displaced,
forever lost.

What are you waiting for? I screamed, I think,
amazed.
In an opportune moment I could hop,
wring the body like a dirty rag
and be forever devoid of desire.
Eroticizing particles
which have separated us and brought us together
are now just a sediment
that can slip away forever.

Translated by Tomislav Longinović

## REMARKABLE EYES
### Božica Jelušić

Yes, remarkable eyes that will see
sunspots, snow in fields of wheat, a metaphor in genitive
all things nonresistant to light and corrosion
the vulnerable inside
of the one who learns by heart the young Pushkin
and built into the expression betrays the source
incessantly whispering
I LOVED YOU WITHOUT WORDS AND HOPE
TORTURED ALTERNATELY BY FEAR AND JEALOUSY
from the bottom of my heart, from a mimetic vessel.

Yes, remarkable eyes, suddenly unaccustomed
on the phosphoric essence of words, on sensitive transition
between the flare of the defeat and the secret flicker,
burns the thin membrane under which a contracted larva
with a human face floats, sensitive matter
that evaporates, that changes, wrinkles and ages
quickly retrieve
all that they gave once, choosing from the best
and building for oneself regardless of adjectival marks
of time place manner
surrealistic booklet, a perfect world
bound in shiny leather.

The dream beyond archetypes pulls the cork and
corrupted air kills the sleeper in a hermetic bottle
the spirit that unifies rises and announces:
Gentlemen, come forward freely, here are eylids, colors and
false eyelashes (sight custom made)
that mirrors now in cold glass
only, the road is narrow and the door is low, the empty sky
for the remarkable eyes of the one who leaves, who
standing too near, does not know that he did not see
WHAT IS DISSOLVING INTO INDIVISIBLE, sparkling
into hundred-faced emptiness
and talking with full lungs.

Translated by Dubravka Juraga

## THIRTY-FIVE LINES FOR POST SCRIPTUM
Božica Jelušić

O my beautiful love, caress me and love
since there is a deserted place, since there is a dark corner
where a child writes hexameters on a wall
milk is boiling in the kitchen, time in between condenses
(chamber music goes on)
one has not been able to live in our poems
for the whole century.

O my beautiful love, peoples sink without splendor
the earth has become cold and coarse, without memory
the language I write in has four hundred
thousand good words, and that is not enough

to inhabit me with your saintly closeness
because you are nothing else but a cold member, rain, NEVERMORE
enter into my body, fall down in a field of wormwood
o, my beautiful love, caress me and love.

O, my beautiful love, everything goes toward the end
and the time of first books and the time of first sighs
we still go on living losing the right of absolution
we shiver with our skins pressed together, against the world
friends encourage us, experience renounces us
a metaphysical house grows out of your rib
a rooster, a walnut tree and a faithful dog
(despair in a mirror changes voiceless forms).
O, my wonderful love, I say ENOUGH thinking MORE
a branch refers to its root, a man to his memories
your prisoners enter the night of NO RETURN
motion pictures disappear
all that is broken within me bears your fingerprints
you, snake in the sun, let me die, forgive
my loved ones
a heart is a lamp, raise its wick, add some oil
that I can find you, everpresent, in water, air, bread and salt
when you breathe me out of your mortal mouth
golden dust, be with me
                    caress me and love.

                                        Translated by Dubravka Juraga


ONLY THESE HOURS WILL STAY, LIKE APPLES
Božica Jelušić

Only these hours will stay, like
apples that peacefully ripen under the wheat.
The rest: the velvet of senses, your fragile breathing
like the shed skin of the moon
will delete isochronous movement of the subconscious pendulum.

OCULI MEI SEMPER AD DOMINUM. There, however:
dark window into nothing. Vegetative movement.
Instead of an embrace, a rose of emptiness will surround me:
ice and morphine.
Hovering BEYOND YOU I will become like others. Now

I am learning to forget. OTHERS forget.
But AHMATOVA'S watch ticks meanings
which escape the style of a comprehensive Encyclopaedia.
For example: death and love, soul, the right to the truth.

Differentiating the right ones from the wrong. (Words-Reasons).
Beware prolixity!

Under the floating eye, in a lean sediment of matter, etc.
only these hours, in which I wrote
love poems for you

will stay as the only real season
meaningless future I dare think of
a winter house, door open like a mouth of wind

and you step over the threshold.

Translated by Dubravka Juraga

## METONYMIC COMPOSITION; K A S T A V
### Božvica Jelušić

A charismatic lancer aims at the airy hawk
try figs and vine, transfigured bread
in which the yeast of history does all your work
respecting the archaic language, leather sandal of the ancestor

on the lip of a scabby saint privation and salt.
He decided to rise to name plants
in the moment while light formed honey-combs
and the sea stretched with a movement glimmering as

the slavic antithesis. What had had to happen
at the level of experience, then slipped into the
darkness of phylogenesis. Now heather is dreamed here.

Gathering the inky black of octopi scarred painter
in his writings cut down, still writes
the experience of description, metonymic multiplier: composition

named the golden lobster, a painting-apartment, a table, a rendezvous
in Kastav.

Translated by Dubravka Juraga

## A BANK OF DEWY DATA
Anka Žagar

*But I have no*
*dress*
*with pockets*
*to remember*

I'll go then I'll return
if from heavenly nostrils
I really left

broken wind a breath
who grazes darkness with lips
who on my skin

a memory for him
a big fragment
but now a big whole

because momentarily
my hands went limp
and so then
fishes became & &
they are already
hands of a clock.
blinked
&& passed. &.

a dot you are the
biggest loneliness in the world

Translated by Dubravka Juraga

## I LIKE THE RHYTHM, BUT NOT THE EVENTS
### Anka Žagar

Part 1.
>
> Slow as a dead fish a line is when I say:
> ah, go and do not remember.
> I'll rise early and remember

Part 2.
>
> where I pass by, there I live
> this room is a street. the things stand
> in two rows. I am in the middle
> and pass by
> like a thread through a needle completely

Part 3.
>
> when I die, I come back, I unstitch and analyze:
> —how many things have I collided with
> —have I grown some while I walked for you
> —and whose clothes does the wind change now that
> it does not reclothe my words

Part 4.
>
> I'll rise early and remember
> I left time outside
> it snows in the mountains and is silent
> precipitations can still be expected
> and then there will be silence
> I keep these words for me
> I am time, sensations out

Part 5.
>
> he who was in a shell
> said I was in a shell
> and he who is now in a shell
> when I say, I am no more

Part 6.
>
> —say, what have you had to give up to play
> —whiteness yes, but the silence of the rising sun never

Translated by Dubravka Juraga

## SMALL HAPPY LINES
### Anka Žagar

and the biggest one among them was a smile

because I slept with apples, well
of course I slept with apples
in the morning a clock will ring in them, frighten
them, roll them, hide not to find them anymore
almost never

archetypal pigeon's ship
now in its breast keeps that dream
that makes
you sail
as into a day
(you and the saddest eyes in the world)

St. Marco night snow
watches over a city
for it I gave birth to a lamb
this floury graphite smile
then I stand a bit apart
trying to see him

but Marco will never return to me
a Marco can't and won't return
my breath pulls away when it's ripe

Translated by Dubravka Juraga

## I SAW DEERS THAT CRIED
### Anka Žagar

as soon as i left the woods, i saw
everything almost grown over, a bush
the woods barely let me pass. it burned and said:
    who has an altar in his eye
    he spoke in his eye: die
    let you die. why don't you die.
i have just arrived. otherwise i would. i would surely
find groping touch that source where cry starts. my

small earring saw. my little silence. that i would not
be able to run away to anyone's ear. because i saw
all made of wilderness and joined with speed. yes i saw
a mountain gray crystal i saw deers that cried their cry went
toward me as a smell of apples and rounded adorned its
pores, to whom, to whom are written these white rivets
i did not lose, otherwise i would. find gropingly the source. where death
comes i'd draw that teary form. and all demonstrative
pronouns. to cry forever
instead that other man
     (and in autumn again when i came
     i saw: everything has its white scarf around itself
     and does not hear me does not hear me)

Translated by Dubravka Juraga

## FAMILY
### Sead Begović

If I fight with my wife in the evening
in the morning, it seems, the apartment is showered with cacti
while she hides her victorious crest
and I brew the tea of conciliation
There is no picture, there is no sound: PRESSURE
Then I hear my
dry skin rustling with tension
like parched paper

Filip wants his pacifier—I give it
I would do it even for Calanhoe
those flowers that Zlata saw first
which shriveled then irradiated
one on top of the other
in that mess a man like me
immediately feels lonesome

I am therefore grateful to Zlata
she taught me to like creamy soups
hot and green
A cup of that soup helps me to
endure carbonated air
and acid rains

They fall all at once
and melt the caulk
from the windows

In the afternoon, the sun cheers me up
I move it close to my face like a hot iron
and it dies in its spots
A moment before, Filip scores
his first goal
The wind aids him

For dinner
we do not lose hope even for a moment
although the sheep was not slaughtered

and we lick one plate in silence
Later we munch the cookies and drink
the juice of crushed apples
Most of what is crushed is inside me
most of crushed guilt

Our family patiently continues
although everything around us is poor
and smells like potatoes and soup
and small domestic protector bugs
stick to our staring eyes

Translated by Tomislav Longinović


## IN EMPTY ROOM A STEADY FORM OF PEACE
### Sead Begović

I was already in the mud
And the swing under my chin
I was a wave of joy
The child of that volcano
Born out of your mouth
pouring fiery and dirty words

I was preserved a bit longer by the night frost
in jars of cold milk
lukewarm lard
and sweet discourse

and thrown to the children
of sexually mature worms
whose ticklish tails
cause laughter
on the long neck of ANAPURNA
and storms

I am interested in the inner side
of that intimacy
Her cool and her chin
floated with a light scent of yarrow
paired with a tortured drawing
of marrow

Oh, if it were possible
To save this world
The steady form of toys
One tear in a grain
That was shed for me
And burned my cheek

I was then an old balcony
And on the balcony the marshmallow leaves
I was surrounded by winter on all sides
Fatherly plants and grandfather's branch
Then a flock of old men descended

Squeezed from a toothpaste
The evil was dripping and it
Sewed me up by the hand
On the clearing of the table
It worshipped me like a statue of horror
In the muddy waters
Where prows and horns stroll by
In the empty room
Where greetings breathe

Stopped by raw rage
Pig headed peace prayer
Entire night he reinforced the cliff
Red houses made of crystal
And paper

Translated by Tomislav Longinović

## HONEY, HERE LIVES A GUARD DOG THAT LOVES YOU WITH A LOT OF SPICE
### Sead Begović

First of all
under your dress I will
stick the wiggling eels

Because I want to kiss you on my own
and for that I need
only saffron, sage and marjoram

Then I carefully remove your skin
which cruel merchants would put on sale
cheaper than bass and pepper
and sell to the producers of moldy patés
beer, vinegar and silk

I steal waterbugs from your eyes
as if they were ponds and puddles
Out of your hair—crabs from the rocks

And I tear down your loveliest
decorum of eyeless foxes
which cause the loud creaking
in the movement of the sun

A tender face appears
spiced with the sacred salt
And before I break its jaw
the thunder of lust bursts
Your slap petrifies
on my fair cook's face

Translated by Tomislav Longinović

## TO CONTINUE LIVING
### Sead Begović

On the reigns of greed you surround me
like flies
Stern Prussians wonder through you, marching
Afterwards everything is still—plucked eyebrows:
with one eye I measure the volume of the room
where your face shone this morning

O, what dull laziness keeps this sun
at one point for hours, why does it let me
suffer the entire afternoon waiting for you
until the twilight
when the suburban powerhouse blasts
and you shake and continue living

Translated by Tomislav Longinović

## ON THE BOTTOM, IN THE ASH
### Sead Begović

I expand the landscape
for that luxurious forehead
Your skin inflames, and disappears
your body transparent like a traitor

And then I wake up
on the bottom, in the ash
in my gray shadow
where you do not exist
I have the bottom
where cold clots of blood
wonder in their dances

The cold has me in its needles
and sharpens me on the shores of frozen rivers
Day is exhausted
Only its pieces shine through
in the eyes and in the grass

However before the last
rabbit's muscle is gone
I am comforted by a warm cup of tea

Translated by Tomislav Longinović

## NARCISSUS IN CLAY
### Drago Štambuk

Close as the bedding I lie on,
dear as the suddenly shining sun.
Like a flowerbed of dewy grass
washing away the heat of my soles.

Approaching you with the face of a mirror
I am a clay fragment in the water of your heart.

Translated by Klara Alcalay

## [UNTITLED]
### Drago Štambuk

On gloomy afternoons harpies
kindly smile at stonemasons.

On gloomy afternoons
when day ascends on earth
and the wind's trumpets announce thunder.

Concubines on gloomy afternoons
cover the wells with metal lids
for stale air
not to sicken the puddles with freshness.

On gloomy afternoons
silence wears a heavy brocade cloak
and in its solitude motionless the birds blacken
tinged with copper fetters.

Translated by Klara Alcalay


SPALATUM
Drago Štambuk

A broken ray sinks into green
and the town which lives on, firm and unreal,
on the distant shore, melts the weft of memory
and falls still deeper into dark cellars.
Dates of happy years are effaced,
and pain and tenderness—can be held on one's palm,
with a pair of names, a square and the smell of the port.

Phantom-like, the dark-ochre Harbour Office
hovers wearily in the span of centuries.
As if I was never there, tiny,
lost amidst the ancient palms,
sensing all possible disasters and delicate
deaths, my back turned on the dark palace.
And before me, alas, was that the sea?

(Hampstead Heath, 2nd June, 1984)

Translated by Bernard Johnson


MARE NOSTRUM
Drago Štambuk

(To Ivo Pogorelich)

Eugenio's well preserved cuttlefish still guard
Xenia in the shadows of cypresses. It is wind
speaking language of limbs and dismemberment
to itself, parched dust and supple goat's hoof.
A trough with mules and wild horses, brambles

stuck to their manes. Courtly neighing before
the chapel. The sun traced out of deep blue sapphire
emits protons, mesons and Ady's pupils. Like a heap
of stones, letters write time upon the summits.
Hygroscopy marks a fall in the black exicator,
the mercury reaches a certain limit, then repulsion,
encrusted eyes and a grey vertical angel upon
an ice-paved bolster. Approaching the landscape
chromatically does not distinguish
primary from secondary. The spectrum dominates
the eyebrows' arch. Egyptian makeup and
Greek apparel. They always dressed lightly
to reduce the burden and certainty.
A lizard could explain the plunge and dizziness
from the height of ripeness that reaches and seizes
with the tip of liquid nitrogen
the nerve wheel of a wart on a sole not given
to quotidian walks. For the action repeats
the wounding and fury of the viruses.
With shaven legs in the sun's wind they expose
knees and armpits with the contours of
their clothing emphasizing the private parts.

Ready to withstand the arrow and foreboding's moan
I take paper, and with a spear, inscribe a circle.

Let there then be a city here, a paved square,
sound arrested in flame. Let there be doors here,
basalt people, a lake, the splendor of many golden
lianas, a polished green lizard with a six-fingered
emerald crown, and fibulae stuck into the muscles
of broken breasts from Ollantaytamba.

Translated by Klara Alcalay

## CROATIAN FULL MOON
### Drago Štambuk

A magician flies
over the sea of blue night
in place of a hollow angel

and the flood of light from a *brazzera*
bears down on the rippling surface
enticing the lush mackerel.

I cannot stop my thoughts
turning the sea into
a boneyard of fish,

where an ancient chant
cleanses and blanches all waste
and transmutes it to silver

flecks and shingle on the shore.
Shall I again hold you
plunged to the mouth in death

as in the sea, swimming
just hard enough to keep
head above open water,

and counting late kisses:
salty tremors
on the crest of the last waves.

Translated by Bernard Johnson

# Serbia, compiled by Aleš Debeljak

## Serbian Poetry in the Eighties
## by Aleš Debeljak

The nation of arguably the richest poetic folklore in southeast Europe, Serbia, found itself in the eighties in the throes of an escruciating historical upheaval that has, for the first time after World War II, brought tanks to the city streets. An animated spirit of pride, long dormant in this traditionally unbowed nation, has rapidly gained currency among the leadership and the populace alike, making them pendulate between aspirations for an open society and a pursuit of ethnic grandeur. While in the early eighties the defiant Serbian Writers Union had mustered a tremendous respect as an all-Yugoslav beacon of anticommunist dissent, the closing of the decade, alas, has seen the rising tide of nationalist sentiments encroach upon the vision of a poetic commitment.

The ensuing discord among writers has ushered in a strong rift. Except for strong poetic voices like those of Miodrag Pavlović, Milorad Petrovič, Ivan L. Lalić,[1] and others, scores of older poets jumped on the bandwagon of ethnically overemphasized writing. These older poets put their muse to the service of volatile daily politics at the time when young writers, including Nikola Vujičić, Milovan Marčetić, Nemanja Mitrovica, and others, made it a point to keep as their paramount concern the precarious equilibrium of intimate and worldly aspects. The flagship for the latter group is an esteemed magazine, *Književna reč (The Literary Word),* in which particularly authors born roughly between 1950 and 1960 sought refuge from the ubiquitous ideologization of literature. The magazine has provided aside from its op-ed pages with exercises in civic courage, an excellent testing ground for writing that refused to be lumped squarely together with more socially preferred poetry ranging from rare gems of *poesie engagé,* at best, to cheap versifications, at worst.

It is in this context that the absence of the luminous vision of the late Vasko Popa,[2] the greatest modern south Slavic poet, makes itself felt ever more conspicuously. By brilliantly manipulating the evasive vocabulary of opposites, rather than taking them for granted, his poems deliver a reader into the ambiguous space wherein the poet's singing of himself already sings of the world. Popa's emblematic penchant for vernacular in which mythological and historical voices call out to each other still commands great respect among young poets.

427

The poetry of Novica Tadić, for one, is by all means indebted to the same dark and lurid imagery that haunts us with the trenchant beauty in Popa's *oeuvre*. Close reading, however, reveals a striking difference between the two. Unlike Popa's comprehensive drawing from the countryside folklore, Tadić is narrower in his themes. With numbing insistence he conjures up exclusively urban horrors. Regardless of his step forward into the realm of the unknown and unknowable chaos of the city, he nevertheless participates in the Serbian poetic continuity to the extent that the experience always assumes a mythological form. While Tadić rarely provides aesthetic pleasure, what he loses to human dignity he gains in persistent clarifications of his loyalty to the outcasts who populate pernicious streets. The varieties of *urban evil* in his poems occupy a central place, thereby shifting altogether the emphasis from the village to the town. In a still largely agricultural Serbia, the incongruence of the urban and rural has been a pivotal topic for many older poets, newcomers to the cosmopolitan city of Belgrade. Tadić, on the contrary, has no remorse for a village as "a paradise lost" since his taste for the obscure and the marginal puts him at ease with poisonous urban emotions. His poems demonstrate a capacity to engage the examinations of a hidden God and the ultimate meaning in the language of everyday banality, which he blasphemously views as the source of all experience—indeed of creation in general.

An entirely different temperament guides the pen of Miloš Komadina. An exceptionally sentient writer, Komadina shaped his work into a grand conceptual project in which the first letters in each title of his poetry books, when put together, spell out *Orpheus!* This in itself speaks volumes about his commitment to the admirable, though unfashionable, faith in the inherent merit of poetry that "makes nothing happen" (W. H. Auden), yet it moves souls and hearts. In this respect, he has set himself up in direct opposition to the more popular currents such as experimentalist and mythopoetic poetry. Komadina's lyrical obsession focuses instead on the illumination of the sensual and endearing values of a locale. By lingering on the particular, he does justice to everything that exists, stressing the muffled nausea and angst of the city dwellers. Thus, despite his traditional style, his richly nuanced poetic documents of evanescent urban reality possess a strangely modern edge. Aligning themselves with the subtle evocation of the metaphysical forces that dominate our deeds and thoughts, these poems quietly languish at the margins of public interest. Yet, one is hard-pressed to find among Komadina's more socially conscious peers a match for his powerful rendition of politically charged despair and hope in the poem *The Autumn Danger*. His lyrical sensibility casts here the melodramatic light on the city streets making them a place of an ongoing existential drama in which, he states, ". . . we wish something new would take place, / it is so boring as soon as we feel secure".

Ivana Milkankova and Nina Živančević, despite their respective alle-

giances to intimist and experimentalist poetics, both partake in the fundamental conviction that the dynamics of everyday life is, despite its ordinary
madness, pain, and sorrow, worthy of celebrating for its inherent beauty.
This beauty, as we are invited to observe, plays itself out against the back-
drop of a pervasive moral inertia and a rising tide of meaninglessness,
because of which the "patience is what we practice to a perfection," as Ivana
Milankova astutely points out in her poem *To One Visiting Belgrade*. This
poem, concerned with the stifling state of mind that the people all over
eastern Europe know first-hand, then presents no argument, but *is* itself
an argument for *joy of living*. In the polarity of the mythic and empiric
aspects of life, Milankova and Živančević, in their unimpeded strike upon
our most hidden feelings, seek out what survives of the human affection
after the damage of totalitarian appeasement has already been done. What
they discover makes us rejoice again—even though the bitter taste of the
troubled past, which persists into the present, remains ominous. The subdued tenderness that gives shape to the hope at the end of the tunnel,
however, is clearly articulated.

Milan Djordjević, who has styled himself originally as a poet of wit and
irony, had, in the late eighties, developed into one of the major voices of
his generation by working within the limits of the rhymed sonnet. Although
his subjects are by no means autobiographical, his poems are intensely
personal. In the light of growing *anomie* that the Serbian social fabric is
currently undergoing, Djordjević's soliloquies about the separation from
loved ones and from the larger cultural context amount to no less than an
impassioned plea for a dialogue in a conflict-ridden society. Ruminating
efforts to strike up a rapport with the "Other," which emerge out of remi-
niscences to what had never happened, allow the author to imaginatively
carry out repeated attempts to establish a viable relation between the sub-
lime and the mundane. Insofar as he stages this self-estrangement in order
to arrive at a catharsis, he reaches far back into poetic tradition, offering,
together with his fellow young writers, a convincing solution to both the
avant-garde myopia and political ardor in Serbian verse.

# Notes

1. See, for example, Ivan V. Lalić, *Roll Call of Mirrors*, trans. Charles Simic (Mid-
dletown, Conn.: Wesleyan University Press, 1988).

2. See, for example, Vasko Popa, *The Little Box*, trans. Charles Simic (Washington,
D.C.: Charioteer Press, 1970); his *Homage to the Lame Wolf*, trans. Charles Simic
(Oberlin, Ohio: Field Translation Service, 1979); etc.

# About the Poets

## MILAN DJORDJEVIĆ

Milan Djordjević (b. 1954) studied world literature at The University of Belgrade. He has four books of poetry to his credit: *Sa ove strane koze* (*On This Side of Skin*, 1979), *Muva i druge pesme* (*Fly and Other Poems*, 1986), *Mumija* (*Mummy*, 1990), and *Ćilibar i vrt* (*Amber and Garden*, 1990). He translates from English and Slovene and is an editor of a Belgrade literary quarterly, *Književna kritika*.

## MILOŠ KOMADINA

Miloš Komadina (b. 1955) makes his home in Belgrade. He is associated with various literary magazines. He has published the following books of poetry: *Obično jutro* (*Normal Morning*, 1978), *Rečnik melankolije* (*Vocabulary of Melancholy*, 1980), *Figure u igri* (*Figures in Play*, 1983), *Etika trave* (*Ethics of Grass*, 1984), and *Južni krst* (*South Cross*, 1987). He translates poetry and fiction from English.

## IVANA MILANKOVA

Ivana Milankova (b. 1952) studied English at and graduated from Belgrade University. She published the following books of poetry: *Meduprostori* (*Spaces in-between*, 1978), *Put do glave* (*A Path to the Head*, 1985), and *Vavilonski praznici* (*Babel's Festivities*, 1987). She translated extensively the works of Emily Dickinson into Serbian in addition to works by other writers.

## NOVICA TADIĆ

Novica Tadić (b. 1949) lives as a free-lance writer in Belgrade. His many books of poetry include *Pogani jezik* (*Pagan Language*, 1984), *Ruglo* (*The Laughing-Stock*, 1987), and *Pesme* (*Selected Poems*, 1988). He won numerous poetry awards in Serbia. His poetry was featured in *Child of Europe: A New Anthology of East European Poetry* (Penguin: 1991).

## NINA ŽIVANČEVIĆ

Nina Živančević (b. 1957) studied English and Spanish at and graduated from The University of Belgrade and got her M.A. in English from Temple University, Philadelphia. She published four books of poetry in Serbia and one in the United States: *More or Less Urgent* (New Rivers Press: 1988). She won a Serbian prize, the Branko Award, for first book of poetry. Since 1985 she writes her poetry in English and Serbian and divides her time between Belgrade and New York.

# Serbian Poems

## A ROGUE
### Novica Tadić

I am dethroned I am a genie
I am a rogue of all the deserts
I solved all riddles
And become an unfathomable secret myself

My frothing minions
At the end of hell are busy
I keep in a little box a small coiled snake
A crescent moon under a nail

I drill like a dog I pee like a dog
On the walls I scribble
I cut noses and ears with a crooked knife
I spit on serene icons

My servants are in my dark service
My masters build things in my name
My devilish apprentices abrade my victims
My twelve mice jump by my knees

Translated by Dubravka Juraga

## THE CABIN
### Novica Tadić

Not for ages
have I been there,
the city's business makes
you walk an objectionable course.

When rats swim in the ditch
and fears spread out huge
then I am certain
that He waits for me on a tiny porch.

I grew up
with the liver wings
of an animal unfamiliar

today
     I'll secretly place
on the table, laying them modestly down
all my gloomy objects
for him to feed on

To nurture his ascent.

Translated by Nina Živanvčević

## CLOCK
Novica Tadić

Beneath it, a pool of blood,
yet it seems to perform
its duty perfectly,
the way it marches, one legend, by itself.

When the cuckoo flies over
it grows silent
        it dares not to make a sound
It covers itself with metal ears
        leaving herself to me
           immobile
             and on guard.

Translated by Nina Živančević

## CAMPAIGN
Novica Tadić

An empty wallet pays me a visit
visits me and my walls
and cawing solitude
and ceiling with loops

Tenants of humid crannies;
insects, mice, and boars
over the high window
make orbits by whipping ropes

I calm myself I calm myself
listening closely for its coming
with a huge centipede
in its base.

Translated by Nina Živančević


RAVEN SNOW
Novica Tadić

He wasn't set outside
the suburban
deserted lands, junk pile grey,
until the snow fell

and the bitter cold delineated
his bright black features, he turned
side to side delirious
like a soul perched
on God's eternal Widow

the somber clerk of the heavens
was now everywhere
visible, totally black

from the closest homes, the voices
of young men and children
lifted him to the sky
            the fire poured
throught the Winter long
      in feathers white and falling
            alone, I shrieked and attacked

Translated by Nina Živančević

## THE AUTUMN DANGER
### Miloš Komadina

The misty rain stops, and already someone
hangs the mottled towels along the terrace.
Still wet, they crackle in the wind like flags,
while clear and steady light
born out of great confusion
spills across the sky and the City.

After the heat wave, this coolness,
seems odd to us from the very beginning.
And then the memories of long gone coolness arise
and we feel safe in the new season.
We wish something new would take place,
it is so boring as soon as we feel secure.

I yearn to hear the cowbell in the midst of the City.
(The barefoot boy walks through the damp grass,
and far in front of him a scattered herd.)
But, the streetcars still pass ding-dong,
and the world, it seems, turns in the only possible way.

Translated by Tomislav Longinović

## THE MAN WALKS TOWARDS THE WATER
### Miloš Komadina

. . . and does not turn around
since your pale shadow runs ahead of you,
and does not turn around
since the water is your destiny wherever you turn.
Since by means of water you will return,
since the water you are and the water you will become.

Since the purple sky spills over into the twilight streets,
since the noxious, black tobacco silently spreads over the city,
since the red sky pours into the rooms with curtains.
Since the white body of the woman on the floor rests as if asleep;
the body whose glassy eyes are motionless,
and the child leaning over the fence
wearing a moon beam on its forehead. . . .

It is summertime.
You left to enter into a chamber of sand.
Under your feet, the no man's land rushes deviously.
The twilight is a sour gelatine for poisoned sweets.
The naked back of a slander woman
in the red summer dress travels into the night,
a distant inverted triangle:
and under the yellow lights by the highway the face
                                    turns green.
The green fungus spreads beyond the reach of light,
and the man does not dare to pause and sink deeper.
That is why he continues to walk.
The man walks towards the water.

Translated by Tomislav Longinović

## THE MONOLOGUE IN THE NOXIOUS AUTUMN NIGHT
### Miloš Komadina

For David

. . . the bones are full and heavy. They are filled with marrow that does not know anything. The time escapes. The sand trickles and falls and rises into the rock into the glass. They sit in the twilight and they are not enraged. The beer bottle tops around them reflect the gelatinous darkness. Little swords of finite light.

The wrong hands reach into the night. When people meet, they believe it has a reason. When something happens, one likes to say: *it is because of this or that reason* . . . and one likes to say: *and if it were different, it would now be different,* and one never knows how it really is. For that reason the hands reaching into the darkness do not bring anything.

The pupil of my eye is so tiny now that it reflects my image. It is so dark that it leaves me without desires. I breathe freely. The facts are for the body. The words are pleasing to the body. They are colored by the mud and polished by the darkness. Little clouds full of nature. The body is scarred. The gray haired sage cannot utter anything that the madman could not.

One should not have intentions, one should forget words. One should exist accidentally. Than more could be given, and not only that which one wants to give. The multicolored stones and the cement are not yet a mosaic.

I know my own vanishing, minute power. I know it.

Look: the keys are everywhere! We walk across the keys. They hang on the walls and fly through the air. And look: the horse has excreted and the keys are inside his droppings.

I offer my time as a present.

The silence is mute like a stone in the abyss, the silence so much talked about: does not exist.

Translated by Tomislav Longinović

## HOW MANY HEARTS DOES MILOŠ HAVE?
### Miloš Komadina

The man whom I will never meet does not feel well. He feels terrible. He is in pain. He acted offensively towards those other people, the ones he will never meet. And now, it is not only the shame that bothers him and weaves black nets around his legs; it is not only the shame. He will continue to live like those other people and I will never meet any of them! But now, that man does not feel well.

*

How many hearts does Miloš have? Certainly one, that beats deceptively with charity. The heart of a whore. The only one?

How many hearts does he have, does he know?

The music boxes ring their comatose bells, unwinding their eternal circular melodies while the day is vanishing. He retreats into innocence as if it were a wound.

"My road is exhausted only when I do not confess."

Translated by Tomislav Longinović

## TOMORROW
### Miloš Komadina

It seems that this is our first encounter
but our paths did cross each other,
a few hundred times,
o, even a few thousand times, my friend.
And what is so odd in my appearance,
why do you stare at me, you unknown individual,
draw your sword, pull the gun from your armpit,

pull the poisoned dagger out of your sleeve,
drive it deep, deep into my throat,
for, although it seems that this is our first encounter,
our glances have already met a thousand times,
and the truth is that maybe even tomorrow,
tomorrow before dawn I will kill you.

Translated by Tomislav Longinović

## THE DAY
Milan Djordjević

How can I depict your fragrance?
Like the one that orange has? Is it made of mother-of-pearl?
Is it blue or perhaps reddish?
Could it be a rose, or instead an iris?

How can I depict a tone and your every sound?
Should I paint it in aniline, in color pigment or in oil?
In acrylic or in pastels?
Or should I endow with pure silence every noise?

How to depict fresh sweetness of fruits—bodies,
whispers of water—leaves—wings,
twitters of the most sensuous springs?

I don't know, my day, I don't know the answers.
Just whenever I feel your fatigued pulse
I light your gorgeousness with the dark.

Translated by Nina Živančević

## ICICLES WHICH MELT ON GLASS
Milan Djordjević

To be icicles as they melt on glass.
To be darkness which at dawn fades away.
To disappear in an ocean scorched by the Tropics
or which is frozen by transparency of the Antarctic.

To disappear in the uniqueness of Tuesday.
To burn in gasoline. To be a drop of iodine
in a glass of water. To be a New York night
to be car's lights, soda's bubbles.

To sleep. To become Labrador's moss.
To be an orange fungus over a naked rock,
as weil as a shimmering opal and phosphorus.

To be asleep. Without those cliffs and fissures——
To become nebulae. And a crust made of basalt.
To be a night bird. Forever bound at the edge of flame.

Translated by Nina Živančević


## DESERT ROSE
Milan Djordjević


High on cocaine, glittery buildings
made of glass burst apart, light feathers snow down,
black grave, my white city,
hot July scatters dry snowflakes.

High on cocaine, pine needles
pierce my hands
the way frost and sparks pierce the night.
High on cocaine, I wipe these hands.

I turn them into blueberry's blood.
Frightened by the sun, I crawl like a snail,
and a sapphire desert rose,
resembling a flu, grows within my flesh.

Translated by Nina Živančević

## WHY, WHY HAVE YOU ABANDONED ME?
### Milan Djordjević

I glance at an overripe apple.
It lies on the table, covered with a layer of dust.
A fiery eye whose flames have been soothed by the seas of ice
stares at me from Your distance.

Now please, transform me into a lonely wolf,
so that I could, drenched in light-borne milk,
get rid of some small human darkness,
so that I could burn and run down an icy river!

Oh You, who have abandoned me, please transform me!
Give me a sign, and drop your honey, whiter than the Athos!
Light up my dusk where I underwent your flood!

Please empty down the strength of all salmon shoals
into silence felt among the blindfolded walls
or turn it into a tender fragrance which pine trees off.

Translated by Nina Živančević


## MORNING
### Milan Djordjević

He wakes up, touches his fur—warmth.
So that there would be a glee in his eyes, like a cat's at night.
He breathes in a morning, drops of amber-freshness.
So that he would be lit by cobalt blue sky, which belongs to no one.
He walks barefoot across a grassy field as if it were water.
Bodily fluids run under his fleece which is cold.
He overhears the sound of pines, a breath of naked country,
in a pine forest where he gets awakened by an evergreen dream.

Translated by Nina Živančević

## TO ONE VISITING BELGRADE
### Ivana Milankova

Patience is what we practice to perfection.
Serenity, even while crossing a dangerous intersection
with the light flashing RED,
because he knows in advance
that everything that might happen,
will happen only to him
and it must happen some day
                    —death or unexpected salvation.

He simply crosses the street,
basking in the traffic light's redness.
He's already on the other side of the street.
He smiles.
It turned out that way, this time.

Translated by Nina Živančević

## EXODUS
### Ivana Milankova

In the land of thrones
there was a bridge: I walked along the dream.
In the land of thrones
there was a city: I existed from events.
In the land of thrones
there was a temple: I passed through two minds.
In the land of thrones
in someone's eye assembled
under the veils remembered.
In the land of thrones
someone from long gone shades
calls to me.
In the underground mass, in swarms, in mirrors
I look, I listen, it echoes
*To crime! To Rome!*
I conquer nature, temper, parade, velvet finesses.
I descend.
And the thrones descend.
And the land descends.

The kingdom enters the sea.
In the other's Mind
the perfect act takes place.
And it could have been so easy, personal
with proud entourage, cortiers, and air.

Translated by Tomislav Longinović


## CELEBRATIONS IN BABYLON, OR ABOUT THE WILL OF GODS
### Ivana Milankova

Everything outside me is image, miracle, sixth sense,
a far off dream, on the border,
maybe the north one.
Beyond him the winds blow
and the great white force
called Nothing.

And one more, below the South,
on a heavenly sledge,
conceals the smoke and laws of young Fire in amphoras,
sends the voice from the aquarium,
the heralds of the Great Southern House
from the twelve sea spirits
and the twelve corners
Into one, abysmal, no one wonders.
Nobody's trace, nobody's alien
in circulation outside the image.
Only the center: I touch it, lose it,
I see it and do not see it, I do not deny.
Neither the star, nor the age, nor the step, nor the trace,
nobody dared to walk
across my face remembered my vulcanoes,
across the skin inscribed by stone.
The short anatomy of destiny:
the memory spoken by triangles
the marble tomb with fireworks from celebrations in Babylon
and all the Forbidden, Inner
with eyes closed in the day
I became their shore.

Translated by Tomislav Longinović

## TO THE TEACHER OF GEOMETRY
Ivana Milankova

Dear Teacher,
I will never arrive
to the fifth degree of knowledge,
I will never touch Your circles
with fingers defiled by shadows,
with palms-traces of the sunken obelisk,
since I was down
in the quarry of souls
among the lonely legions,
—where the Cunning One bowed down,
honored, listened
and supposedly returned.
I returned too
with the weight of lower things
and the Great Memory.
This light blinds me.
Therefore rather NO.
I do not engage with You
in a dialogue about parallel planes
until I parallelly endure
my own life.
Only the longing
—neither truth nor lie: silence, silk,
invisible herald, a hunting scene.
Only longing. Yes, that is my weight.
—I am the water:
30,000 demons drain me simultaneously.

Translated by Tomislav Longinović

## CALL ME ATLANTIS
Ivana Milankova

Until the end of dying
    there will be one wind in your throat
    and one train, voices and the storm.
When the landscapes are gone and the end comes to a stop
    you will be a trace on a distant ice.

And when the final face takes place
   only the sky and your face will remain unfinished.
The stone will take long to end, the soil will be deep.
   And you will breathe beyond the heaven.
And only this image will last long on the skin
   and afterwards, beyond some other and some alien:
the cathedral with the bottom of fog and leaves.
Just the image, the experience. Do not confuse. Forbid the thought,
   because of you, because of the cathedral and leaves.
So the solitude will not remain personal.
   And the light will breathe beyond the heaven,
unperfected.
Before the soul there will be certain signs:
   bracelets, rings, pearls, and mother-of-pearl buttons—
spaces and objects of prophecy.
   And then from the Atlantic
the land of mirrors appears.
   And you slowly remember the city where your eyes
began, for the first time.

Translated by Tomislav Longinović

## POEM FOR ALL SENTIENT BEINGS
### Nina Živančević

Joyful! Practitioner of great Adi Yoga,
happy prisoner of self-discipline who
endures the coldest breaths of
the freezing January air
in the midst of all East Village poverty and beauty,
Joyful! Think of the beings who
were never born, never will be, or ceased to exist—
to them this poem belongs and not to Carlo
whose sweet sweet voice lifts me up
from all these phenomena and
like the purest oil keeps
my lamp burning in such a dark, murky night

(Written in English)

POETS' SONG
Nina Živančević

We must be tigers,
and lions too
and roar in the big thick forest
(all animals surrender to them,
they are here to destroy our ego,
pride, arrogance and folly.)
Action is like an insect—
it should not hurt
anyone's place,
our principle is
infinite like the sky
as we are the real
kings of the state.

(Written in English)

MYTHOLOGY
Nina Živančević

A punk woman is dancing in the street,
her tits bouncing and her glossy zebra-hair
standing five feet high;

A punk woman is dancing along First Avenue,
her nipples smeared with relish from a pizza parlour.

Perhaps she did not lose her number which she
wanted to call last night, as the bass player
makes her ERRORS   ERRORS   ERRORS

almost EROs like a love, or a tattoo print
on her pelvic bone, like a
constrictor/transvestite's touch
TENDER   TENDER   TENDER

       Mythologies we create for ourselves,
thus they do not create us—
a punk woman, like a golden panache
dances in the street

(Written in English)

## LINED UP
### Nina Živančević

They were all lined up
as if they had something important to say,
as if they had somewhere to go!
(Staten Island pigeons)
And if you stared at me instead of
at the Statue of Liberty, it's only because
the more transparent I grow, the more cryptic I become,
or as Neruda put it "I loved her, and sometimes
she would love me too," well, I don't know
what happens in the summer—only one
certainty in November's fog: biting this sandwich.
sliced ham, swiss and lettuce—
the first one I ever got
in this town the way I really liked it,
or cared to like

(Written in English)


## TRANSPARENCY
### Nina Živančević

I don't know who
all these people are
this woman in a courtroom who killed
her husband telling me that she did it
because he was still in love with his first wife
who left his baby five months old at their doorstep
and then she, the stepmother, had to bring her up,
take care of her as if she "was her own daughter"
and then the father decided to return to his child's mother,
and I am wondering
—whose circus is this, anyway?
—and whose world, whose justice applies
to us all, and don't I have my own worlds
to attend to, worlds much less complex
deprived and personal where advice

is fed to the birds and where "folly" replaces
words such as "truth" and "justice,"
beyond the impossible dwells the grey quietness
of absence, which becomes a mode for moods
like "let it be" and "let it go"
which I hear as I listen
to the voices in my skull
sharp and dull sounds of an outer echo
which we perceive as a hectic hour

(Written in English)

# Slovenia, compiled by Aleš Debeljak

## Slovene Poetry in the Eighties
## by Aleš Debeljak

Unlike their repression-savvy predecessors in the fifties and sixties—such as the leading modernist poets Veno Taufer, Dane Zajc, and Gregor Strniša—young Slovene writers in the eighties never lived under life-threatening totalitarianism. Hardly a time of absolute freedom, the eighties in Slovenia were nonetheless marked by the growing civil disobedience that has brought about an unexperienced "open space." This accounted for the uncanny problem of identity that hadn't forced itself with such magnitude upon the older writers. They knew all along that their writing was, at its source, speaking on behalf of the oppressed masses regardless of how personal their messages might be on the surface.

In a communist regime, constantly eroding under the radical criticism spearheaded by prominent members of the Slovene Writers Union, young *literati* were left with few ideological taboos to debunk, almost no political blacklists to challenge, and virtually no censors peeking over their shoulders. They had to design their own responses to a predicament that currently haunts so many an east European writer: "How to address broader moral and social dilemmas of the time when they seem to be better dealt with by anti-totalitarian activists?"

As a moral authority, a writer was, until the eighties, prompted to shape the popular imagination, thereby resonating the rich tradition of Slovene *literati qua* politicians. Young writers had thus two strikes against them. A sense of palpable danger present in their older colleagues' poems—nearly always backed up by a personal experience of jail or persecution—was evidently not their turf. The vocation of a writer as a people's mouthpiece has, by the same token, dwindled, thanks to the improved conditions of public discourse. In short, prospects for carving out a recognizable niche in a larger cultural frame seemed to be rather unpromising.

The writers who came into their own in the eighties were born between 1955 and 1965. Their social outlets were the cultural quarterly, *Literature*, and a small publishing house, *Aleph Press*. As a generation, they quickly overcame the obstacles of existing social void created by a move away from the literary matters and started charting the heretofore neglected realm, the depths of idiosyncratic poetic mythologies. They steered clear from an activist commitment, opting instead for an "anti-political" identity.[1] It comes then as a small surprise that Tomaž Šalamun, a seminal avant-gardist, was embraced as a writer who didn't succumb to the allure of explicit political critique, thus coming right up their alley.[2] To be sure, young poets were at odds with his experimental poetic strategies. What appealed to them was his sensibility in finding a transcendental meaning in the rituals of mundane life. On more than one account, the young authors defined their individual poetics in a poignant dialectic of rejection and acceptance of what Šalamun's poetry represents.

In the mid eighties, the lowest common denominator of the young writers was a belief that a creative self can only flourish beyond the political divisions of progressive versus conservative. More so than was the case with the authors in the seventies—including Milan Jesih, Boris A. Novak, Milan Dekleva, Jure Detela, and others—an individual voice now had a chance to be fully spelled out in expressive artistic rather than tacit ideological terms. Arguing for a critical separation of civil engagement on the one hand and autonomous writing on the other— long overdue in eastern Europe as a whole—the young authors championed a distinct attitude: a writer can only aspire to be a witness of his or her times if the writing itself is free of any external prescriptions, no matter what "the cause" might be.

While less gripping than a metaphysical vortex and its horrid political implications in the poetry of Gregor Strniša, the poetic vision of Jure Potokar exercises the same participation in the noble tradition of a poet as a clairvoyant. This time around, however, the existential scope has considerably narrowed, compelling the poet to dwell at length upon his disappointment with a redemption through the written word. Unlike his mentors, he doesn't believe in the healing power of words any more. In Potokar's poems, one can see how the struggle against the silence gives way to an abstract mysticism, replete with the perseverance that bears true witness to a postmodern condition. From under the layers of mass media generated glossolalia, the poet unearths the authentic human experience of longing for something that is forever lost. In a paradoxical reversal of poetic mission, he demonstrates that a need for communication and community governs our lives even when it gets dwarfed by seemingly more pressing concerns.

Aleš Debeljak is, alongside with Potokar, also an heir to Gregor Strniša and, by extension, to Rilke. Trakl, and Celan. In his poems, the dark vision of the world as a place with no exit takes on a nomadic dimension. The melancholic subject of his poems, a veteran of loneliness and voluntary exile, is traversing various landscapes of geography that gradually become a metaphor for a landscape of the restive mind. At the core of his poems is the impossible pursuit—the pursuit of the impossible: an effort to "break through to the other side," much as it ceased to use the language of ancient sages and resorted to everyday vocabulary, still very much underscores his poetic incantations.

While the public at large focused on heated political debates by older writers who, by and large, stopped writing literature *stricto sensu*, the young generation quietly labored to win the hearts of the sophisticated readers. By no means an escapist lot, "a generation without charismatic leaders" contemplated ordinary stories of ordinary people, discovering the spiritual consequences of social change in marginal sentiments and ephemeral feelings.

Maja Haderlap is a good case in point. Writing from the vantage point of a member of an indigenous Slovene minority in Austria, she managed to marry the elegiac tones of an assertion of her ethnic place with larger observations of nature. By drawing upon the semiforgotten language of change in nature she developed a sensitive eye for the transformations that her social habitat is currently undergoing.

Her popularity among readers and critics alike is perhaps rivaled by Alojz Ihan, who established himself with the publication of *Silver Coin* (1986), a collection of poetry that carried his voice well beyond the boundaries of the traditional public. His adamant opposition to the avangardist demands to push the limits of language has led him to model his poetry on the prewar poetics of Edvard Kocbek, a renown visionary and essayist.[3] Under the influence of Kocbek's premise that a poet must speak with an awareness of transcendence in mind, Ihan cast doubt on corruptible moralism while pursuing a coherent personal ethic. His accessible verses retain the sensitive touch of a naive child who dares to expose the naked emperor.

In as much as the Slovene poets in the eighties comprehend public matters in terms of private trials, they continue to raise the right questions. With the diminishing importance of literature in social reality they strive to seize another reality, that of spiritual and metaphysical experience. For a culture where plain bad writing with political pretensions quite often passed for exquisite work of art, this is perhaps no negligible accomplishment.

# Notes

1. Georgy Konrad, *Anti-Politics: Central European Meditations*, trans. Richard Allen (San Diego: Harcourt, Brace, Jovanovich, 1984).
2. See Tomaž Šalamun, *Selected Poems*, ed. Charles Simic (New York: Ecco Press, 1988).

3. See Edvard Kocbek, *Na vratih zvečer/At the Door at Evening,* trans. Tom Ložar (Dorian, Quebec, Canada: The Muses Co./Aleph, 1990).

# About the Poets

## ALEŠ DEBELJAK

Aleš Debeljak (b. 1961) studied comparative literature at and graduated from the University of Ljubljana and is now a doctoral candidate in social thought at Syracuse University, New York. He published four books of poetry and two of cultural criticism and edited a book of American short stories in Slovenia. There he won a number of awards, including Prešeren Prize (Slovene National Book Award). He also won Hayden Carruth Poetry Prize at Syracuse University. His poetry books are translated into Serbo-Croatian, Polish, and Italian. In the United States, he published a chapbook *Chronicle of Melancholy* (1989). His poems were featured in *Child of Europe: A New Anthology of East European Poetry* (Penguin, 1991).

## MAJA HADERLAP

Maja Haderlap (b. 1961) studied theater studies at the University of Vienna, Austria. She is the editor of a literary magazine, *Mladje* in the Carinthia region of Austria where she makes her home. She published two collections of poems, *Žalik pesmi (Nymph Poems)* and *Bajalice (Spellbound Poems).* She won several awards, including prestigious Presseren Prize (Slovene National Book Award). She translates from and into German and writes criticism, particularly on literature by Slovene minority in Austria.

## ALOJZ IHAN

Alojz Ihan (b. 1961), an M.D., is a research fellow at the Institute of Microbiology, University of Ljubljana. He published the following books of poetry: *Srebrnik (Silver Coin,* 1985), *Igralci pokra (The Poker Players,* 1989), and *Selected Poems* (1990). The first two were translated into Serbo-Croatian and Macedonian. He won numerous literary awards in Yugoslavia, including prestigious Prešeren Prize (Slovene National Book Award). He was a chief editor for Ljubljana-based Aleph Press and is on the editoral board of an important literary quarterly, *Literatura.*

## JURE POTOKAR

Jure Potokar (b. 1956) studied Slavic literatures at the University of Ljubljana. He works as a music editor and a translator in Ljubljana. *Aiton*

(1980), *Pokrajina se tu nagiba proti jugu* (*The Landscape Here Bends toward the South*, 1982), *Ambienti zvočnih pokrajin* (*The Ambients of Sonic Landscapes*, 1986), and *Stvari v praznini* (*Things in Void*, 1990) are among his books of poetry. He has a number of translations from English to his credit, including sections in an authoritative *Anthology of American Poetry in 20th Century*.

## TOMAŽ ŠALAMUN

Tomaž Šalamun (b. 1941) studied art history at the University of Ljubljana. As a member of the avant-garde group OHO, he exhibited worldwide, including the Museum of Modern Art, New York. In 1971–73 he was a member of International Writing Program at the University of Iowa. In Slovenia he published more than twenty books of poetry. He won many awards, including prestigious Prešeren Prize (Slovene National Book Award). His poetry books have appeared in German, Serbo-Croatian, and Polish. His book in English is *Selected Poems* (Ecco, 1988).

# Slovene Poetry

### WHITE ITHACA
### Tomaž Šalamun

stars, that you salute me
that you set the fire, the nape of beasts
ignite the cold, arcadia
grape flames in shadows, the sound of helmets

that you reveal the sea, greed, christening to me
straying of white sheep, scorched flesh
that once more I see color sailing
hear peals of our lady, collapsed railings

that I grant flight to animals, bread to people
sin to gentle breezes, a razor to wine
that I see ships of bauxite, sun in the earth
chains on walls, the tribe of days

that you join stars together, burn down in blueness
that you leave behind no scent no crumbs, no silence no pictures
that I yet see the bamboo, native fields
the chewing of deer, white ithaca

Translated by Michael Biggins

## AIR
### Tomaz Šalamun

Your body is a pipe
through which wheat, food, oil flow,
a bridge that horseman race down.
Your hands are a window,
your words are a window,
your body a window.
Whatever you touch
you stroke in your thoughts,
it burns in frightful mountains and gives scent,
in every movement,
in every breath you guide me.
I bend over,
I bend over,
and get up,
and get up and go.
You tell me not to use
bloated, clever weapons,
the hungry, emaciated weapons of air,
I should be careful,
You tell me to be pleasant and I'm pleasant.
You tell me to be wealthy and I'm wealthy.
Sky-blue,
powerful my strongholds,
so I go shooting through the souls of kings
and travel to Nineveh from the Balkans,
from Nineveh to Babylon.
You've named me:
I am handsome and contemptuous, because I'm strong and moist.
Your body is a pipe
through which wheat, food, oil flow,
a bridge that horsemen race down.
Your hands are a window,
your words are a window,
your body a window.
Whatever you touch
you stroke in your thoughts,
it burns in frightful mountains and gives scent.

Translated by Michael Biggins

## I AM A MASON
Tomaž Šalamun

I am a mason, a priest of dust
hardened as a monster, as bread's crust
I am a water-lily, a warrior of sacred trees
sacred dreams, I shout with angels

I am a castle, a dead wall
I said ships, am a ferryman to travellers
o wood! wood!
come herons, blood

come gardeners, shine light
come open hand, glass
blue whirlpools, come water surface
the sliding wind of creatures from different fields

here the pastures are burnt, the lava boils
the shepherds are waiting, they impatiently stamp their wings
dogs smell each other, wolves
here dwell memory, order, omens

Translated by Sonja Kravanja

## PRAYER FOR BREAD
Tomaž Šalamun

He, who will not know how to drink the miracle,
will burn down. It is that powerful. And he,
who in the miracle won't grasp the soil like a bulldozer,
will be like the wing birds discarded.
We are humans, not flowers.
Their tranquility blossoms only out of dead flesh,
so let's not run ahead of time.
The spirit never loses itself in haste,
which, if it runs ahead empty, returns.
I am a circle until I become power.
And if I hurt your face,
hit your screams when you sleep,
if I dispossess you over and over like the poison
of chaos,

kneel like a sacred animal
that just finished nursing.
Kiss the ground and cast
a curse on me.
Chain me down with your hatred,
so I can crush you into
love.

Translated by Sonja Kravanja

## TORTURING THE SLAVE
### Tomaž Šalamun

Slave, will your breath halt?
Will the Slavs destroy the geography of their cabbage?
In the throat of she-deer lies a lacquer globe
that my mother had eaten.
On it the picture of Jerusalem, on it only.
Did you make the grass grow?
Tie threads on bombshells?
Make gold out of fireclay?
My blotting paper lies in a crystal moor
and it is your fault, slave!
Just look at my optical gargantua.
Knives, like the bubbling water of occult races,
are uniting with the gauze on my finger.
What are you waiting for?
Why don't you stop the weather just
like highlanders used to in olden times?
They cut down everything obstructing the wind,
snapped brambles and chopped them up.
Rolled oak-trees down.
Timber-slides came later,
after gravitation had won.
You are crying, son, because of being soaked,
but your calendar is not in the spirit of the Maya.

Your hips seem to be stolen from
my mountains in Crete and when
barbarians will stamp on them with their boots
you'll leave the revolving door
so white-hot from the solitude
of the she-deer, that stags will dash into
the forest, already smelling of other burned
stags, and sing the last pious accord of their
suicide.

Translated by Sonja Kravanja

## NEW POEMS
### Alojz Ihan

I had to decide to start
writing poems again. Besides the ones I've
steadily been writing for some years now. To write
for each new poem one more, a parallel,
different poem. In secret. I feel that there's some sense to
this. Something similar happens
to a man with a woman he has loved, really loved,
for a long time. There comes a need
to start loving her again. To begin a new love
next to the old. Parallel to it. In silence.
In secret. And if the love is really longstanding,
it needs more silence all the time, more composure.
For new and new beginnings and continuations.
For nothing must be noticed on the outside.
I write this in all sincerity, without irony.
My girl, before we make love, still
draws the curtains because of the neighbors.
Though in some silence of hers she may be stepping naked
into a city bus, her monthly pass in her hand.
What is essential is to know and despite that to play
an old, simple fairytale. To celebrate a rite
whose gods died long ago. Precisely
because.

Translated by Tom Ložar

## THE SIXTH DAY
### Alojz Ihan

I know, the fifth night is when the doubts come,
and unpleasant dreams, for everything is done, everything
set into motion, and then and there You realized that
one day Your stars would be left without light,
that Your sun would cool, and the plants
would wither, the animals die, for
no being come from the word is created
for a dark sun, for the cold, and endless aloneness,
for suffering, and no way out. And when You saw
that one day amid all this you would again be left
all alone, terrified, on the sixth day, you grabbed for the clay.

Translated by Tom Ložar

## ACTRESSES
### Alojz Ihan

They have an uncanny ability to watch themselves
even when not in front of a looking class, and, with at least   a
tiny part of their gaze, they monitor themselves unceasingly.
Their every expression they diligently inspect,
they see precisely how it suits them, this or that
smile, gaze, wrinkle on the cheek, and therefore
they seem always a little absent, except the ones,
the very best, who are capable of eyeing themselves in
the faces and, above all, the eyes of others, and are thus
happiest when there are faces galore, before which
they then stroll, screech, sing, dance;
before which they are happy little girls in a house of
a thousand curved mirrors; hours on end they could spend
watching themselves as if believing that with each new
image they become much more beautiful still.

Translated by Tom Ložar

## LITTLE SOLDIER OF THE BIG ARMY
### Alojz Ihan

Little soldier of the big army, don't be afraid,
your war will be won, you cannot make
a mistake so big that you could lose it, and defeated
will the soldiers of the little armies be, they cannot
perform heroics grand enough to be victorious;
don't be afraid, little soldier of the big army,
proudly will you march down the streets of captured
cities, on the highest steeples will you hang your
flags, in taverns the frightened waiters
will commandeer for you the best tables, and the beautiful
foreign women will answer to your slightest gesture;
no one will ever force you to flee, and you will be used
only to victories, always, as long as you are a little soldier
of the big army, so don't be afraid, your war will be won,
you cannot make a mistake so big that you could
lose it, and defeated will the soldiers of the little armies be,
they cannot perform heroics grand enough to be
victorious; don't be afraid, little soldier of the big army!

Translated by Tom Ložar

## THE BOY IN THE TREE
### Alojz Ihan

for Edvard Kocbek

Then they begin to search for him. Torches aflame,
people scatter through the forest
calling out his name. Boatmen
take to the lake and sink
their poles into its murky depths. The dogs
are let loose from their chains. The boy squats
in the tree and watches in distress.
A little while longer and he'll hear the weeping,
the bells will ring, out of the house
a prayer will sound. Then the boy will slide
stealthily down from his tree
and, comforted now, head
for the precipice.

Translated by Tom Ložar

## NORTHERN ELEGIES I
### Aleš Debeljak

Horses sculpted in black marble. In town squares swept by gusts of winter wind. Rip themselves off their pedestals? No: perhaps they're tempted to go with the boy. The one who woke this morning, serious and dizzy. Woke from sleep overrun by a faint image, blurring. His companions try to keep him from leaving right away. He walks in silence toward the North. Across wheat fields, through birch groves. He won't rest till he reaches the glacier. While he ages like wine. Will he return? Eskimos lead him safely through snowfields and over the Bering Strait. In their boats he sleeps easily. Like anyone would: this is his home. Not that he would erase memory. Only in the glint of frozen water, in crystals and smooth ice does day become bitter enough for him. Only one move—and what was once solid disappears. The only thing that lasts is the careless flow of time. In the dreams of other men the boy looks calmly over the dark backs of horses and knows what I don't know how to say. Others would need a lifetime. Today, tomorrow, yesterday: it's all the same. I, too, will do what I should have done long ago.

Translated by Christopher Merrill and the author

## NORTHERN ELEGIES II
### Aleš Debeljak

The image—lost forever—comes to life again. Always the same room, embedded in darkness. Flies on the cracked walls. In the stale air, the smell of stomach acids and urine. A child immersed in a picture book of exotic plants, frozen in an endless moment. A blue labyrinth of veins shines through his white skin. Was he raised in love by Albanian women in the damp and dark? A face bitterness turned pale. Dry pears on the windowsill. Still life. The sand in the hourglass crumbles into dust. Someday, somewhere, perhaps this boy, now at rest, will become a man who travels, cries, causes pain. Who will think of home only when he catches a reflection of eyes—as lonely as ours—staring back at him from mirrors, sand, and grass. Doubts will ravage him. Visions of abandoned ports, pride, drunkenness—everything will haunt him. Like the one who writes these lines, he'll know we all share the memory of empty rooms and blind windows.

Translated by Christopher Merrill and the author

## NORTHERN ELEGIES III
Aleš Debeljak

After all, why sadness? Why fear? We don't know the depths of Finnish lakes, the cold of the Siberian taiga, the map of the Gobi desert. We don't even know what's in your dreams. Mine, too. That's the way it is. But you, as always: listening in the dark, lighting matches, gazing straight ahead. The man whose name you won't forget—even in the middle of the night— still hasn't called. You're hungry. In the corner of the room an old man in a rocking chair creaks back and forth, the shining keys of the sax laid on its side reflect your soft face, which you hide from yourself and others. Framed by the window, horses hover above the ground, wandering aimlessly through men's destinies, silk tails sailing in the wind. And for a moment, while the old man leans over a book—leafed through hundreds of times—you see the riders galloping across the fields, through the woods, heads down, black hair waving in the setting sun, the vanishing sun. Gone. Is that why you can't remember the short poem describing the whole world as it was and will be, why dusk blinds you to the stories of everyone, stories known only to the man whose name you won't forget—even in the middle of the night, the man who stands somewhere in the open, alone, in the dark, on the high plains?

Translated by Christopher Merrill and the author

## NORTHERN ELEGIES IV
Aleš Debeljak

It could also be a church. Lacking portals, frescoes, stucco work. Smoothly cut from fragile stone, perhaps. As though dropped into the hot desert sand from far off, from some unknown world. In this space I remain as I was. You're the one who changes. The watch hands gradually transport you to February. You sit, possibly all afternoon, beneath arches clearly the result of a mad dream. The sun's warmth filters through fissures in the roof. Patches of light, whole nets of them, fumble over blackened canvasses. I couldn't say if you can even distinguish shadows from the darkened wall. You hold your breath. Don't move. The outlines of faces you've met and forgotten, their brothers and sisters, the Russian steppe traversed so many times—all congeal in a mass, and fade from vision. As in high mountains, silence saturates the air. Though some muffled noise or even murmuring, it's true, emanates from somewhere. It echoes emptily. Gently settles in you. It softens you, so that you're wholly changed. More receptive to passion, longing. To the fluttering of titmice, the way you hiked (and in a sense still do) through the Karst's meadows and to the sea. What that whispering is exactly, I can't say. A song of dervishes from Konya? The half-completed poem of some Romanian, homesick, dying far from the Danube's shores? I can't say. But this at least: what interests me is you, the way you sink into the twilight. Your face covered in your hands. Seeing nothing. Your eyes will only open once day is finally through. And you'll be older by as many years as flashed by all the monks that lived here. Riper for the insight. The love that outlasts separations.

Translated by Michael Biggins

## NORTHERN ELEGIES V
### Aleš Debeljak

The ink runs in the bowels of cuttlefish. A bird calls sharply from low-hanging clouds. A windhover perhaps. The glowing surfaces of rock formations cool. Summer melts. A cicada's crushed wing gives scent. And you, where are you in this picture? Staring over waves of grapeleaves? If that's really you, then you're not speaking with the person who stands beside you. Bent slightly forward, as though trying to identify in the depths of fields the thing that's drawing your attention. Condensing in a point on the edge of the horizon. Dimly shining, as before a thunderburst. No more threatening than the wavering shadows that cast the portrait of a stranger on your wall at dusk. This moment, seeming to last ages. A boy runs over the dunes. Does he know that language provides many words for the same things?

Translated by Michael Biggins

## ANATHEMA
### Jure Potokar

I don't trust that deeply in myself, nor do I trust
that deeply in changes *outside* myself. All these syllables
withering on soaked paper are just a pretense,

clumsy attempts at exact definition, as we know.
the anathema has been pronounced, become a cry
whose resonance confirms the power and persistence of the cold

within numbed selves, where it's meant to flourish.
afterwards how calm I am, loquacious in my solitude,
and how belief wanders in and out of the cobwebbed church.
yet I don't trust that deeply in myself. for that the stone's too hard.

Translated by Michael Biggins

## AFTER A DEFEAT
Jure Potokar

after a defeat your movements are more guarded.
it's hard to stop the fissures that let the cold
seep through your bleached, divided self.

yet blind endurance drags on. the words
you've spoken have exposed only you, and this
is why silence can so often be such balm,

the counterpart to gusts of air in a broken flute
as it gathers speed. in silence's carminic shadings
you lose your warm breath, and the capillaries in you

burst with such a strange and wonderful sound.

Translated by Michael Biggins


## TOUCHING
Jure Potokar

you're left with a body that has passed into memory, like
a nomad's dwelling that layers and layers of sand
bury with unmatched persistence. bitter, barely discernible,

yet so final. you'll count, and with intolerable
clarity, perhaps, make out a coin ringing against
cement, snow falling softly into the November nights.

you'll be alone in this listless time of bitter colors,
where there is no space for irony, alone among
bloodthirsty smells of times gone by, alone and in company

thinking of a touch that will never again be yours.

Translated by Michael Biggins

## NIGHTS WITH NO MORNING (V)
### Jure Potokar

it's all here: the gust of wind in young girls' hair,
the crude joke provoking laughter, the shiver of lovers
in a close room that smells of musk, childrens'

longing that fills clouds, the silent persistence of rust
in metal seams, the plan of a house that someone
will build, the gait of an animal prowling the savannah

and the unseeing gaze of party ideologues.
all this and much more is revealed in the landscape
that evaporates before your eyes each day here

when the steely pain of loneliness fills your lungs.

Translated by Michael Biggins

## TONALITE
### Jure Potokar

if time improves us, then why these trembling lips,
blenching face and cold, faint shudder?
why do the grass's awful spikelets lash

our faces like a whip,
reduce our range of vision, and then
eclipse it altogether?

so it's true, just as the world reveals each night
in dreams, that the usually pliant core
of blazing magma turns all too quick

to hard, unyielding tonalite.

Translated by Michael Biggins

## [UNTITLED]
### Maja Haderlap

who as a stranger openly offers you effacement and loneliness? who
  stops and
turns back and sees their own uninhabitedness? who grows blind from
  the days
which make their appearance with weary dimness, pallid is everything
  that
powerfully imposes itself on space: the bridge, the house, the person.

a modest shudder arcs into blisters of sweat, such is the deaf sense,
  that everything
rounds itself into foreign worlds, and the forced termination prowls
  furtively,
and the silence becomes golden-tongued and does not comprehend
  what it cannot believe.
finally the emptiness goes through the corneas into a net and stops
  being.

Translated by Tom Priestly

## [UNTITLED]
### Maja Haderlap

there are days when tapestries are hanging in the town for the curious
  japanese and
platinum lights shimmer like silver over the entrances. there is a time
  when memory
comes from the promised land quite absently and deceptively, and
  death is cool only
when touched. the day is all jagged, trampled, and there is no plea for
  life.

there are cramped times when I choose incarnate stupidities anywhere,
  I approach on tiptoe,
I swallow them and would believe something of it all; the singing, the
  sentence which
deserves to be reconciled a bit later and becomes numb with
  repetition, sensuous is
the good whom I have wooed and who, with opium lips, makes fun of
  the orphan, of anyone.

Translated by Tom Priestly

## [UNTITLED]
### Maja Haderlap

nothing remains of the illusion of security, which settles like a sickness
    in the
memory and persists, impatient. the endless knot here, so that I am at
    a loss for words;
the elevator of the year descends to a hallway too low and the
    vineyards
outside recall the place. impermanence has seized the walls and the
    innuendoes.

total alarm veils the audacious charm; anew I choose among the
    phantoms of home
and abroad, and attempts at domestication come to naught in flight. I
    note the ancient grievance
and the idea of the experience of weakness, as if it could not increase,
and remembrance is shortened into the fleeting sensation that the
    microbes are trembling.

Translated by Tom Priestly

## [UNTITLED]
### Maja Haderlap

I have walked
after days without peace
full of words of ill repute
in among the larches.

the earth
this day has been
bloated with a clammy heat.

perspiring and
breathing heavily
I am aware
that I am walking on and on.

in a clearing
I wrap myself
in the smell of pitch,
I pick a full fist
of strawberries,
with my mouth full
I sit through till evening,
happy as beetles
in spring.

Translated by Tom Priestly

## FEAR
### Maja Haderlap

I breathe in
and hold my breath,
in on myself
I am huddled.

fearfully
through the door,
I clutch the handle
to find out
if it is shut fast
behind me.

then I breathe out
and again breathe in,
perhaps
there is still someone
behind the door.
I take a look
and I know
there is no one.

bewildered,
pressed close to myself
in the iron-and-concrete building
alone
out into the narrow
undeafened night
I slide.

Translated by Tom Priestly

# Section Editors and Introduction Authors

## General Introduction

BURTON RAFFEL is a author, critic, and translator well-known for his translations of works from many languages, including his highly praised editions of *Beowulf* and Rabelais's *Gargantua and Pantagruel*. He is now preparing a new English version of *Don Quixote*. His discussions of the craft of translation are *Art of Translating Poetry* and *The Forked Tongue: A Study of the Translation Process*. He also has written studies of Ezra Pound, Robert Lowell, and T. S. Eliot as well as *How to Read a Poem* and two works on Victorian America.

## Estonian Poetry Editor

DORIS KAREVA (b. 1958) has published six books of poetry; *Buudutus (Touch*, (1981), *Salateadvus (The Secret Consciousness*, 1983), *Vari ja viiv (Shadow and While*, 1986), and *Armuaeg (Days of Grace*, 1991) are among them. She has also translated works by Emily Dickinson, Anna Ahmatova, Hasso Krull (Mas Harnoon), and others.

## Latvian Poetry Editor

AINA KRAUJIETE (b. 1923), after studies in medicine at the W. von Goethe Institute in Frankfurt, Germany, worked at the Sloan-Kettering Institute for Cancer Research and other similar institutions. She is the author of five collections of poetry. Her poems have been translated into several languages, and she has translated works by E. Pound, M. Moore, C. Sandburg, R. Frost, O. Paz, C. Miłosz, and A. Vosnesensky. Kraujiete is the poetry editor of the Latvian literary journal *Jaună Gaita* (New Way), and is the recipient of major Latvian literary awards, including Z. Lazda Prize of Poetry. She resides in New York and writes critical essays and scripts for Radio Free Europe.

# Latvian Poetry Introduction

Jurius Silenieks (b. 1925 in Riga, Lavita), after graduating from high school in Riga, fled to Germany in 1944, and in 1950 he emigrated to the U.S. After military service, he studied French at the University of Nebraska where in 1963 he earned his Ph.D. In 1960 he joined the faculty of Carnegie Mellon University, where he taught and later served as department head and director of Modern Languages until his retirement in 1990. Silenieks is author and editor of several books on Latvian and Caribbean Francophone literatures. He has published numerous articles and reviews in American, Latvian, French, and African publications.

# Lithuanian Poetry Editor

Rimvydas Šilbajoris, an essayist and student of literature, was born in 1926 in Kretinga, Lithuania. He studied at the University of Mainz, Germany, and graduated from Columbia University in 1962. He has taught Russian language and literature at Oberlin College and at The Ohio State University, and he has published several books dealing with Russian and Lithuanian languages and literatures.

# Bulgarian Poetry Editor

Ludmilla Popova-Wightman was born in Sofia, Bulgaria. She translates and teaches Bulgarian and Russian at the Princeton Language Group. Her translations have appeared in *The New York Review of Books, The New England Review and Bread Loaf Quarterly, The Southerly* (Australia), and *Mr. Cogito.*

# Czech and Slovak Poetry Editors

Edward J. Czerwinski holds a BA degree from Grove City College, an M.A. in English and Theater from Pennsylvania State University, and an M.A. in Russian literature—as well as a Ph.D.—from the University of Wisconsin. He has spent several years (1962–64, 1967–68, 1973–74, 1983–84, 1987–88, 1990–91) on research grants in Poland, Yugoslavia, Czechoslovakia, Romania, and the Soviet Union. His publications include more than a hundred articles on east European theater and drama, translations from Polish, Russian, and Serbo-Croatian, and hundreds of reviews of east European literatures. The editor of *Slavic and East European Arts,* he is also on the editorial board of *World Literature Today, Comparative Drama,* and *Twentieth-*

*Century Literature.* The founder and director of the Slavic Cultural Center in Port Jefferson, New York, he was instrumental in introducing American audiences to the works of east European dramatists. In 1990 he was invited to become a member of the PEN American Center.

STANA DOLEZIAL was born in Prague, Czechoslovakia, and graduated from Charles University, Prague. She taught in a prestigious high school and the College of Arts in Prague until 1968. At the State University of New York at Stony Brook, she has taught Russian and Czech. She was director and coordinator of a summer intensive course in Russian. She is at presently assistant to the editor of the *Slavic and East European Arts* journal. Her publications include: *Translations of Eighteen Short Stories by Jaroslav Hasek* (1991).

# Hungarian Poetry Editor

BRUCE BERLIND's translations of modern Hungarian poetry, for which he was awarded the PEN Memorial Medal, include *Selected Poems of Àgnes Nemes Nagy* and *Birds and Other Relations: Selected Poems of Dezsö Tandori.* He is Charles A. Dana Professor of English Emeritus at Colgate University.

# Polish Poetry Editor

DANIEL BOURNE spent 1985–87 in Poland on a Fulbright fellowship working on a translation of works by younger Polish poets. He teaches at The College of Wooster where he also edits *Artful Dodge.* A chapbook of his own poetry, *Boys Who Go Aloft,* appeared in 1987 from Sparrow Press, and his poems and translations have appeared in *American Poetry Review, Field, Salmagundi, Partisan Review,* and elsewhere.

# Romanian Poetry Editor

STAVROS DELIGIORGIS (b. 1933), is a Greek who has both studied and taught in Romania. He specializes in the European middle ages (early and more recent) and was a frequent beneficiary of the Romanian Writers Union and its members during the late nineteen seventies.

# Ukrainian Poetry Editor

Larissa M. L. Z. Onyshkevych taught Ukranian literature at Rutgers University. She is literary editor of *Suchasnist* and vice-president of Princeton Research Forum.

# Croatian, Serbian, and Slovenian Poetry Editor

Aleš Debeljak (b. 1961), a comparative literature graduate from The University of Ljubljana, is now a doctoral candidate in social thought at Syracuse University, New York. He published four books of poetry and two of cultural criticism and edited a book of American short stories in Slovenia. There he won a number of awards, aincluding Prešeren Prize (Slovene National Book Award). He also won Hayden Carruth Poetry Prize at Syracuse University. His poetry books are translated into Serbo-Croatian, Polish, and Italian. In the United States, he published a chapbook *Chronicle of Melancholy* (1989). His poems were featured in *Child of Europe: A New Anthology of East European Poetry* (Penguin, 1991).

# About the Translators

## Estonian Translators

BILLY COLLINS is the author of four books of poetry, the most recent *Questions About Angels* (Morrow), a 1990 National Poetry Series selection. He teaches in the English Department at Lehman College (City University of New York).

SAM HAMILL has published several books of original poetry, translations from the Chinese, and critical essays.

GEORGE KURMAN has published articles on a variety of literary topics and has translated the Estonian national epic, *Kalevipoeg* (1982). He is a professor of English at Western Illinois University.

TALVI LAEV translates from various European languages into both English and Estonian. She has worked at the United Nations and Voice of America and currently edits scholarly monographs for a New York-based publisher.

ELMAR MARIPUU is a playwright whose works have been staged in New York, Toronto, and Estonia.

W. K. MATTHEWS (1901–1958) of the University of London edited *Modern Estonian Poetry* for the University of Florida Press in 1953.

GABRIELLA MIROLLO is a native New Yorker who works as a library assistant by day and divides her remaining time between collaborative translations of contemporary Estonian poetry and her own writing.

RIINA TAMM is a college instructor of English as a Second Language in Vancouver, British Columbia, and she is co-translator of Jaan Kaplinski's *The Wandering Border* (Copper Canyon Press, 1987).

MARDI VALGEMÄE has translated Betti Alver, Paul-Eerik Rummo, and Mati Unt and is author of *Accelerated Grimace: Expressionism in the American Drama of the 1920s* and *Ikka teatrist môteldes (Theatre on My Mind)*, which won two prizes in Estonia for best critical book of 1990. He is chairman of the Department of English at Lehman College (City University of New York).

# Latvian Translators

BITĪTE VINKLERS BLUĶIS, born in Latvia, lives in New York. She holds M.A. degrees in English literature and art history, and works as an editor and as a translator of Latvian poetry, prose, and folklore.

INARA CEDRIŅŠ has a B.A. in Writing from Columbia College, Chicago, and attended the School of the Art Institute of Chicago on a graduate level in Printmaking. From illustrating her own poetry with wood engravings, she now focuses mainly on the visual arts. Her writing and translations have appeared in numerous magazines and in book publication. A book of Aleksandrs Čaks' imagist poetry in her translation will be published in 1992 by Barbarian Press, Canada.

GUNA KUPČS CHABEREK (b. 1949) studied Linguistics and Philosophy at the University of Connecticut, graduating magna cum laude in 1982. Recently, her translation of R.Mūks' poem "Amrita, or How To Die" won second prize in the William Kushner Annual Award sponsored by *Bitterroot* magazine; she is pursuing a Master's in Linguistics at the University of Montana and is currently researching Latvian "intonation" or tonal patterns, as well as the vowel system.

ROBERT FEARNLEY is an English poet who has mastered Latvian among other languages. He achieves great poetic precision and clarity in his translations.

ILZE MUELLER KĻAVIŅA (b. 1935 in Latvia) teaches German in Minnesota, and translates Latvian and German poetry and prose. She is winner of the 1983 *Jaunā Gaita* literary translation contest.

J. KĻAVIŅŠ is a translator of Latvian poetry.

VALTERS NOLLENDORFS (b. 1931 in Riga, Latvia) is a Professor of German at the University of Wisconsin-Madison. He has published scholarly work on German and Latvian literature. A Latvian-language poet in his own right, he has translated both from Latvian into English and from English into Latvian.

ASTRIDA STAHNKE (b. 1935, Latvia) lived in Latvia until 1944, when her family escaped from Communist occupation; she lived in Germany, then emigrated to the USA; attended Western Reserve University and Bethel College, St. Paul, Minn. A freelance writer and translator of Latvian literature dramas by Rainis and his wife Aspazija, she has published a 382-page book, *Aspazija: Her life and Her Drama* that offers the only modern analysis of Aspazija's role as an important European writer. Forthcoming (in *Lituanus*) is her article "Vizma Belševica and her Poetry".

MONIKA ZARIŅA (b. 1932 in Riga, Latvia) is a poet and translator. After the tragic death of her husband, the Latvian novelist Guntis Zariņš, she moved with her two sons to Scotland, where she has resided since 1964.

# Lithuanian Translators

MIRGA GIRNIUS was born in 1948 in a displaced person's camp in Oldenberg, Germany. Holder of a Ph.D. in philosophy from the University of Pittsburgh, she is a systems analyst for AT&T and author of poems, essays, reviews, and two children's books published in Lithuania.

RANDALL JARRELL is a well-known American poet.

DEMIE JONAITIS, formerly editor of *Voyager, American Traveler,* and the Lithuanian-American journal *Bridges,* was first published in *Poet Lore* with an essay and translations: "The Lithuanian Folk Song—Its Influence on the Survival of a Denationalized People." She edited and translated refugee Rev. L. Andriekus' book of poetry, *Amens in Amber.* Her translations have appeared in A. Landsbergis's two anthologies and in *Lithuanian Writers of the West.*

CLARK MILLS is the pen name of Clark McBurney, the poet, editor, and publisher who created Voyages Press, which was active in the 1970s.

DORIAN ROTTENBERG's translations were first published in Moscow.

RIMVYDAS ŠILBAJORIS, an essayist and student of literature, was born in 1926 in Kretinga, Lithuania. He studied at the University of Mainz, Germany, and graduated from Columbia University in 1962. He has taught Russian language and literature at Oberlin College and at The Ohio State University, and he has published several books dealing with Russian and Lithuanian languages and literatures.

JONAS ZDANYS, Assistant to the President of Yale University, has published twelve volumes of poetry and translations. Forthcoming is *Four Poets of Lithuania* from the Press of PEN in Lithuania. Holder of a B.A. from Yale and Ph.D. from the State University of New York at Buffalo, he teaches courses in translation theory and practice.

## Bulgarian Translator

LUDMILLA POPOVA-WIGHTMAN was born in Sofia, Bulgaria. She translates and teaches Bulgarian and Russian at the Princeton Language Group. Her translations have appeared in *The New York Review of Books, The New England Review and Bread Loaf Quarterly, The Southerly* (Australia), and *Mr. Cogito.*

## Czech and Slovak Translators

EDWARD J. CZERWINSKI holds the B.A. degree from Grove City College, the M.A. in English and theater from Pennsylvania State University, the M.A. in Russian literature from the University of Wisconsin, and the Ph.D. from the latter university (1965). He has spent several years (1962–64, 1967–68, 1973–74, 1983–84, 1987–88,and 1990–91) on research grants in Poland, Yugoslavia, Czechoslovakia, Romania, and the Soviet Union. His publications include more than a hundred articles on east European the-ater and drama, translations from Polish, Russian, and Serbo-Croatian, and hundreds of reviews of east European literatures. The editor of *Slavic and East European Arts,* he is also on the editorial board of *World Literature Today, Comparative Drama,* and *Twentieth-Century Literature.* The founder and director of the Slavic Cultural Center in Port Jefferson, New York, he was instrumental in introducing American audiences to the works of east European dramatists. In 1990 he was invited to become a member of the PEN American Center.

STANA DOLEZAL was born in Prague, Czechoslovakia, and graduated from Charles University, Prague. She taught in a prestigious high school and the College of Arts in Prague until 1968. At the State University of New York at Stony Brook, she has taught Russian and Czech. She was director and coordinator of a summer intensive course in Russian. She is at present assistant to the editor of the *Slavic and East European Arts* journal. Her publications include *Translations of Eighteen Short Stories by Jaroslav Hasek* (1991).

## Hungarian Translators

BRUCE BERLIND's translations of modern Hungarian poetry, for which he was awarded the PEN Memorial Medal, include *Selected Poems of Ágnes*

*Nemes Nagy* and *Birds and Other Relations: Selected Poems of Dezsö Tandori.* He is Charles A. Dana Professor of English Emeritus at Colgate University.

JASCHA KESSLER, also a winner of the Hungarian PEN Memorial Medal, has translated *The Magician's Garden: 24 Stories of Géza Csath, Under Gemini: The Selected Poetry of Miklós Radnóti,* and an anthology, *The Face of Creation: Contemporary Hungarian Poetry.* He is professor of English and modern literature at the University of California at Los Angeles.

MÁRIA KŐRÖSY holds the M.A. degree in English literature from Budapest University. As English secretary of the Hungarian PEN Club with expertise in producing rough translations for American poets, she has worked for many years with both Bruce Berlind and Jascha Kessler.

LEN ROBERTS was a Fulbright Lecturer at Janus Pannonius University in Pécs, Hungary, in 1988–89 and again in 1990–91. He is on the English Department faculty of Northampton Community College in Bethlehem, Pennsylvania.

# Polish Translators

DANIEL BOURNE spent 1985–87 in Poland on a Fulbright fellowship working on translation of works by younger polish poets. He teaches at The College of Wooster where he also edits *Artful Dodge.* A chapbook of his own poetry, *Boys Who Go Aloft,* appeared in 1987 from Sparrow Press, and his poems and translations have appeared in *American Poetry Review, Field, Salmagundi, Partisan Review,* and elsewhere.

JOHN AND BOGDANA CARPENTER have been responsible for the translation of a wide and impressive array of Polish literature into English but are especially known for their translations of Zbigniew Herbert. In fall 1991 Bogdana became chair of the Slavic Department at the University of Michigan.

RICHARD CHETWYND is a graduate of the Iowa Writers' Workshop, where he worked with Grzegorz Musiał on the translation of Musiał's poetry. Other translations appear in *Poetry East, Mr. Cogito* and *Poet Lore.* He currently teaches in the English Department at Emerson College.

GRAŻYNA DRABIK is a Polish poet, sociologist, and translator. She has taught in the Slavic Department at Columbia University and currently lives in New York City.

PETER HARRIS spent the year of Solidarity (1980–81) teaching in Poland at Marie-Curie Skłodowska University in Lublin. He is currently Professor of English at Colby College and has published poetry in *Chariton Review, College English,* and *Beloit Poetry Journal.*

KAREN KARLESKI is an assistant editor for *Poetry East.* Her own poems currently appear in *Blue Buildings.*

KAREN KOVACIK won the 1990 Poetry Atlanta Chapbook competition with her collection *Return of the Prodigal.* She was the 1991–92 Poetry Fellow at the Institute of Creative Writing at the University of Wisconsin. Other of her translations of Katarzyna Boruń-Jagodzińska recently appeared in *American Poetry Review.*

FRANK KUJAWINSKI has translated a chapbook of the poetry of Stanisław Barańczak, *Where Did I Wake Up?,* published by Mr. Cogito Press. His other translations have appeared in *Manhattan Review* (where "Much Simpler" originally appeared), *Artful Dodge,* and elsewhere.

DANUTA ŁOPOSZKO is an instructor of English at Marie-Curie Skłodowska University.

BOGUSŁAW ROSTWOROWSKI, a Polish poet and the author of several collections of work, including *Rycerskie rozrywki (Knightly Entertainments), Złote czasy (Golden Times),* and *Pier śi pięść (Breast and Fist),* is also a noted translator from Polish into English. His version of Zbigniew Herbert's famous long-poem "Report from a City Under Siege" appeared in *TriQuarterly's* 1983 special issue on Polish Martial Law literature.

# Romanian Translators

SERGIU CELAC is currently Romania's ambassador to the Court of Saint James. A prolific translator—among others of Constanța Buzea's *Tip of the Iceberg*—editor, and publishing director, he has also written fiction and verse.

STAVROS DELIGIORGIS (b. 1933), is a Greek who has both studied and taught in Romania. He specializes in the European middle ages (early and more recent) and was a frequent beneficiary of the Romanian Writers Union and its members during the late nineteen seventies.

MARGUERITE DORIAN is a novelist, a poet, and a critic. She and Elliott B.

Urdang have published a biligual edition of the poetry of Ion Caraion (Ohio University Press, 1981).

ADAM J. SORKIN is a university professor at Pennsylvania State University, and the recipient of numerous awards to travel and translate. His published work includes studies on politics and literature, popular culture, and film.

LILIANA URSU (b. 1949) studied English at the University of Bucharest. She is an experienced translator from and into Romanian and the author of more than four books of her own poetry, one of which received the Romanian Writers Union Prize in 1980.

ELLIOTT B. URDANG, M.D., is a child psychiatrist. He has collaborated with Marguerite Dorian on numerous publications of Romanian poetry in English translation.

LIDIA VIANU is on the English faculty of the University of Bucharest. She is a specialist on T. S. Eliot and on post-World War II American poetry.

# Ukrainian Translators

VOLODYMYR HRUSZKEWYCZ is a graphic artist and translator from Detroit, Michigan.

VERA KACZMARSKYJ is an editor and translator. She is currently assistant editor of *Ukrainian Business Digest,* formerly having been editor of *Soviet Ukrainian Affairs.*

IRENA EVA MOSTOVYCH is a psychologist and translator from Washington, D.C.

MICHAEL M. NAYDAN is professor of Slavic languages and literatures at Pennsylvania State University. He is the translator of a book of poetry by Lina Kostenko and of poems by other writers.

LARISSA M. L. Z. ONYSHKEVYCH taught Ukrainian literature at Rutgers University. She is literary editor of *Suchasnist* and president of Princeton Research Forum.

MYROSIA STEFANIUK is a geographer and free-lance writer and translator. She lives in Detroit.

# Crotian Translators

BERNARD JOHNSON is a senior lecturer at the London School of Economics and has translated poetry and fiction from Russian, Croatian, and Serbian. His publications include *New Writing in Yugoslavia* [editor] (Penguin, 1970), *Miodrag Pavlović: The Slavs Beneath Parnassus* (Angel Press & New Rivers Press, 1985), *Slavko Mihalić: Black Apples* (Exile Editions, 1989), *Borislav Pekić: The Houses of Belgrade* (Harcourt, Brace, Jovanovich), and *Aleksandar Tišma: The Usage of Man* (Harcourt, Brace, Jovanovich).

DUBRAVKA JURAGA graduated after studying English at the University of Novi Sad and received her M.A. in English from the University of Belgrade. She was a Visiting Fulbright Scholar in the United States in 1988. She works in the Literary Translation Program at the University of Arkansas-Fayetteville.

TOMISLAV LONGINOVIĆ studied psychology at the University of Belgrade and received his Ph.D. in comparative literature from the University of Iowa. He teaches in the Department of Slavic Studies at the University of Wisconsin-Madison. He has published a novel *Moment of Silence* (Burning Books, 1990) and has a nonfiction book, *The Improbable Universe,* forthcoming from the University of Arkansas Press in 1992.

KLARA MIŠIĆ-ALKALAY was born in Split, Croatia. She graduated, after studying world literature, from the University of Belgrade and has studied art history in Jerusalem. She now lives and works in New York. Her translations of contemporary writers from Yugoslavia, including Danilo Kiš and David Albahari, have appeared in a number of American literary magazines.

# Serbian Translators

DUBRAVKA JURAGA graduated after studying English at the University of Novi Sad and received her M.A. in English from the University of Belgrade. She was a visiting Fulbright Scholar to the United States in 1988. She works for the Literary Translation Program at the University of Arkansas-Fayetteville.

TOMISLAV LONGINOVIĆ studied in psychology at the University of Belgrade and received his Ph.D. in comparative literature from the University of Iowa. He teaches in the Department of Slavic Studies at the University of Wisconsin-Madison. He has published a novel, *Moment of Silence* (Burning

Books, 1990) and has a nonfiction book, *The Improbable Universe,* forthcoming from the University of Arkansas Press, 1992.

NINA ŽIVANČEVIĆ studied English and Spanish at and graduated from the Universify of Belgrade and received her M.A. in English from Temple University. She published four books of poetry in Serbia and one in the United States: *More or Less Urgent* (New Rivers Press, 1988). She won a Serbian prize for first book of poetry (Branko Award). Since 1985, she writes her poetry in English and Serbian and divides her time between Belgrade and New York.

# Slovenian Translators

MICHAEL BIGGINS is a Slavic collection librarian at the University of Kansas, Lawrence, where he received his Ph.D. in Russian and Slavic studies. He has taught at Middlebury College and Knox College. His translations of Slovenian poetry appeared (among other magazines) in a special section of *New England Review/Bread Loaf Quarterly.*

SONJA KRAVANJA lives in Santa Fe, New Mexico. She graduated after studying comparative literature at the University of Ljubljana. She was an IREX Visiting Scholar at the University of Colorado-Boulder and received a translation fellowship from Witter Bynner Foundation for Poetry in 1990–91. Her translation of *Selected Poems of Tomaž Šalamun* is forthcoming from Racoorsos Books in 1992.

TOM LOŽAR came from his native Ljubljana, Slovenia, to Canada at the age of eight. He received a Ph.D. in American literature from the University of Toronto. He teaches in the Department of English at Vanier College, Montreal, and is a translator of a book of selected poems by Edvard Kocbek, *Na vratih zvečer/At The Door of Evening* (Muses & Co. 1990).

CHRISTOPHER MERRILL is the author of two collections of poetry, *Workbook* and *Fevers & Tides,* cotranslator of *Constellations by Andre Breton* and *Slow Down Construction by Breton, Rene Char, and Paul Eluard,* and editor of *Outcroppings: John McPhee in the West* and, most recently, of *The Forgotten Language: Contemporary Poets and Nature* (Peregrine Smith, 1991).

TOM PRIESTLY teaches in the Department of Slavic and East European Studies, University of Alberta, Edmonton, Canada. His research publications focus on the Slovenian dialects of Carintia region of Austria. He is the editor-in-chief of *Slovene Studies.*

# Index of Poets